I enjoy looking at the house-for-sale fliers that are mailed to me. I look at the floor plans and think, "I'd make this room the home office, this one the bedroom," even though I know I'll never live there. But I still like to pretend I will. When I tell people about this, I'm surprised that so many other people share this same hobby! *Toriko* is themed around food, but someday I'd like to make a housing-themed manga! Though I doubt it'd make for a very interesting story (laughs)… (My current weight…71 kg!! Ha!… I've got to get more serious about this!)

—Mitsutoshi Shimabukuro, 2016

Mitsutoshi Shimabukuro made his debut in **Weekly Shonen Jump** in 1996. He is best known for **Seikimatsu Leader Den Takeshi!**, for which he won the 46th Shogakukan Manga Award for children's manga in 2001. His current series, **Toriko**, began serialization in Japan in 2008.

TORIKO

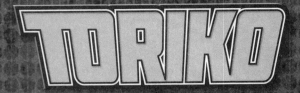

TORIKO VOL. 39
SHONEN JUMP Manga Edition

STORY AND ART BY **MITSUTOSHI SHIMABUKURO**

Translation/Christine Dashiell
Weekly Shonen Jump Lettering/ Erika Terriquez
Graphic Novel Touch-Up Art & Lettering/ Paolo Gattone and Chiara Antonelli
Design/Veronica Casson
Editor/Marlene First

Printed in the U.S.A.

Published by VIZ Media, LLC
P.O. Box 77010
San Francisco, CA 94107

10 9 8 7 6 5 4 3 2 1
First printing, August 2017

viz media
www.viz.com

RATED T FOR TEEN

PARENTAL ADVISORY
TORIKO is rated T for Teen and is recommended for ages 13 and up. This volume contains realistic and fantasy violence.
ratings.viz.com

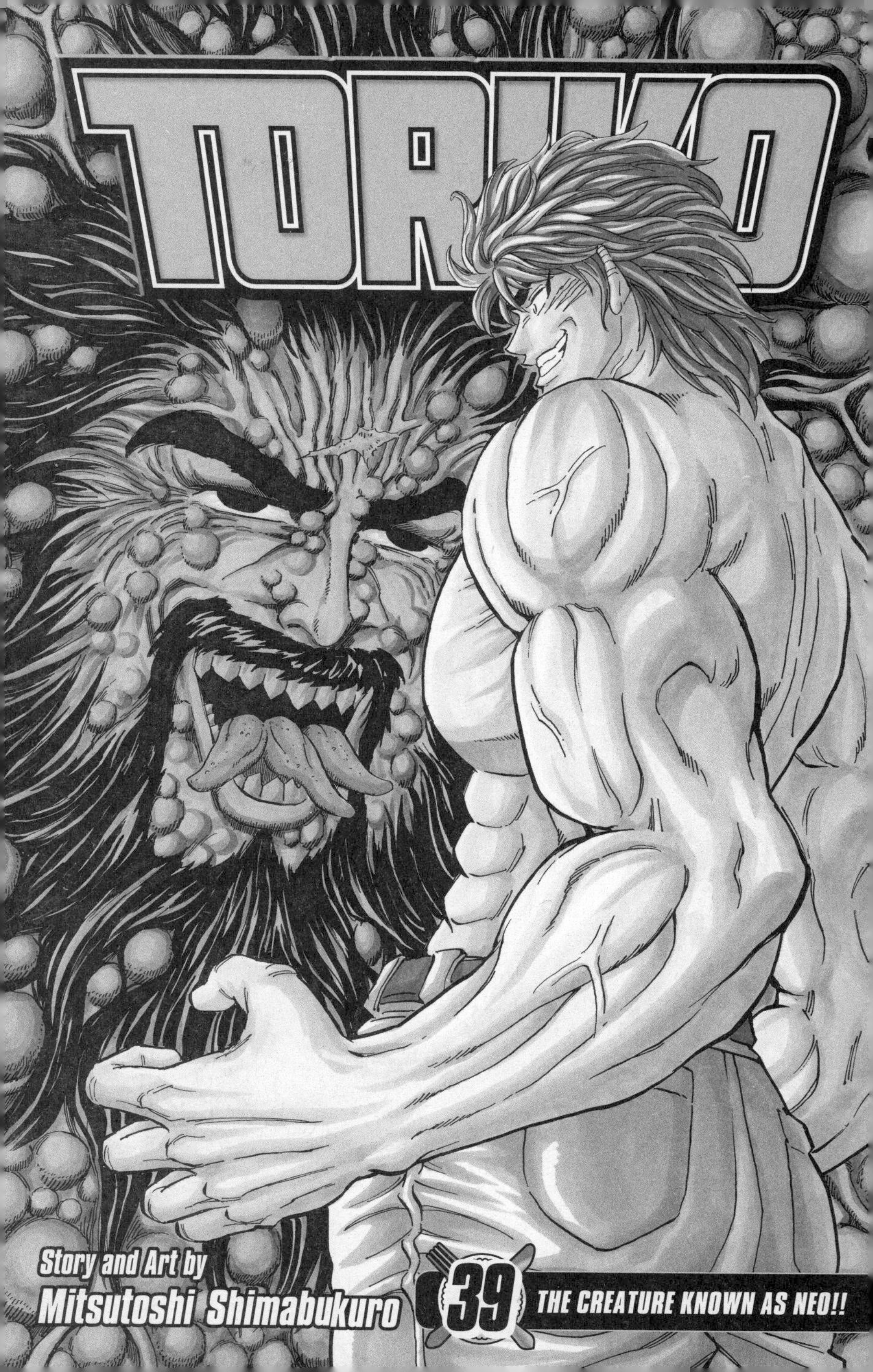
TORIKO
Story and Art by
Mitsutoshi Shimabukuro
39
THE CREATURE KNOWN AS NEO!!

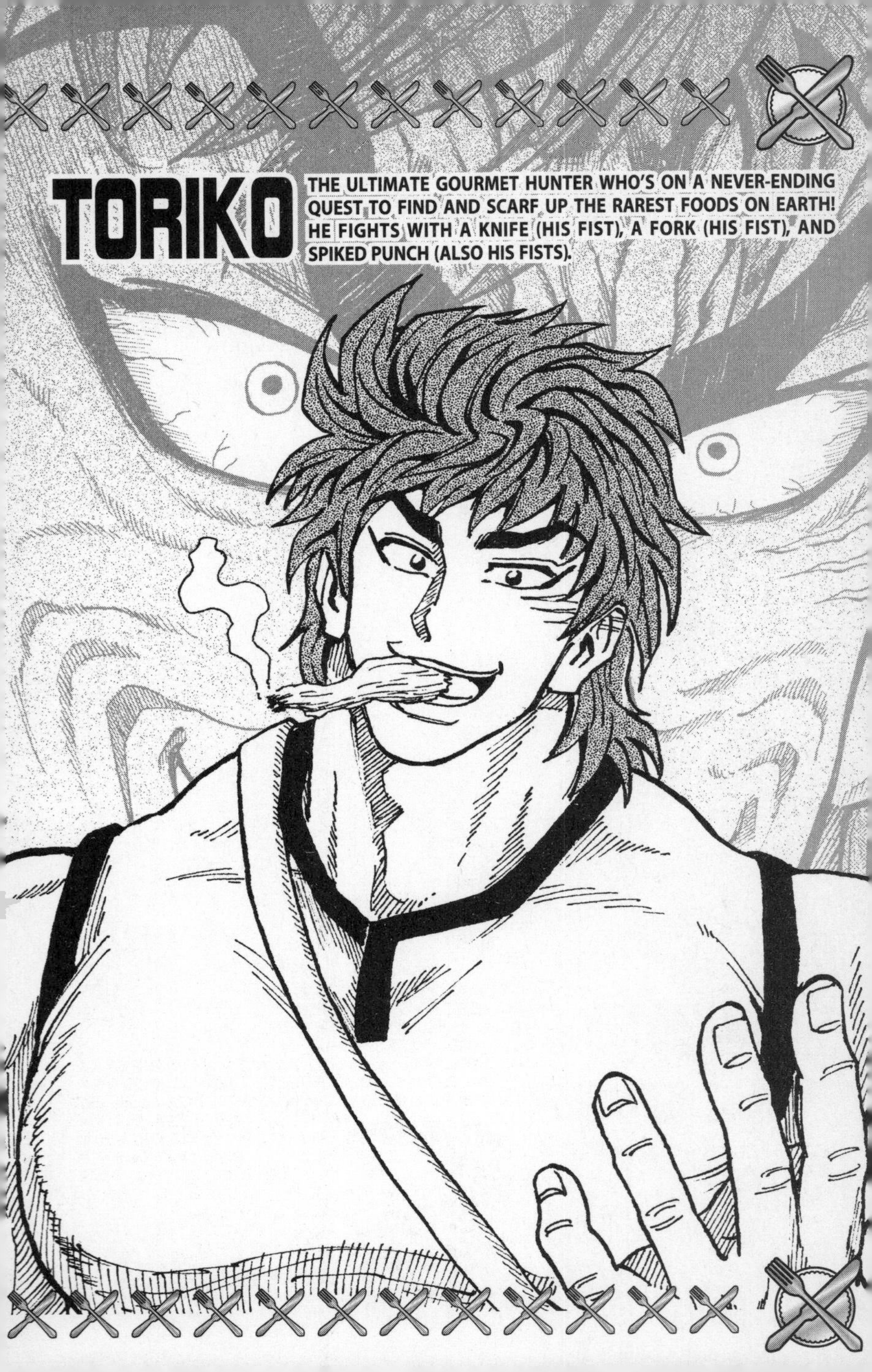
TORIKO
THE ULTIMATE GOURMET HUNTER WHO'S ON A NEVER-ENDING QUEST TO FIND AND SCARF UP THE RAREST FOODS ON EARTH! HE FIGHTS WITH A KNIFE (HIS FIST), A FORK (HIS FIST), AND SPIKED PUNCH (ALSO HIS FISTS).

WHAT'S FOR DINNER

THE WORLD IS IN THE AGE OF GOURMET! THE GOURMET HUNTER, TORIKO AND HIS FRIEND KOMATSU, A CHEF WHO POSSESSES THE UNIQUE ASSET OF "FOOD LUCK," HAVE A FATEFUL MEETING AND EMBARK ON NUMEROUS ADVENTURES TOGETHER. MEANWHILE, THE IGO AND THE EVIL ORGANIZATION GOURMET CORP. WAGE AN ALL-OUR WAR. THE WAR DESTROYS MOST OF THE INGREDIENTS ON EARTH AND THE HUMAN WORLD ENTERS A FOOD SHORTAGE CRISIS! GOURMET CORP. TAKES THE BRUNT OF THE DAMAGE THANKS TO A NEW EVIL POWER KNOWN AS NEO, LED BY THE INFAMOUS CHEF JOIE!

IN ORDER TO SAVE HUMANITY, TORIKO AND KOMATSU, ALONG WITH THE OTHER FOUR KINGS, COCO, SUNNY AND ZEBRA, EMBARK ON AN ADVENTURE TO THE GOURMET WORLD TO GO AFTER ACACIA'S FULL-COURSE MEAL!

MEANWHILE, THE GOURMET ARISTOCRATS, THE BLUE NITRO, HAVE SPENT THOUSANDS OF YEARS WORKING TO PREPARE ACACIA'S FULL-COURSE MEAL ON THEIR OWN. THEIR GOAL IS TO FULLY RESURRECT ACACIA'S GOURMET CELL DEMON, NEO, AND SEAL HIM AWAY. BUT RIGHT AS THEY ARE SUCCESSFULLY ABOUT TO RESURRECT HIM, PIECES OF NEO ESCAPE THE BLUE NITRO'S BASE AND HEAD TO EACH AREA. TO MAKE MATTERS WORSE, ACACIA HIMSELF DISAPPEARS TOO!!

TO PREVENT NEO FROM DESTROYING THE WORLD AND STOP HIS RESURRECTION, TORIKO AND THE GANG SPLIT UP TO CAPTURE THE REMAINING INGREDIENTS IN THE FULL COURSE. TORIKO AND STARJUN FACE OFF AGAINST THE WOLF KING, GUINNESS, IN AREA 2. KOMATSU ARRIVES IN THE DEEP SEA CIVILIZATION OF BLUE GRILL IN AREA 6, BUT SOON LEARNS OF THE CRUEL PROJECT TAKING PLACE BENEATH THE DEPTHS. THE KING OF BLUE GRILL, DON SLIME, WANTS TO RESURRECT THE ONLY PERSON WHO CAN POSSIBLY DEFEAT NEO–ICHIRYU! BUT TO DO THIS, HE HAS BEEN FORCING THE PEOPLE OF BLUE GRILL TO SACRIFICE THEMSELVES FOR THE REBIRTH AND PREPARATION OF ACACIA'S FULL-COURSE MEAL. KOMATSU AIMS TO COMPLETE THE PROJECT AND HEADS TO THE SPIRIT WORLD WITH DON SLIME, SO THAT HE CAN PREPARE THE FINAL INGREDIENT OF THE FULL-COURSE MEAL–ANOTHER! JUST AS THE FOOD SPIRITS ARE CLOSING IN ON THEM, SOMETHING UNBELIEVABLE HAPPENS RIGHT BEFORE THEIR EYES...!

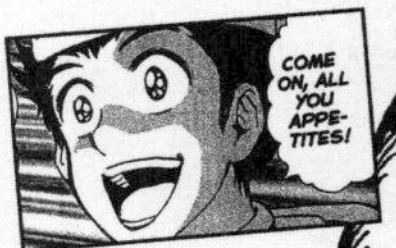
COME ON, ALL YOU APPETITES!

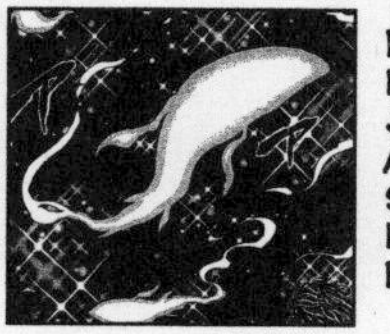

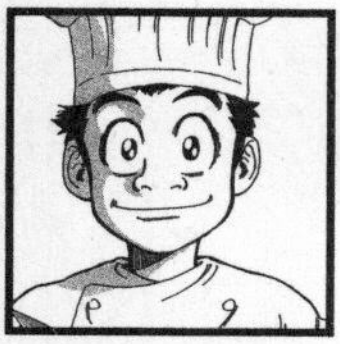

● KOMATSU

TALENTED IGO HOTEL CHEF AND TORIKO'S #1 FAN.

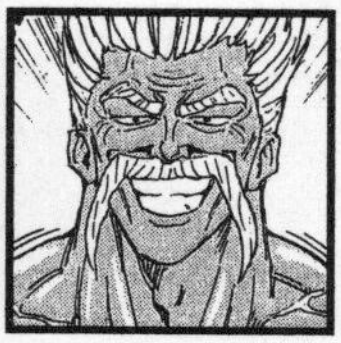

● ICHIRYU

THE FORMER IGO PRESIDENT AND DISCIPLE OF THE LATE GOURMET GOD ACACIA. HE DIES WHILE FIGHTING MIDORA.

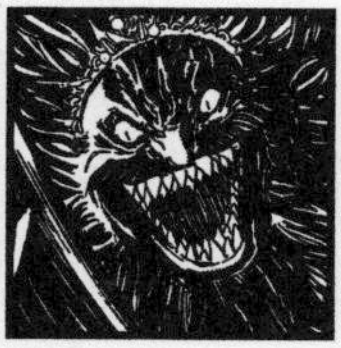

● DON SLIME

THE KING OF BLUE GRILL. HE'S A FOOD SPIRIT SHROUDED IN MYSTERY WHO HAS JOINED FORCES WITH KOMATSU AND THE GANG ON THEIR MISSION.

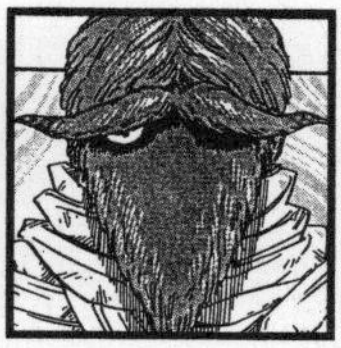

● JIJI

A TASTE HERMIT AND THE GOLDEN CHEF. HE KNOWS HOW TO PREPARE ACACIA'S FULL-COURSE MEAL

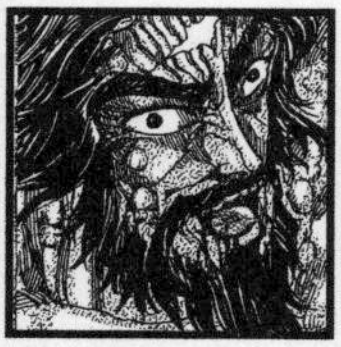

● ACACIA

A LEGENDARY GOURMET HUNTER ALSO KNOWN AS THE GOURMET GOD. HE'S WORKING WITH THE BLUE NITRO TO BE COMPLETELY REVIVED.

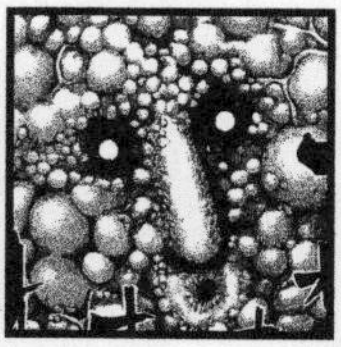

● NEO

A DANGEROUS GOURMET CELL DEMON THAT'S BEEN REBORN COUNTLESS TIMES OVER THE PAST TEN BILLION YEARS. HE RESIDES WITHIN ACACIA.

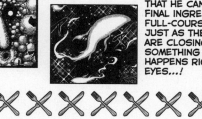

Contents

TORIKO

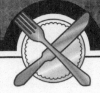

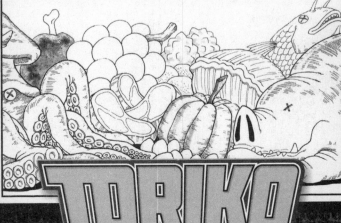

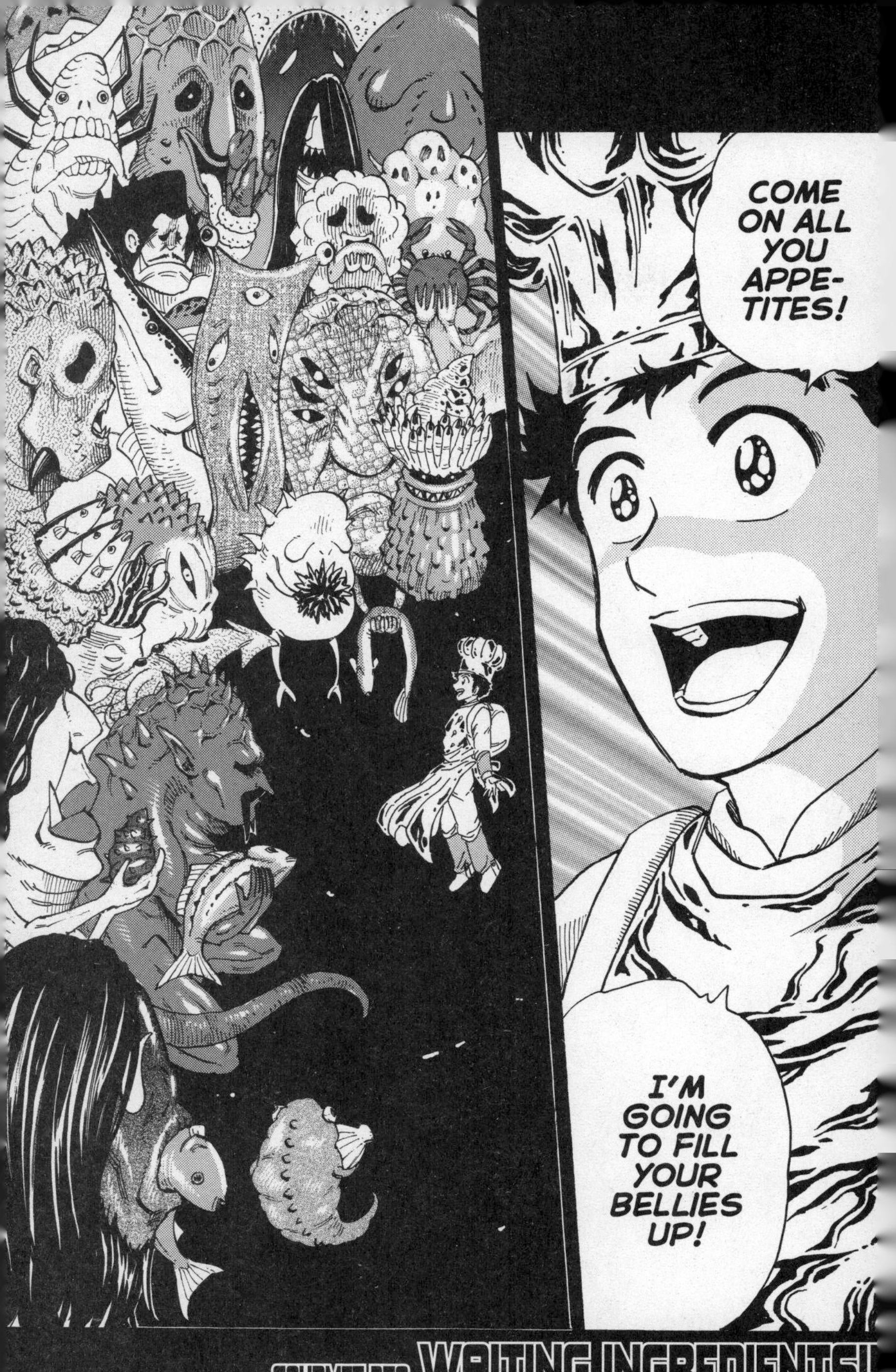
COME ON ALL YOU APPE-TITES!
I'M GOING TO FILL YOUR BELLIES UP!

GOURMET 350: WAITING INGREDIENTS!!

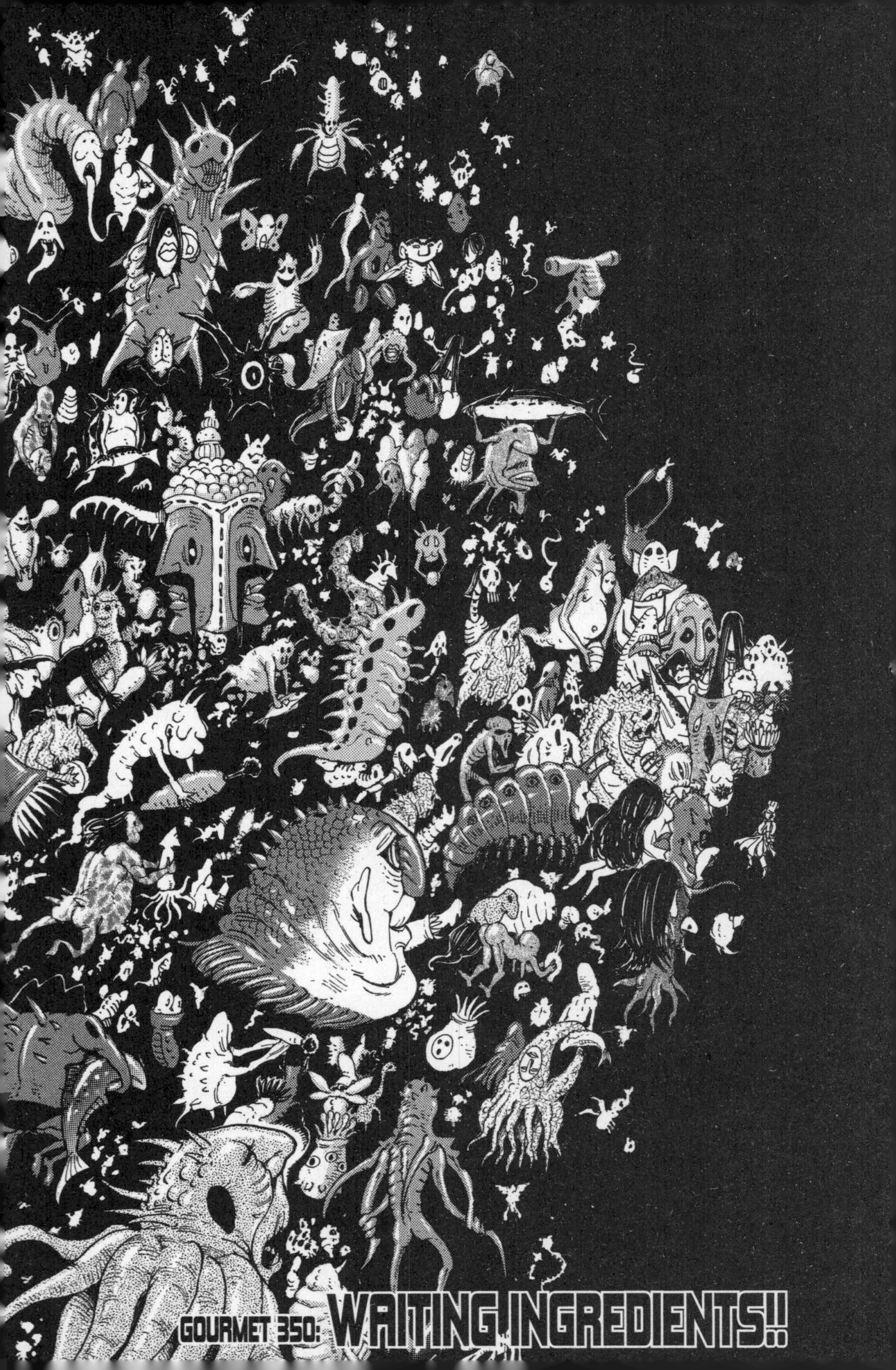
GOURMET 350: WAITING INGREDIENTS!!

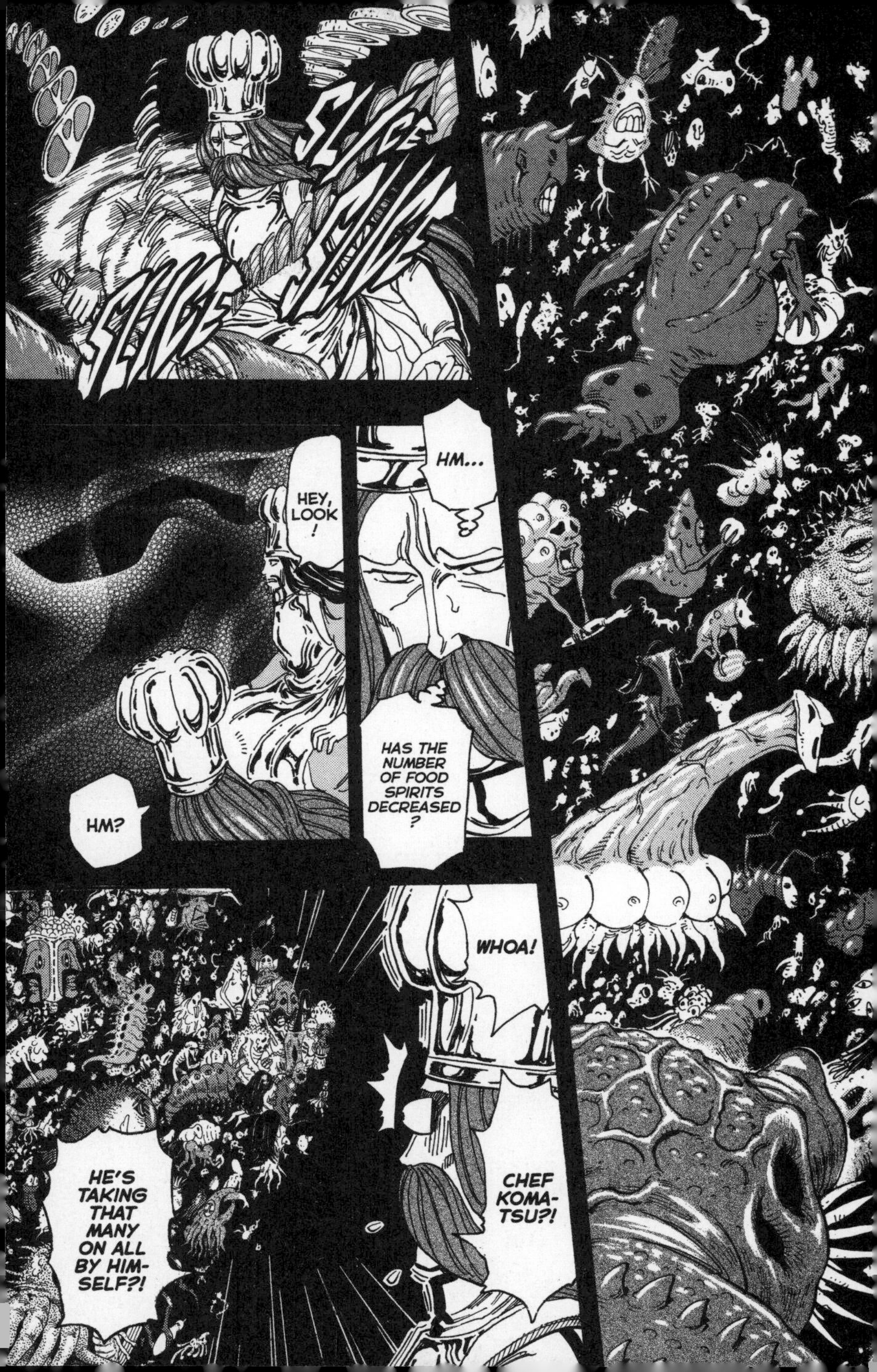
SLICE
SLICE
SLICE
HM...
HAS THE NUMBER OF FOOD SPIRITS DECREASED?
HEY, LOOK!
HM?
WHOA!
CHEF KOMATSU?!
HE'S TAKING THAT MANY ON ALL BY HIMSELF?!

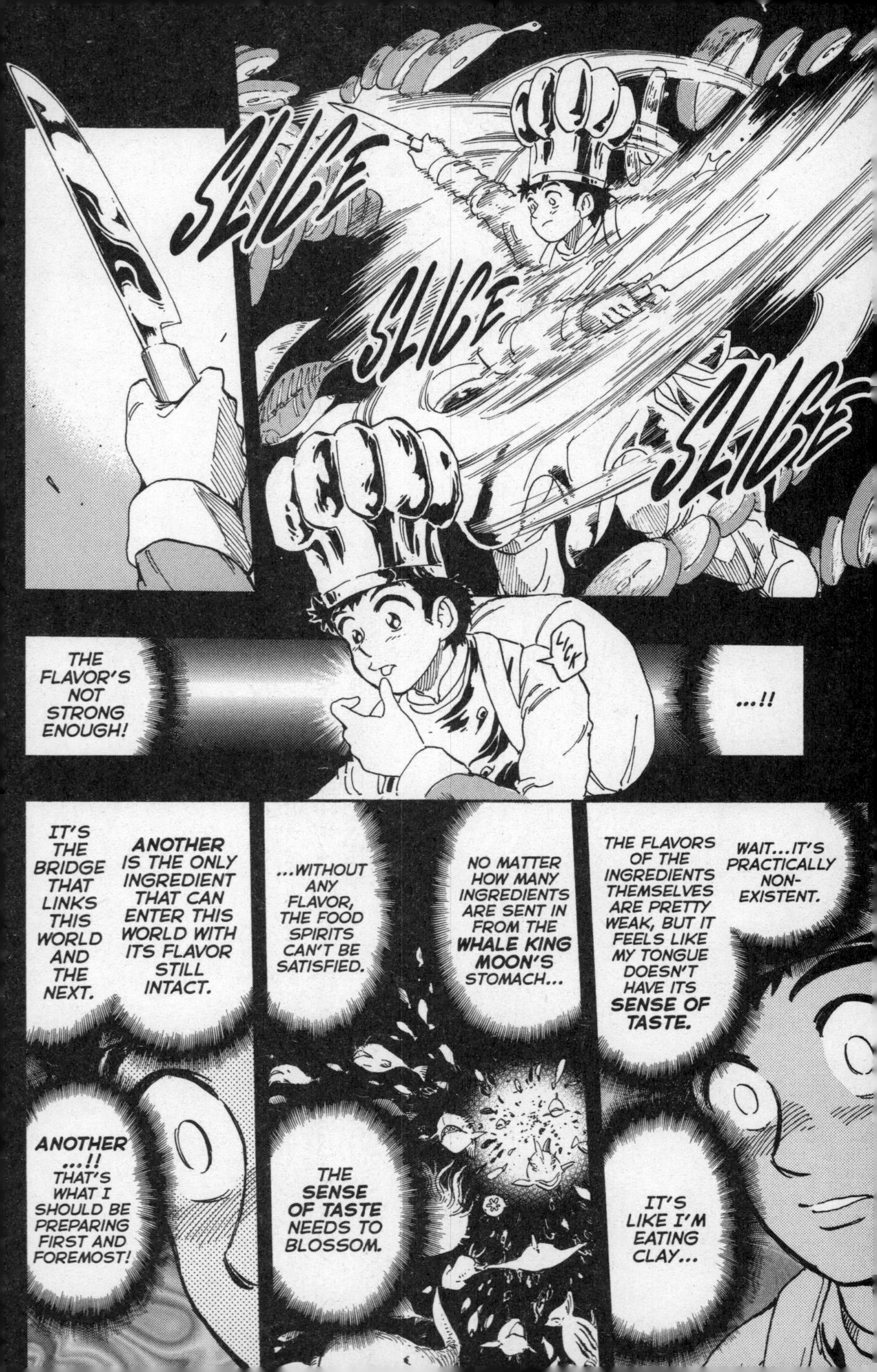
SLICE
SLICE
SLICE
...!!
LICK
THE FLAVOR'S NOT STRONG ENOUGH!
WAIT...IT'S PRACTICALLY NON-EXISTENT.
THE FLAVORS OF THE INGREDIENTS THEMSELVES ARE PRETTY WEAK, BUT IT FEELS LIKE MY TONGUE DOESN'T HAVE ITS **SENSE OF TASTE.**
IT'S LIKE I'M EATING CLAY...
NO MATTER HOW MANY INGREDIENTS ARE SENT IN FROM THE **WHALE KING MOON'S** STOMACH...
...WITHOUT ANY FLAVOR, THE FOOD SPIRITS CAN'T BE SATISFIED.
THE **SENSE OF TASTE** NEEDS TO BLOSSOM.
ANOTHER IS THE ONLY INGREDIENT THAT CAN ENTER THIS WORLD WITH ITS FLAVOR STILL INTACT.
IT'S THE BRIDGE THAT LINKS THIS WORLD AND THE NEXT.
ANOTHER ...!! THAT'S WHAT I SHOULD BE PREPARING FIRST AND FOREMOST!

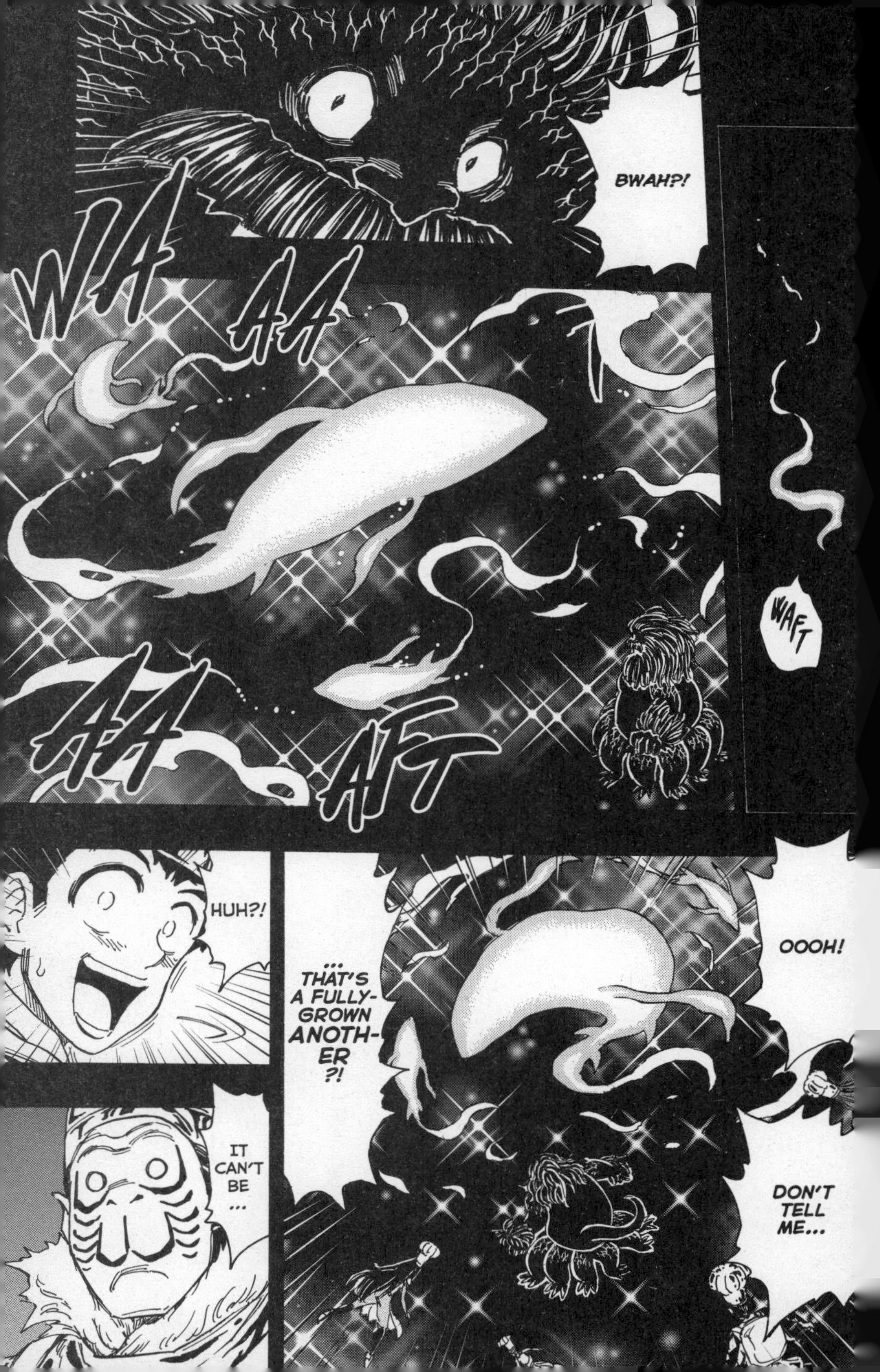
BWAH?!
WAFT
WHAAAAAAFT
OOOH!
DON'T TELL ME...
...THAT'S A FULLY-GROWN ANOTHER?!
HUH?!
IT CAN'T BE...

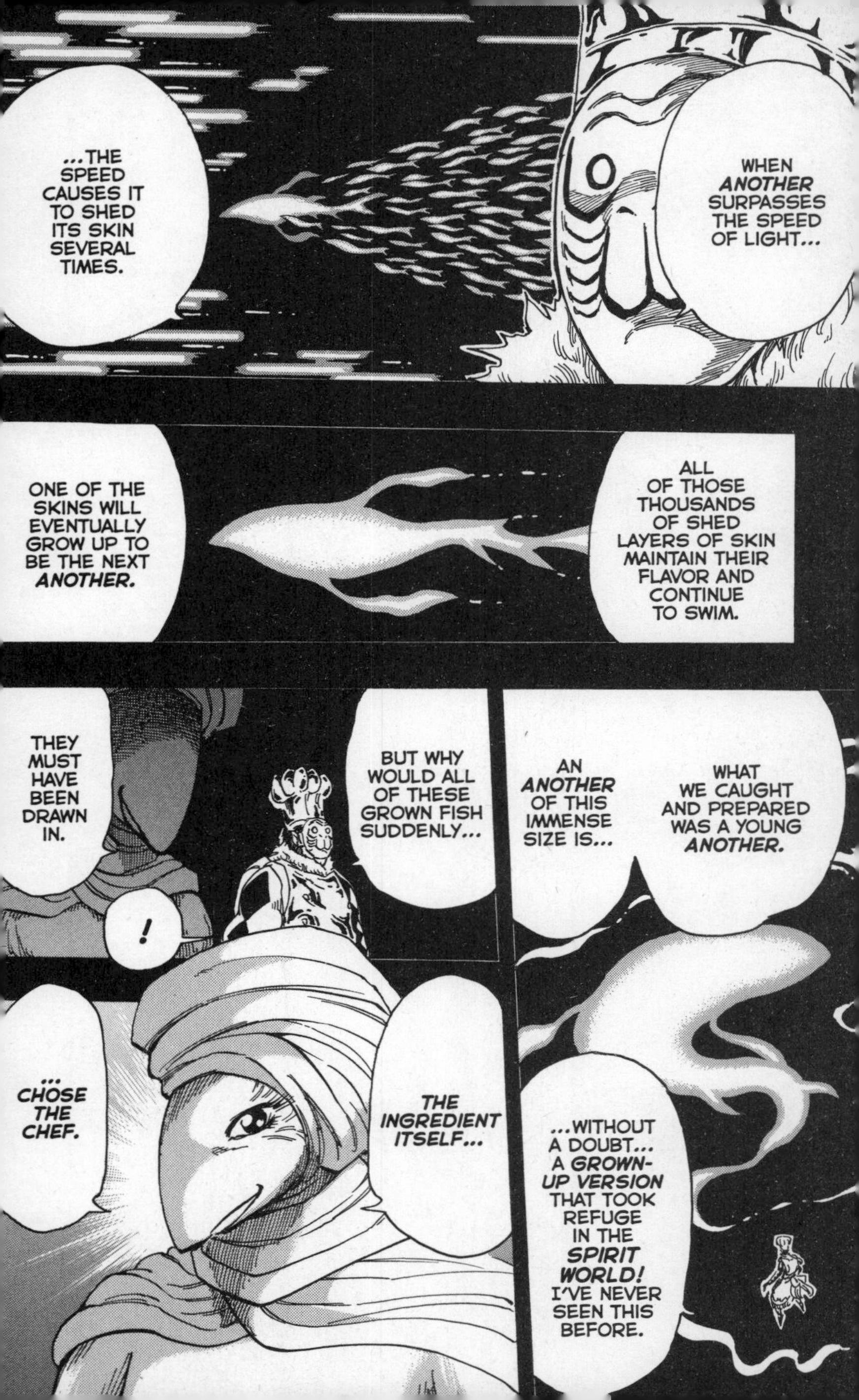
WHEN ANOTHER SURPASSES THE SPEED OF LIGHT...
...THE SPEED CAUSES IT TO SHED ITS SKIN SEVERAL TIMES.
ALL OF THOSE THOUSANDS OF SHED LAYERS OF SKIN MAINTAIN THEIR FLAVOR AND CONTINUE TO SWIM.
ONE OF THE SKINS WILL EVENTUALLY GROW UP TO BE THE NEXT ANOTHER.
WHAT WE CAUGHT AND PREPARED WAS A YOUNG ANOTHER.
AN ANOTHER OF THIS IMMENSE SIZE IS...
...WITHOUT A DOUBT... A GROWN-UP VERSION THAT TOOK REFUGE IN THE SPIRIT WORLD! I'VE NEVER SEEN THIS BEFORE.
BUT WHY WOULD ALL OF THESE GROWN FISH SUDDENLY...
THEY MUST HAVE BEEN DRAWN IN.
!
THE INGREDIENT ITSELF...
...CHOSE THE CHEF.

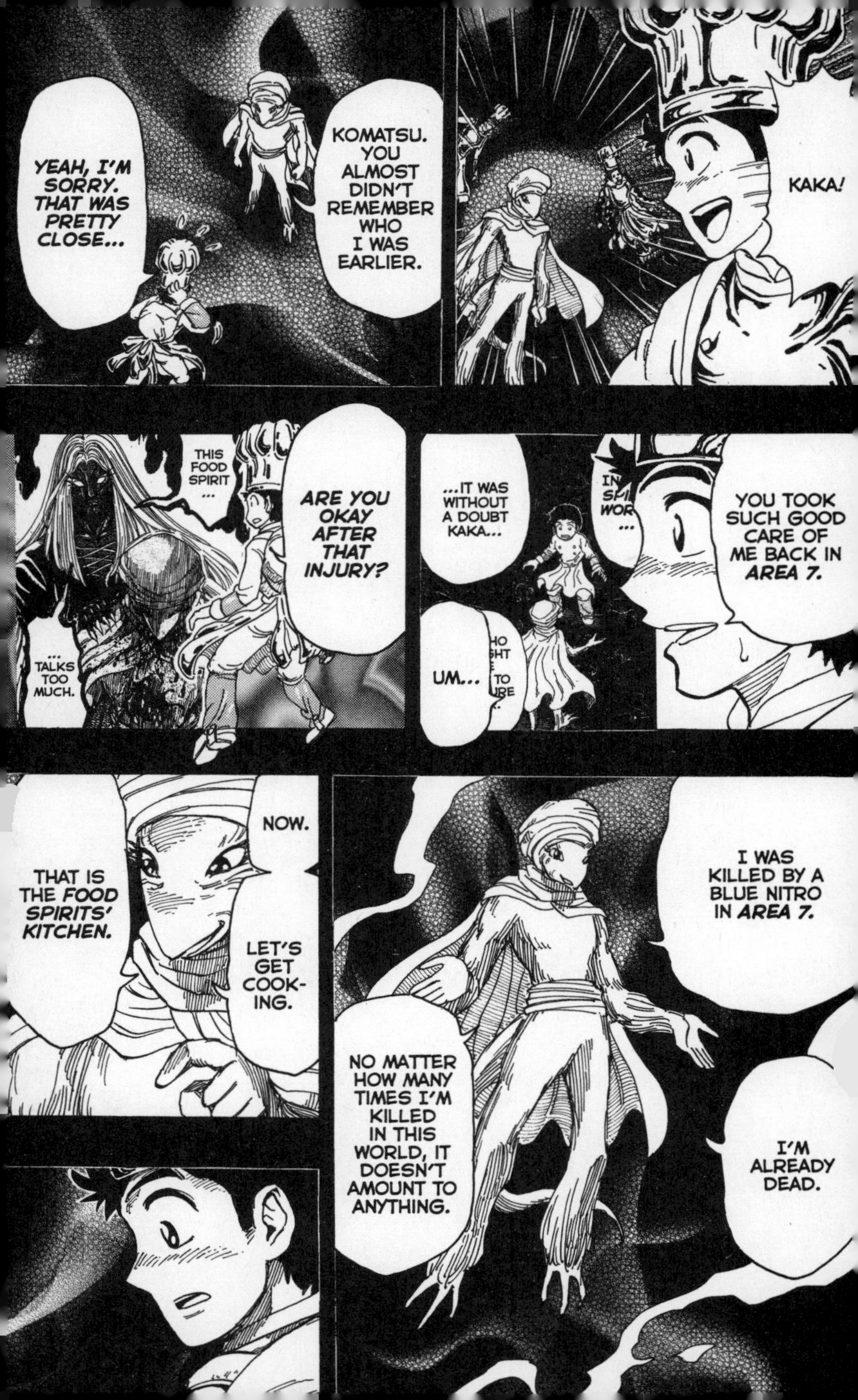
KAKA!
KOMATSU. YOU ALMOST DIDN'T REMEMBER WHO I WAS EARLIER.
YEAH, I'M SORRY. THAT WAS PRETTY CLOSE...
YOU TOOK SUCH GOOD CARE OF ME BACK IN AREA 7.
...IT WAS WITHOUT A DOUBT KAKA...
UM...
ARE YOU OKAY AFTER THAT INJURY?
THIS FOOD SPIRIT...
...TALKS TOO MUCH.
I WAS KILLED BY A BLUE NITRO IN AREA 7.
I'M ALREADY DEAD.
NO MATTER HOW MANY TIMES I'M KILLED IN THIS WORLD, IT DOESN'T AMOUNT TO ANYTHING.
THAT IS THE FOOD SPIRITS' KITCHEN.
NOW.
LET'S GET COOKING.

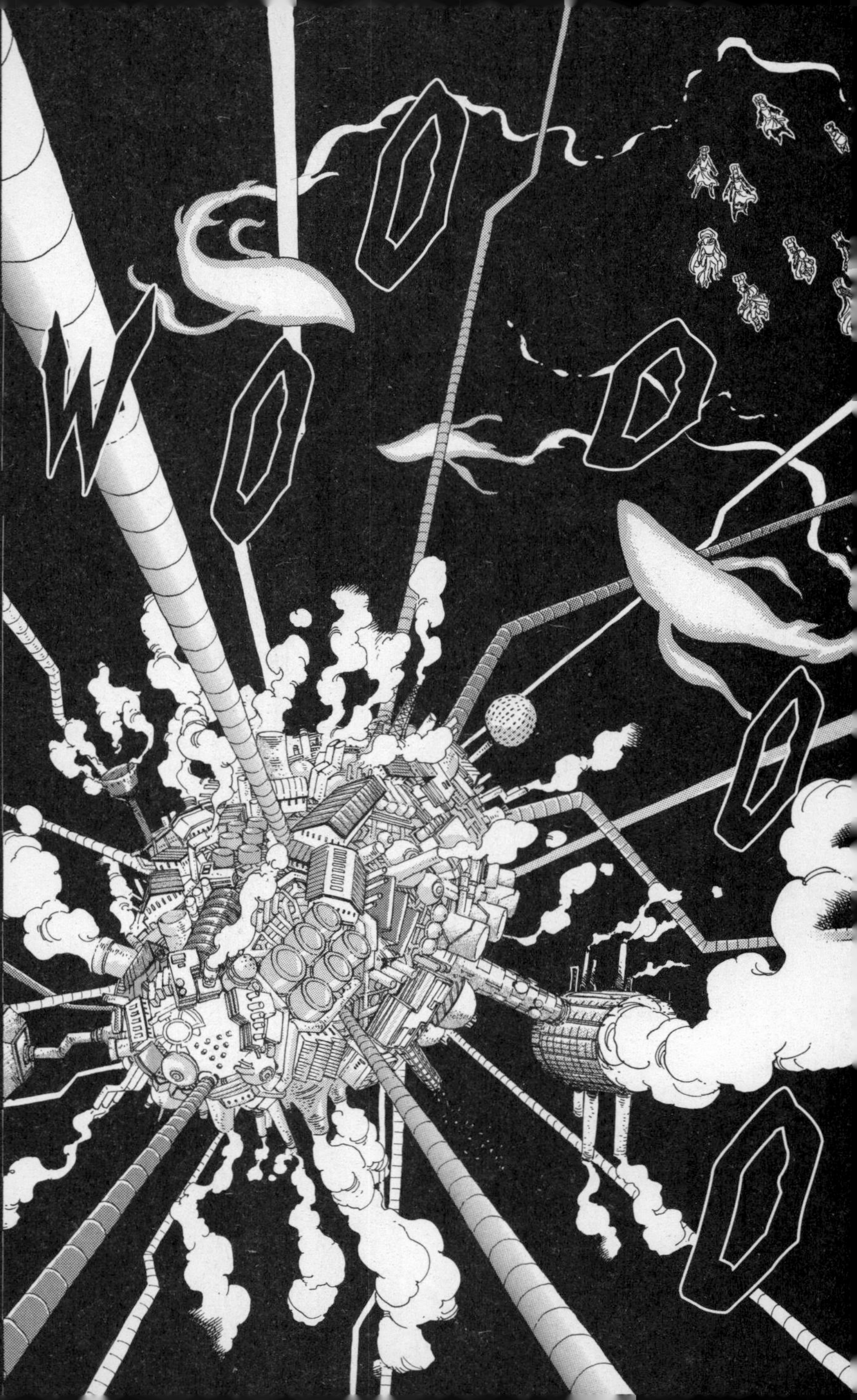
WOOOOO

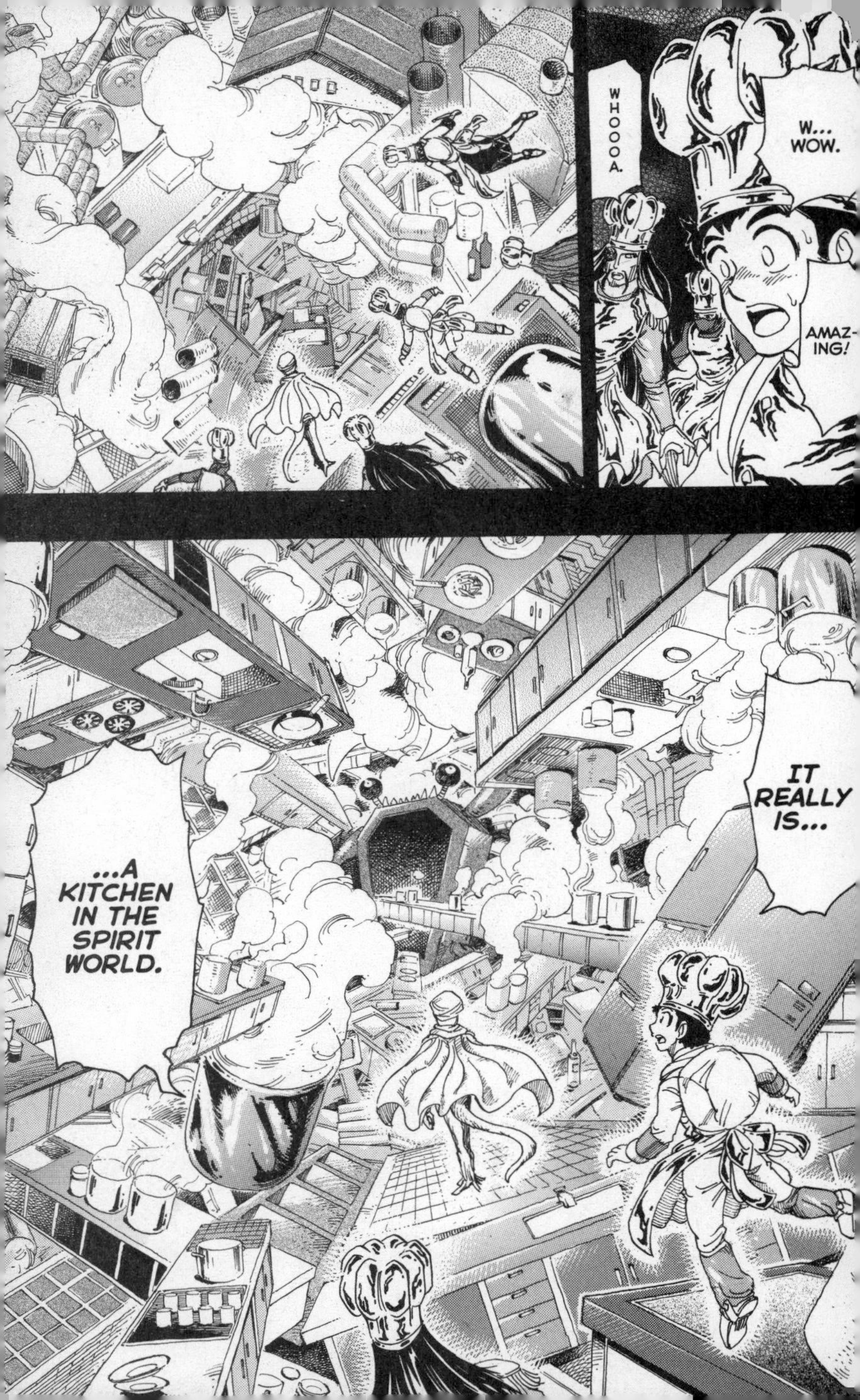
W... WOW.
WHOOOA.
AMAZ-ING!
IT REALLY IS...
...A KITCHEN IN THE SPIRIT WORLD.

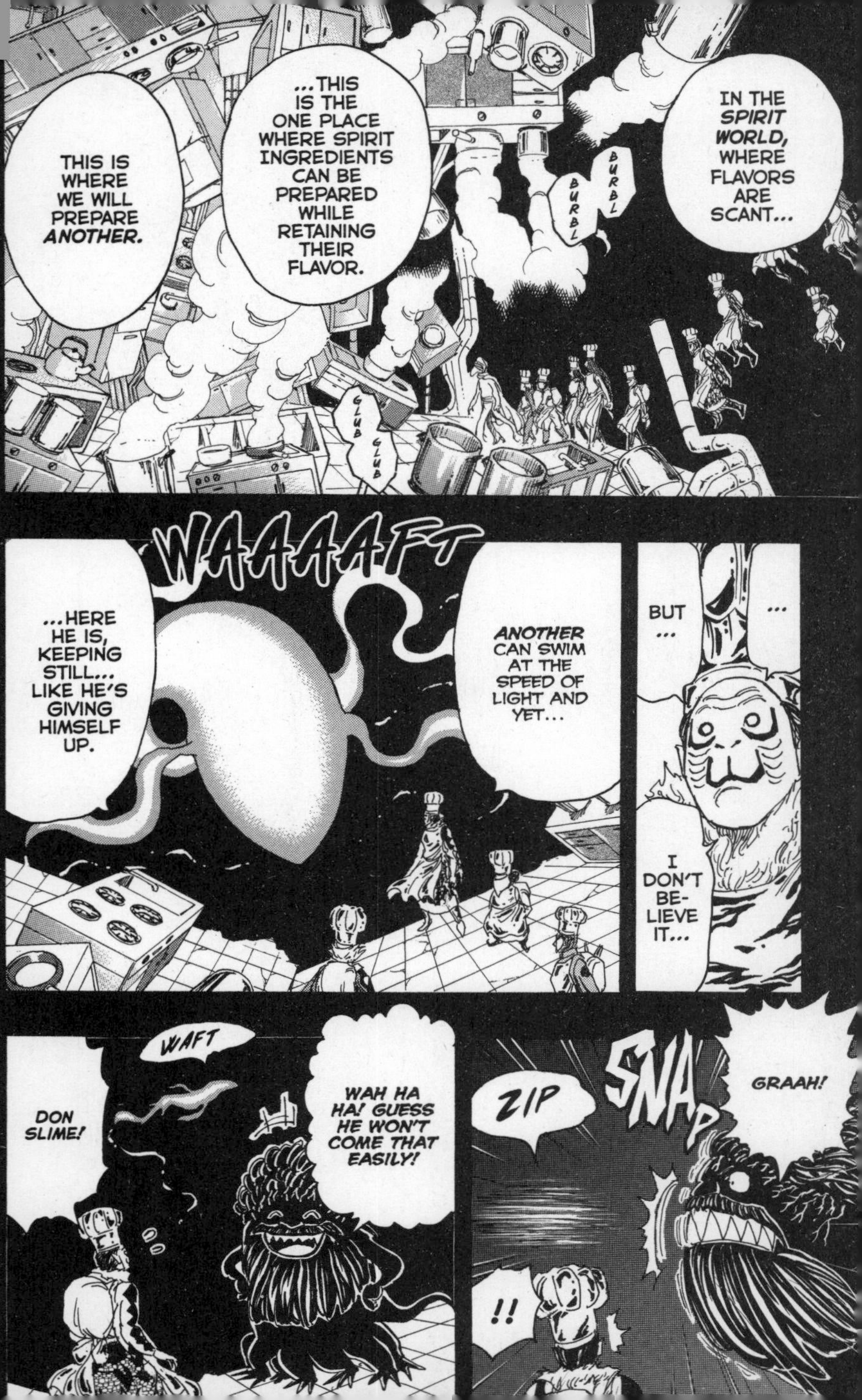
IN THE SPIRIT WORLD, WHERE FLAVORS ARE SCANT...
BURBL BURBL
...THIS IS THE ONE PLACE WHERE SPIRIT INGREDIENTS CAN BE PREPARED WHILE RETAINING THEIR FLAVOR.
THIS IS WHERE WE WILL PREPARE ANOTHER.
GLUB GLUB
...
BUT...
I DON'T BE-LIEVE IT...
WAAAAAFT
ANOTHER CAN SWIM AT THE SPEED OF LIGHT AND YET...
...HERE HE IS, KEEPING STILL... LIKE HE'S GIVING HIMSELF UP.
GRAAH!
SNAP
ZIP
!!
WAH HA HA! GUESS HE WON'T COME THAT EASILY!
WAFT
DON SLIME!

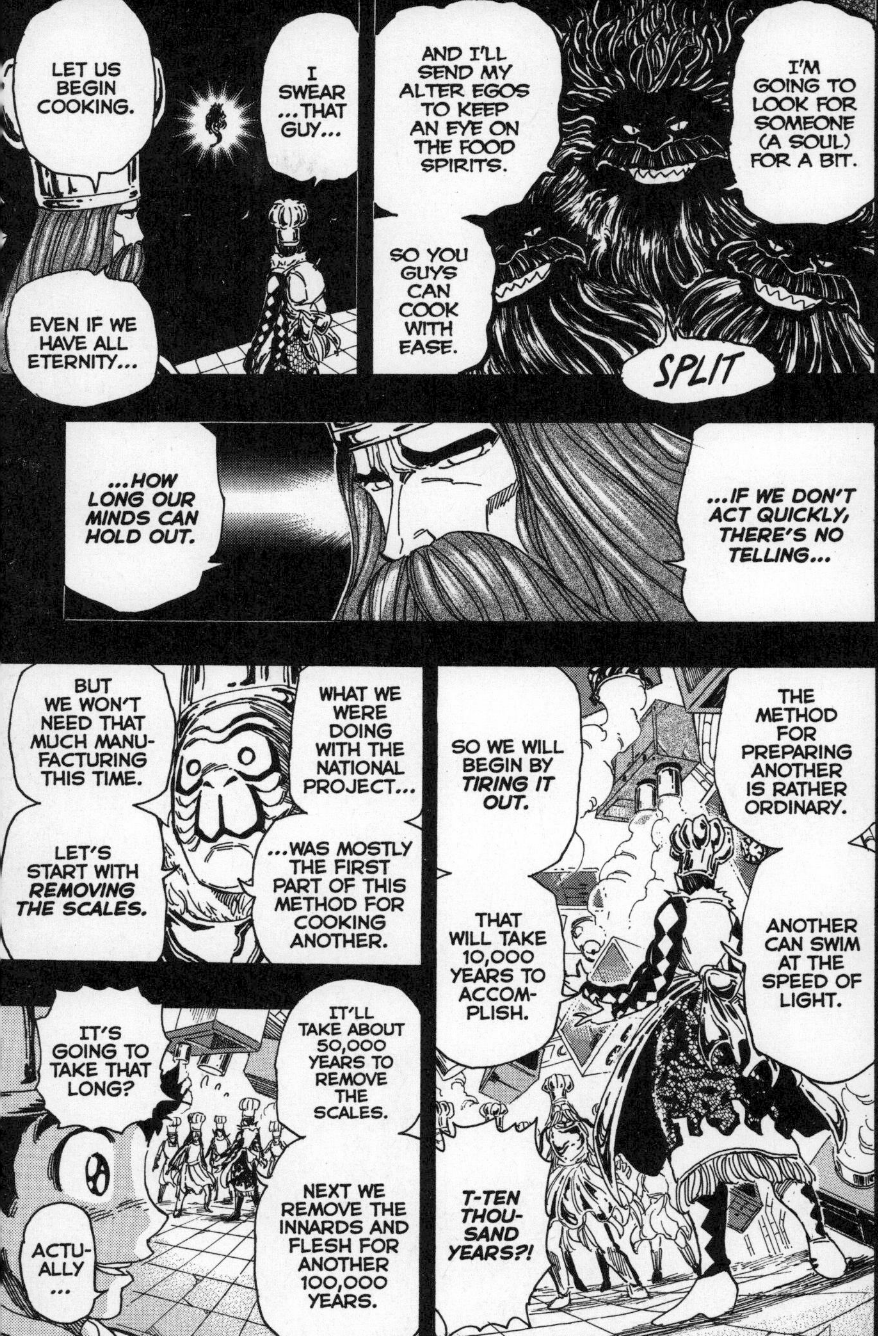
I'M GOING TO LOOK FOR SOMEONE (A SOUL) FOR A BIT.
AND I'LL SEND MY ALTER EGOS TO KEEP AN EYE ON THE FOOD SPIRITS.
SO YOU GUYS CAN COOK WITH EASE.
SPLIT
I SWEAR ...THAT GUY...
LET US BEGIN COOKING.
EVEN IF WE HAVE ALL ETERNITY...
...IF WE DON'T ACT QUICKLY, THERE'S NO TELLING...
...HOW LONG OUR MINDS CAN HOLD OUT.
THE METHOD FOR PREPARING ANOTHER IS RATHER ORDINARY.
ANOTHER CAN SWIM AT THE SPEED OF LIGHT.
SO WE WILL BEGIN BY TIRING IT OUT.
THAT WILL TAKE 10,000 YEARS TO ACCOMPLISH.
T-TEN THOUSAND YEARS?!
WHAT WE WERE DOING WITH THE NATIONAL PROJECT...
...WAS MOSTLY THE FIRST PART OF THIS METHOD FOR COOKING ANOTHER.
BUT WE WON'T NEED THAT MUCH MANUFACTURING THIS TIME.
LET'S START WITH REMOVING THE SCALES.
IT'LL TAKE ABOUT 50,000 YEARS TO REMOVE THE SCALES.
NEXT WE REMOVE THE INNARDS AND FLESH FOR ANOTHER 100,000 YEARS.
IT'S GOING TO TAKE THAT LONG?
ACTUALLY...

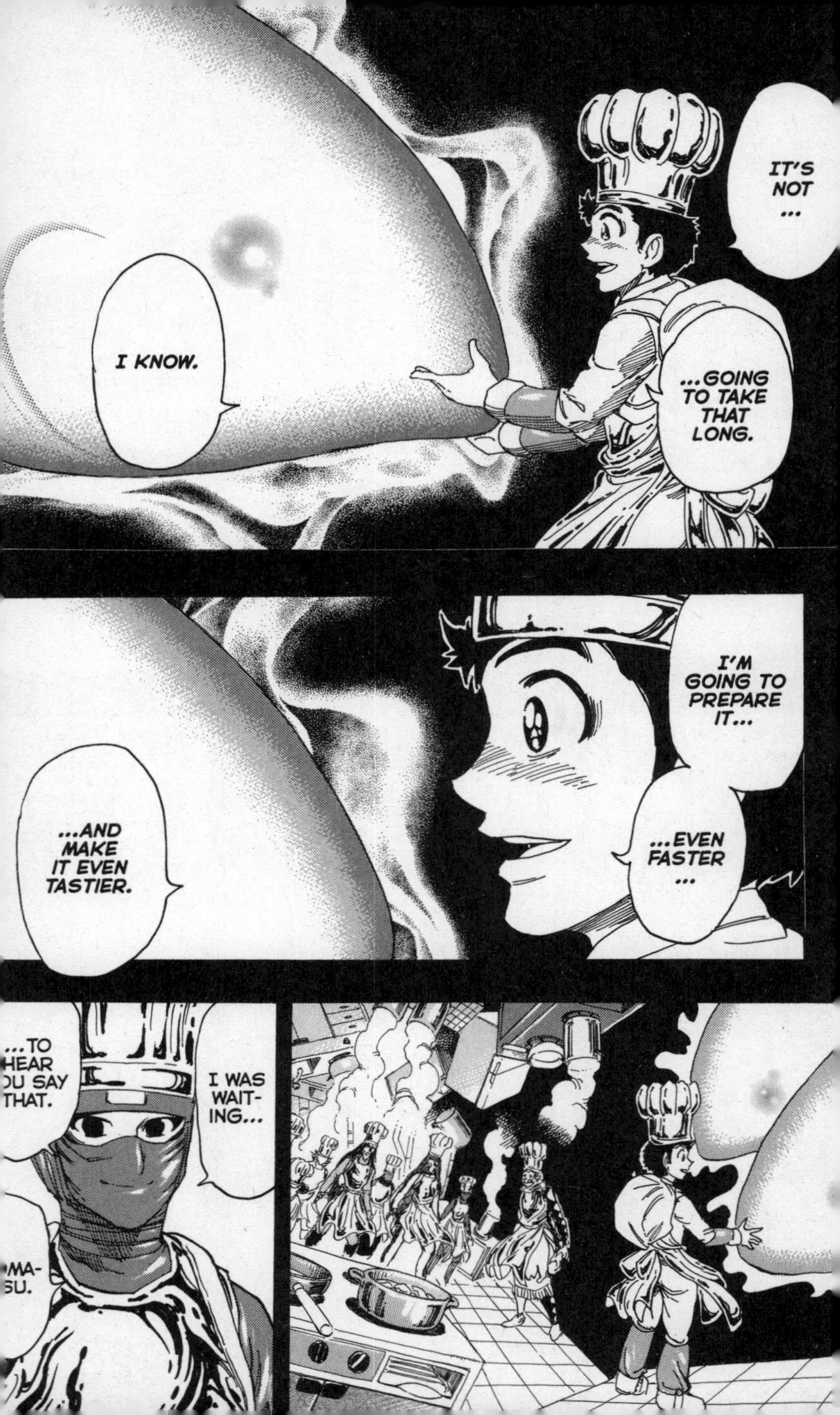
IT'S NOT ...
...GOING TO TAKE THAT LONG.
I KNOW.
I'M GOING TO PREPARE IT...
...EVEN FASTER ...
...AND MAKE IT EVEN TASTIER.
I WAS WAIT-ING...
...TO HEAR OU SAY THAT.
OMA- SU.

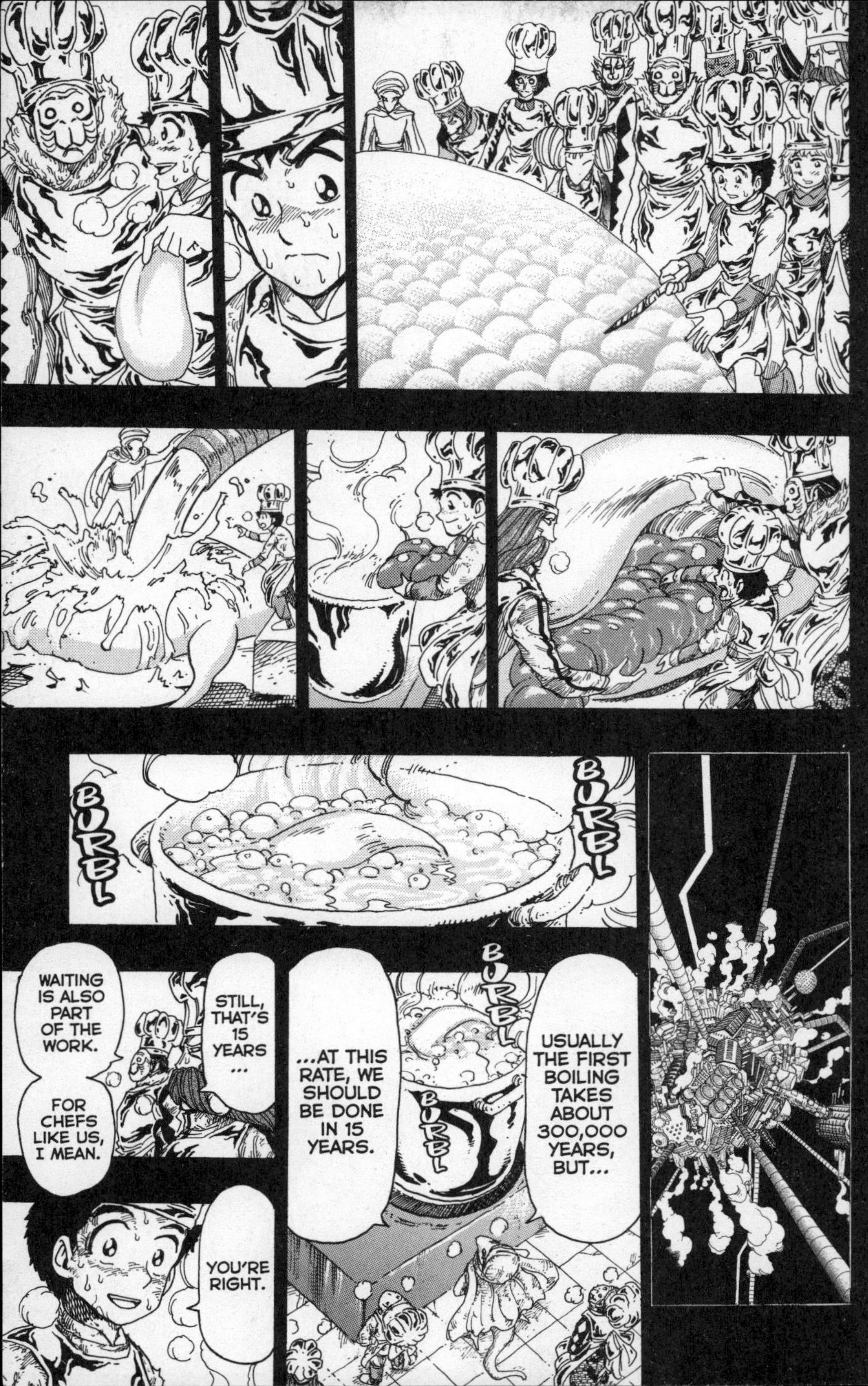
BURBL
BURBL
BURBL
USUALLY THE FIRST BOILING TAKES ABOUT 300,000 YEARS, BUT...
BURBL
...AT THIS RATE, WE SHOULD BE DONE IN 15 YEARS.
STILL, THAT'S 15 YEARS...
WAITING IS ALSO PART OF THE WORK.
FOR CHEFS LIKE US, I MEAN.
YOU'RE RIGHT.

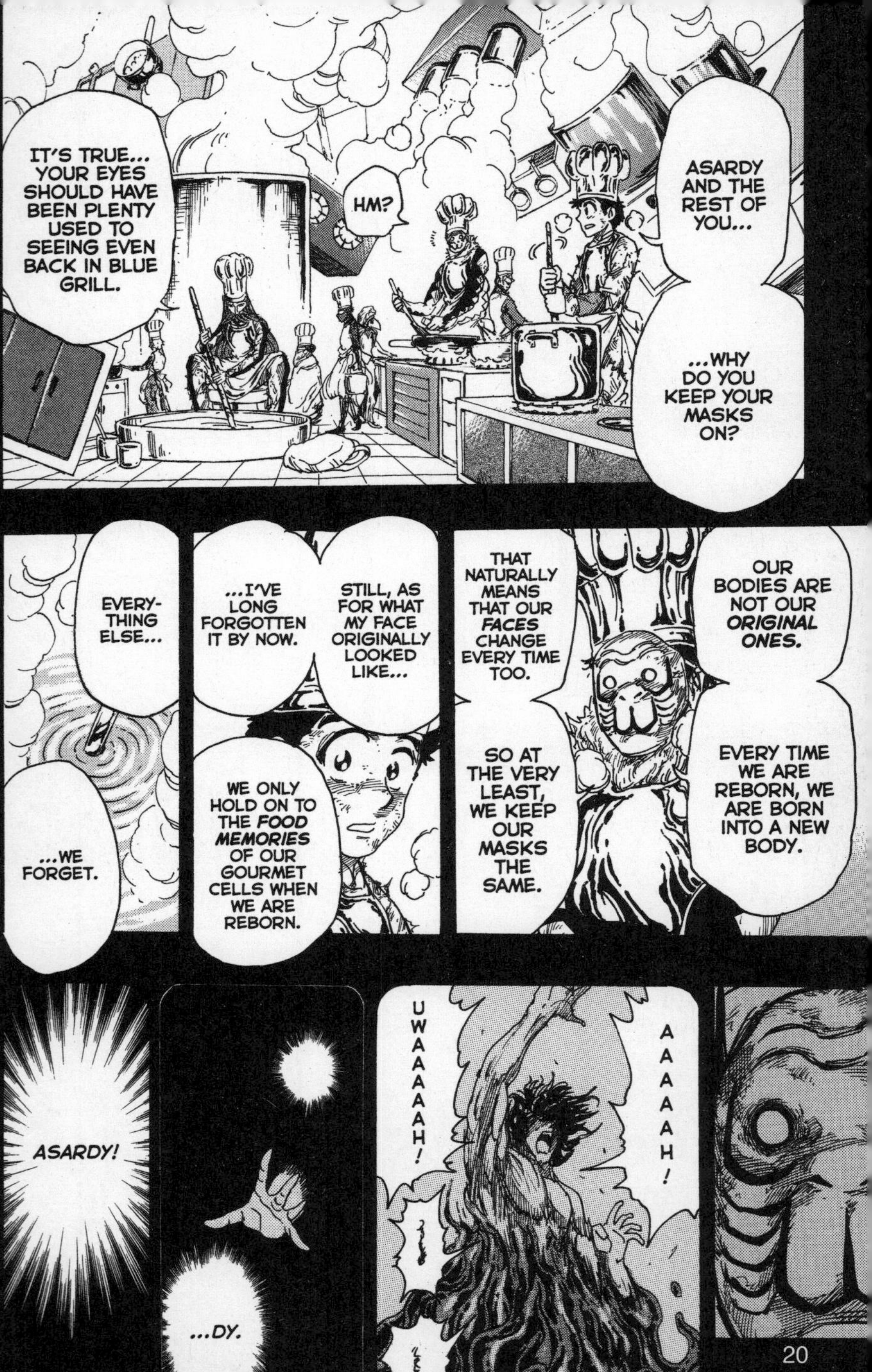
ASARDY AND THE REST OF YOU...
...WHY DO YOU KEEP YOUR MASKS ON?
HM?
IT'S TRUE... YOUR EYES SHOULD HAVE BEEN PLENTY USED TO SEEING EVEN BACK IN BLUE GRILL.
OUR BODIES ARE NOT OUR *ORIGINAL ONES.*
EVERY TIME WE ARE REBORN, WE ARE BORN INTO A NEW BODY.
THAT NATURALLY MEANS THAT OUR *FACES* CHANGE EVERY TIME TOO.
SO AT THE VERY LEAST, WE KEEP OUR MASKS THE SAME.
STILL, AS FOR WHAT MY FACE ORIGINALLY LOOKED LIKE...
...I'VE LONG FORGOTTEN IT BY NOW.
WE ONLY HOLD ON TO THE *FOOD MEMORIES* OF OUR GOURMET CELLS WHEN WE ARE REBORN.
EVERYTHING ELSE...
...WE FORGET.
UWAAAAAH!
AAAAAH!
...DY.
ASARDY!

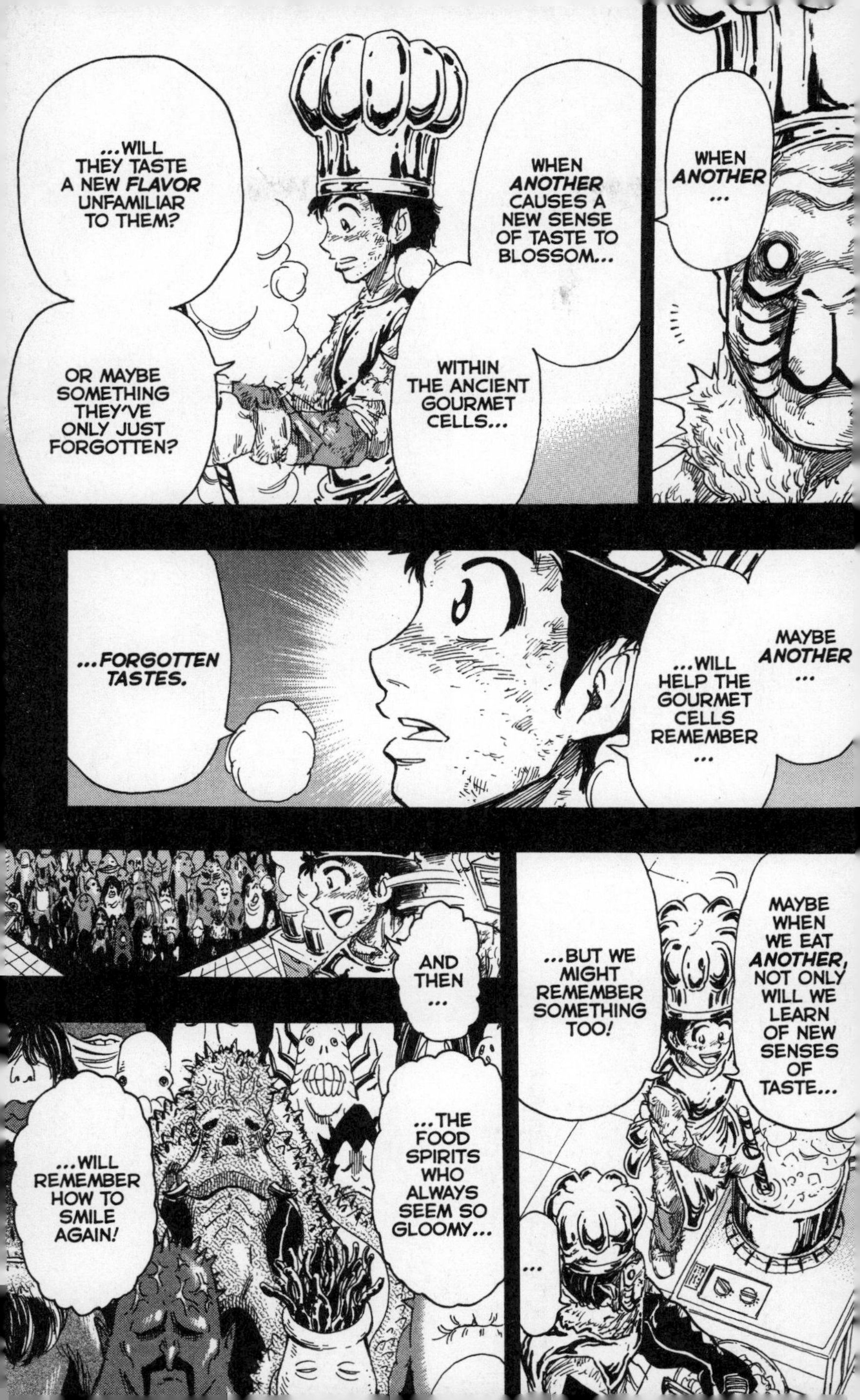
WHEN ANOTHER ...
WHEN ANOTHER CAUSES A NEW SENSE OF TASTE TO BLOSSOM...
WITHIN THE ANCIENT GOURMET CELLS...
...WILL THEY TASTE A NEW FLAVOR UNFAMILIAR TO THEM?
OR MAYBE SOMETHING THEY'VE ONLY JUST FORGOTTEN?
MAYBE ANOTHER ...
...WILL HELP THE GOURMET CELLS REMEMBER ...
...FORGOTTEN TASTES.
MAYBE WHEN WE EAT ANOTHER, NOT ONLY WILL WE LEARN OF NEW SENSES OF TASTE...
...BUT WE MIGHT REMEMBER SOMETHING TOO!
...
AND THEN ...
...THE FOOD SPIRITS WHO ALWAYS SEEM SO GLOOMY...
...WILL REMEMBER HOW TO SMILE AGAIN!

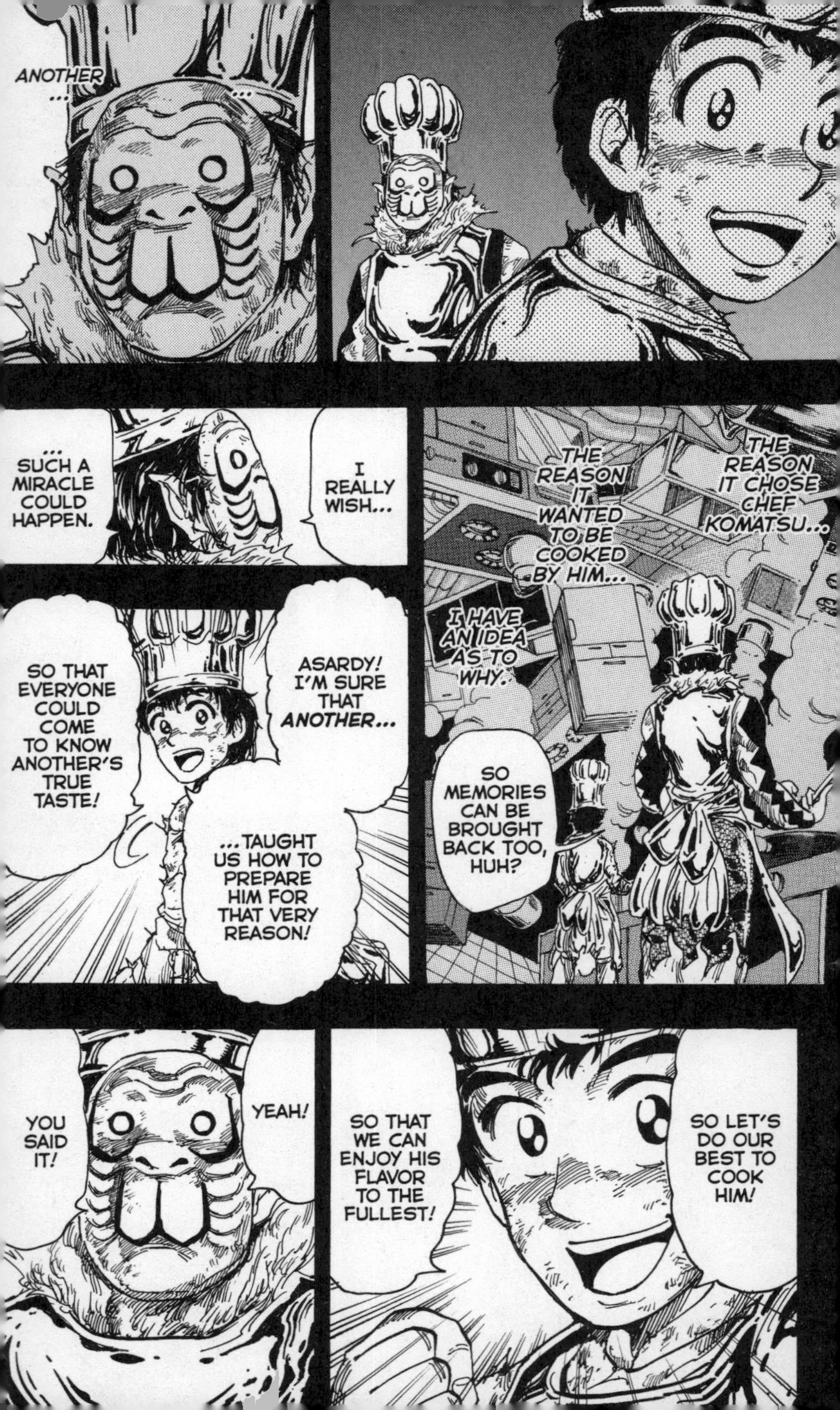
ANOTHER ...
...
THE REASON IT CHOSE CHEF KOMATSU...
THE REASON IT WANTED TO BE COOKED BY HIM...
I HAVE AN IDEA AS TO WHY.
SO MEMORIES CAN BE BROUGHT BACK TOO, HUH?
I REALLY WISH...
...SUCH A MIRACLE COULD HAPPEN.
ASARDY! I'M SURE THAT ANOTHER...
...TAUGHT US HOW TO PREPARE HIM FOR THAT VERY REASON!
SO THAT EVERYONE COULD COME TO KNOW ANOTHER'S TRUE TASTE!
SO LET'S DO OUR BEST TO COOK HIM!
SO THAT WE CAN ENJOY HIS FLAVOR TO THE FULLEST!
YEAH!
YOU SAID IT!

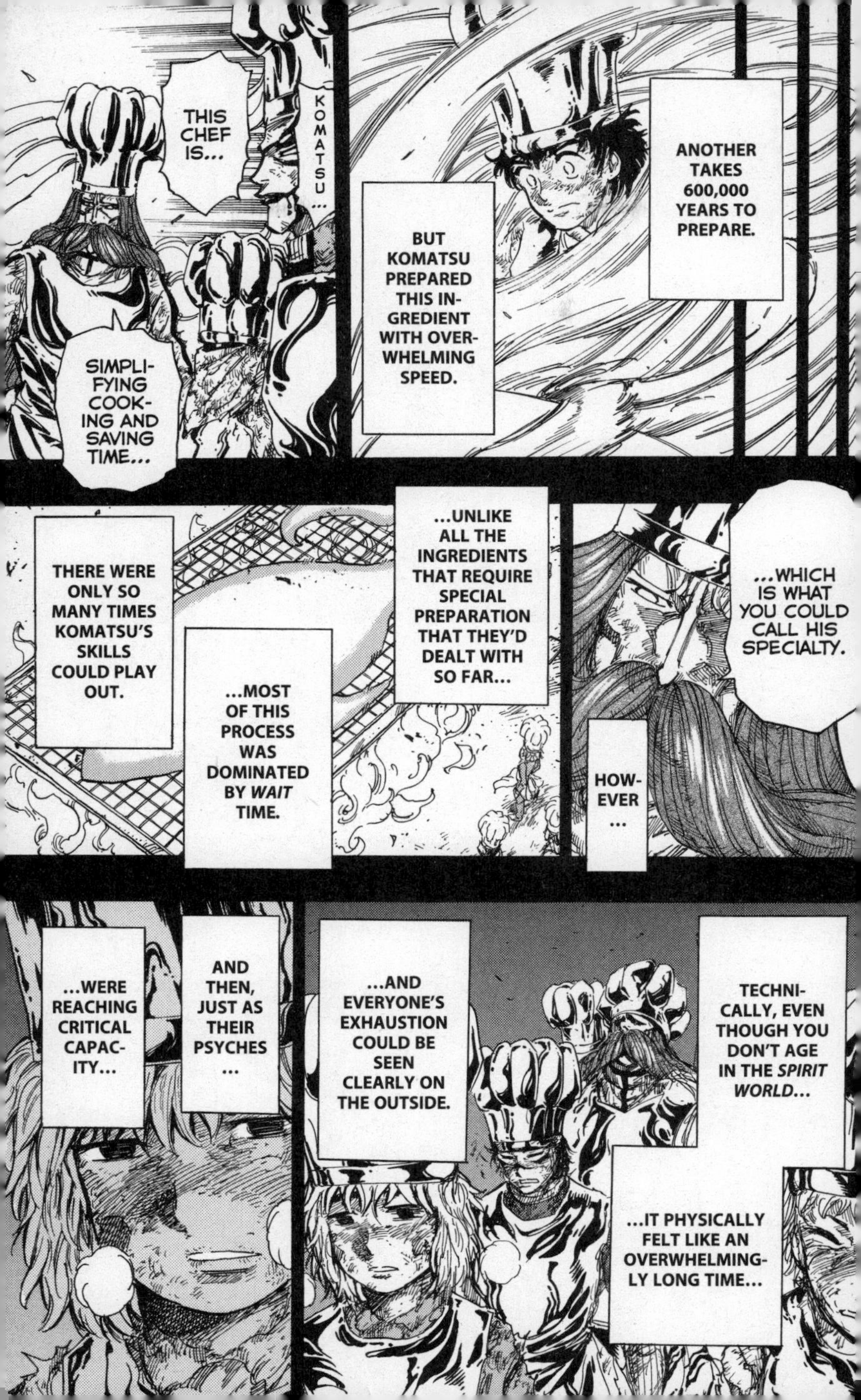
ANOTHER TAKES 600,000 YEARS TO PREPARE.
BUT KOMATSU PREPARED THIS INGREDIENT WITH OVERWHELMING SPEED.
KOMATSU...
THIS CHEF IS...
SIMPLIFYING COOKING AND SAVING TIME...
...WHICH IS WHAT YOU COULD CALL HIS SPECIALTY.
HOWEVER...
...UNLIKE ALL THE INGREDIENTS THAT REQUIRE SPECIAL PREPARATION THAT THEY'D DEALT WITH SO FAR...
...MOST OF THIS PROCESS WAS DOMINATED BY *WAIT* TIME.
THERE WERE ONLY SO MANY TIMES KOMATSU'S SKILLS COULD PLAY OUT.
TECHNICALLY, EVEN THOUGH YOU DON'T AGE IN THE *SPIRIT WORLD*...
...IT PHYSICALLY FELT LIKE AN OVERWHELMINGLY LONG TIME...
...AND EVERYONE'S EXHAUSTION COULD BE SEEN CLEARLY ON THE OUTSIDE.
AND THEN, JUST AS THEIR PSYCHES...
...WERE REACHING CRITICAL CAPACITY...

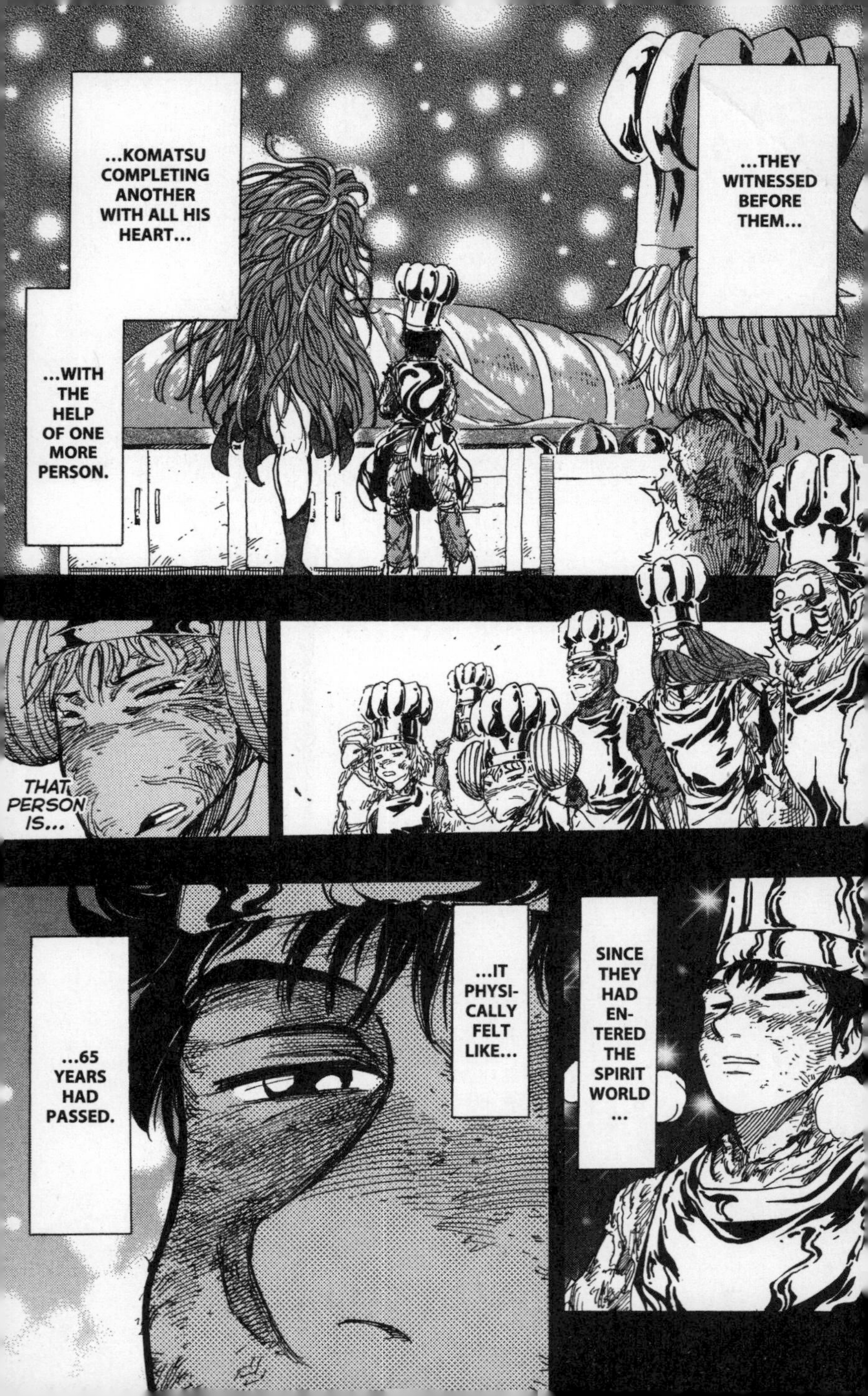
...THEY WITNESSED BEFORE THEM...
...KOMATSU COMPLETING ANOTHER WITH ALL HIS HEART...
...WITH THE HELP OF ONE MORE PERSON.
THAT PERSON IS...
SINCE THEY HAD ENTERED THE SPIRIT WORLD...
...IT PHYSICALLY FELT LIKE...
...65 YEARS HAD PASSED.

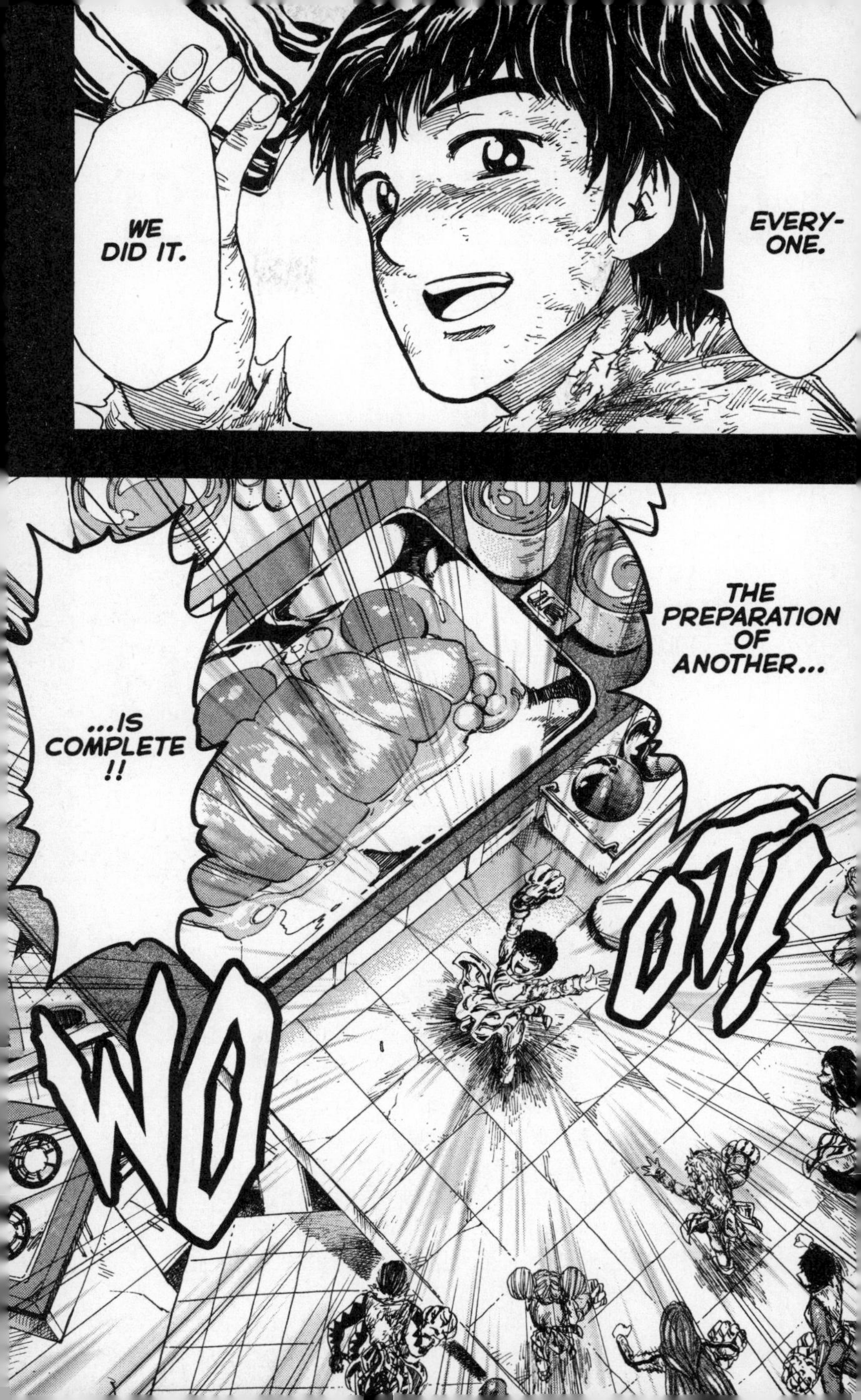
EVERY-ONE.
WE DID IT.
THE PREPARATION OF ANOTHER...
...IS COMPLETE!!
WOOT!

TORIKO

GOURMET CHECKLIST

Vol. 381

CRABUS
(CRUSTACEAN)

CAPTURE LEVEL: 500

HABITAT: GOURMET WORLD

SIZE: 20 M

HEIGHT: 5 M

WEIGHT: 10 TONS

PRICE: 7 MILLION YEN PER CLAW

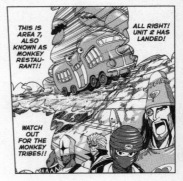

ALL RIGHT! UNIT 2 HAS LANDED!
THIS IS AREA 7, ALSO KNOWN AS MONKEY RESTAURANT!!
WATCH OUT FOR THE MONKEY TRIBES!!

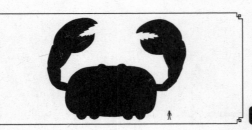

SCALE

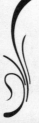

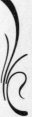

A CRAB IN THE SHAPE OF A BUS. IT'S AN INDISPENSABLE CAMPING MONSTER WHEN IT COMES TO TRAVELING SAFELY THROUGH THE GOURMET WORLD AND CARRYING INGREDIENTS BACK TO THE HUMAN WORLD. LIKE A REGULAR CRAB, IT CAN ONLY MOVE SIDEWAYS. BUT UNLIKE A REGULAR CRAB, IT CAN SURPASS AN F-1 RACECAR IN TERMS OF SPEED! ITS CLAWS ARE PACKED WITH FATTY MEAT THAT IS SO DELICIOUS THAT IT'LL HAVE YOU HOOKED!

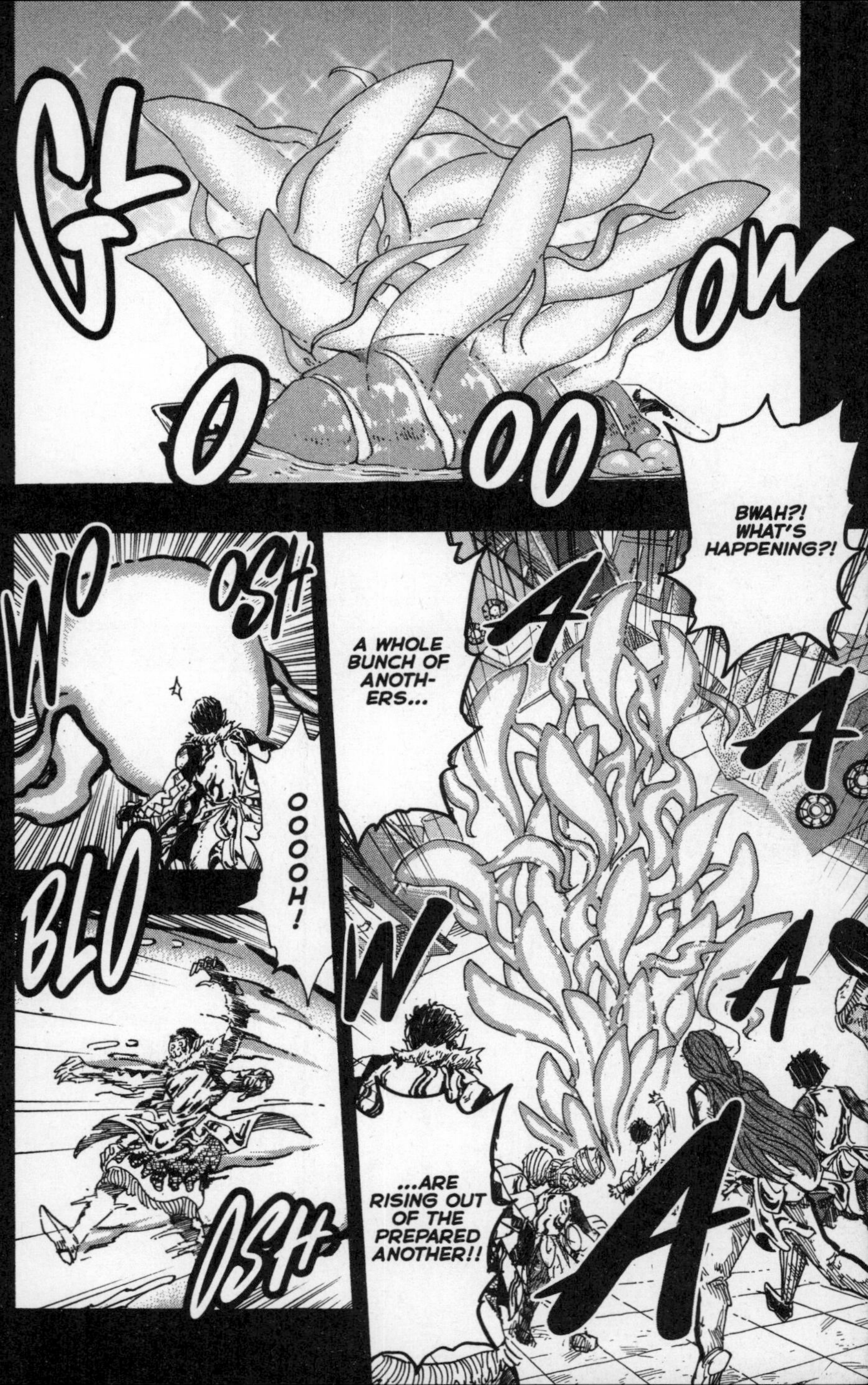
GLOOOOW
BWAH?! WHAT'S HAPPENING?!
A WHOLE BUNCH OF ANOTH-ERS...
...ARE RISING OUT OF THE PREPARED ANOTHER!!
WAAAA
WOOSH
OOOOOH!
BLOOSH

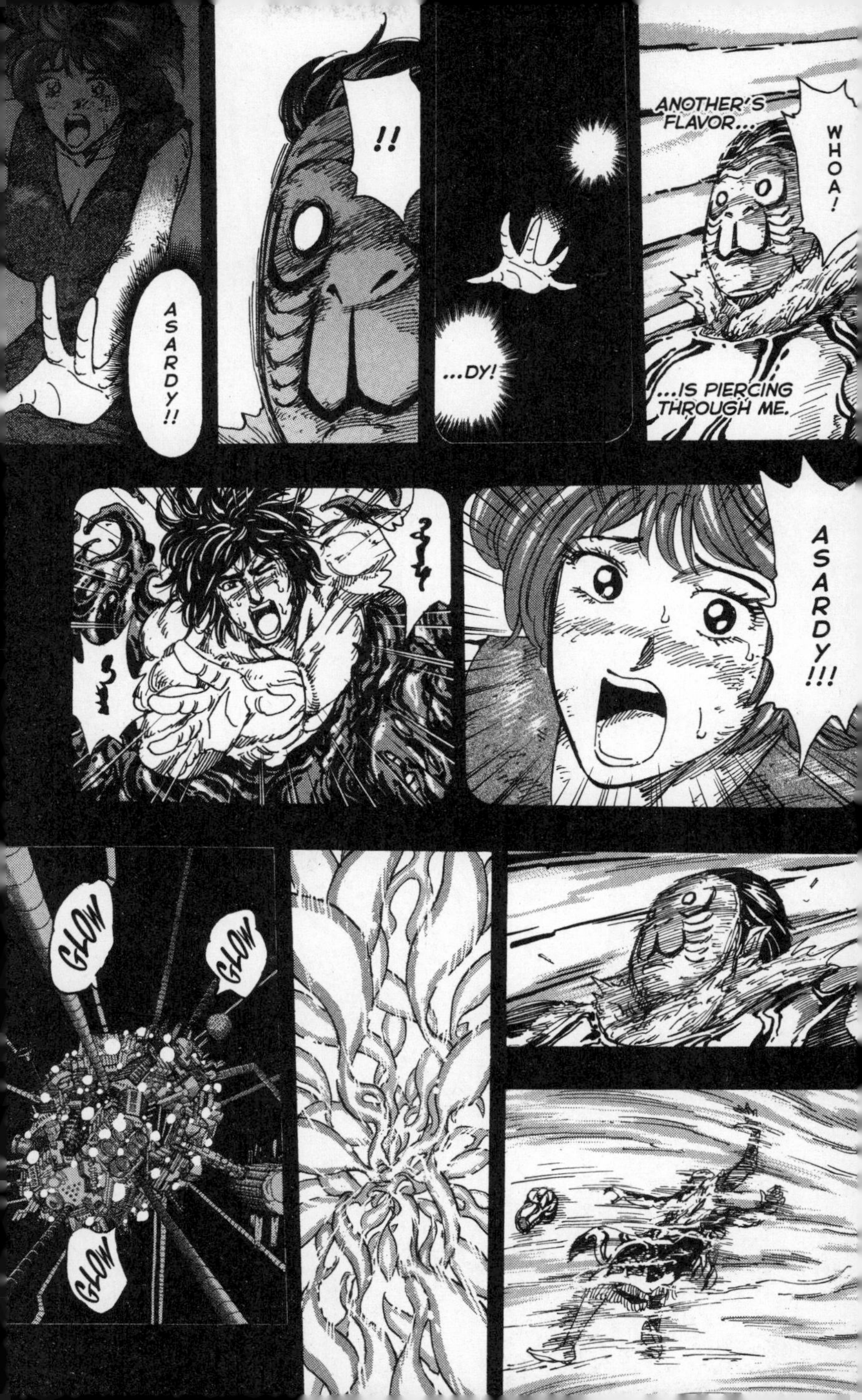
WHOA!
ANOTHER'S FLAVOR...
...IS PIERCING THROUGH ME.
...DY!
!!
ASARDY!!
ASARDY!!!
GLOW
GLOW
GLOW

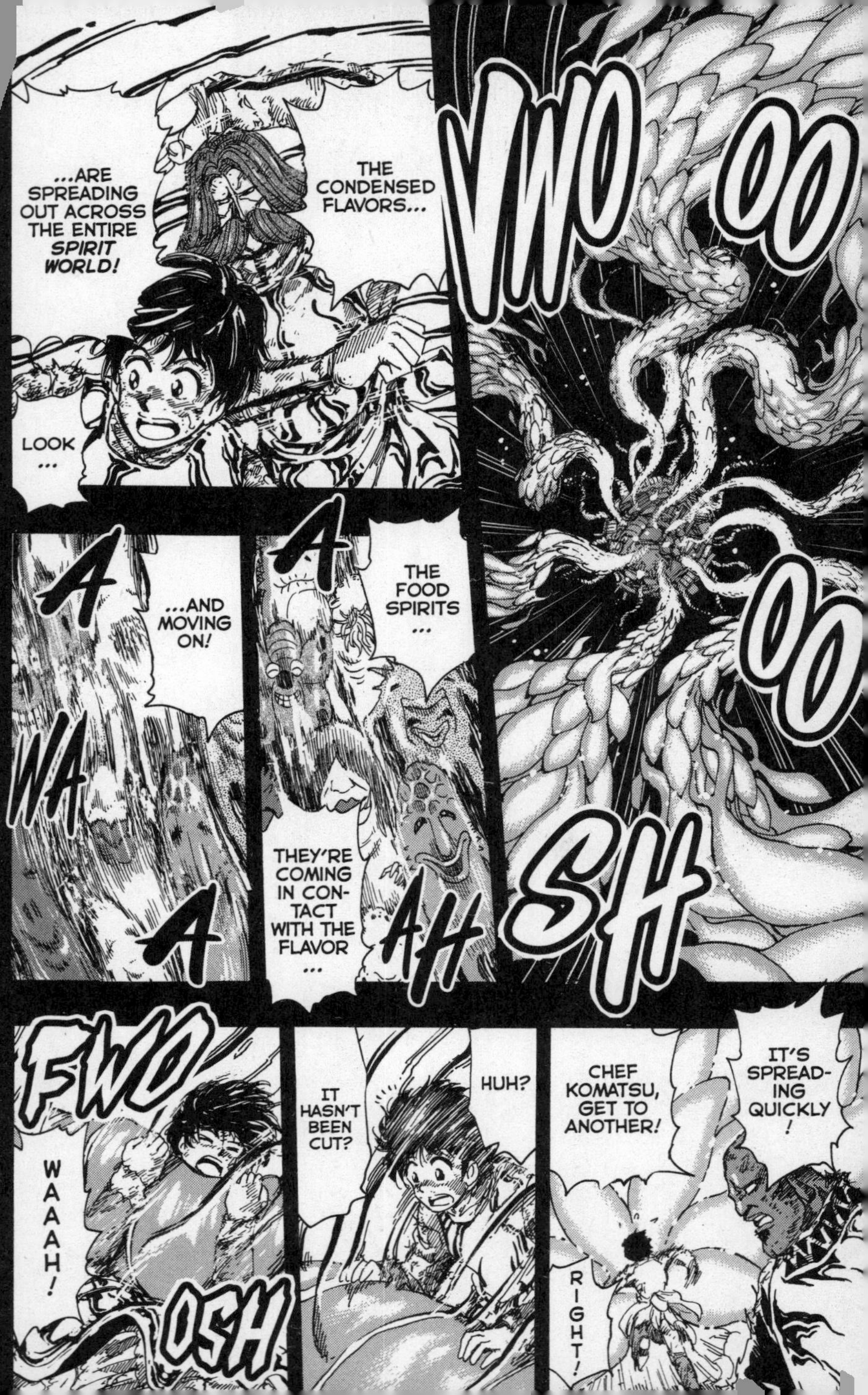
VWOOOOOO
SH
THE CONDENSED FLAVORS...
...ARE SPREADING OUT ACROSS THE ENTIRE SPIRIT WORLD!
LOOK...
A
THE FOOD SPIRITS...
THEY'RE COMING IN CON-TACT WITH THE FLAVOR...
AH
A
...AND MOVING ON!
WA
A
IT'S SPREAD-ING QUICKLY!
CHEF KOMATSU, GET TO ANOTHER!
RIGHT!
HUH?
IT HASN'T BEEN CUT?
FWO
WAAAAH!
OSH

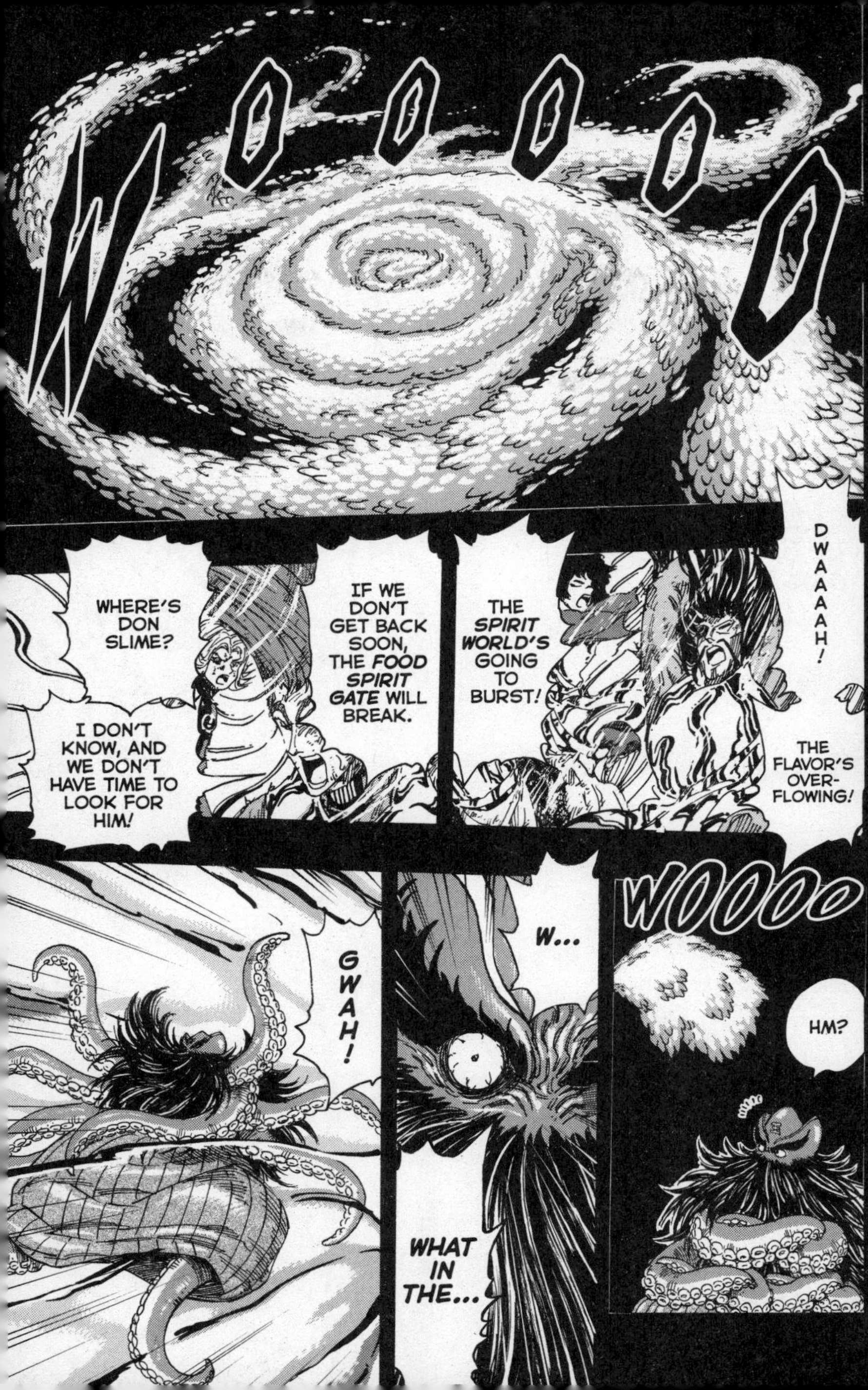
WOOOOOO
DWAAAAAH!
THE SPIRIT WORLD'S GOING TO BURST!
THE FLAVOR'S OVER-FLOWING!
IF WE DON'T GET BACK SOON, THE FOOD SPIRIT GATE WILL BREAK.
WHERE'S DON SLIME?
I DON'T KNOW, AND WE DON'T HAVE TIME TO LOOK FOR HIM!
WOOOo
HM?
W...
WHAT IN THE...
GWAH!

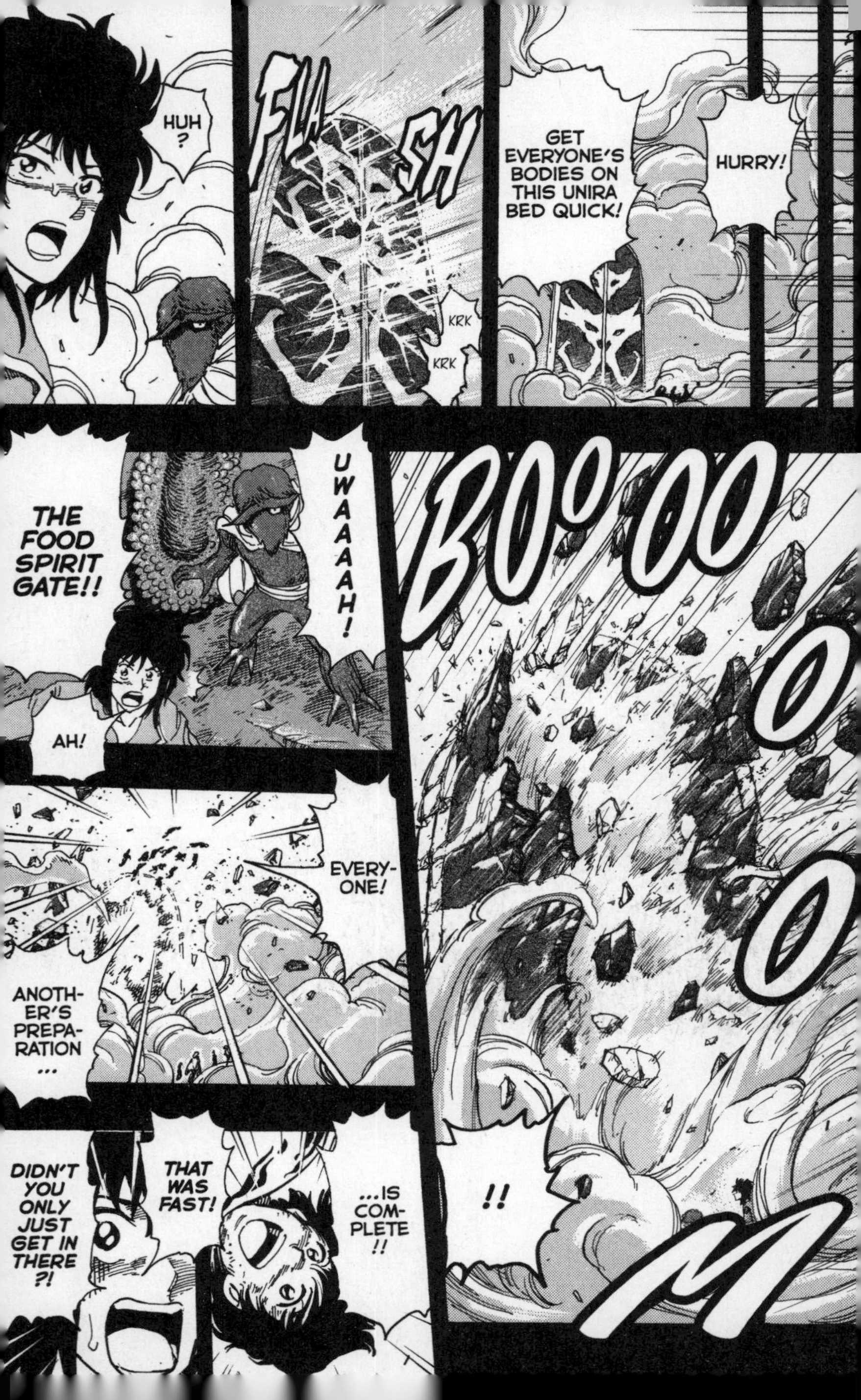
HURRY!
GET EVERYONE'S BODIES ON THIS UNIRA BED QUICK!
FLASH
KRK
KRK
HUH?
BOOOOOOM
!!
UWAAAAAH!
THE FOOD SPIRIT GATE!!
AH!
EVERYONE!
ANOTHER'S PREPARATION...
...IS COMPLETE!!
THAT WAS FAST!
DIDN'T YOU ONLY JUST GET IN THERE?!

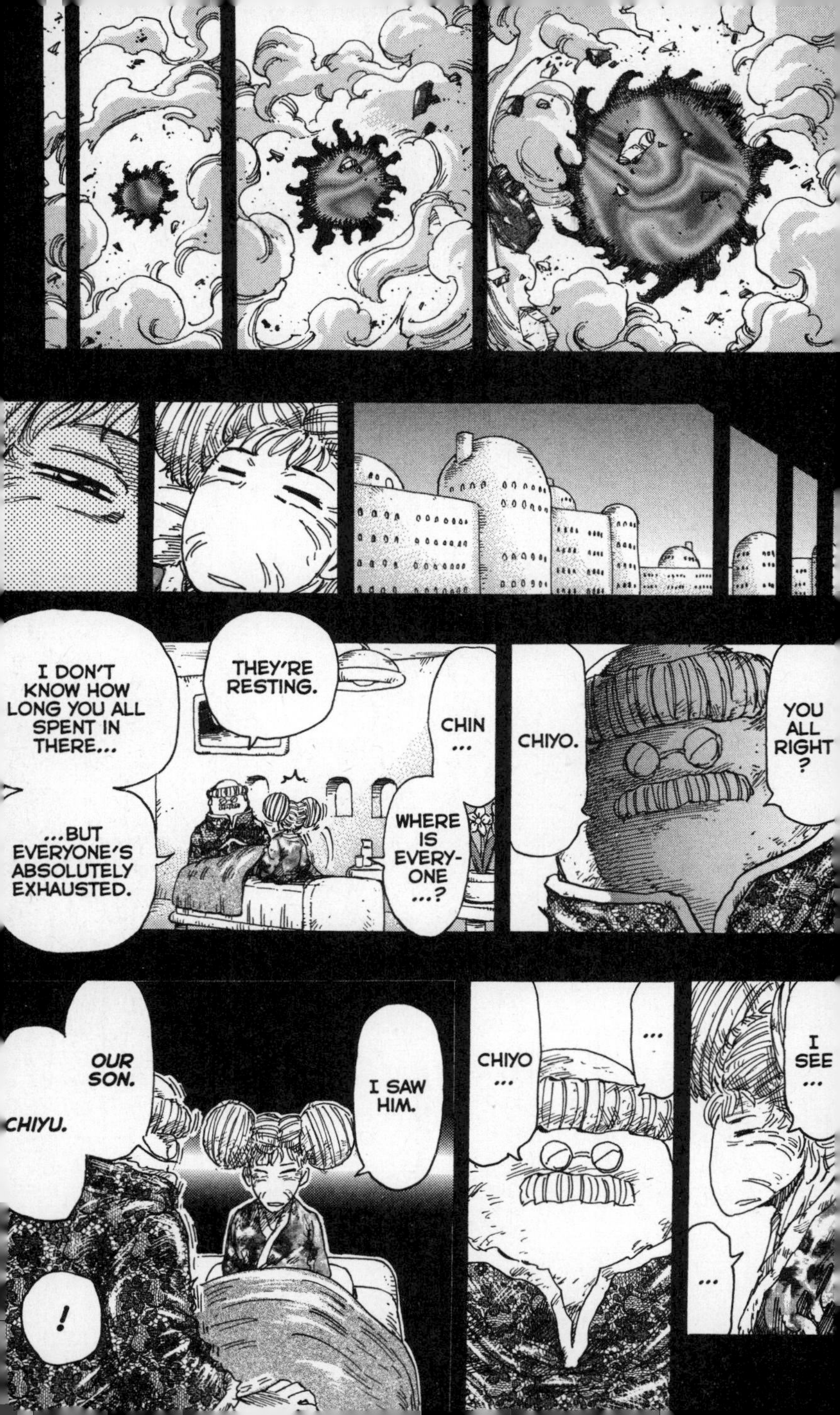
YOU ALL RIGHT?
CHIYO.
CHIN...
WHERE IS EVERYONE...?
THEY'RE RESTING.
I DON'T KNOW HOW LONG YOU ALL SPENT IN THERE...
...BUT EVERYONE'S ABSOLUTELY EXHAUSTED.
I SEE...
...
...
CHIYO...
I SAW HIM.
OUR SON.
CHIYU.
!

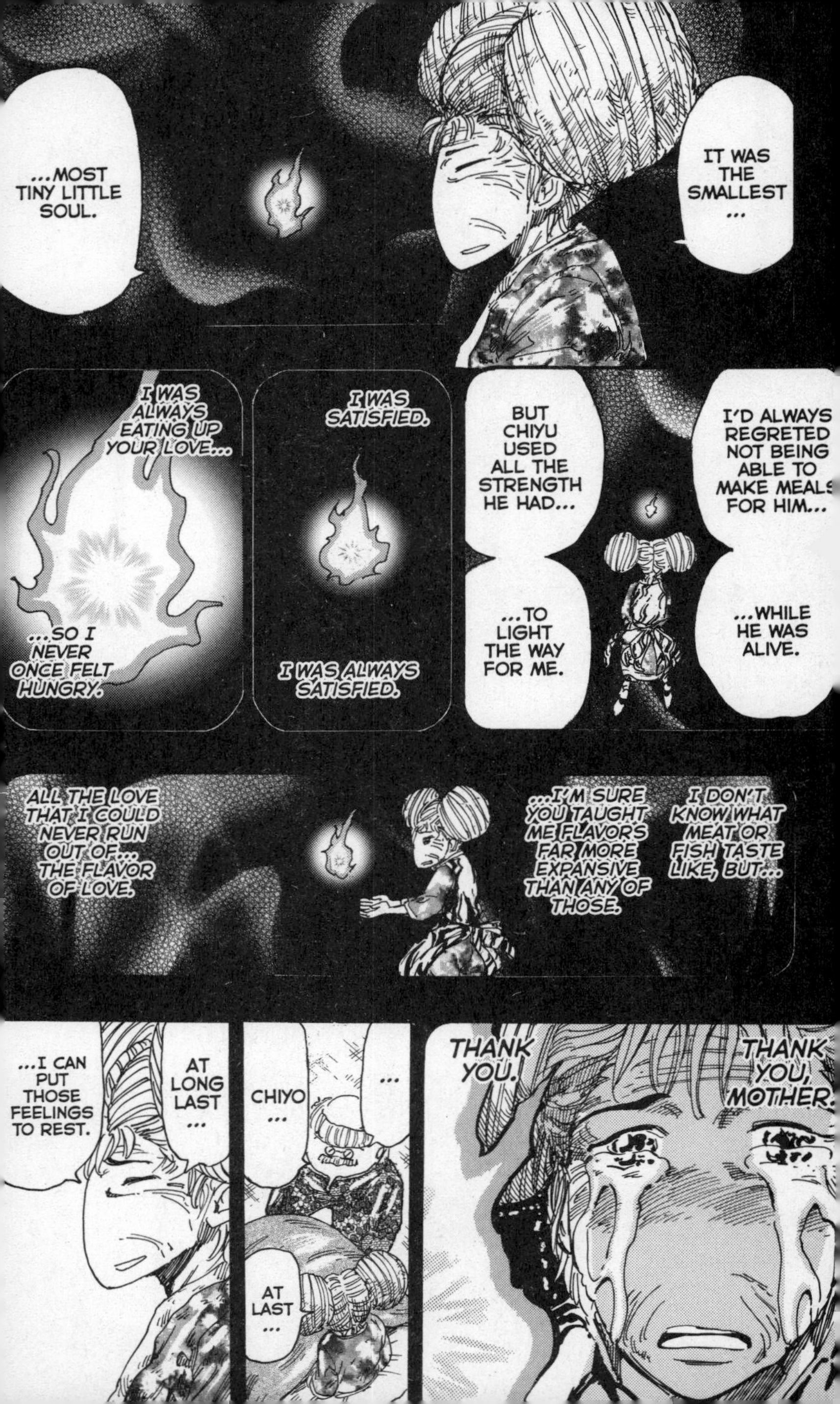
IT WAS THE SMALLEST ...
...MOST TINY LITTLE SOUL.
I'D ALWAYS REGRETED NOT BEING ABLE TO MAKE MEALS FOR HIM...
...WHILE HE WAS ALIVE.
BUT CHIYU USED ALL THE STRENGTH HE HAD...
...TO LIGHT THE WAY FOR ME.
I WAS SATISFIED.
I WAS ALWAYS SATISFIED.
I WAS ALWAYS EATING UP YOUR LOVE...
...SO I NEVER ONCE FELT HUNGRY.
I DON'T KNOW WHAT MEAT OR FISH TASTE LIKE, BUT...
...I'M SURE YOU TAUGHT ME FLAVORS FAR MORE EXPANSIVE THAN ANY OF THOSE.
ALL THE LOVE THAT I COULD NEVER RUN OUT OF... THE FLAVOR OF LOVE.
THANK YOU, MOTHER.
THANK YOU.
...
CHIYO ...
AT LAST ...
AT LONG LAST ...
...I CAN PUT THOSE FEELINGS TO REST.

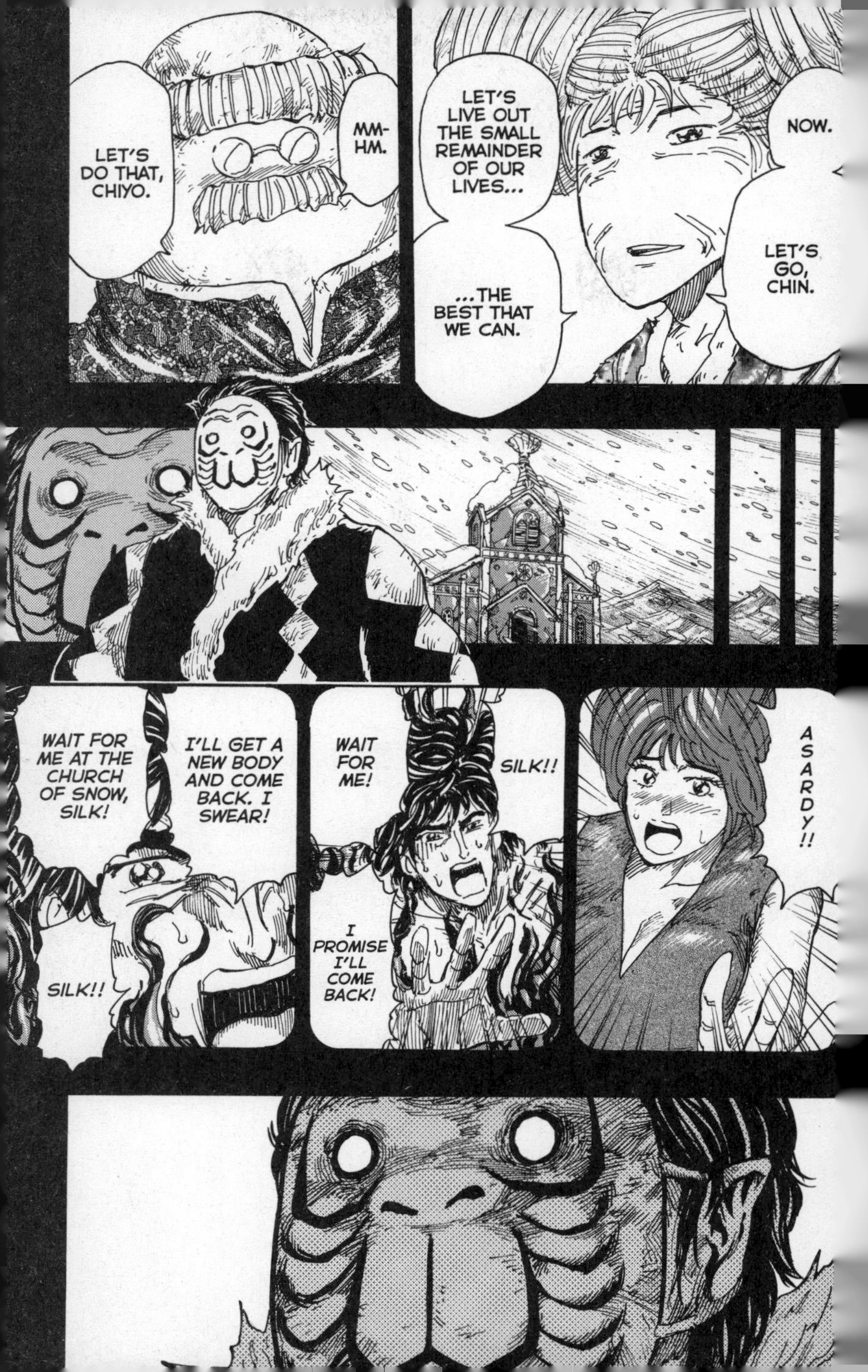
NOW.
LET'S GO, CHIN.
LET'S LIVE OUT THE SMALL REMAINDER OF OUR LIVES...
...THE BEST THAT WE CAN.
MM-HM.
LET'S DO THAT, CHIYO.
ASARDY!!
SILK!!
WAIT FOR ME!
I PROMISE I'LL COME BACK!
I'LL GET A NEW BODY AND COME BACK. I SWEAR!
WAIT FOR ME AT THE CHURCH OF SNOW, SILK!
SILK!!

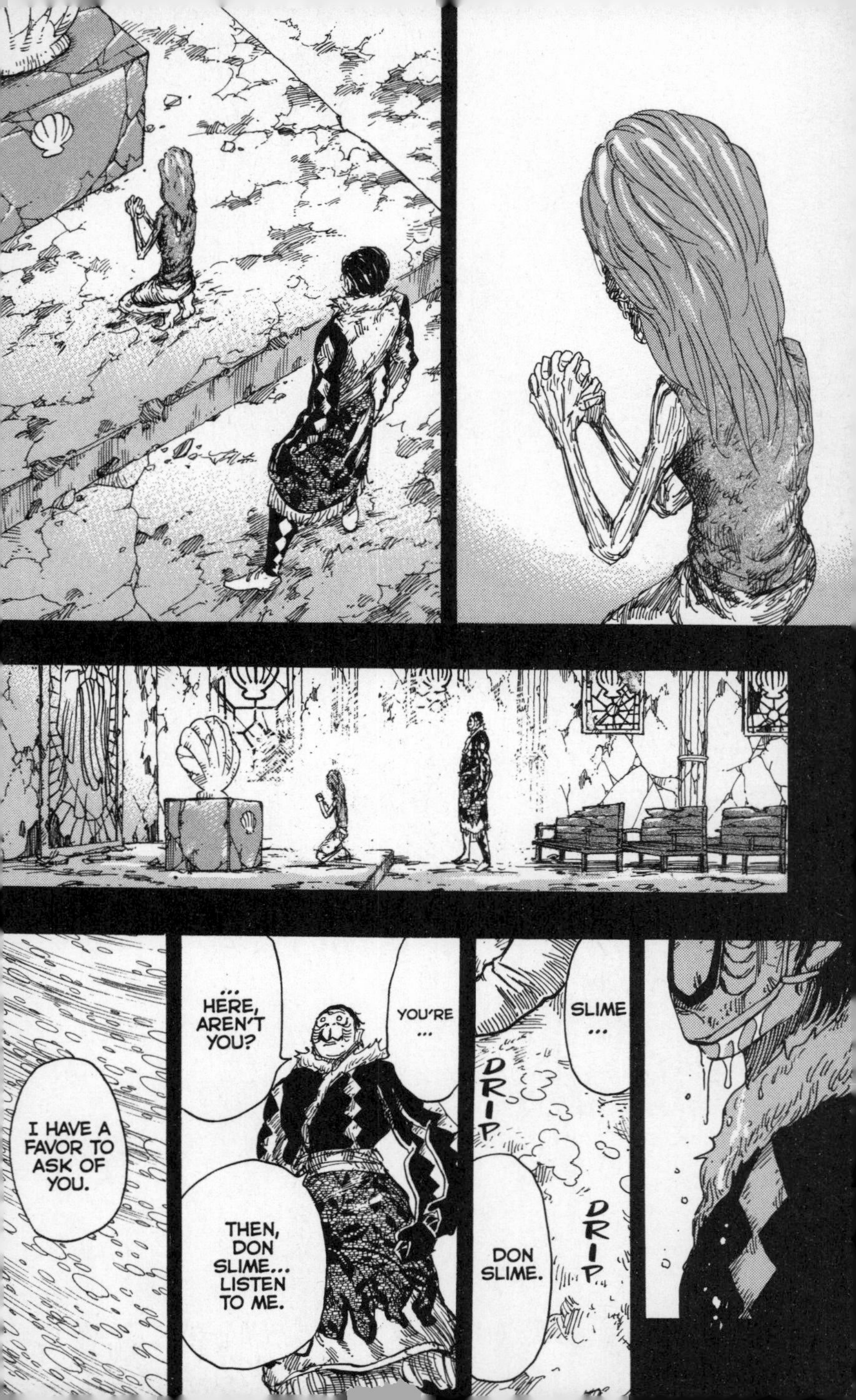
SLIME ...
DRIP
DRIP
DON SLIME.
YOU'RE ...
... HERE, AREN'T YOU?
THEN, DON SLIME... LISTEN TO ME.
I HAVE A FAVOR TO ASK OF YOU.

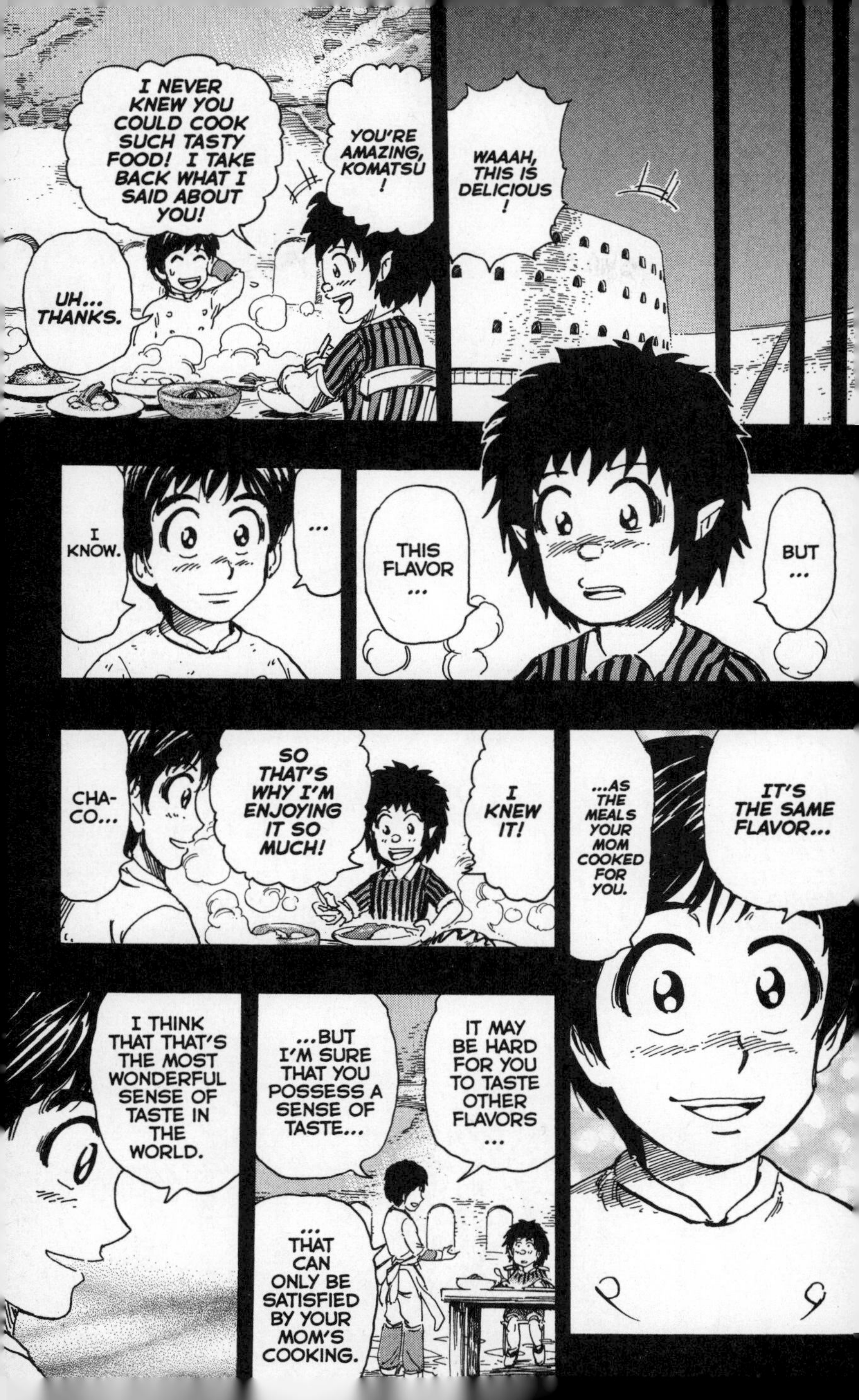
WAAAH, THIS IS DELICIOUS!
YOU'RE AMAZING, KOMATSU!
I NEVER KNEW YOU COULD COOK SUCH TASTY FOOD! I TAKE BACK WHAT I SAID ABOUT YOU!
UH... THANKS.
BUT...
THIS FLAVOR...
...
I KNOW.
IT'S THE SAME FLAVOR...
...AS THE MEALS YOUR MOM COOKED FOR YOU.
I KNEW IT!
SO THAT'S WHY I'M ENJOYING IT SO MUCH!
CHA-CO...
IT MAY BE HARD FOR YOU TO TASTE OTHER FLAVORS...
...BUT I'M SURE THAT YOU POSSESS A SENSE OF TASTE...
...THAT CAN ONLY BE SATISFIED BY YOUR MOM'S COOKING.
I THINK THAT THAT'S THE MOST WONDERFUL SENSE OF TASTE IN THE WORLD.

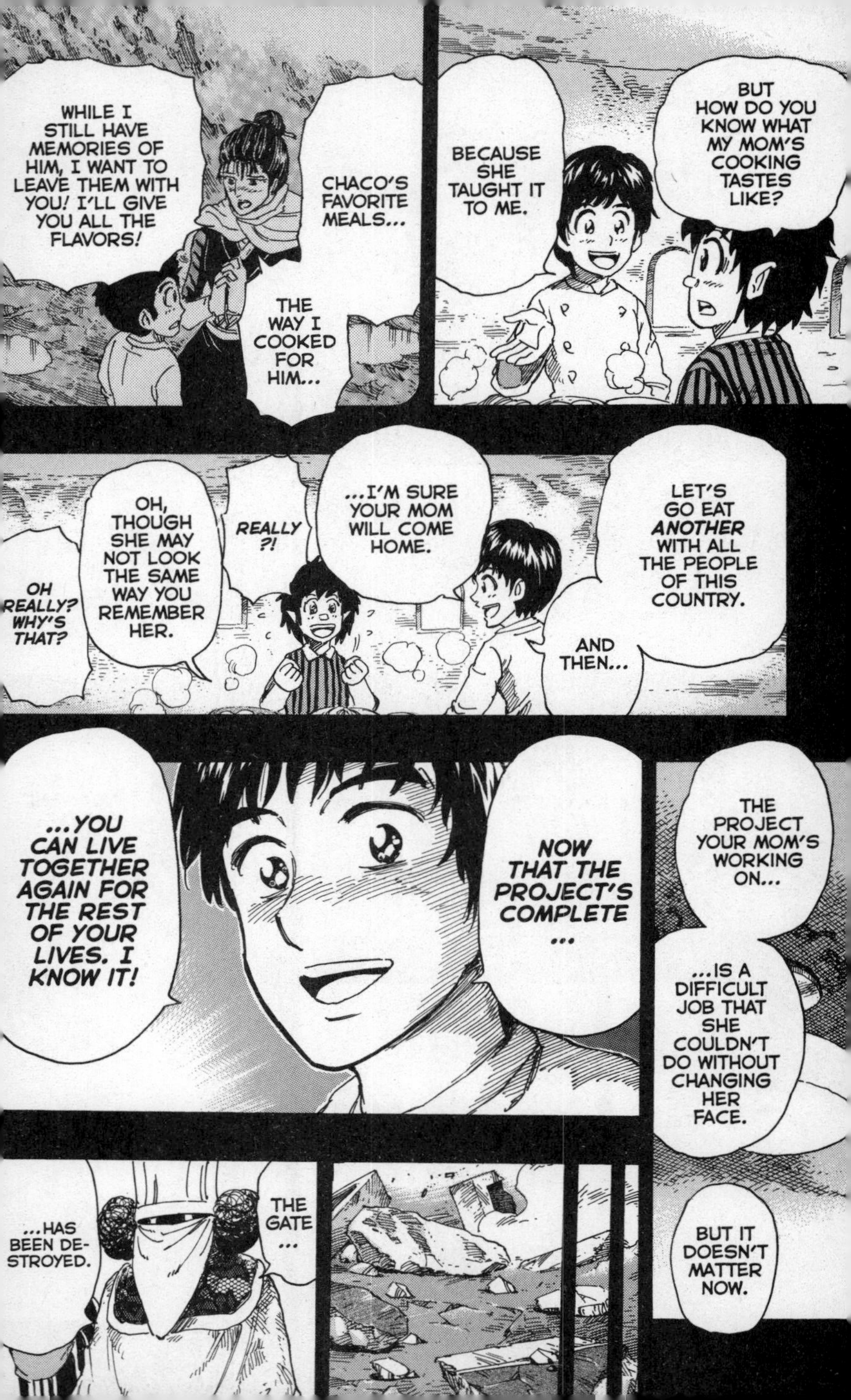
BUT HOW DO YOU KNOW WHAT MY MOM'S COOKING TASTES LIKE?
BECAUSE SHE TAUGHT IT TO ME.
CHACO'S FAVORITE MEALS...
THE WAY I COOKED FOR HIM...
WHILE I STILL HAVE MEMORIES OF HIM, I WANT TO LEAVE THEM WITH YOU! I'LL GIVE YOU ALL THE FLAVORS!
LET'S GO EAT ANOTHER WITH ALL THE PEOPLE OF THIS COUNTRY.
AND THEN...
...I'M SURE YOUR MOM WILL COME HOME.
REALLY?!
OH, THOUGH SHE MAY NOT LOOK THE SAME WAY YOU REMEMBER HER.
OH REALLY? WHY'S THAT?
THE PROJECT YOUR MOM'S WORKING ON...
...IS A DIFFICULT JOB THAT SHE COULDN'T DO WITHOUT CHANGING HER FACE.
NOW THAT THE PROJECT'S COMPLETE...
...YOU CAN LIVE TOGETHER AGAIN FOR THE REST OF YOUR LIVES. I KNOW IT!
BUT IT DOESN'T MATTER NOW.
THE GATE...
...HAS BEEN DE-STROYED.

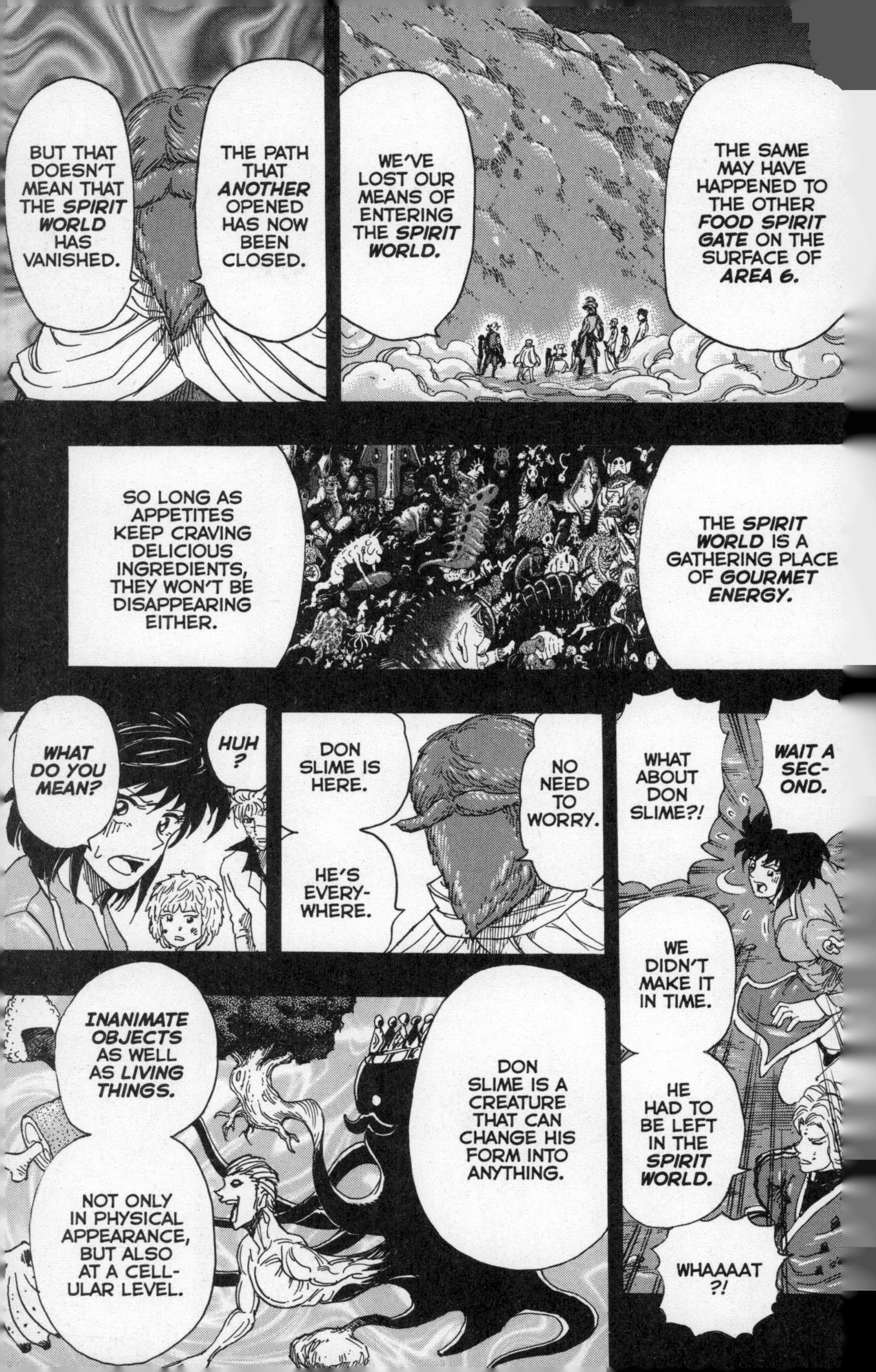
WE'VE LOST OUR MEANS OF ENTERING THE SPIRIT WORLD.
THE SAME MAY HAVE HAPPENED TO THE OTHER FOOD SPIRIT GATE ON THE SURFACE OF AREA 6.
THE PATH THAT ANOTHER OPENED HAS NOW BEEN CLOSED.
BUT THAT DOESN'T MEAN THAT THE SPIRIT WORLD HAS VANISHED.
THE SPIRIT WORLD IS A GATHERING PLACE OF GOURMET ENERGY.
SO LONG AS APPETITES KEEP CRAVING DELICIOUS INGREDIENTS, THEY WON'T BE DISAPPEARING EITHER.
WAIT A SEC-OND.
WHAT ABOUT DON SLIME?!
WE DIDN'T MAKE IT IN TIME.
HE HAD TO BE LEFT IN THE SPIRIT WORLD.
WHAAAAT ?!
NO NEED TO WORRY.
DON SLIME IS HERE.
HE'S EVERY-WHERE.
HUH ?
WHAT DO YOU MEAN?
DON SLIME IS A CREATURE THAT CAN CHANGE HIS FORM INTO ANYTHING.
INANIMATE OBJECTS AS WELL AS LIVING THINGS.
NOT ONLY IN PHYSICAL APPEARANCE, BUT ALSO AT A CELL-ULAR LEVEL.

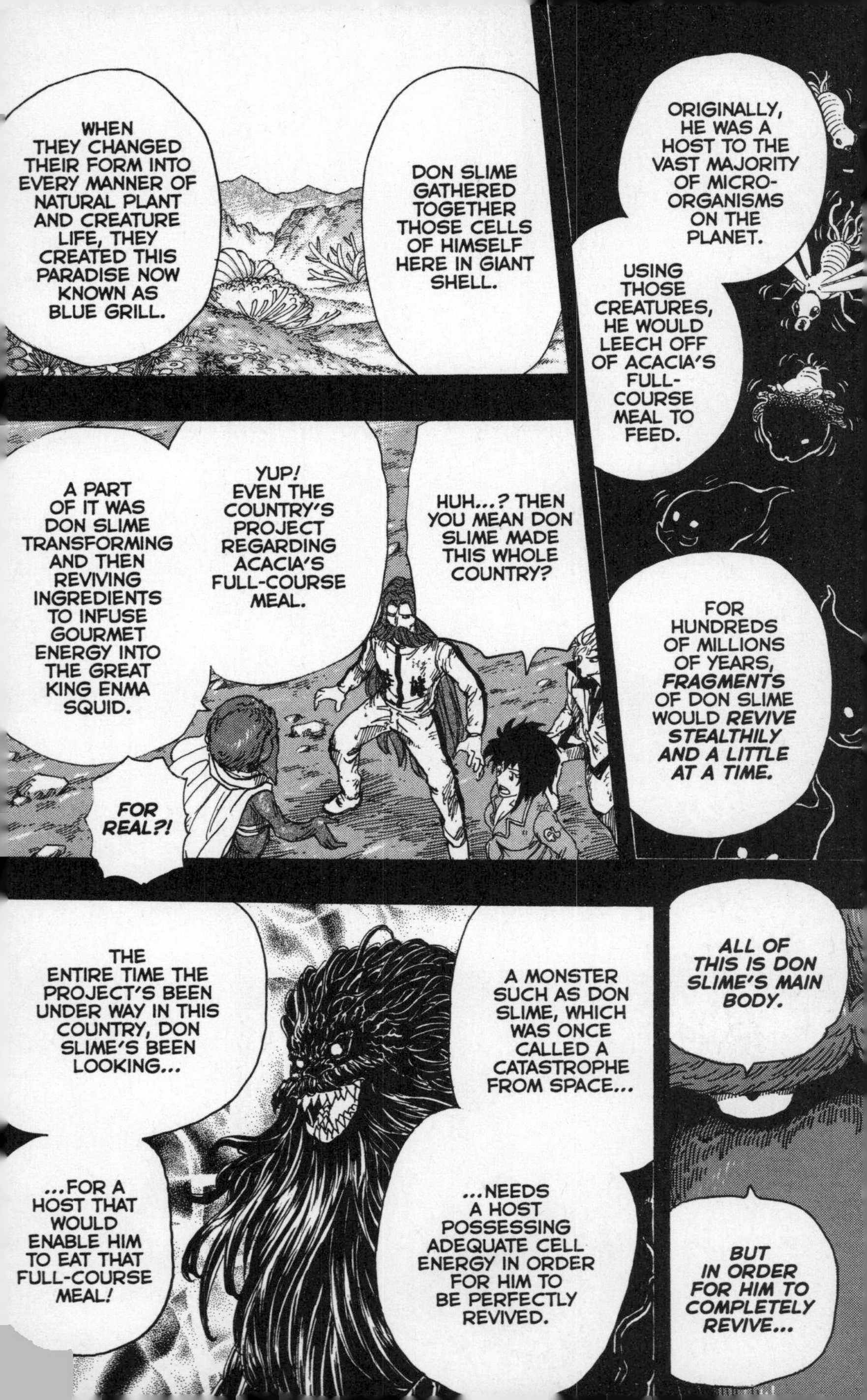
ORIGINALLY, HE WAS A HOST TO THE VAST MAJORITY OF MICRO-ORGANISMS ON THE PLANET.
USING THOSE CREATURES, HE WOULD LEECH OFF OF ACACIA'S FULL-COURSE MEAL TO FEED.
FOR HUNDREDS OF MILLIONS OF YEARS, *FRAGMENTS* OF DON SLIME WOULD *REVIVE STEALTHILY AND A LITTLE AT A TIME.*
DON SLIME GATHERED TOGETHER THOSE CELLS OF HIMSELF HERE IN GIANT SHELL.
WHEN THEY CHANGED THEIR FORM INTO EVERY MANNER OF NATURAL PLANT AND CREATURE LIFE, THEY CREATED THIS PARADISE NOW KNOWN AS BLUE GRILL.
HUH...? THEN YOU MEAN DON SLIME MADE THIS WHOLE COUNTRY?
YUP! EVEN THE COUNTRY'S PROJECT REGARDING ACACIA'S FULL-COURSE MEAL.
A PART OF IT WAS DON SLIME TRANSFORMING AND THEN REVIVING INGREDIENTS TO INFUSE GOURMET ENERGY INTO THE GREAT KING ENMA SQUID.
FOR REAL?!
ALL OF THIS IS DON SLIME'S MAIN BODY.
BUT IN ORDER FOR HIM TO COMPLETELY REVIVE...
A MONSTER SUCH AS DON SLIME, WHICH WAS ONCE CALLED A CATASTROPHE FROM SPACE...
...NEEDS A HOST POSSESSING ADEQUATE CELL ENERGY IN ORDER FOR HIM TO BE PERFECTLY REVIVED.
THE ENTIRE TIME THE PROJECT'S BEEN UNDER WAY IN THIS COUNTRY, DON SLIME'S BEEN LOOKING...
...FOR A HOST THAT WOULD ENABLE HIM TO EAT THAT FULL-COURSE MEAL!

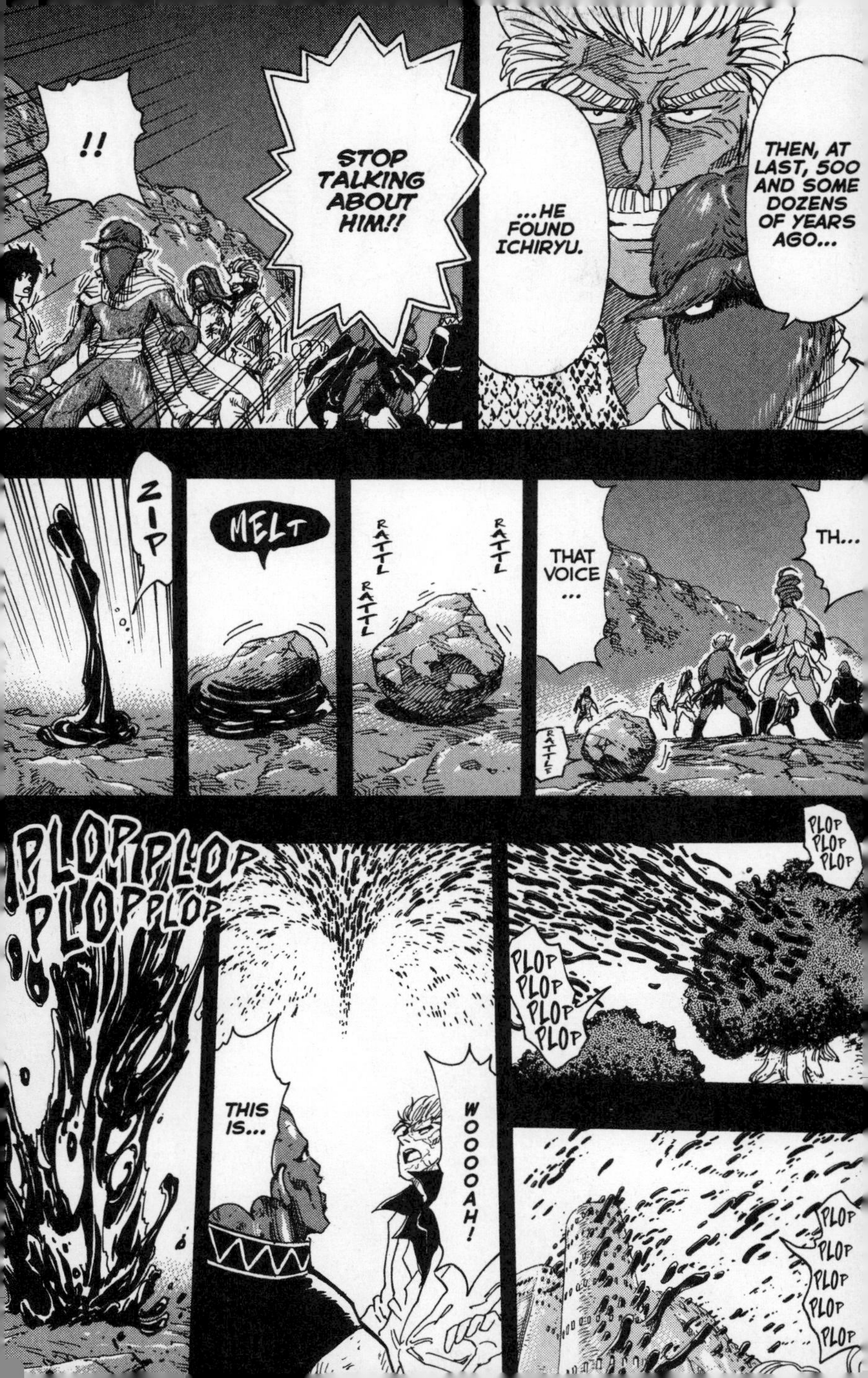

THEN, AT LAST, 500 AND SOME DOZENS OF YEARS AGO...
...HE FOUND ICHIRYU.
STOP TALKING ABOUT HIM!!
!!
TH...
THAT VOICE ...
RATTL
RATTL
RATTL
RATTL
MELT
ZIP
PLOP PLOP PLOP
PLOP PLOP PLOP PLOP
PLOP PLOP PLOP PLOP PLOP
WOOOOOAH!
THIS IS...
PLOPPLOP PLOPPLOP

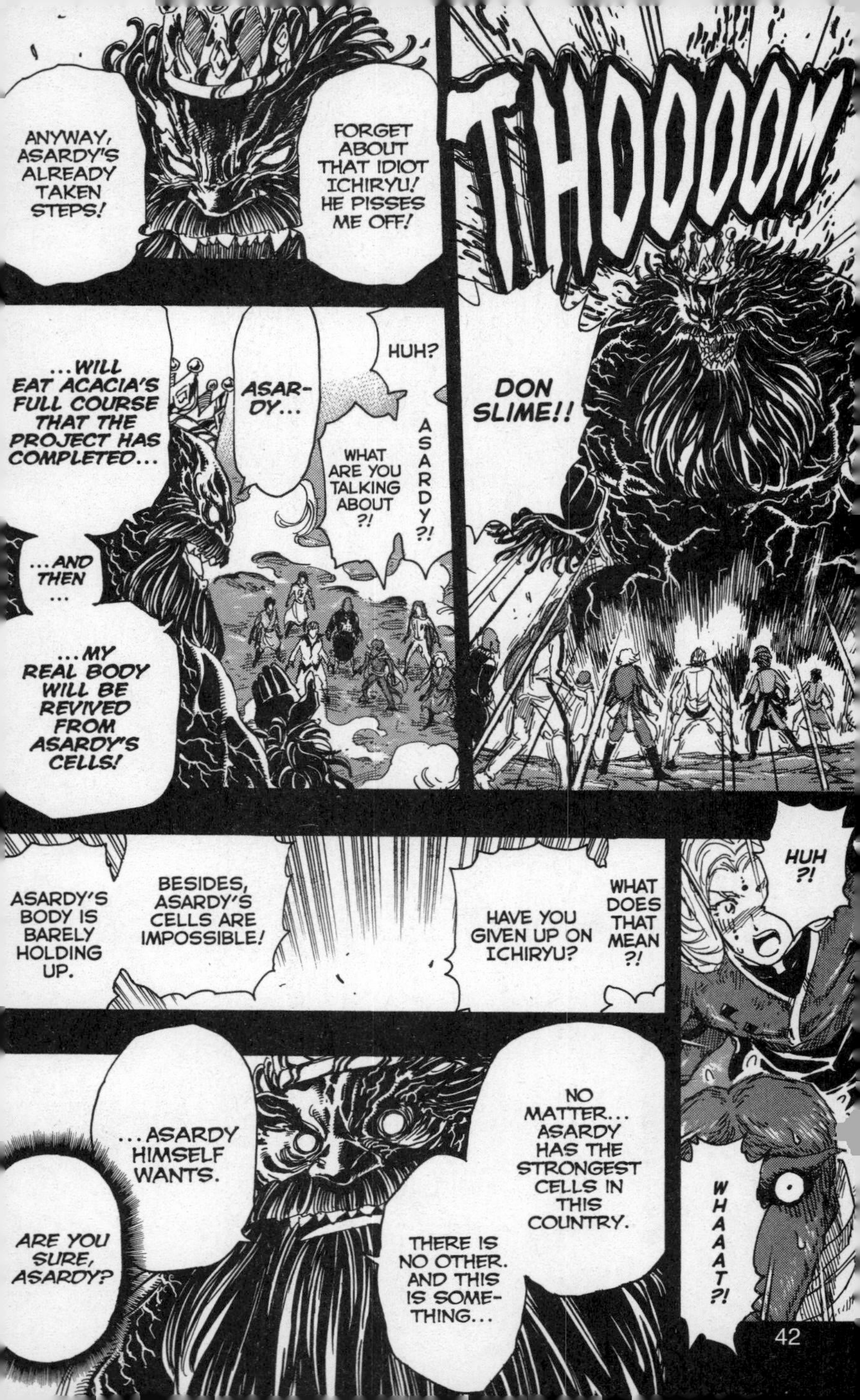
THOOOOM
DON SLIME!!
FORGET ABOUT THAT IDIOT ICHIRYU! HE PISSES ME OFF!
ANYWAY, ASARDY'S ALREADY TAKEN STEPS!
HUH?
ASARDY?!
WHAT ARE YOU TALKING ABOUT?!
ASARDY...
...WILL EAT ACACIA'S FULL COURSE THAT THE PROJECT HAS COMPLETED...
...AND THEN...
...MY REAL BODY WILL BE REVIVED FROM ASARDY'S CELLS!
HUH?!
WHAAAAT?!
WHAT DOES THAT MEAN?!
HAVE YOU GIVEN UP ON ICHIRYU?
BESIDES, ASARDY'S CELLS ARE IMPOSSIBLE!
ASARDY'S BODY IS BARELY HOLDING UP.
NO MATTER... ASARDY HAS THE STRONGEST CELLS IN THIS COUNTRY.
THERE IS NO OTHER. AND THIS IS SOME-THING...
...ASARDY HIMSELF WANTS.
ARE YOU SURE, ASARDY?

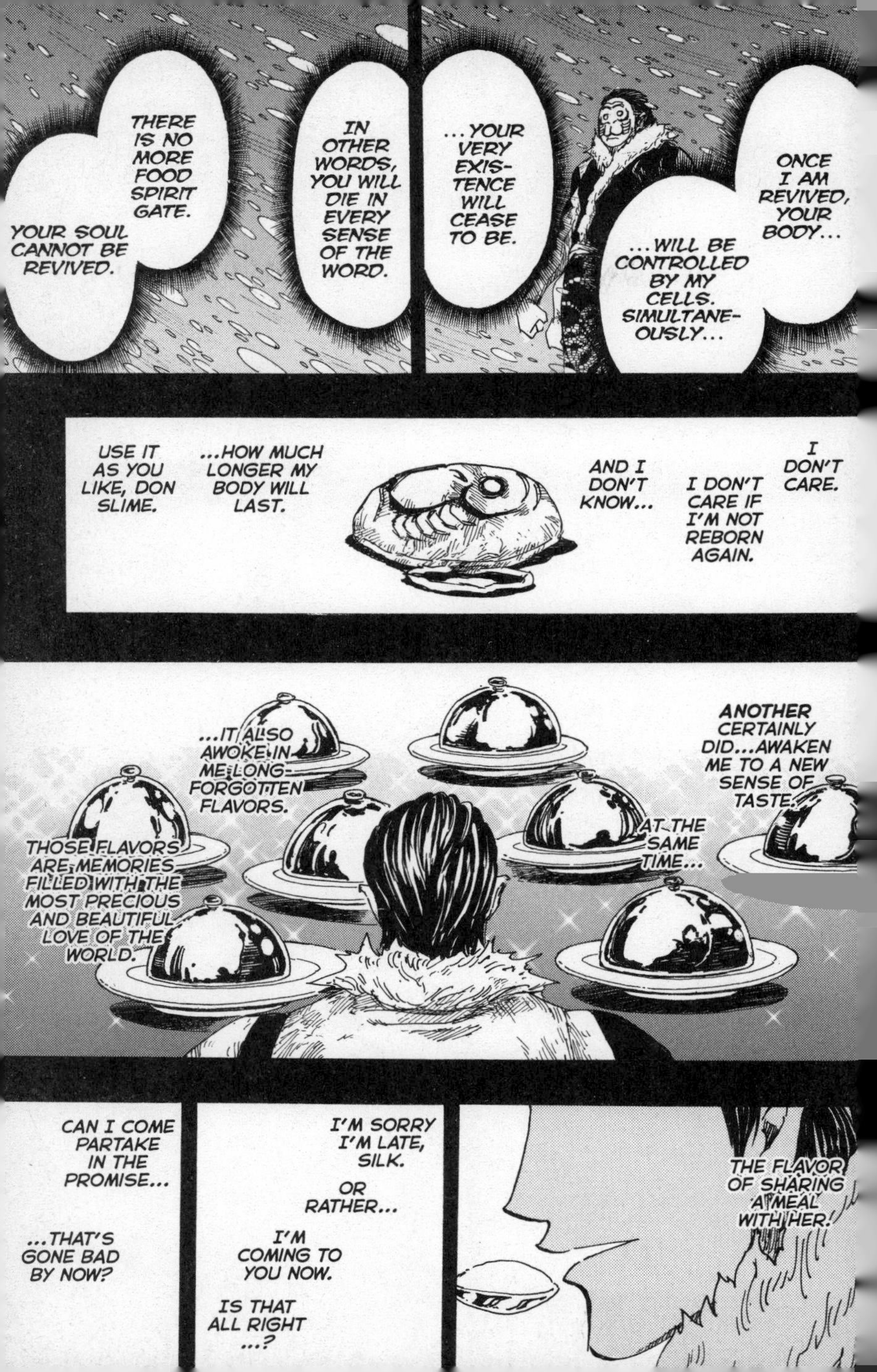
ONCE I AM REVIVED, YOUR BODY...
...WILL BE CONTROLLED BY MY CELLS. SIMULTANEOUSLY...
...YOUR VERY EXISTENCE WILL CEASE TO BE.
IN OTHER WORDS, YOU WILL DIE IN EVERY SENSE OF THE WORD.
THERE IS NO MORE FOOD SPIRIT GATE.
YOUR SOUL CANNOT BE REVIVED.
I DON'T CARE.
I DON'T CARE IF I'M NOT REBORN AGAIN.
AND I DON'T KNOW...
...HOW MUCH LONGER MY BODY WILL LAST.
USE IT AS YOU LIKE, DON SLIME.
ANOTHER CERTAINLY DID...AWAKEN ME TO A NEW SENSE OF TASTE.
AT THE SAME TIME...
...IT ALSO AWOKE IN ME LONG-FORGOTTEN FLAVORS.
THOSE FLAVORS ARE MEMORIES FILLED WITH THE MOST PRECIOUS AND BEAUTIFUL LOVE OF THE WORLD.
THE FLAVOR OF SHARING A MEAL WITH HER.
I'M SORRY I'M LATE, SILK.
OR RATHER...
I'M COMING TO YOU NOW.
IS THAT ALL RIGHT...?
CAN I COME PARTAKE IN THE PROMISE...
...THAT'S GONE BAD BY NOW?

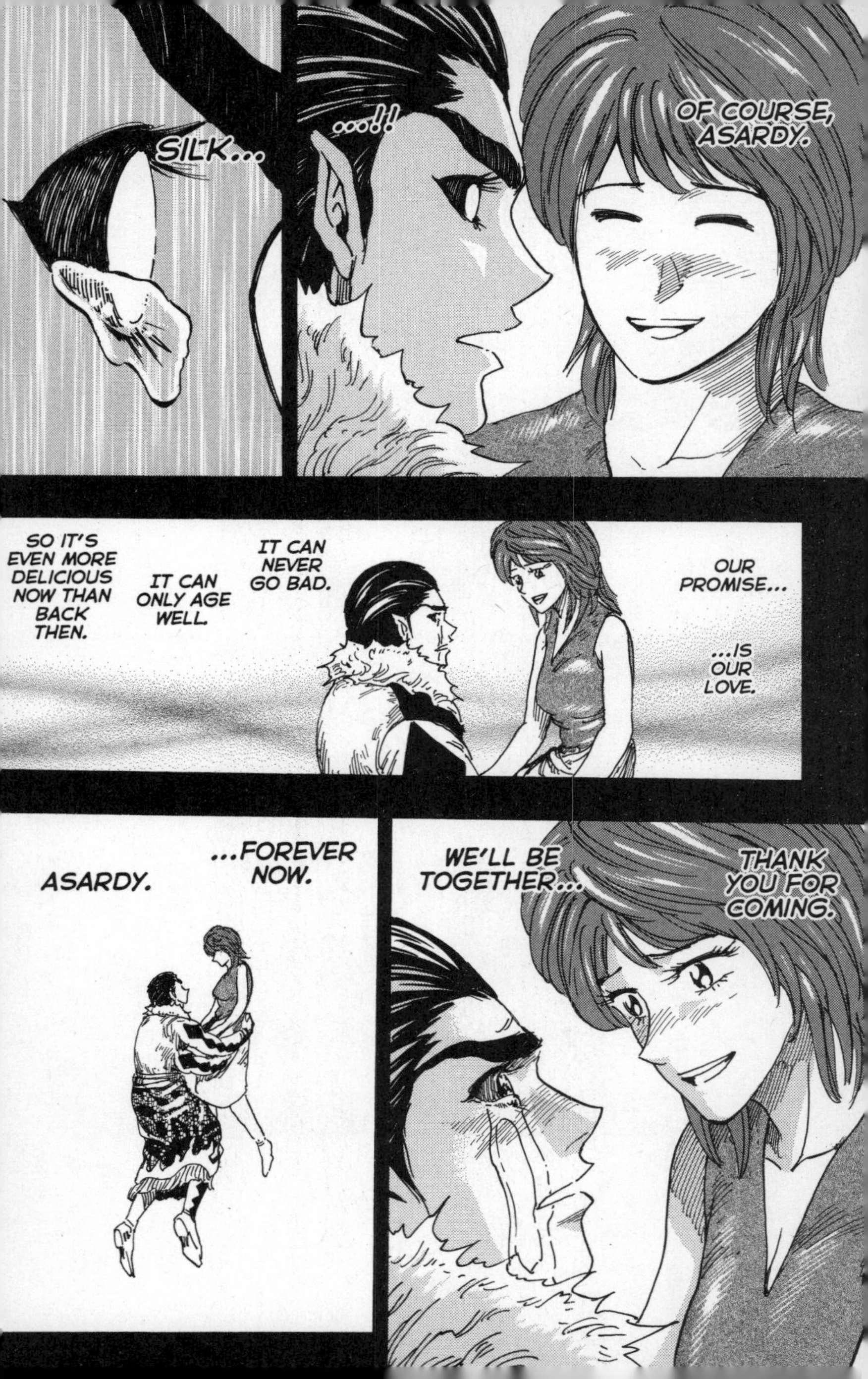
OF COURSE, ASARDY.
...!!
SILK...
OUR PROMISE...
...IS OUR LOVE.
IT CAN NEVER GO BAD.
IT CAN ONLY AGE WELL.
SO IT'S EVEN MORE DELICIOUS NOW THAN BACK THEN.
THANK YOU FOR COMING.
WE'LL BE TOGETHER...
...FOREVER NOW.
ASARDY.

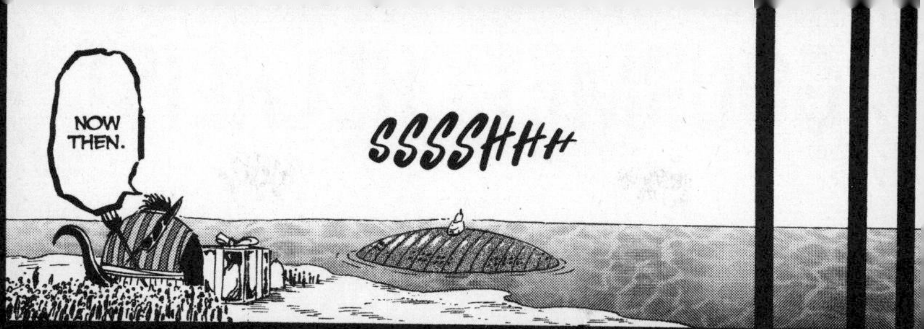
SSSSHHH
NOW THEN.

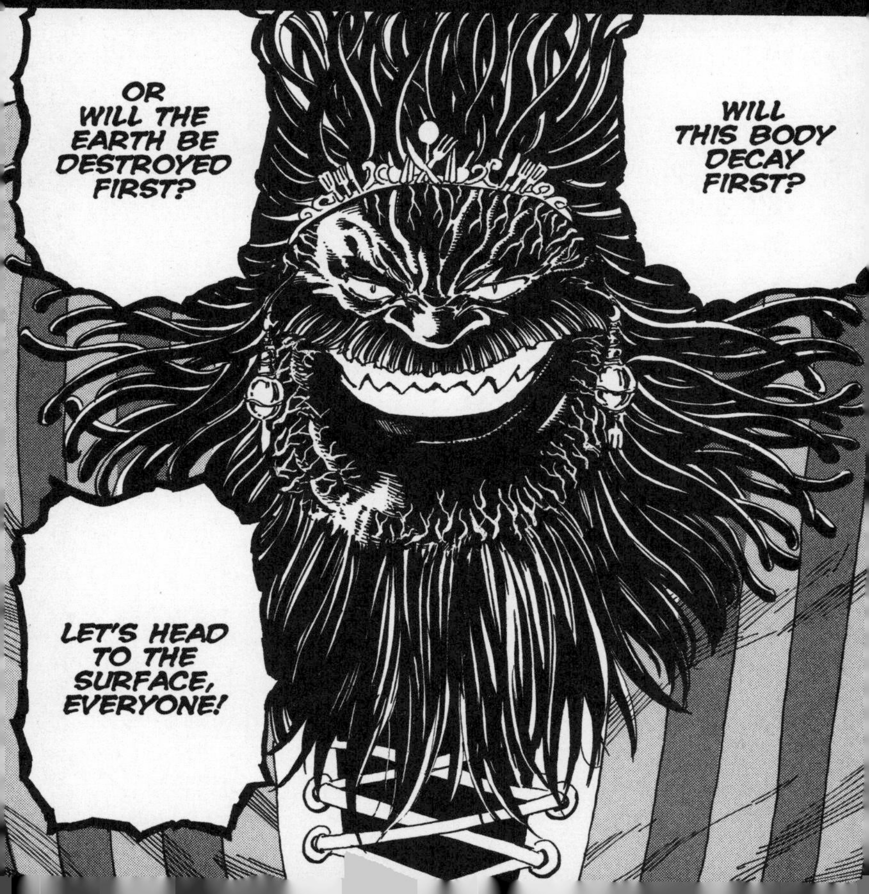
WILL THIS BODY DECAY FIRST?
OR WILL THE EARTH BE DESTROYED FIRST?
LET'S HEAD TO THE SURFACE, EVERYONE!

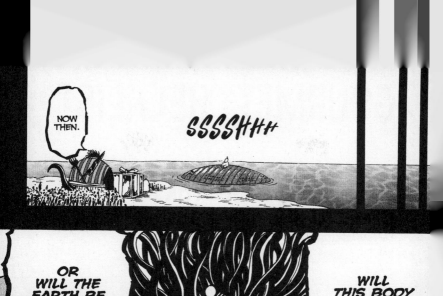

TORIKO

GOURMET CHECKLIST

Vol. 382

DIRIGIBLE TURTLE

(REPTILE)

CAPTURE LEVEL: 820
HABITAT: GOURMET WORLD
SIZE: 300 M
HEIGHT: 60 M
WEIGHT: 50,000 TONS
PRICE: 50,000 YEN PER 100 GRAMS

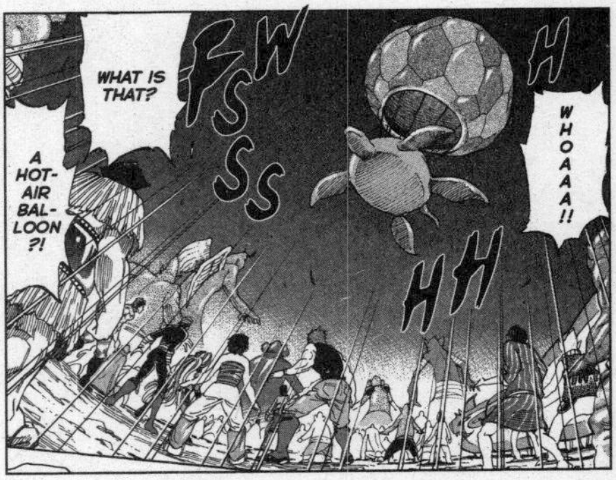
WHOAAAA!!
WHAT IS THAT?
A HOT-AIR BALLOON ?!

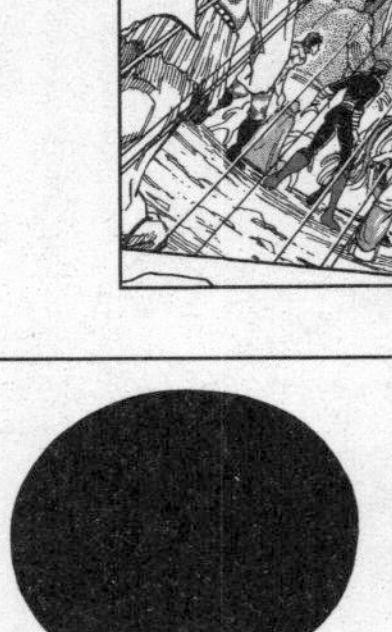

SCALE

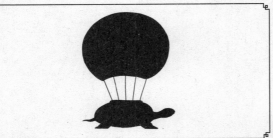

A TURTLE THAT'S ALSO A HOT AIR BALLOON! IT'S A CAMPING MONSTER THAT CAN TRAVERSE LAND, SEA AND SKY. IT'S THE FINEST SPECIMEN OF SAFE ZONE COMPARED TO ALL THE CAMPING MONSTERS IN THE GOURMET WORLD. WHEN ITS SHELL IS FILLED WITH HOT AIR, IT SWIMS THROUGH THE AIR. WHEN THE AIR IS REMOVED, THE SHELL IS STORED BACK IN ITS BODY AND WILL BECOME SUBMERSIBLE FOR UNDERWATER TRAVEL.

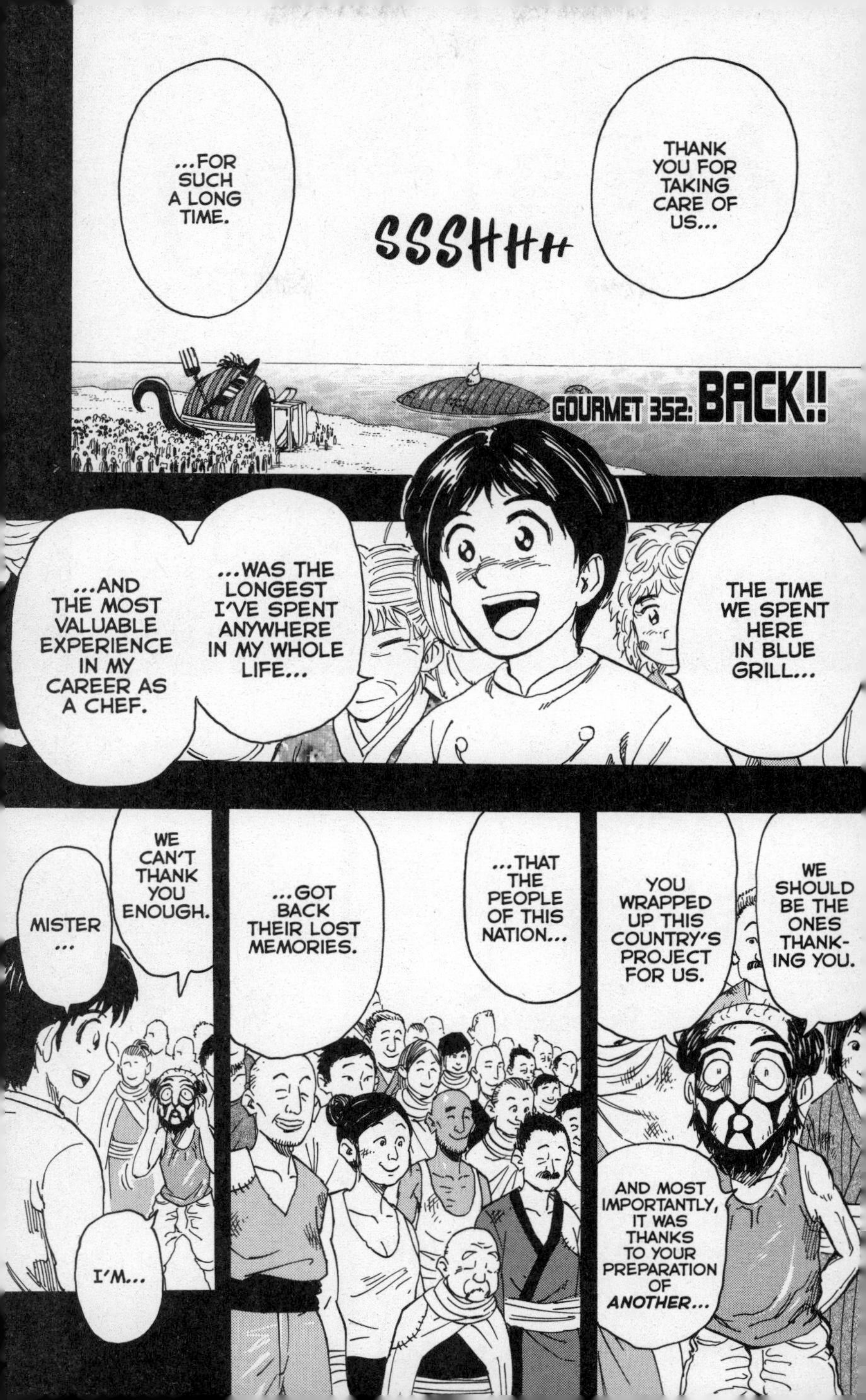
THANK YOU FOR TAKING CARE OF US...
SSSHHH
...FOR SUCH A LONG TIME.
GOURMET 352: BACK!!
THE TIME WE SPENT HERE IN BLUE GRILL...
...WAS THE LONGEST I'VE SPENT ANYWHERE IN MY WHOLE LIFE...
...AND THE MOST VALUABLE EXPERIENCE IN MY CAREER AS A CHEF.
WE SHOULD BE THE ONES THANKING YOU.
YOU WRAPPED UP THIS COUNTRY'S PROJECT FOR US.
AND MOST IMPORTANTLY, IT WAS THANKS TO YOUR PREPARATION OF *ANOTHER*...
...THAT THE PEOPLE OF THIS NATION...
...GOT BACK THEIR LOST MEMORIES.
WE CAN'T THANK YOU ENOUGH.
MISTER...
I'M...

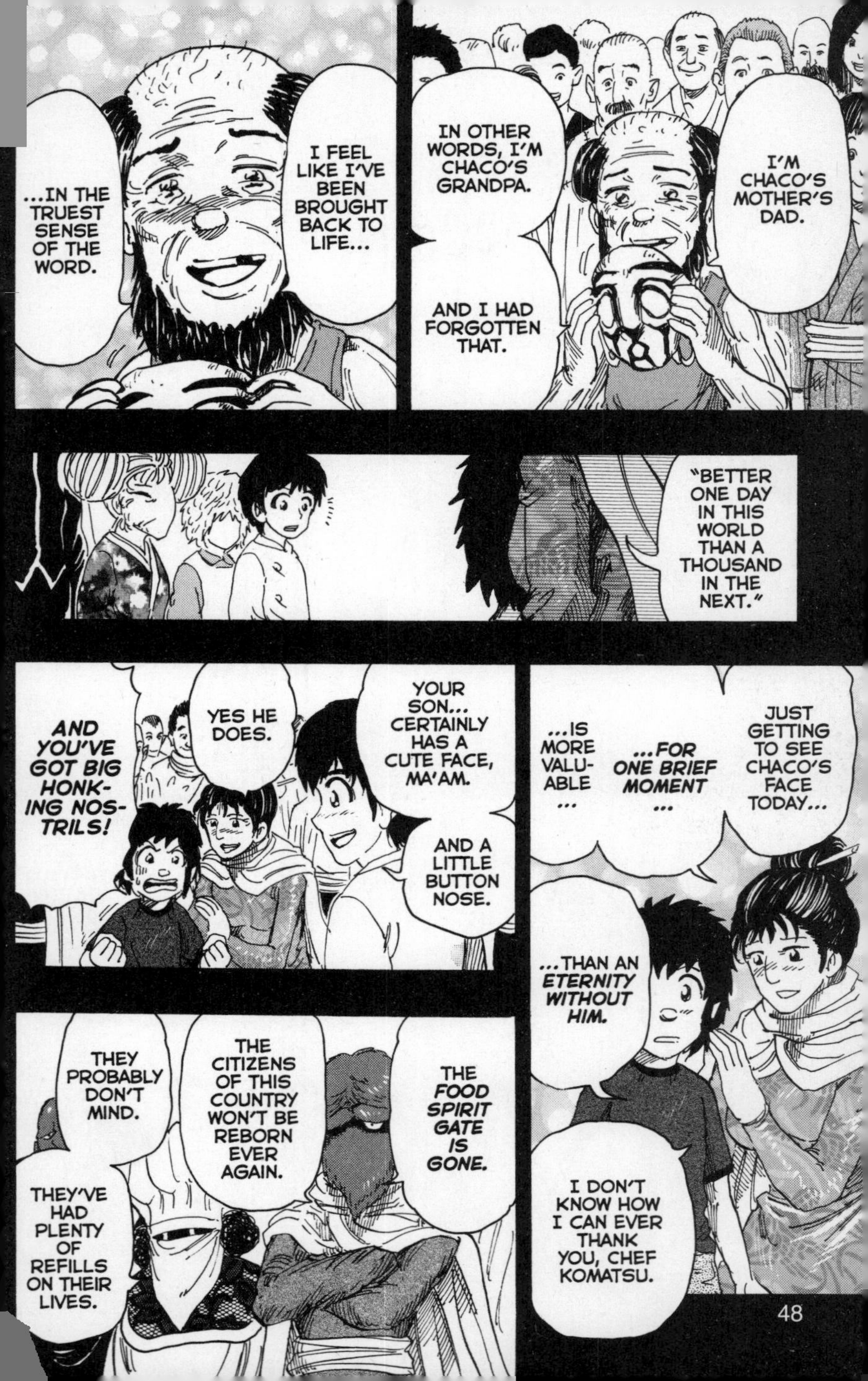
I'M CHACO'S MOTHER'S DAD.
IN OTHER WORDS, I'M CHACO'S GRANDPA.
AND I HAD FORGOTTEN THAT.
I FEEL LIKE I'VE BEEN BROUGHT BACK TO LIFE...
...IN THE TRUEST SENSE OF THE WORD.
"BETTER ONE DAY IN THIS WORLD THAN A THOUSAND IN THE NEXT."
JUST GETTING TO SEE CHACO'S FACE TODAY...
...FOR ONE BRIEF MOMENT...
...IS MORE VALUABLE...
...THAN AN *ETERNITY WITHOUT HIM.*
I DON'T KNOW HOW I CAN EVER THANK YOU, CHEF KOMATSU.
YOUR SON... CERTAINLY HAS A CUTE FACE, MA'AM.
YES HE DOES.
AND A LITTLE BUTTON NOSE.
AND YOU'VE GOT BIG HONKING NOSTRILS!
THE *FOOD SPIRIT GATE* IS *GONE.*
THE CITIZENS OF THIS COUNTRY WON'T BE REBORN EVER AGAIN.
THEY PROBABLY DON'T MIND.
THEY'VE HAD PLENTY OF REFILLS ON THEIR LIVES.

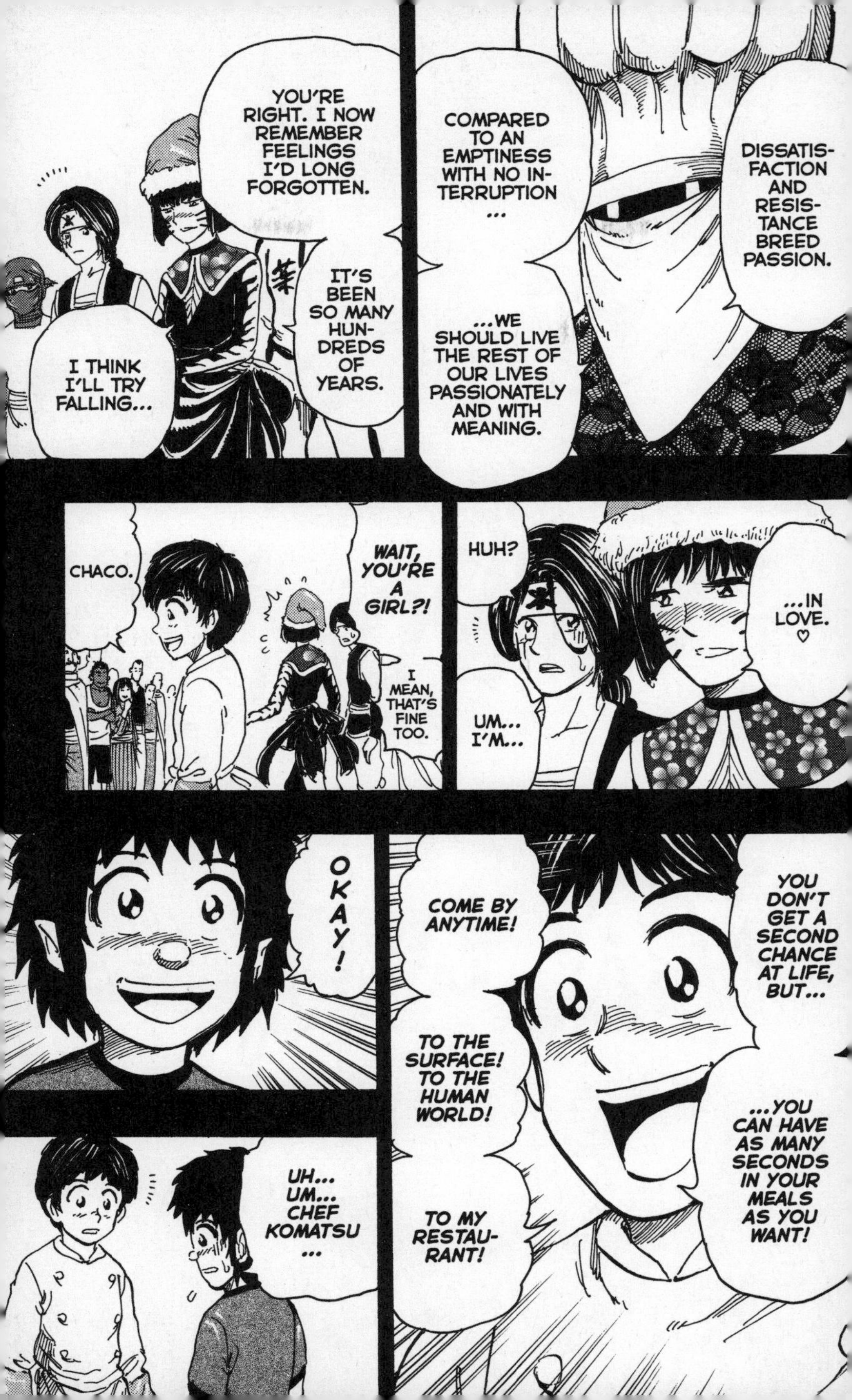
DISSATIS-FACTION AND RESIS-TANCE BREED PASSION.
COMPARED TO AN EMPTINESS WITH NO IN-TERRUPTION...
...WE SHOULD LIVE THE REST OF OUR LIVES PASSIONATELY AND WITH MEANING.
YOU'RE RIGHT. I NOW REMEMBER FEELINGS I'D LONG FORGOTTEN.
IT'S BEEN SO MANY HUN-DREDS OF YEARS.
I THINK I'LL TRY FALLING...
...IN LOVE. ♡
HUH?
UM... I'M...
WAIT, YOU'RE A GIRL?!
I MEAN, THAT'S FINE TOO.
CHACO.
YOU DON'T GET A SECOND CHANCE AT LIFE, BUT...
...YOU CAN HAVE AS MANY SECONDS IN YOUR MEALS AS YOU WANT!
COME BY ANYTIME!
TO THE SURFACE! TO THE HUMAN WORLD!
TO MY RESTAU-RANT!
OKAY!
UH... UM... CHEF KOMATSU...

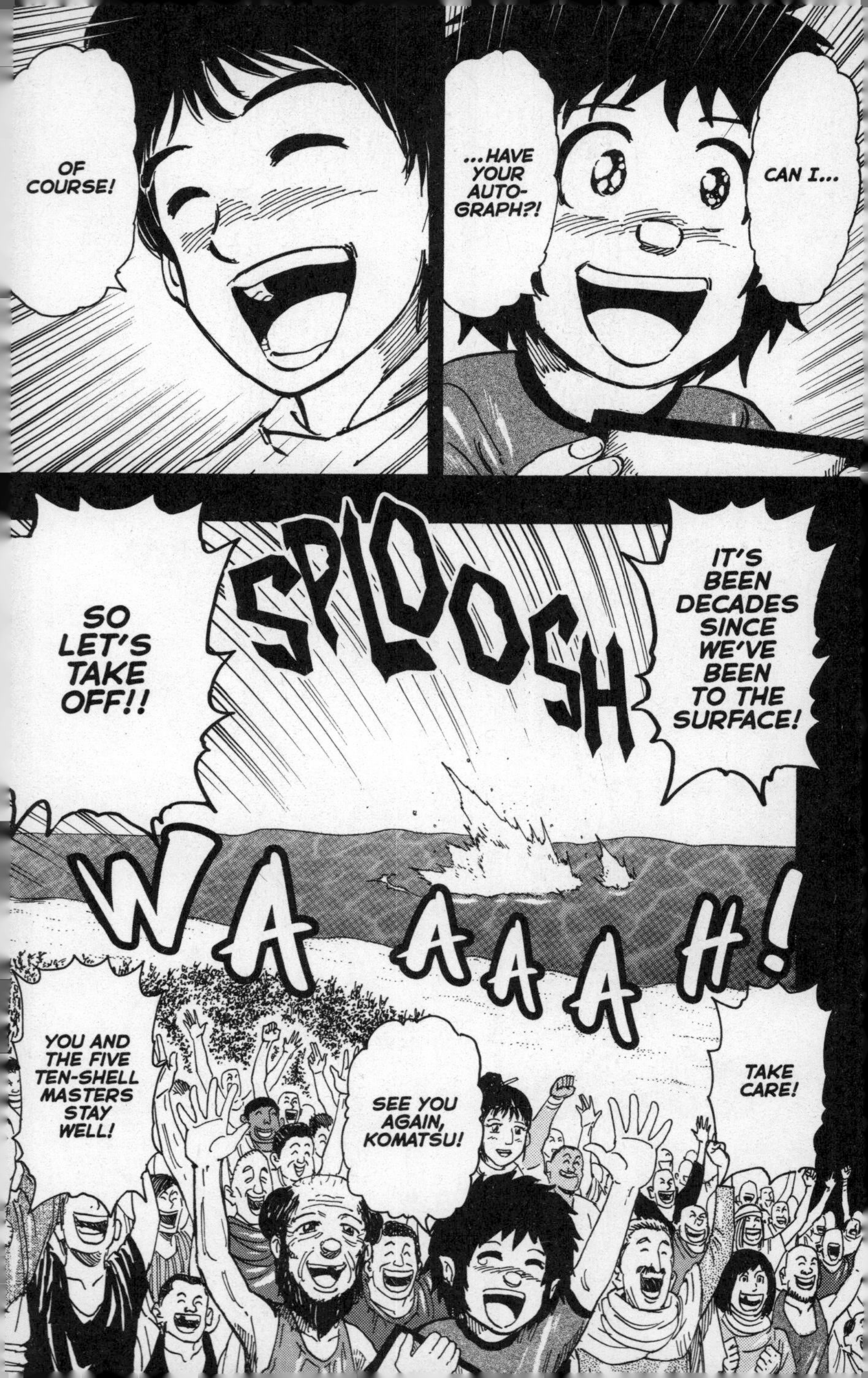
CAN I...
...HAVE YOUR AUTO-GRAPH?!
OF COURSE!
IT'S BEEN DECADES SINCE WE'VE BEEN TO THE SURFACE!
SPLOOSH
SO LET'S TAKE OFF!!
WAAAAH!
TAKE CARE!
SEE YOU AGAIN, KOMATSU!
YOU AND THE FIVE TEN-SHELL MASTERS STAY WELL!

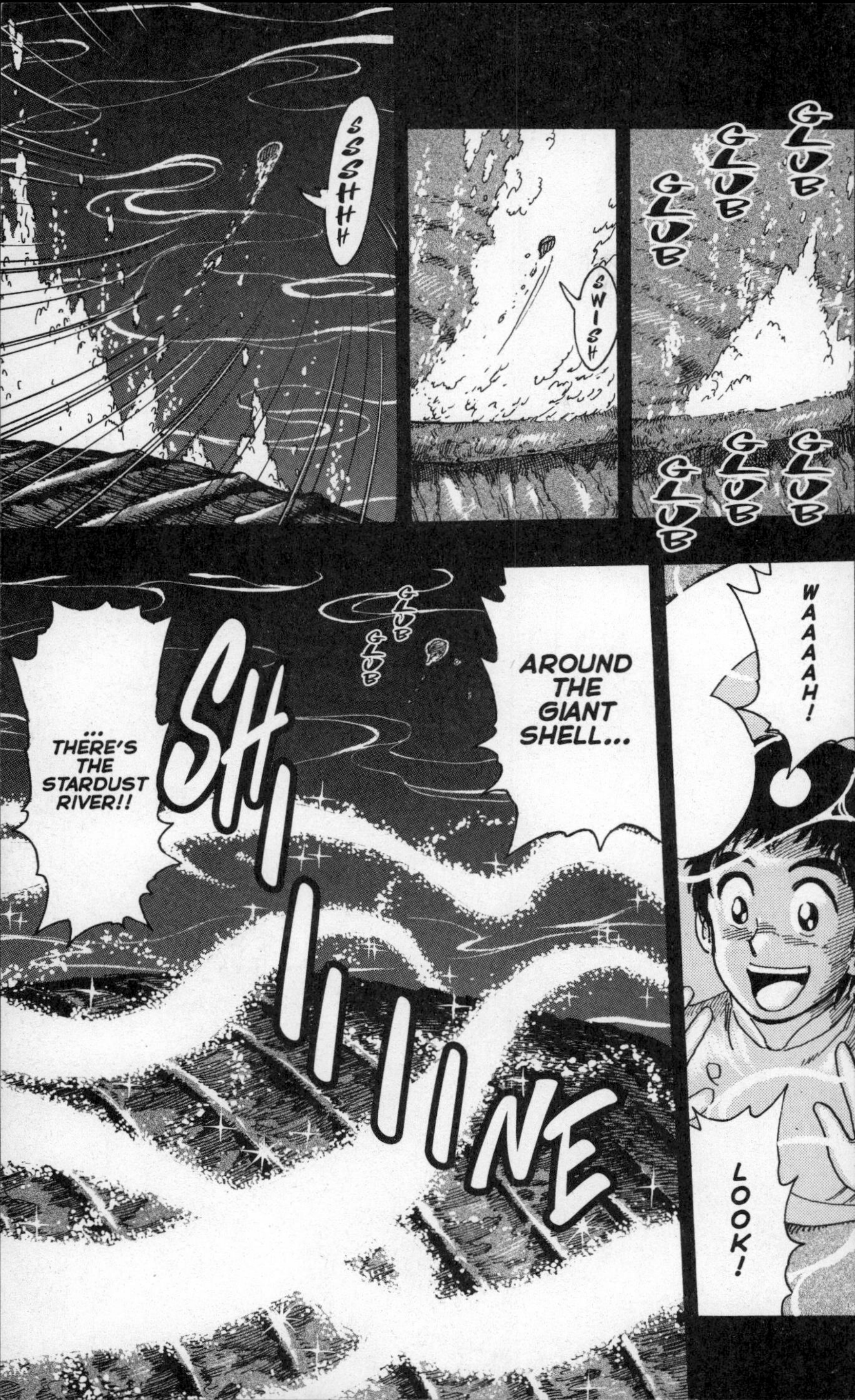

GLUB
GLUB
GLUB
GLUB
GLUB
GLUB
SWISH
SSSHHH
WAAAAH!
LOOK!
AROUND THE GIANT SHELL...
GLUB
GLUB
SHIIIINE
...THERE'S THE STARDUST RIVER!!

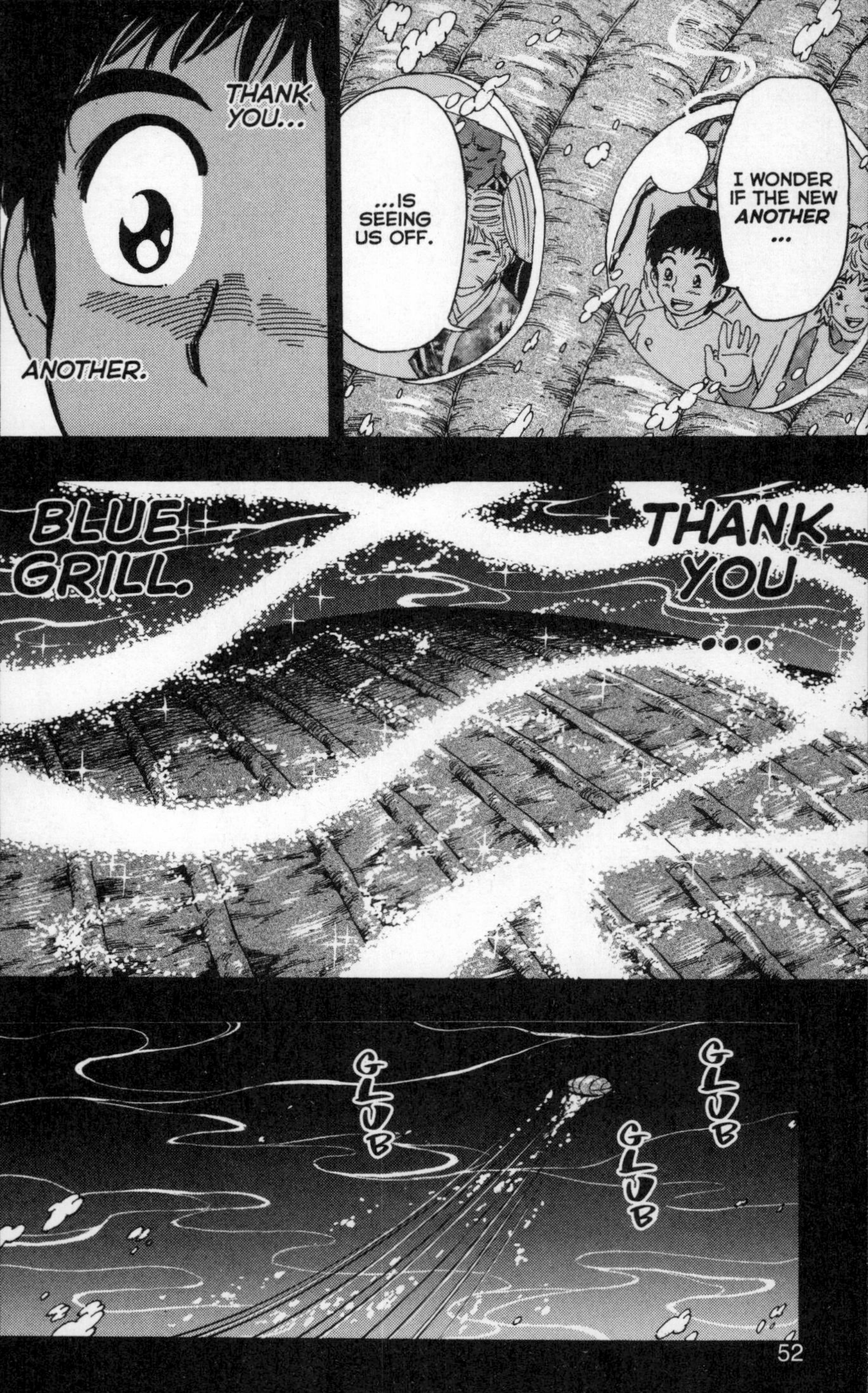
I WONDER IF THE NEW ANOTHER ...
...IS SEEING US OFF.
THANK YOU...
ANOTHER.
THANK YOU ...
BLUE GRILL.
GLUB
GLUB
GLUB

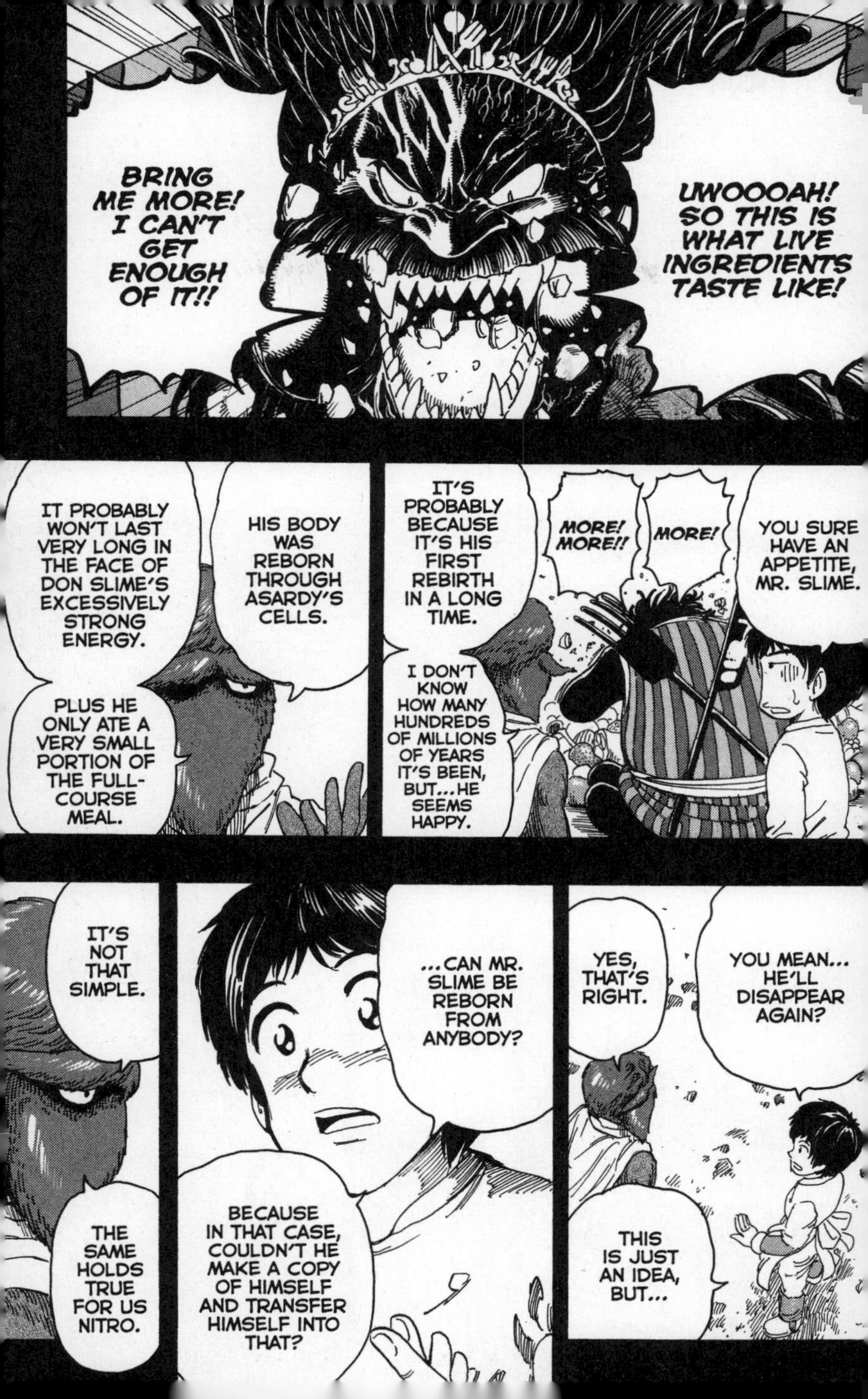
UWOOOAH! SO THIS IS WHAT LIVE INGREDIENTS TASTE LIKE!
BRING ME MORE! I CAN'T GET ENOUGH OF IT!!
YOU SURE HAVE AN APPETITE, MR. SLIME.
MORE!
MORE! MORE!!
IT'S PROBABLY BECAUSE IT'S HIS FIRST REBIRTH IN A LONG TIME.
I DON'T KNOW HOW MANY HUNDREDS OF MILLIONS OF YEARS IT'S BEEN, BUT...HE SEEMS HAPPY.
HIS BODY WAS REBORN THROUGH ASARDY'S CELLS.
IT PROBABLY WON'T LAST VERY LONG IN THE FACE OF DON SLIME'S EXCESSIVELY STRONG ENERGY.
PLUS HE ONLY ATE A VERY SMALL PORTION OF THE FULL-COURSE MEAL.
YOU MEAN... HE'LL DISAPPEAR AGAIN?
YES, THAT'S RIGHT.
THIS IS JUST AN IDEA, BUT...
...CAN MR. SLIME BE REBORN FROM ANYBODY?
BECAUSE IN THAT CASE, COULDN'T HE MAKE A COPY OF HIMSELF AND TRANSFER HIMSELF INTO THAT?
IT'S NOT THAT SIMPLE.
THE SAME HOLDS TRUE FOR US NITRO.

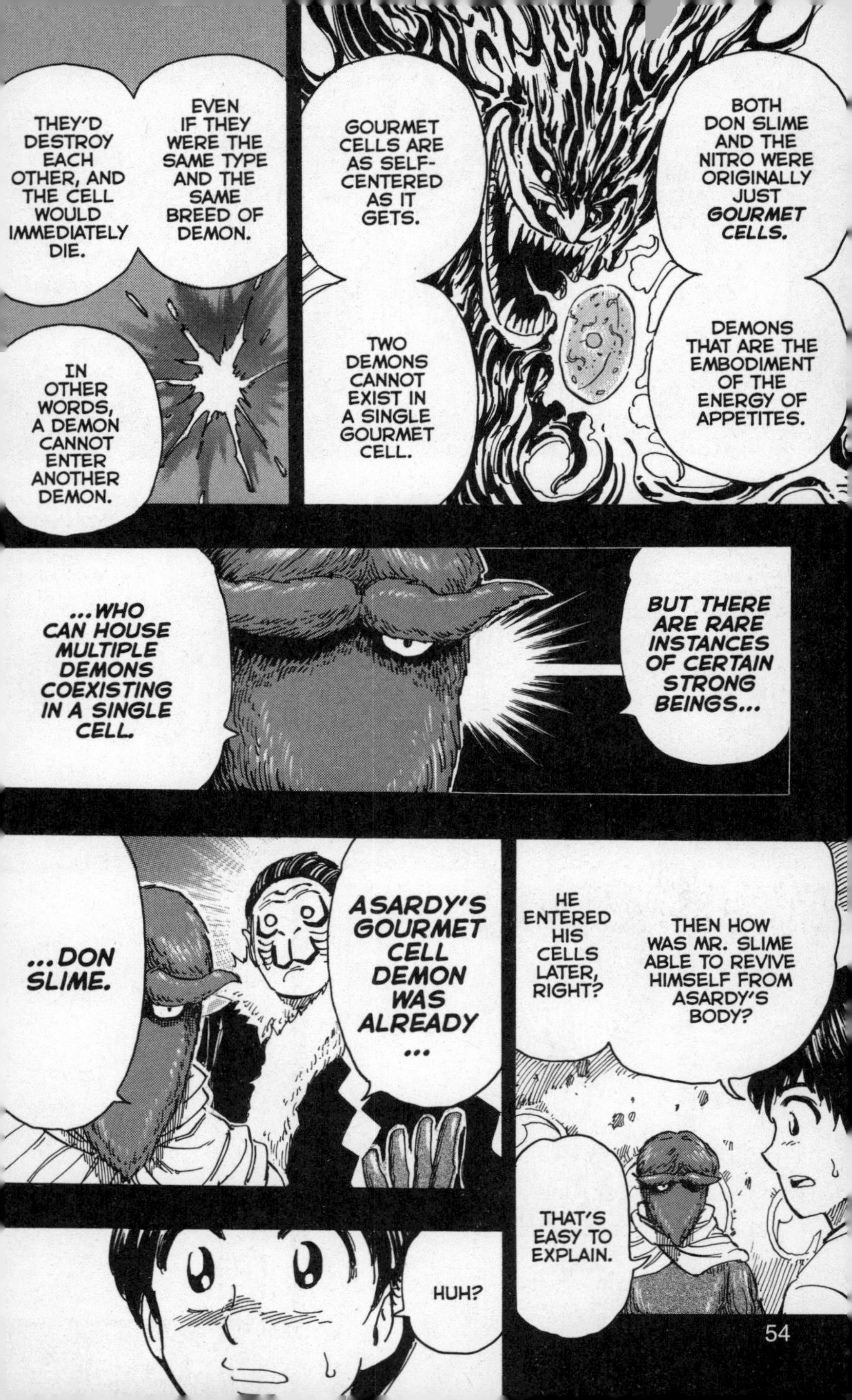
BOTH DON SLIME AND THE NITRO WERE ORIGINALLY JUST GOURMET CELLS.
DEMONS THAT ARE THE EMBODIMENT OF THE ENERGY OF APPETITES.
GOURMET CELLS ARE AS SELF-CENTERED AS IT GETS.
TWO DEMONS CANNOT EXIST IN A SINGLE GOURMET CELL.
EVEN IF THEY WERE THE SAME TYPE AND THE SAME BREED OF DEMON.
THEY'D DESTROY EACH OTHER, AND THE CELL WOULD IMMEDIATELY DIE.
IN OTHER WORDS, A DEMON CANNOT ENTER ANOTHER DEMON.
BUT THERE ARE RARE INSTANCES OF CERTAIN STRONG BEINGS...
...WHO CAN HOUSE MULTIPLE DEMONS COEXISTING IN A SINGLE CELL.
THEN HOW WAS MR. SLIME ABLE TO REVIVE HIMSELF FROM ASARDY'S BODY?
HE ENTERED HIS CELLS LATER, RIGHT?
THAT'S EASY TO EXPLAIN.
ASARDY'S GOURMET CELL DEMON WAS ALREADY...
...DON SLIME.
HUH?

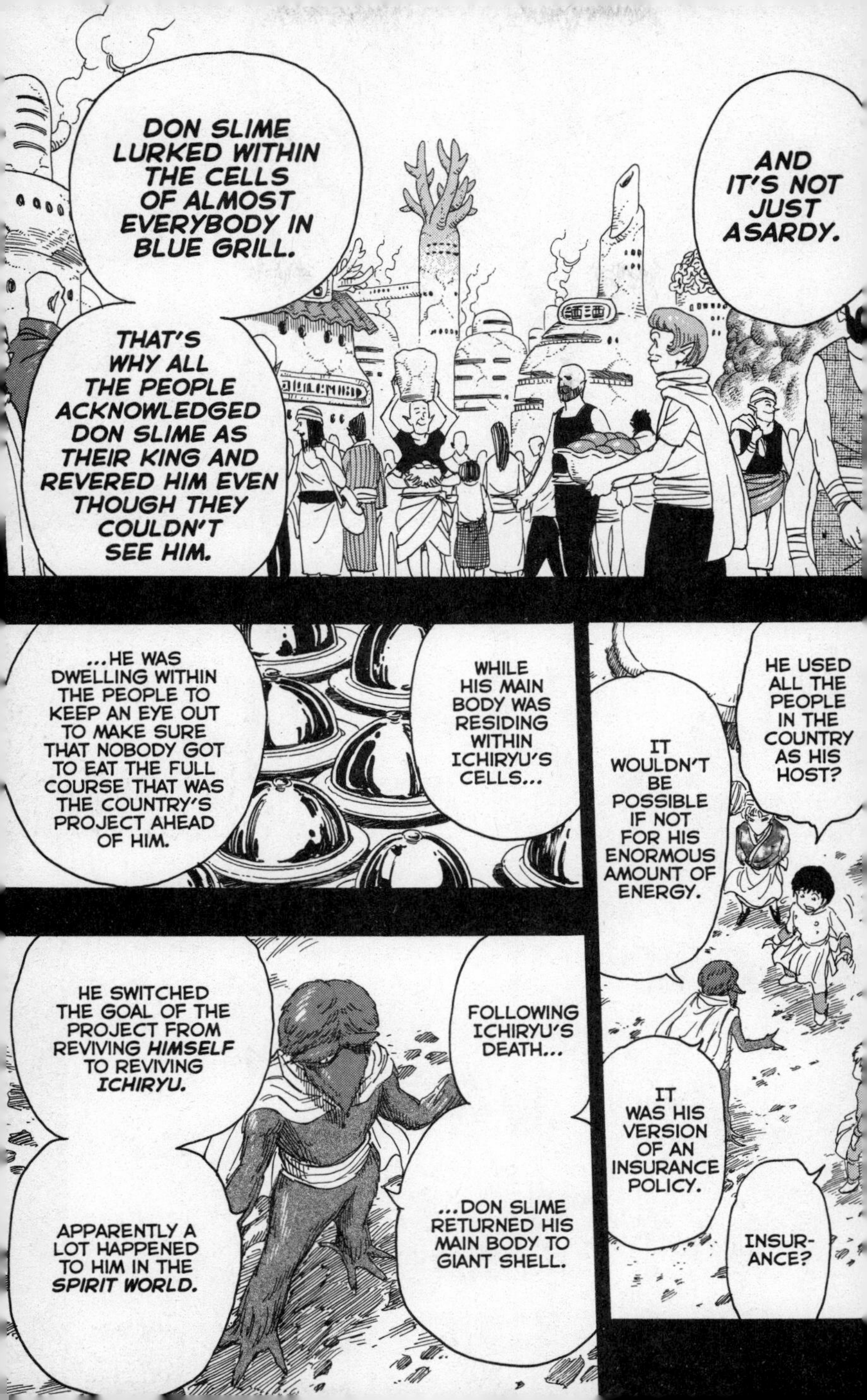
AND IT'S NOT JUST ASARDY.
DON SLIME LURKED WITHIN THE CELLS OF ALMOST EVERYBODY IN BLUE GRILL.
THAT'S WHY ALL THE PEOPLE ACKNOWLEDGED DON SLIME AS THEIR KING AND REVERED HIM EVEN THOUGH THEY COULDN'T SEE HIM.
HE USED ALL THE PEOPLE IN THE COUNTRY AS HIS HOST?
IT WOULDN'T BE POSSIBLE IF NOT FOR HIS ENORMOUS AMOUNT OF ENERGY.
IT WAS HIS VERSION OF AN INSURANCE POLICY.
INSUR-ANCE?
WHILE HIS MAIN BODY WAS RESIDING WITHIN ICHIRYU'S CELLS...
...HE WAS DWELLING WITHIN THE PEOPLE TO KEEP AN EYE OUT TO MAKE SURE THAT NOBODY GOT TO EAT THE FULL COURSE THAT WAS THE COUNTRY'S PROJECT AHEAD OF HIM.
FOLLOWING ICHIRYU'S DEATH...
...DON SLIME RETURNED HIS MAIN BODY TO GIANT SHELL.
HE SWITCHED THE GOAL OF THE PROJECT FROM REVIVING *HIMSELF* TO REVIVING *ICHIRYU*.
APPARENTLY A LOT HAPPENED TO HIM IN THE *SPIRIT WORLD*.

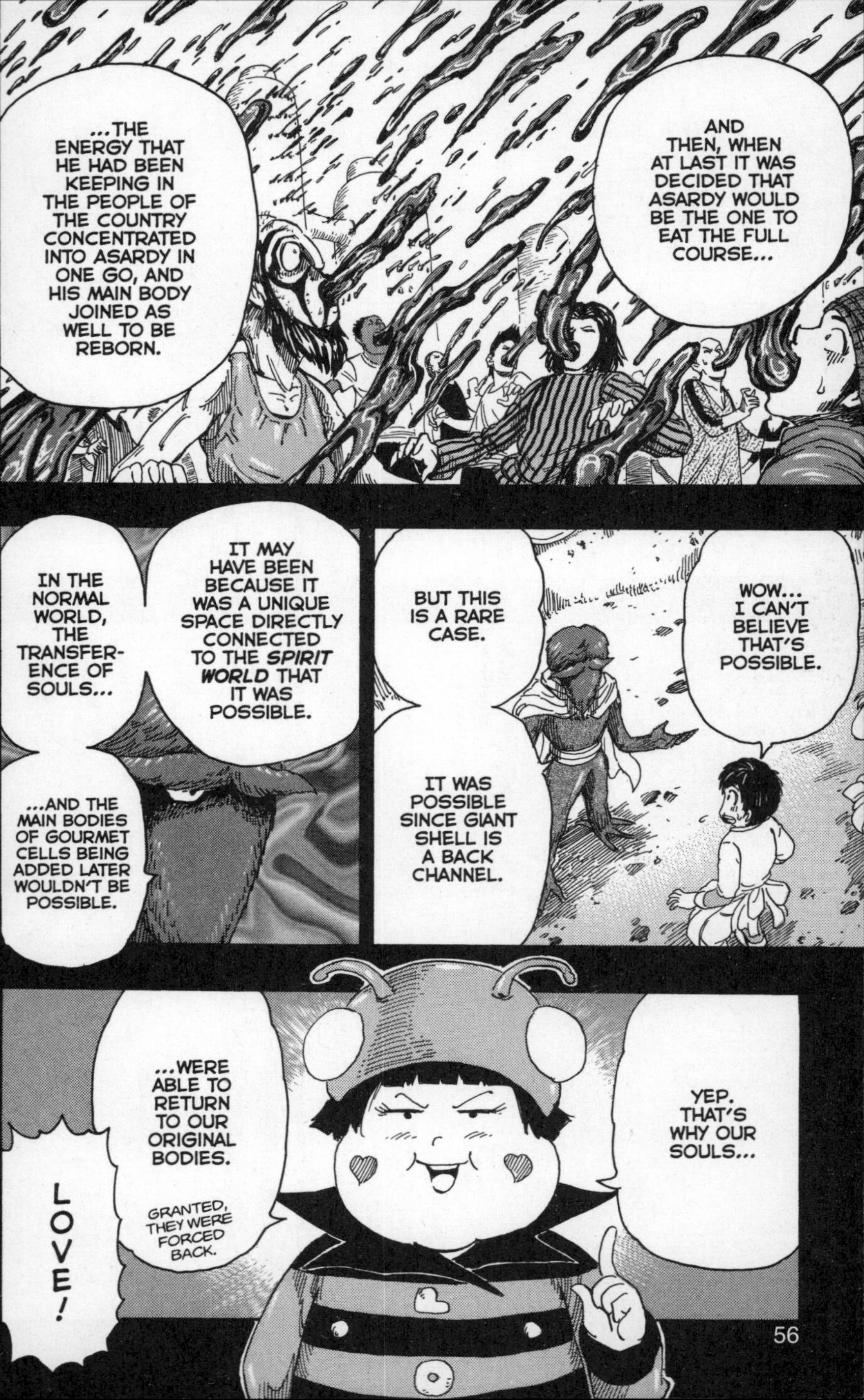
AND THEN, WHEN AT LAST IT WAS DECIDED THAT ASARDY WOULD BE THE ONE TO EAT THE FULL COURSE...
...THE ENERGY THAT HE HAD BEEN KEEPING IN THE PEOPLE OF THE COUNTRY CONCENTRATED INTO ASARDY IN ONE GO, AND HIS MAIN BODY JOINED AS WELL TO BE REBORN.
WOW... I CAN'T BELIEVE THAT'S POSSIBLE.
BUT THIS IS A RARE CASE.
IT WAS POSSIBLE SINCE GIANT SHELL IS A BACK CHANNEL.
IT MAY HAVE BEEN BECAUSE IT WAS A UNIQUE SPACE DIRECTLY CONNECTED TO THE *SPIRIT WORLD* THAT IT WAS POSSIBLE.
IN THE NORMAL WORLD, THE TRANSFERENCE OF SOULS...
...AND THE MAIN BODIES OF GOURMET CELLS BEING ADDED LATER WOULDN'T BE POSSIBLE.
YEP. THAT'S WHY OUR SOULS...
...WERE ABLE TO RETURN TO OUR ORIGINAL BODIES.
GRANTED, THEY WERE FORCED BACK.
LOVE!

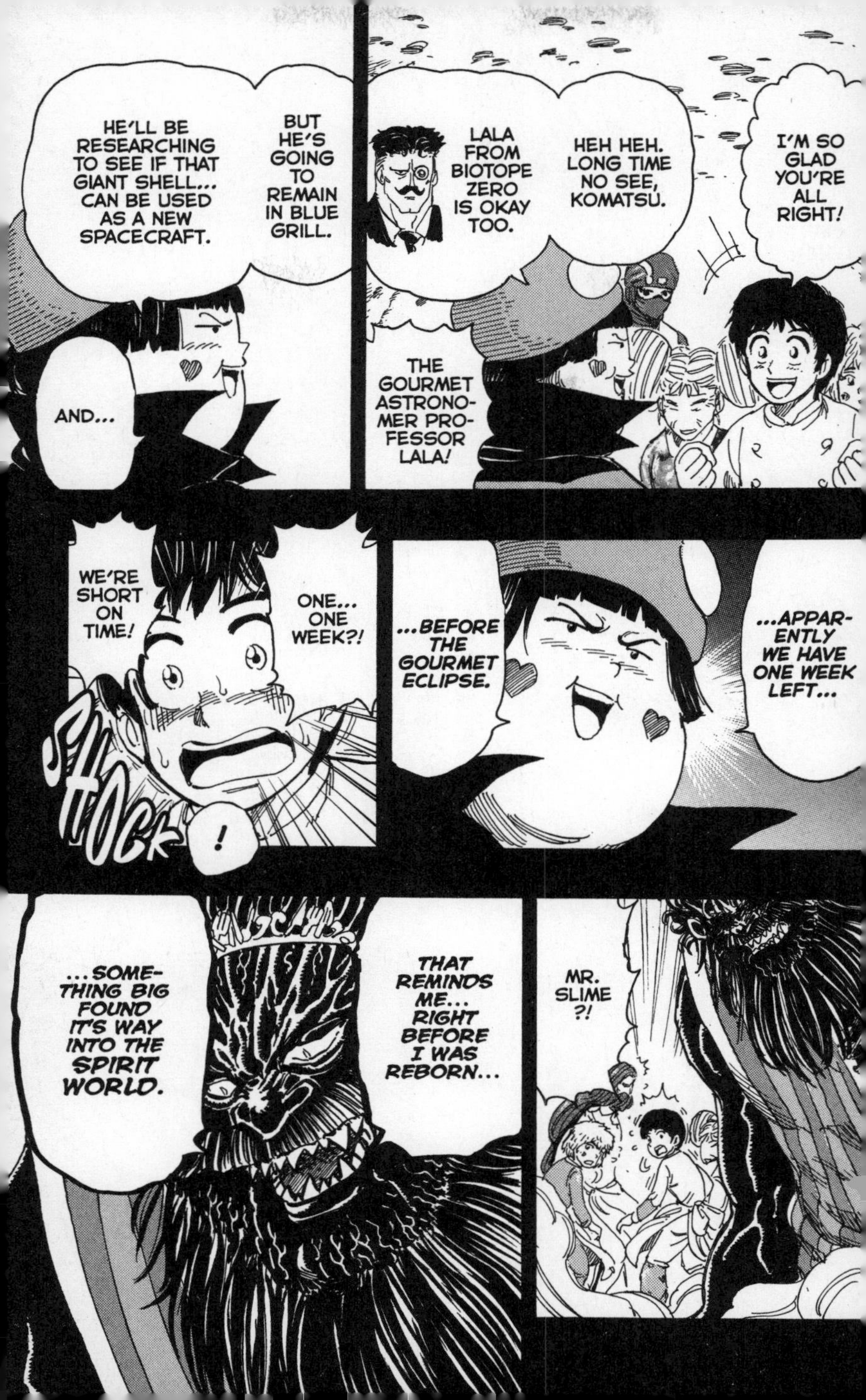
I'M SO GLAD YOU'RE ALL RIGHT!
HEH HEH. LONG TIME NO SEE, KOMATSU.
LALA FROM BIOTOPE ZERO IS OKAY TOO.
THE GOURMET ASTRONOMER PROFESSOR LALA!
BUT HE'S GOING TO REMAIN IN BLUE GRILL.
HE'LL BE RESEARCHING TO SEE IF THAT GIANT SHELL... CAN BE USED AS A NEW SPACECRAFT.
AND...
...APPARENTLY WE HAVE ONE WEEK LEFT...
...BEFORE THE GOURMET ECLIPSE.
ONE... ONE WEEK?!
WE'RE SHORT ON TIME!
SHOCK
!
MR. SLIME?!
THAT REMINDS ME... RIGHT BEFORE I WAS REBORN...
...SOMETHING BIG FOUND IT'S WAY INTO THE SPIRIT WORLD.

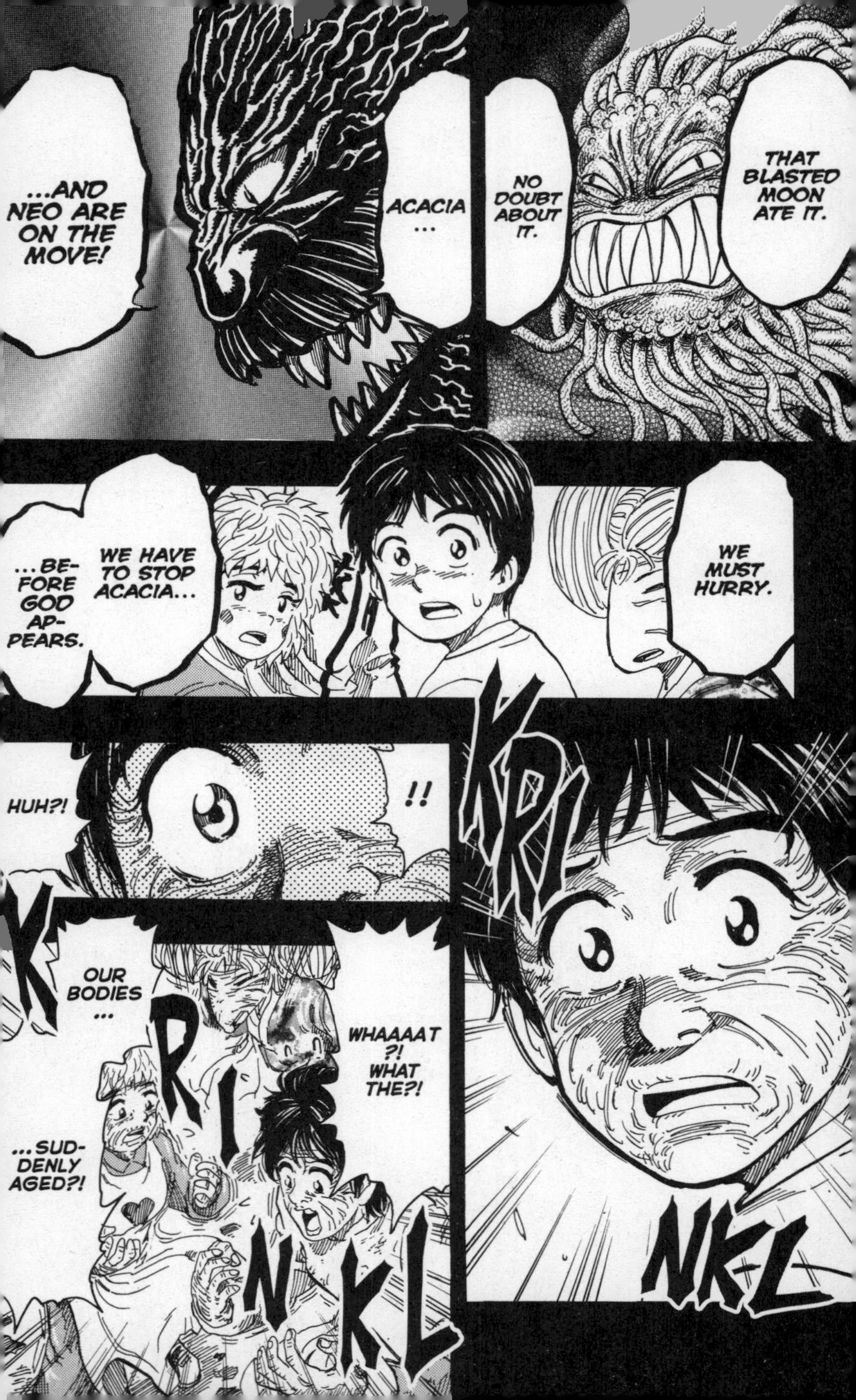
THAT BLASTED MOON ATE IT.
NO DOUBT ABOUT IT.
ACACIA...
...AND NEO ARE ON THE MOVE!
WE MUST HURRY.
WE HAVE TO STOP ACACIA...
...BEFORE GOD APPEARS.
KRI
NKL
!!
HUH?!
KRINKL
WHAAAAT?! WHAT THE?!
OUR BODIES...
...SUDDENLY AGED?!

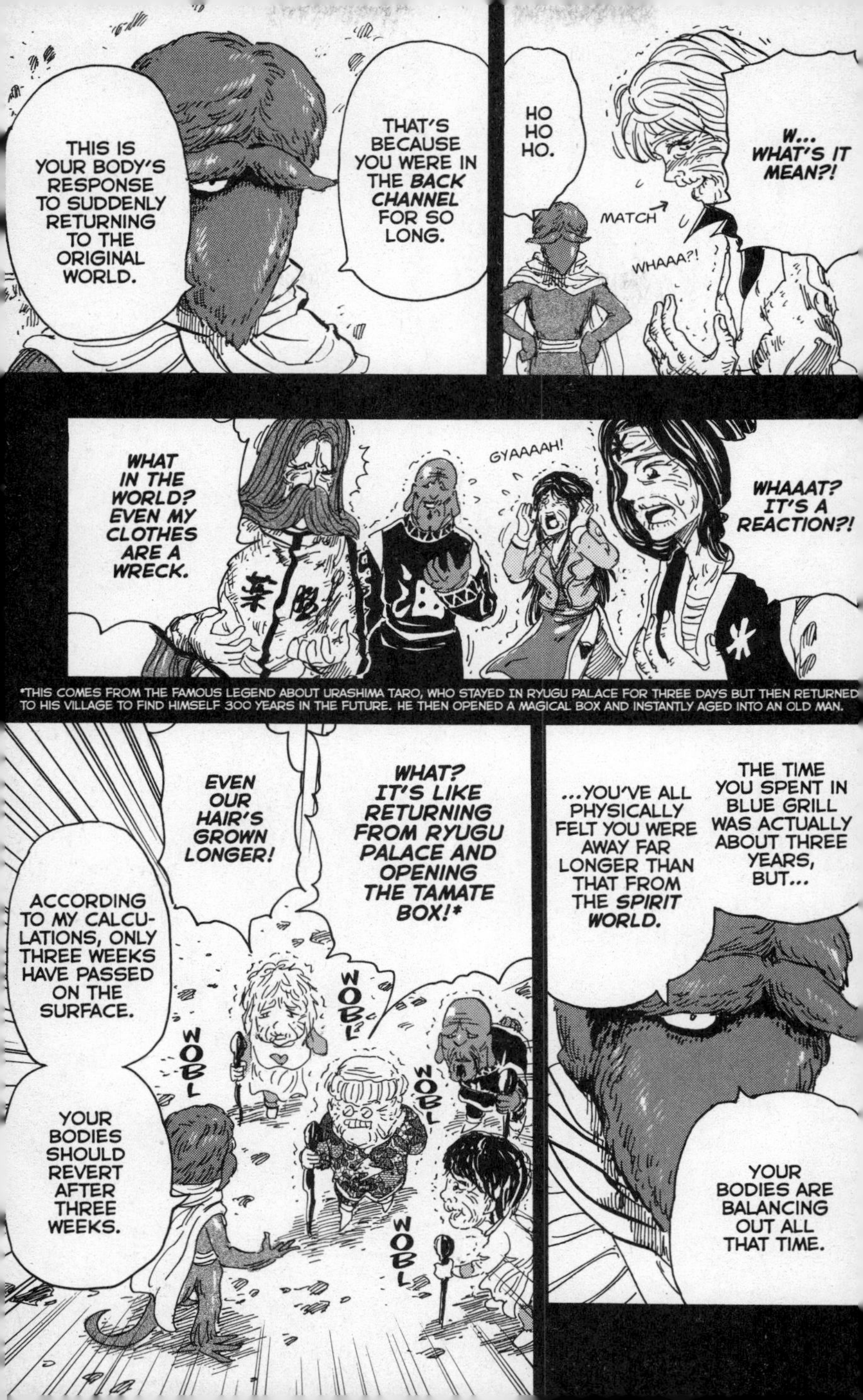
W... WHAT'S IT MEAN?!
MATCH
WHAAA?!
HO HO HO.
THAT'S BECAUSE YOU WERE IN THE *BACK CHANNEL* FOR SO LONG.
THIS IS YOUR BODY'S RESPONSE TO SUDDENLY RETURNING TO THE ORIGINAL WORLD.
WHAAAT? IT'S A REACTION?!
GYAAAAH!
WHAT IN THE WORLD? EVEN MY CLOTHES ARE A WRECK.
THE TIME YOU SPENT IN BLUE GRILL WAS ACTUALLY ABOUT THREE YEARS, BUT...
...YOU'VE ALL PHYSICALLY FELT YOU WERE AWAY FAR LONGER THAN THAT FROM THE *SPIRIT WORLD.*
YOUR BODIES ARE BALANCING OUT ALL THAT TIME.
WHAT? IT'S LIKE RETURNING FROM RYUGU PALACE AND OPENING THE TAMATE BOX!*
EVEN OUR HAIR'S GROWN LONGER!
WOBL
WOBL
WOBL
WOBL
ACCORDING TO MY CALCULATIONS, ONLY THREE WEEKS HAVE PASSED ON THE SURFACE.
YOUR BODIES SHOULD REVERT AFTER THREE WEEKS.

*THIS COMES FROM THE FAMOUS LEGEND ABOUT URASHIMA TARO, WHO STAYED IN RYUGU PALACE FOR THREE DAYS BUT THEN RETURNED TO HIS VILLAGE TO FIND HIMSELF 300 YEARS IN THE FUTURE. HE THEN OPENED A MAGICAL BOX AND INSTANTLY AGED INTO AN OLD MAN.

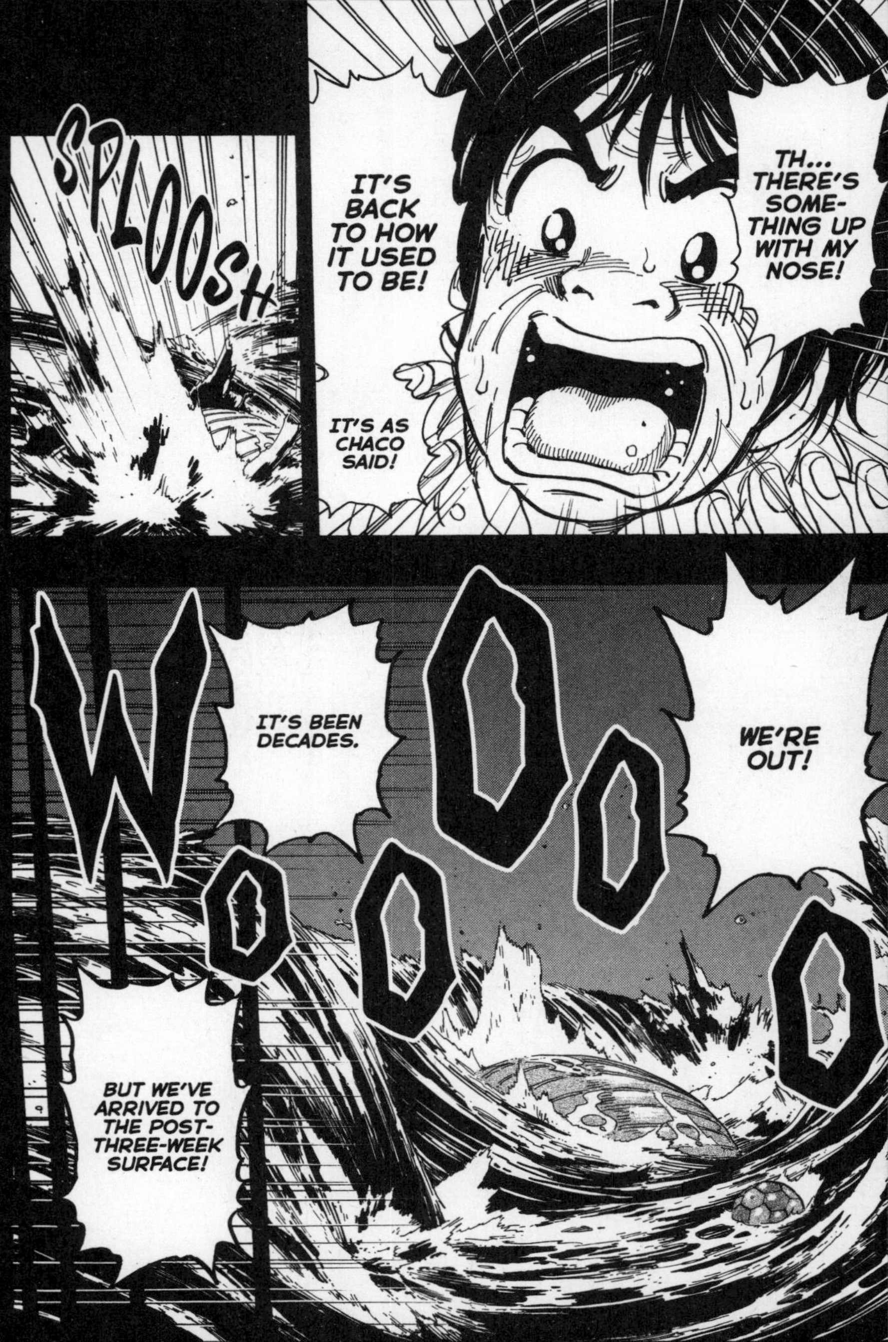
TH... THERE'S SOME-THING UP WITH MY NOSE!
IT'S BACK TO HOW IT USED TO BE!
IT'S AS CHACO SAID!
SPLOOSH
WE'RE OUT!
IT'S BEEN DECADES.
WOOOOO
BUT WE'VE ARRIVED TO THE POST-THREE-WEEK SURFACE!

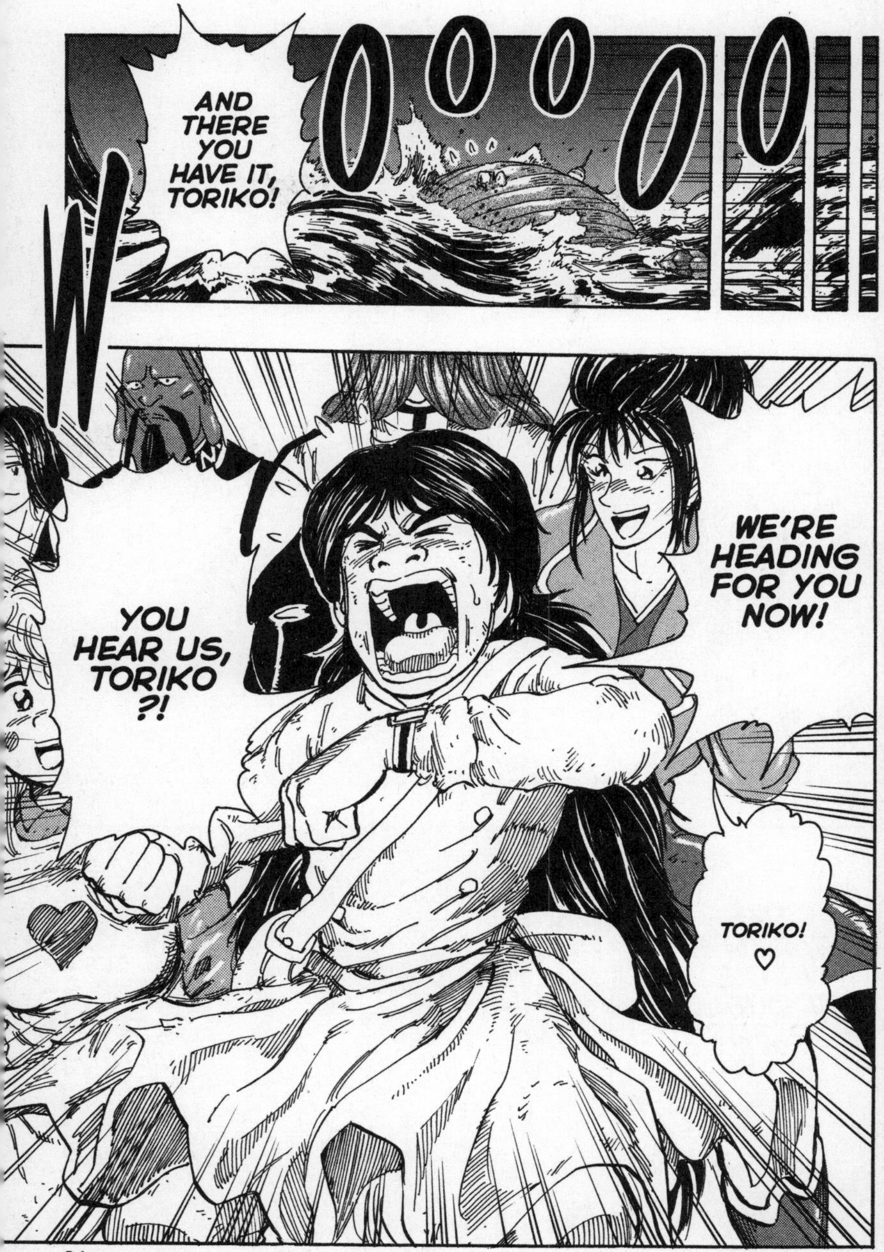
WOOOOO
AND THERE YOU HAVE IT, TORIKO!
WE'RE HEADING FOR YOU NOW!
TORIKO! ♡
YOU HEAR US, TORIKO?!

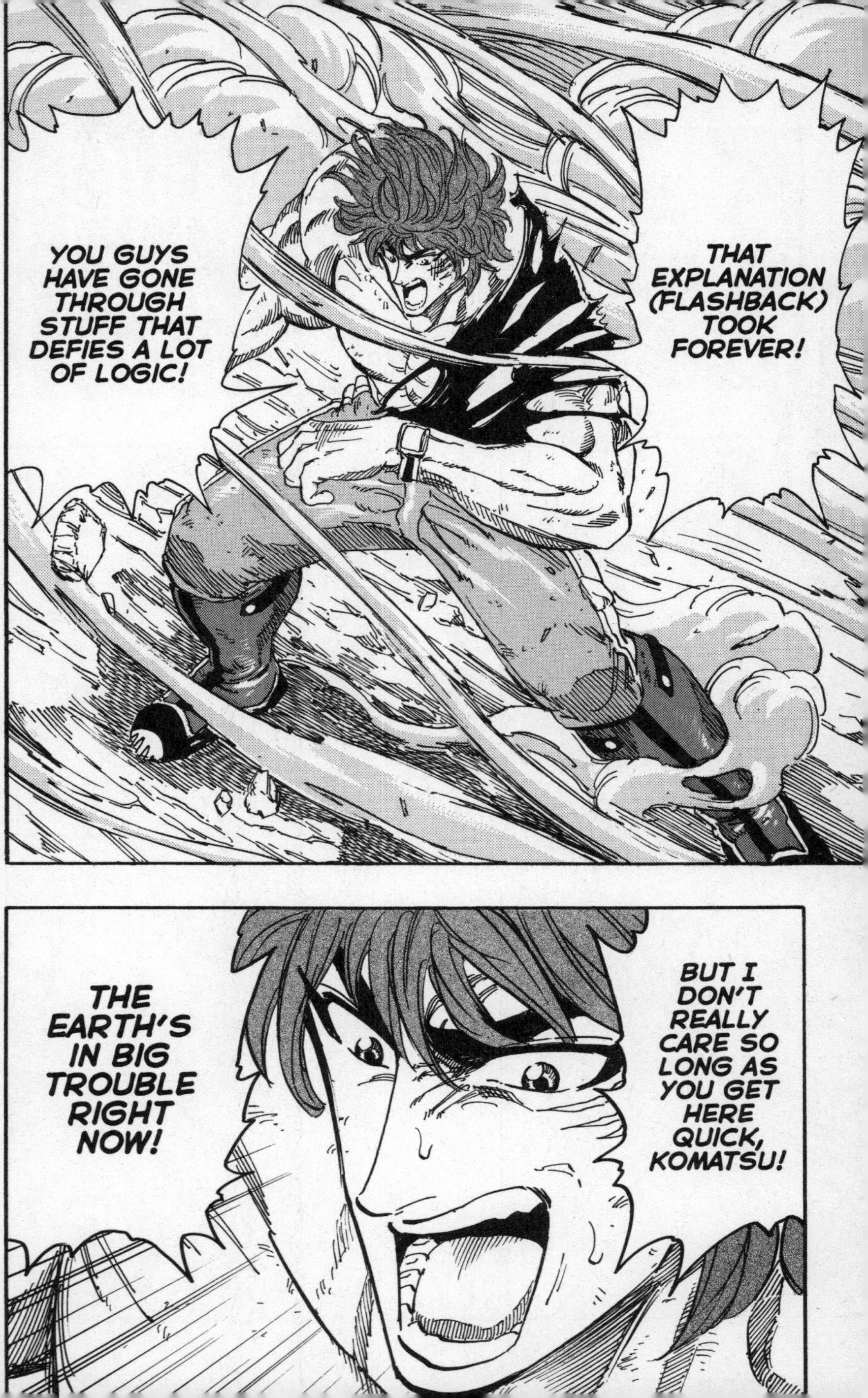
THAT EXPLANATION (FLASHBACK) TOOK FOREVER!
YOU GUYS HAVE GONE THROUGH STUFF THAT DEFIES A LOT OF LOGIC!
BUT I DON'T REALLY CARE SO LONG AS YOU GET HERE QUICK, KOMATSU!
THE EARTH'S IN BIG TROUBLE RIGHT NOW!

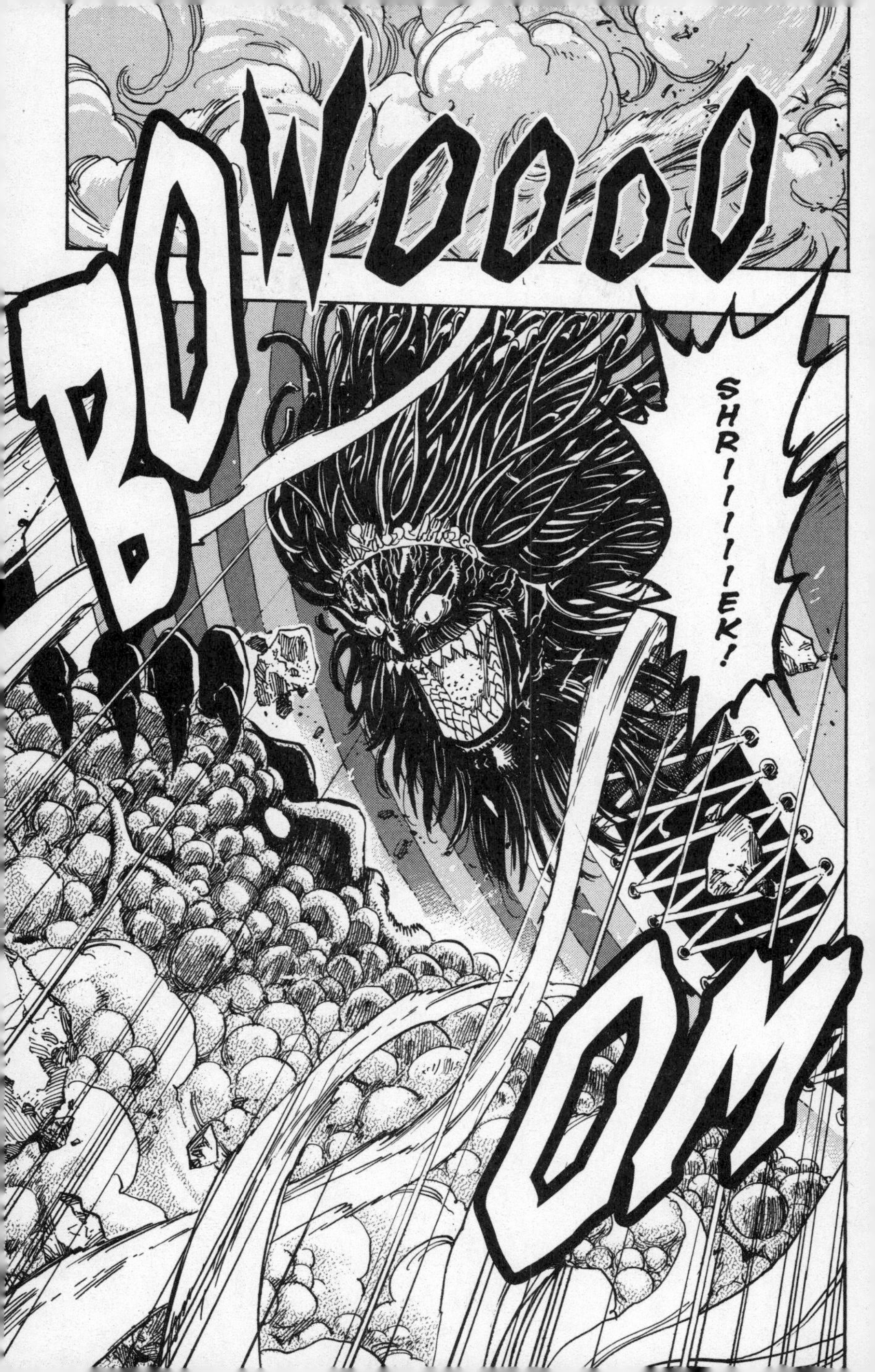
BOWOOOOOM
SHRIIIIIEK!

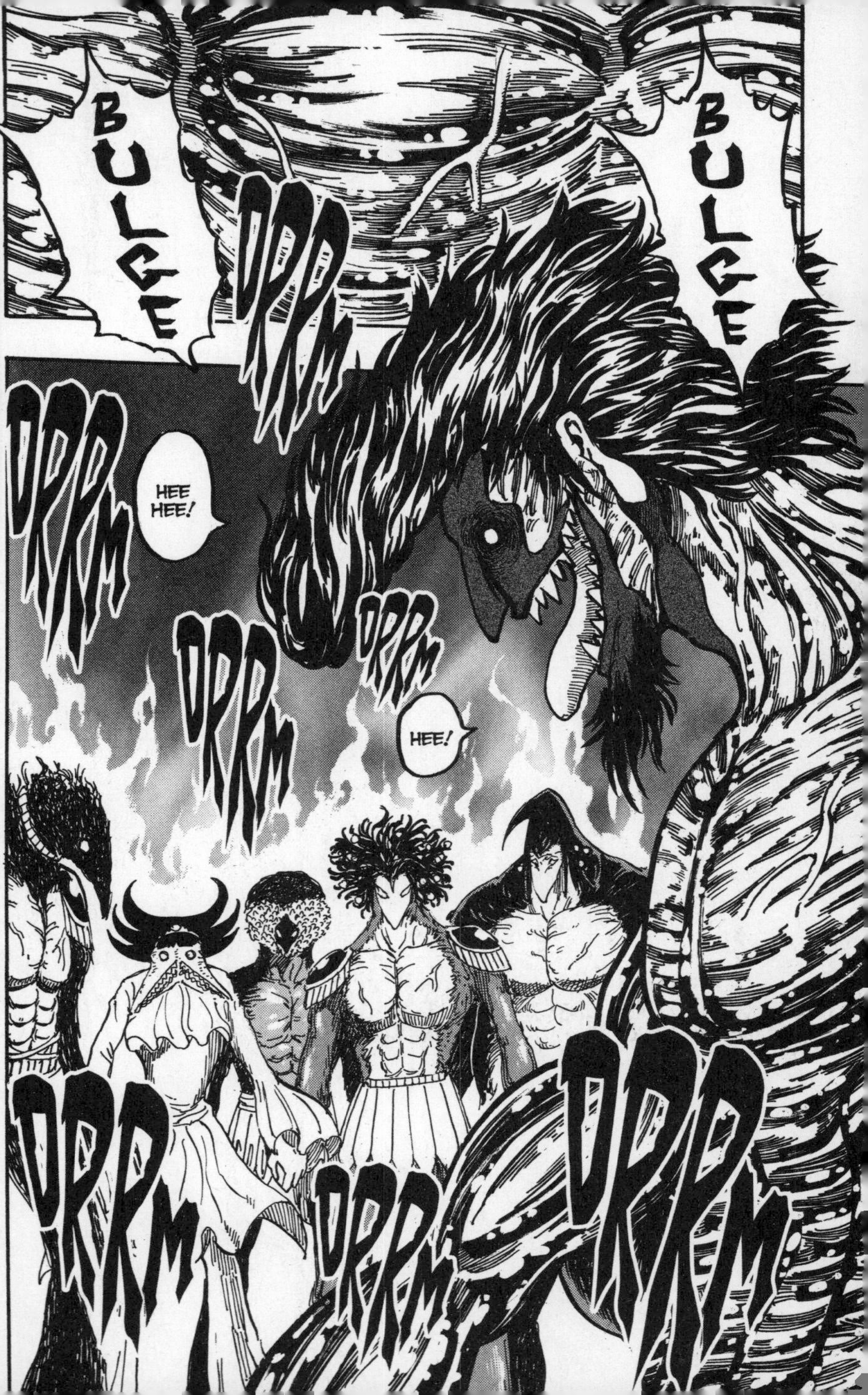
BULGE
BULGE
DRRM
HEE HEE!
DRRM
DRRM
HEE!
DRRM
DRRM
DRRM
DRRM

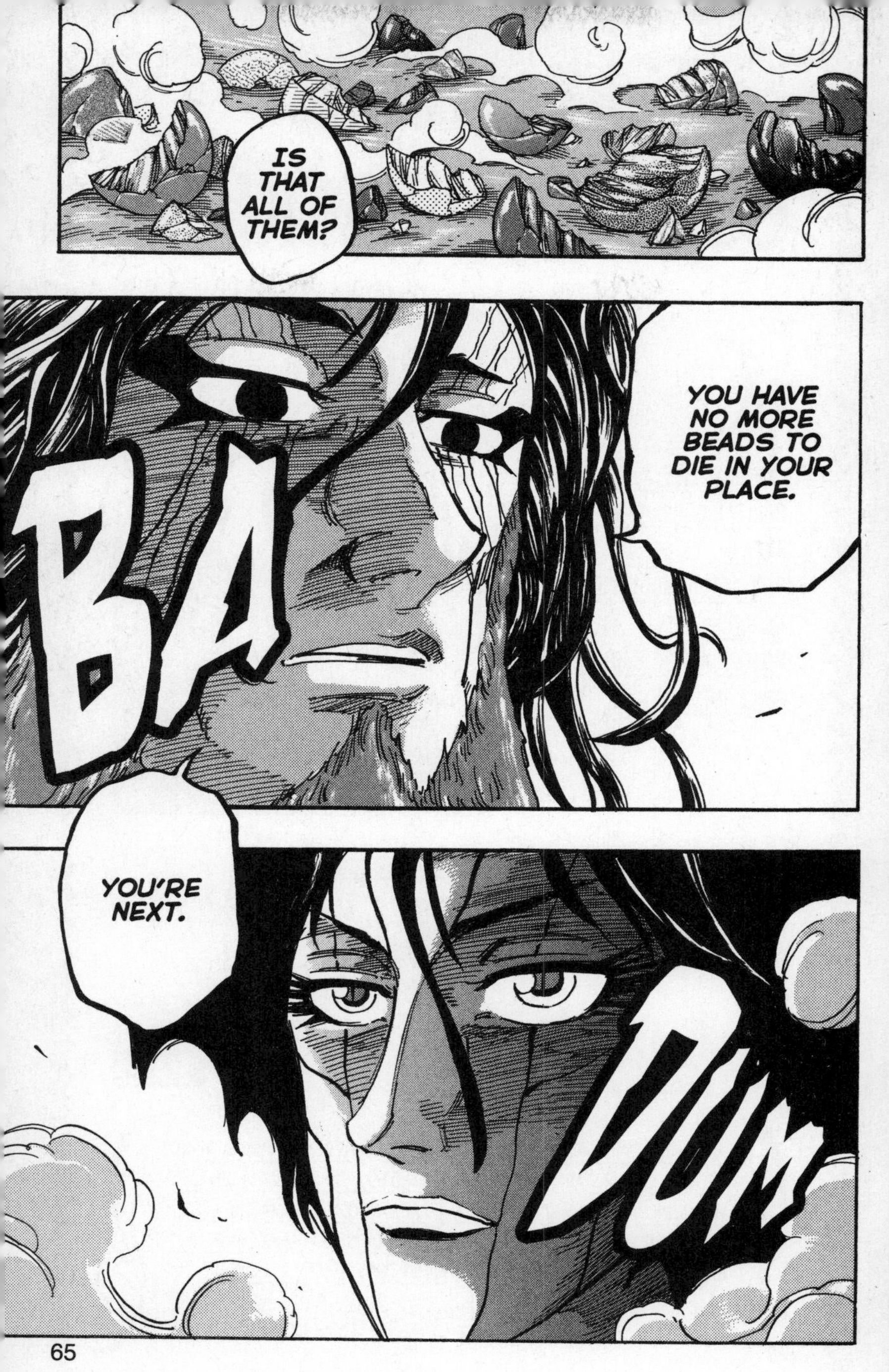
IS THAT ALL OF THEM?
YOU HAVE NO MORE BEADS TO DIE IN YOUR PLACE.
BA
YOU'RE NEXT.
DUM

TORIKO

GOURMET CHECKLIST

Vol. 383

WAVE BOY
(OCEAN CURRENT MONSTER)

CAPTURE LEVEL: 1,600
HABITAT: GOURMET WORLD'S AREA 6
SIZE: ACTUAL BODY / 10 CM
HEIGHT: ---
WEIGHT: ACTUAL BODY / 200 G
PRICE: INEDIBLE

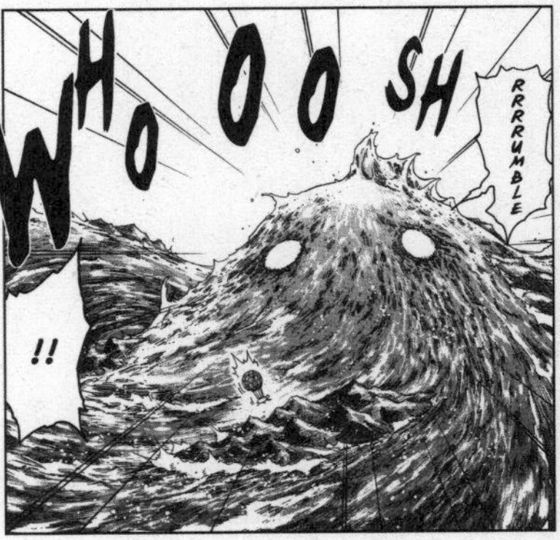
WHOOOSH
RRRRUMBLE
!!

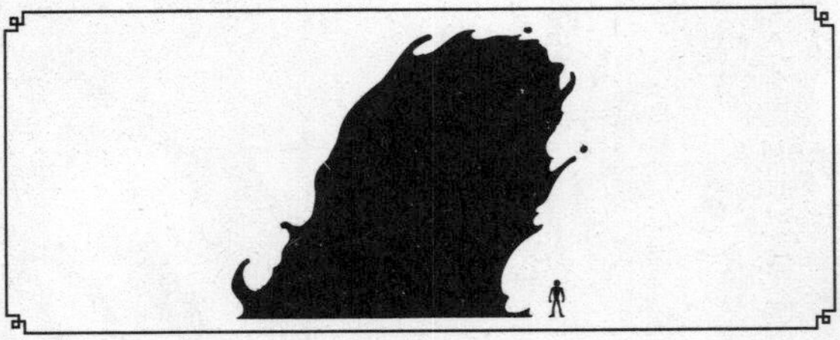

SCALE

AN OCEAN CURRENT MONSTER THAT RESIDES IN THE OCEANS OF THE GOURMET WORLD'S AREA 6. IT CAN CONSTANTLY CHANGE ITS BODY AND TAKE ON A NUMBER OF DIFFERENT FORMS, INCLUDING A GIANT OR A DRAGON. ITS ACTUAL BODY IS AS SMALL AS A SEA ANGEL, SO IT'S VERY DIFFICULT TO ATTACK DIRECTLY OR INFLICT DAMAGE ON IT. THE MOST EFFECTIVE ATTACKS ARE ELECTRIC AND FIRE TYPES DIRECTLY AT ITS HEAD.

GOURMET 353: TO THE MAIN ONE!!

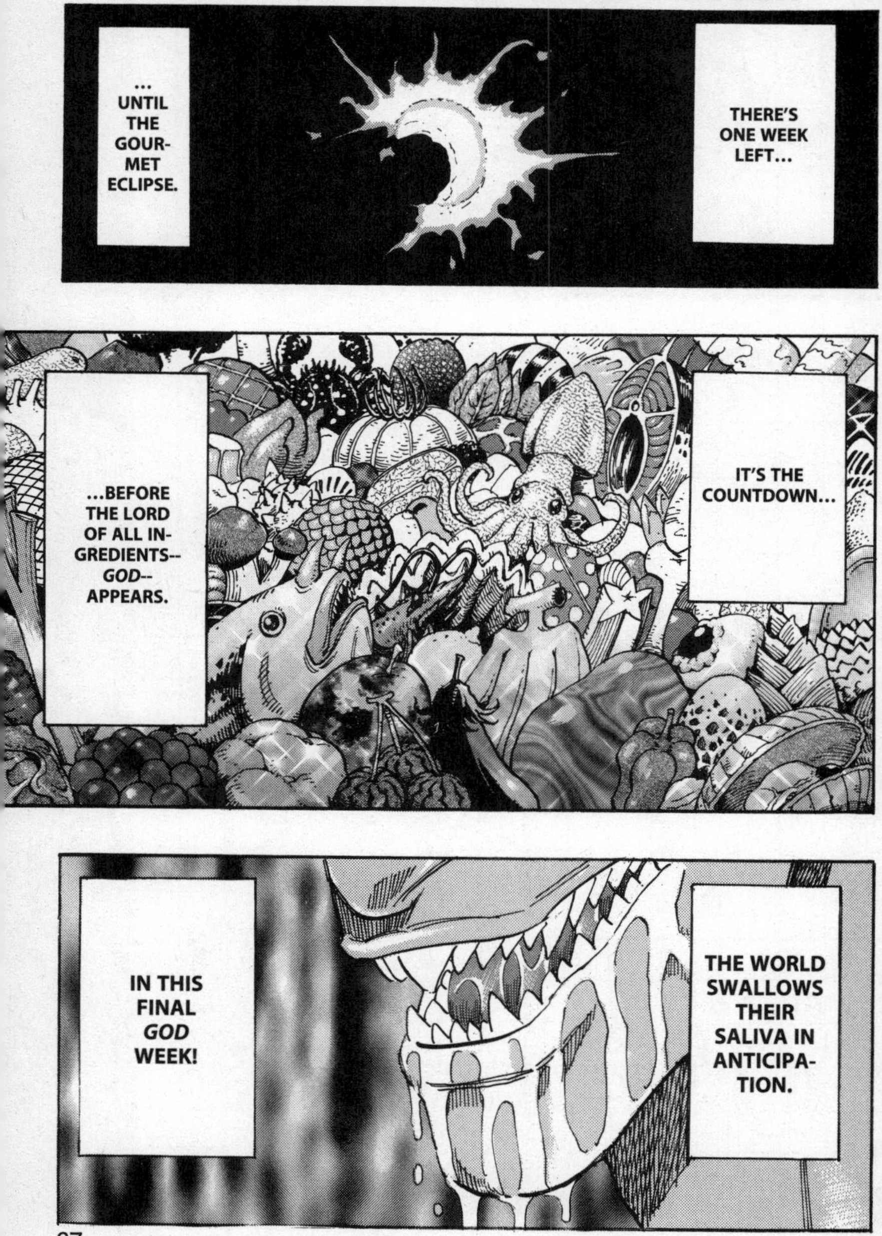

THERE'S ONE WEEK LEFT...
... UNTIL THE GOUR-MET ECLIPSE.
IT'S THE COUNTDOWN...
...BEFORE THE LORD OF ALL IN-GREDIENTS-- *GOD*-- APPEARS.
THE WORLD SWALLOWS THEIR SALIVA IN ANTICIPA-TION.
IN THIS FINAL *GOD* WEEK!

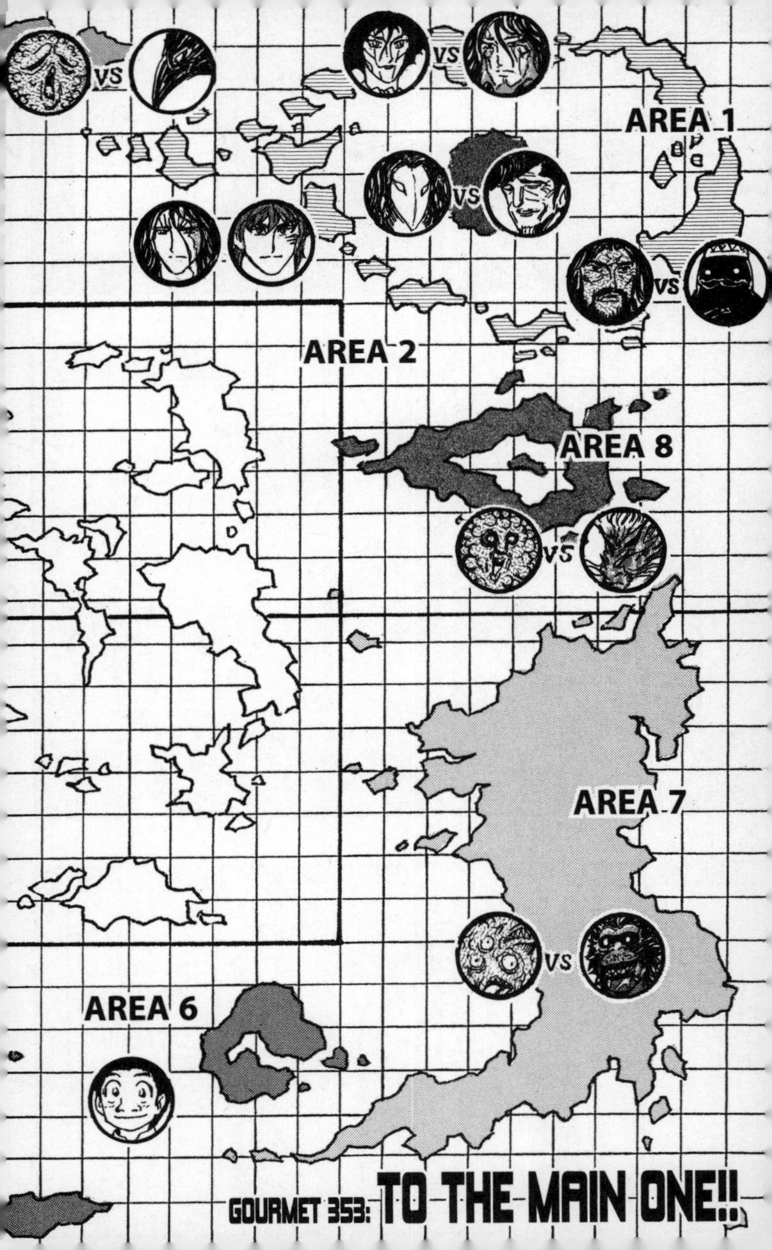
VS
VS
AREA 1
VS
VS
AREA 2
AREA 8
VS
AREA 7
VS
AREA 6

GOURMET 353: TO THE MAIN ONE!!

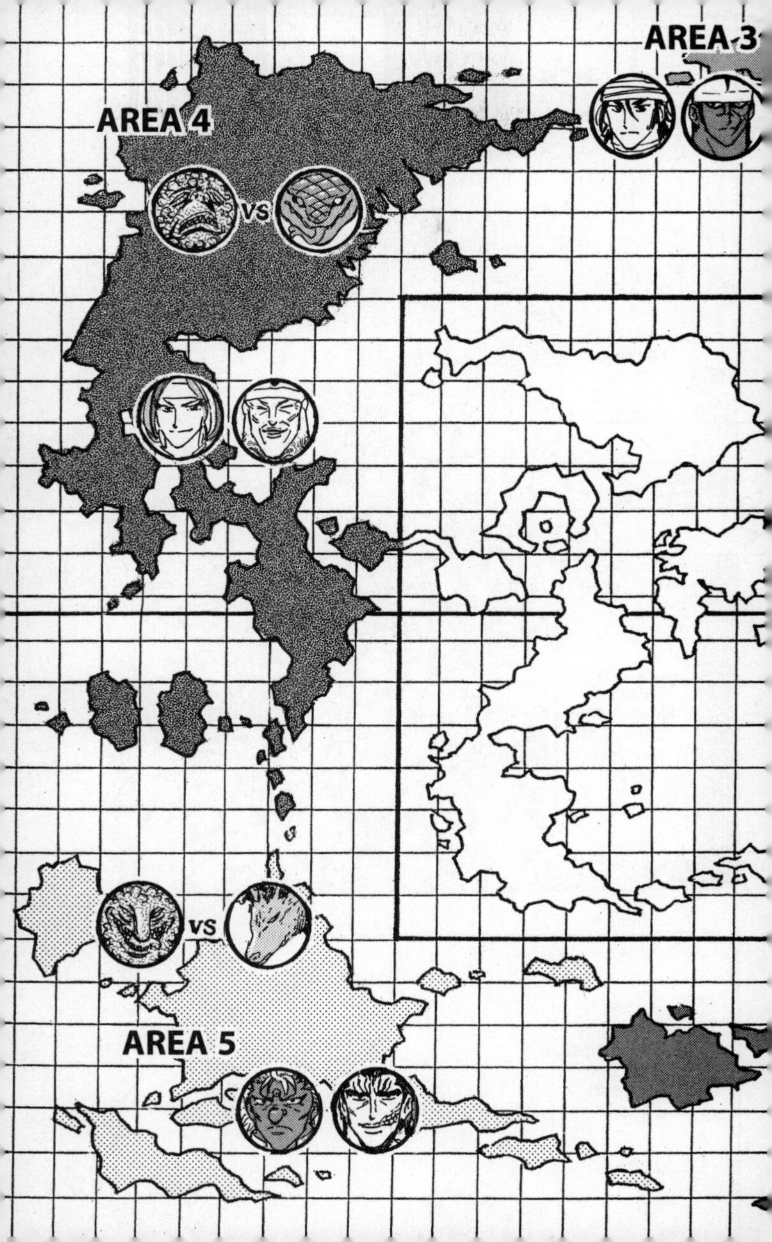
AREA 3
AREA 4
VS
AREA 5
VS

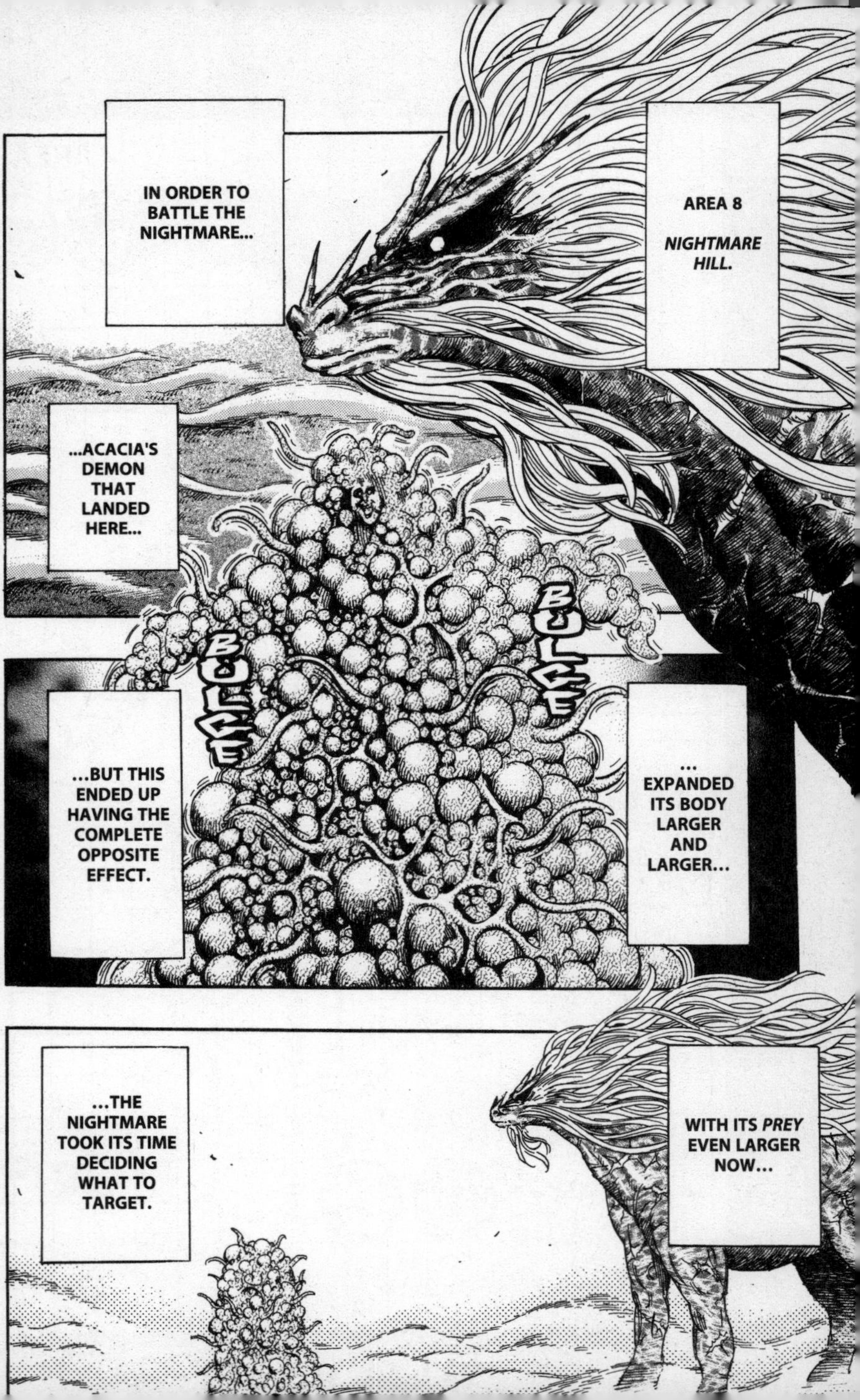
AREA 8
NIGHTMARE HILL.
IN ORDER TO BATTLE THE NIGHTMARE...
...ACACIA'S DEMON THAT LANDED HERE...
... EXPANDED ITS BODY LARGER AND LARGER...
BULGE
BULGE
...BUT THIS ENDED UP HAVING THE COMPLETE OPPOSITE EFFECT.
WITH ITS *PREY* EVEN LARGER NOW...
...THE NIGHTMARE TOOK ITS TIME DECIDING WHAT TO TARGET.

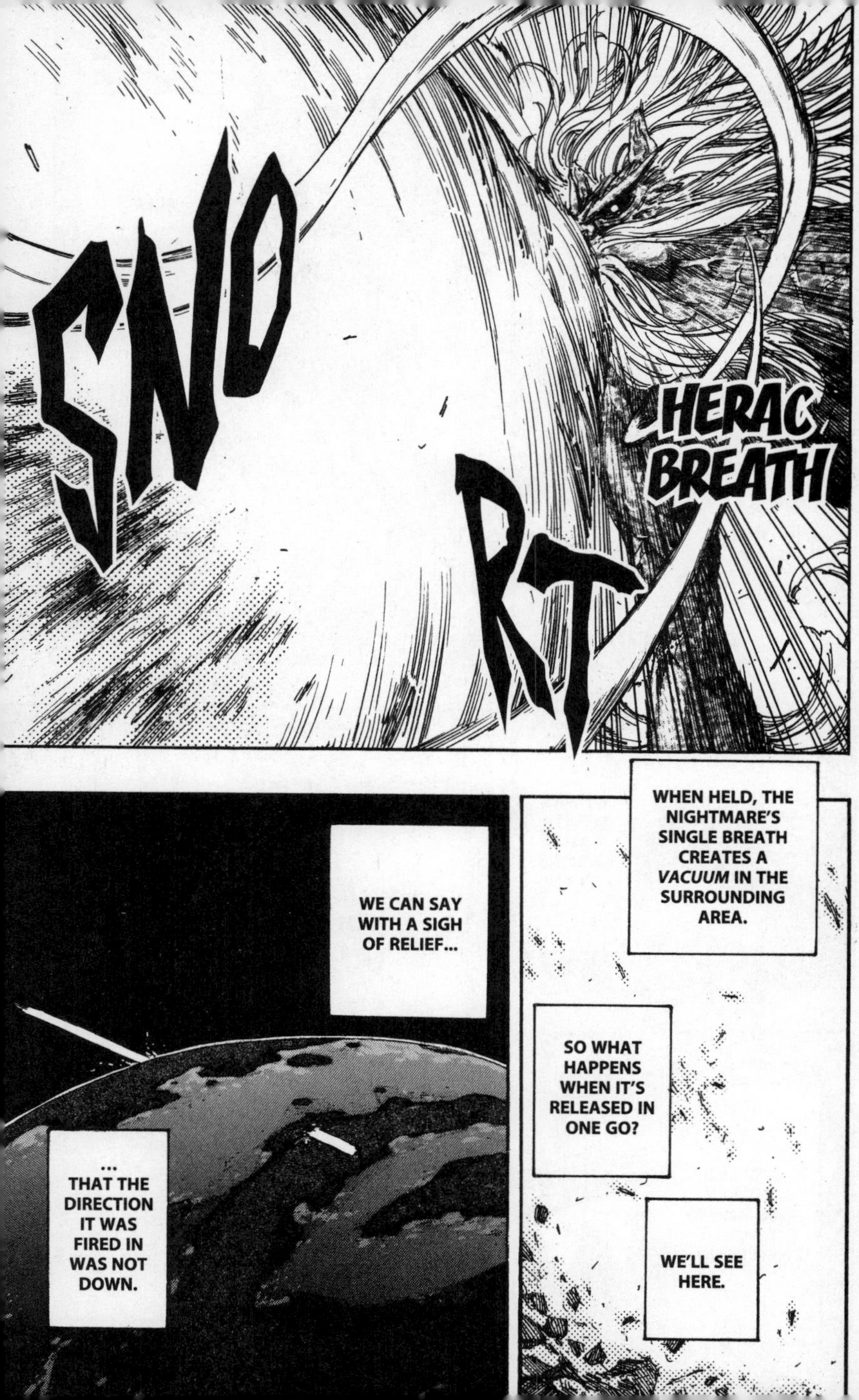
HERAC BREATH
SNORT
WHEN HELD, THE NIGHTMARE'S SINGLE BREATH CREATES A *VACUUM* IN THE SURROUNDING AREA.
SO WHAT HAPPENS WHEN IT'S RELEASED IN ONE GO?
WE'LL SEE HERE.
WE CAN SAY WITH A SIGH OF RELIEF...
... THAT THE DIRECTION IT WAS FIRED IN WAS NOT DOWN.

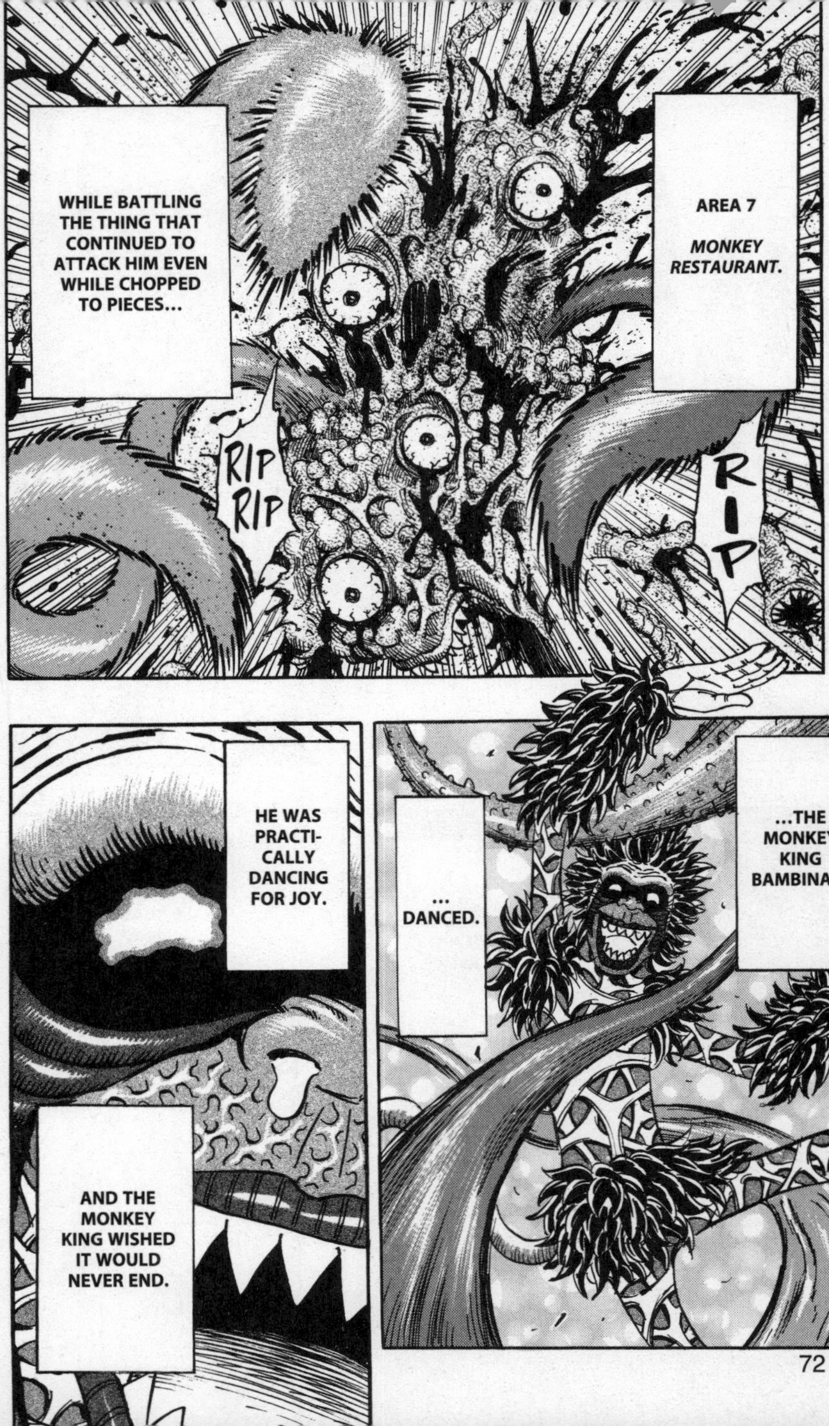
AREA 7
MONKEY RESTAURANT.
WHILE BATTLING THE THING THAT CONTINUED TO ATTACK HIM EVEN WHILE CHOPPED TO PIECES...
RIP
RIP RIP
...THE MONKEY KING BAMBINA...
...DANCED.
HE WAS PRACTI-CALLY DANCING FOR JOY.
AND THE MONKEY KING WISHED IT WOULD NEVER END.

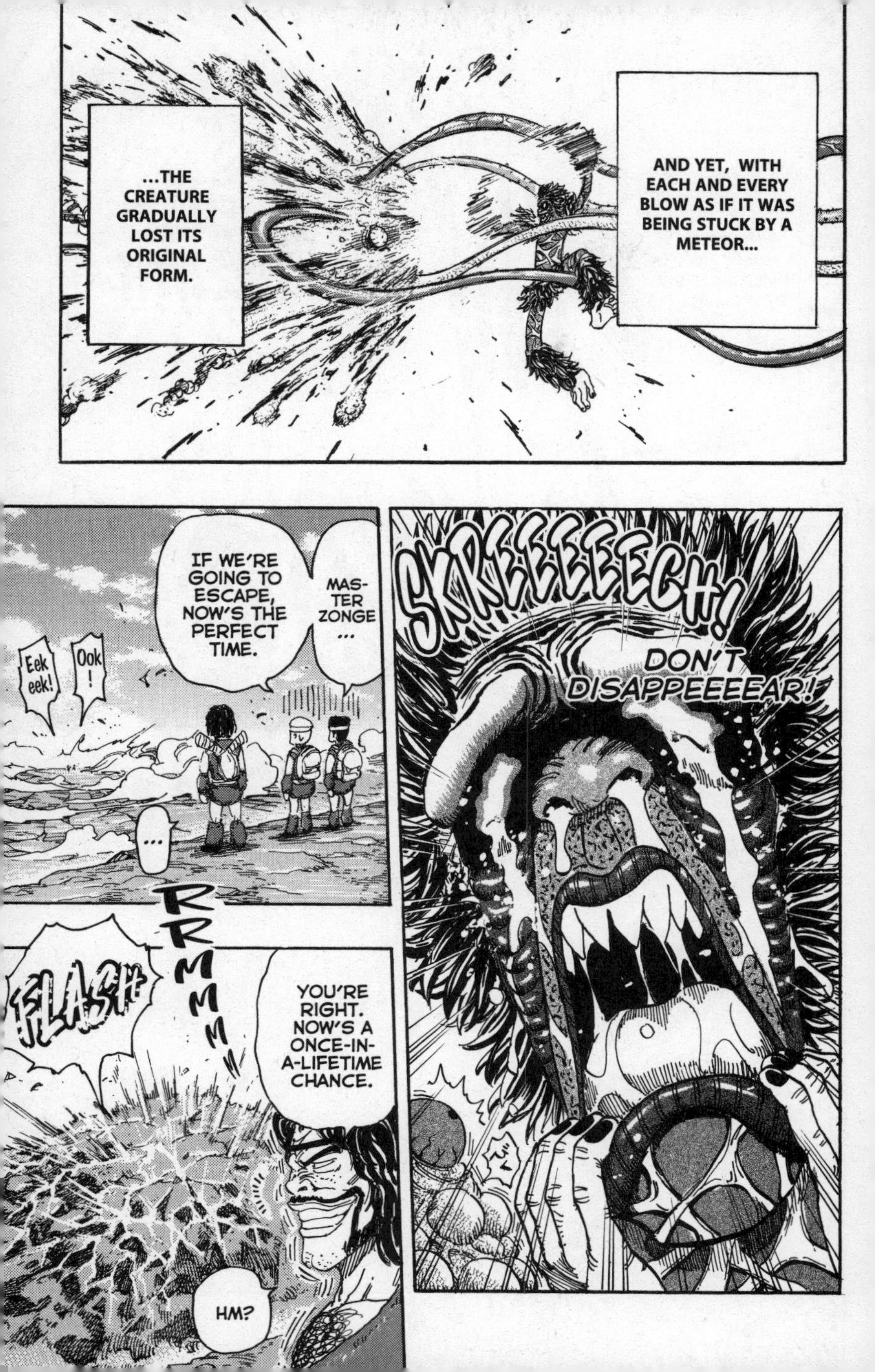
AND YET, WITH EACH AND EVERY BLOW AS IF IT WAS BEING STUCK BY A METEOR...
...THE CREATURE GRADUALLY LOST ITS ORIGINAL FORM.
SKREEEEECH!
DON'T DISAPPEEEEEAR!
MAS-TER ZONGE ...
IF WE'RE GOING TO ESCAPE, NOW'S THE PERFECT TIME.
Ook!
Eek eek!
...
RRMMMM
YOU'RE RIGHT. NOW'S A ONCE-IN-A-LIFETIME CHANCE.
FLASH
HM?

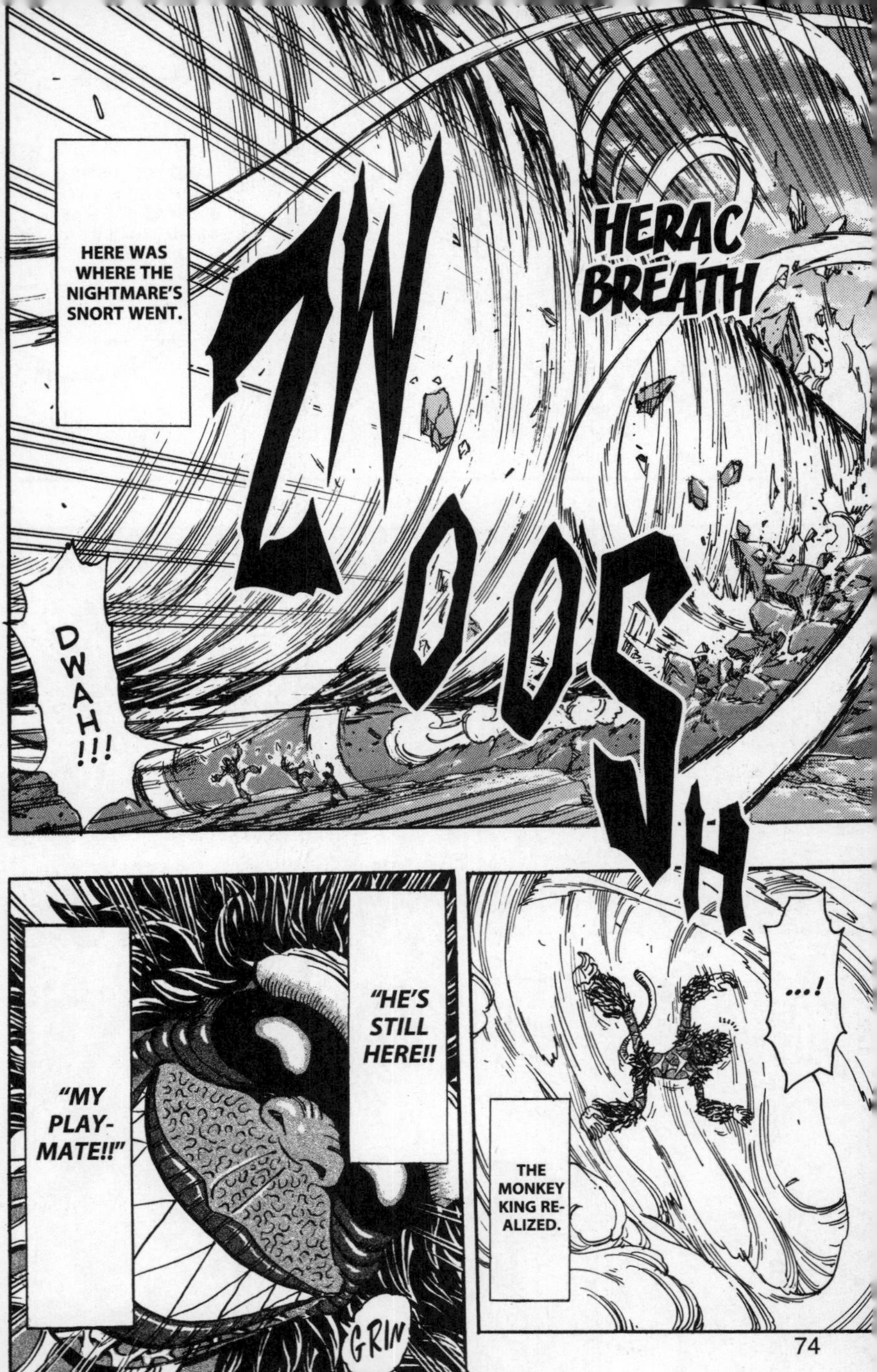
HERAC BREATH
ZWOOSH
HERE WAS WHERE THE NIGHTMARE'S SNORT WENT.
DWAH!!!
...!
THE MONKEY KING RE-ALIZED.
"HE'S STILL HERE!!
"MY PLAY-MATE!!"
GRIN

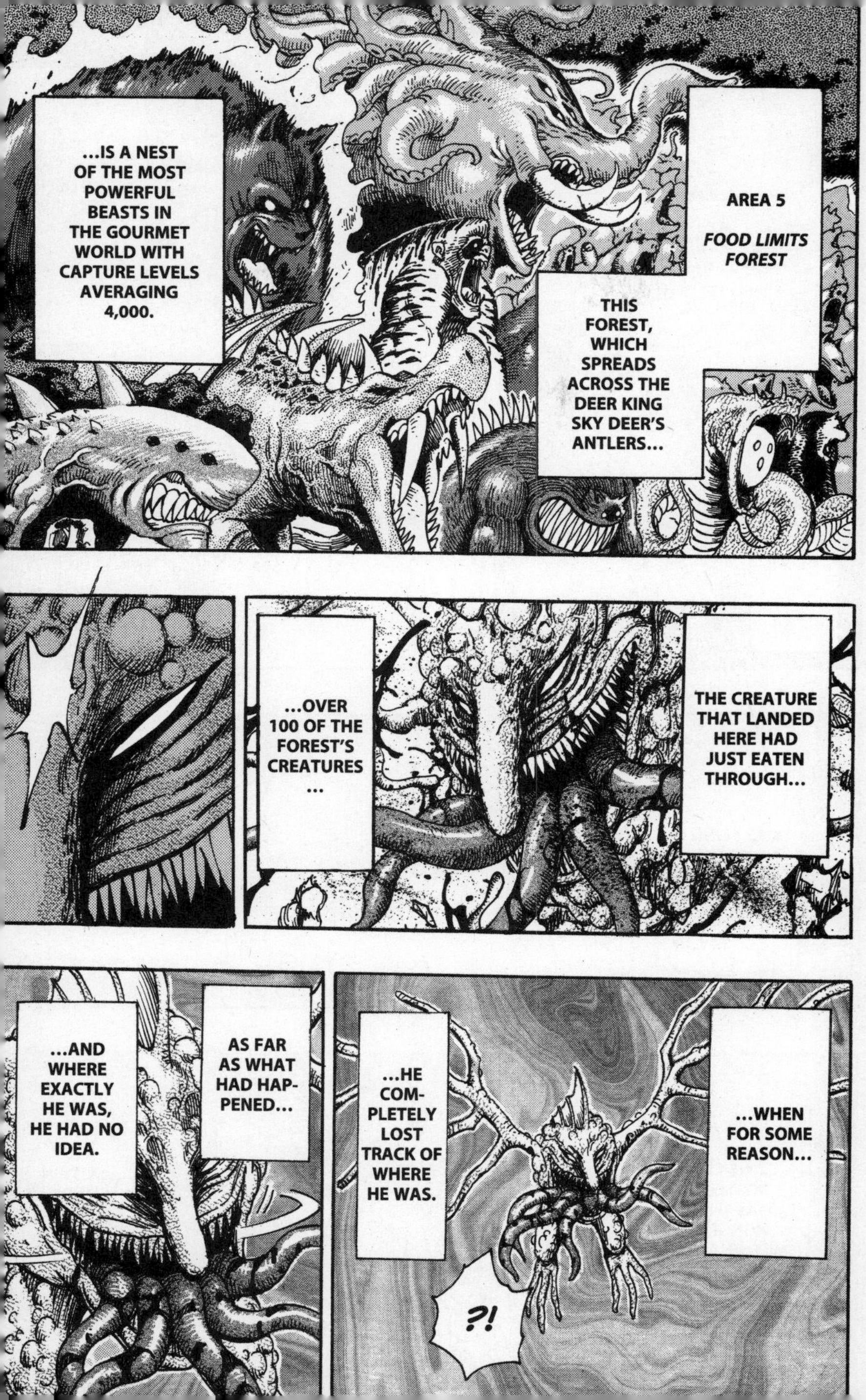
AREA 5
FOOD LIMITS FOREST
THIS FOREST, WHICH SPREADS ACROSS THE DEER KING SKY DEER'S ANTLERS...
...IS A NEST OF THE MOST POWERFUL BEASTS IN THE GOURMET WORLD WITH CAPTURE LEVELS AVERAGING 4,000.
THE CREATURE THAT LANDED HERE HAD JUST EATEN THROUGH...
...OVER 100 OF THE FOREST'S CREATURES ...
...WHEN FOR SOME REASON...
...HE COMPLETELY LOST TRACK OF WHERE HE WAS.
?!
AS FAR AS WHAT HAD HAPPENED...
...AND WHERE EXACTLY HE WAS, HE HAD NO IDEA.

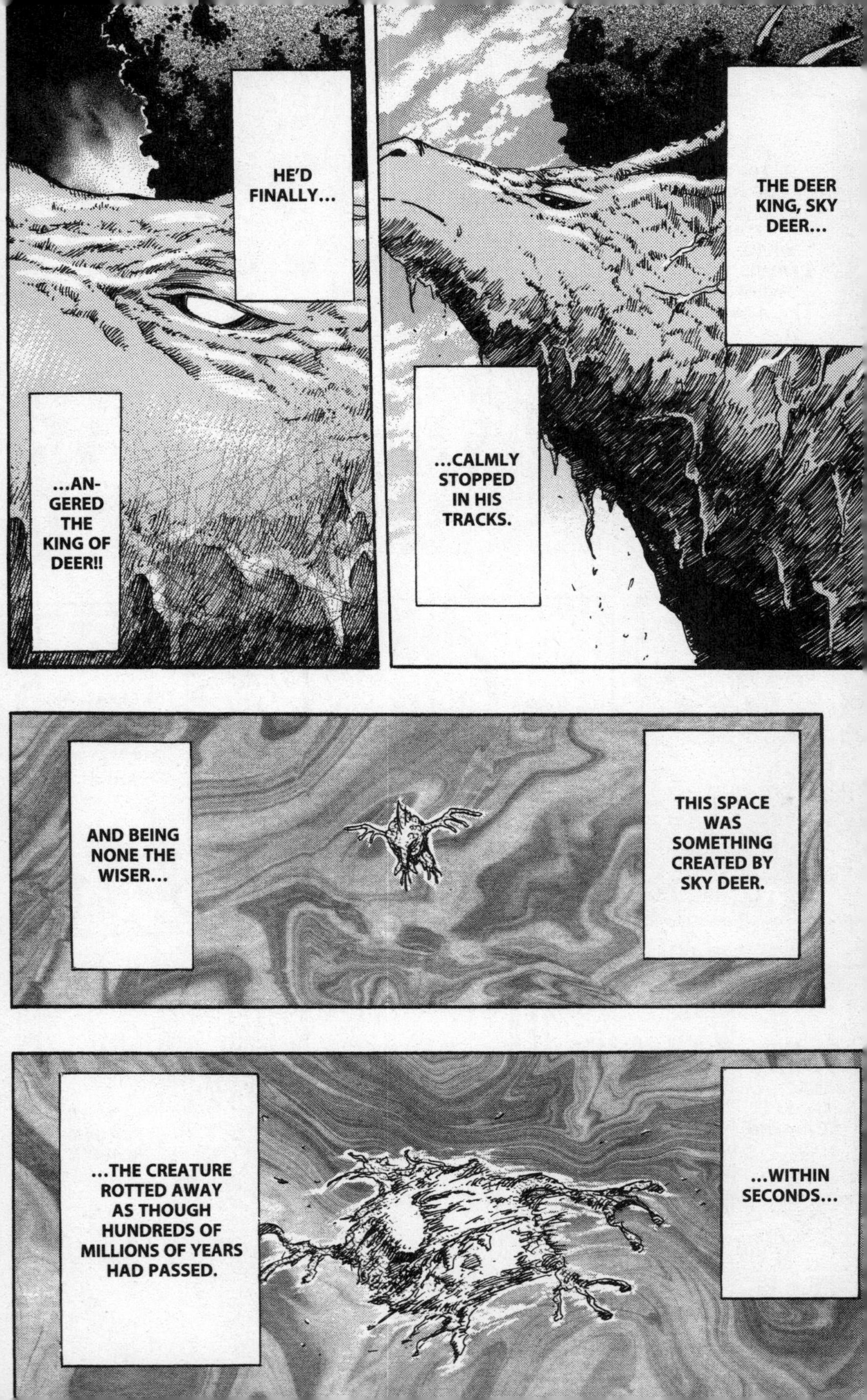
THE DEER KING, SKY DEER...
...CALMLY STOPPED IN HIS TRACKS.
HE'D FINALLY...
...AN-GERED THE KING OF DEER!!
THIS SPACE WAS SOMETHING CREATED BY SKY DEER.
AND BEING NONE THE WISER...
...WITHIN SECONDS...
...THE CREATURE ROTTED AWAY AS THOUGH HUNDREDS OF MILLIONS OF YEARS HAD PASSED.

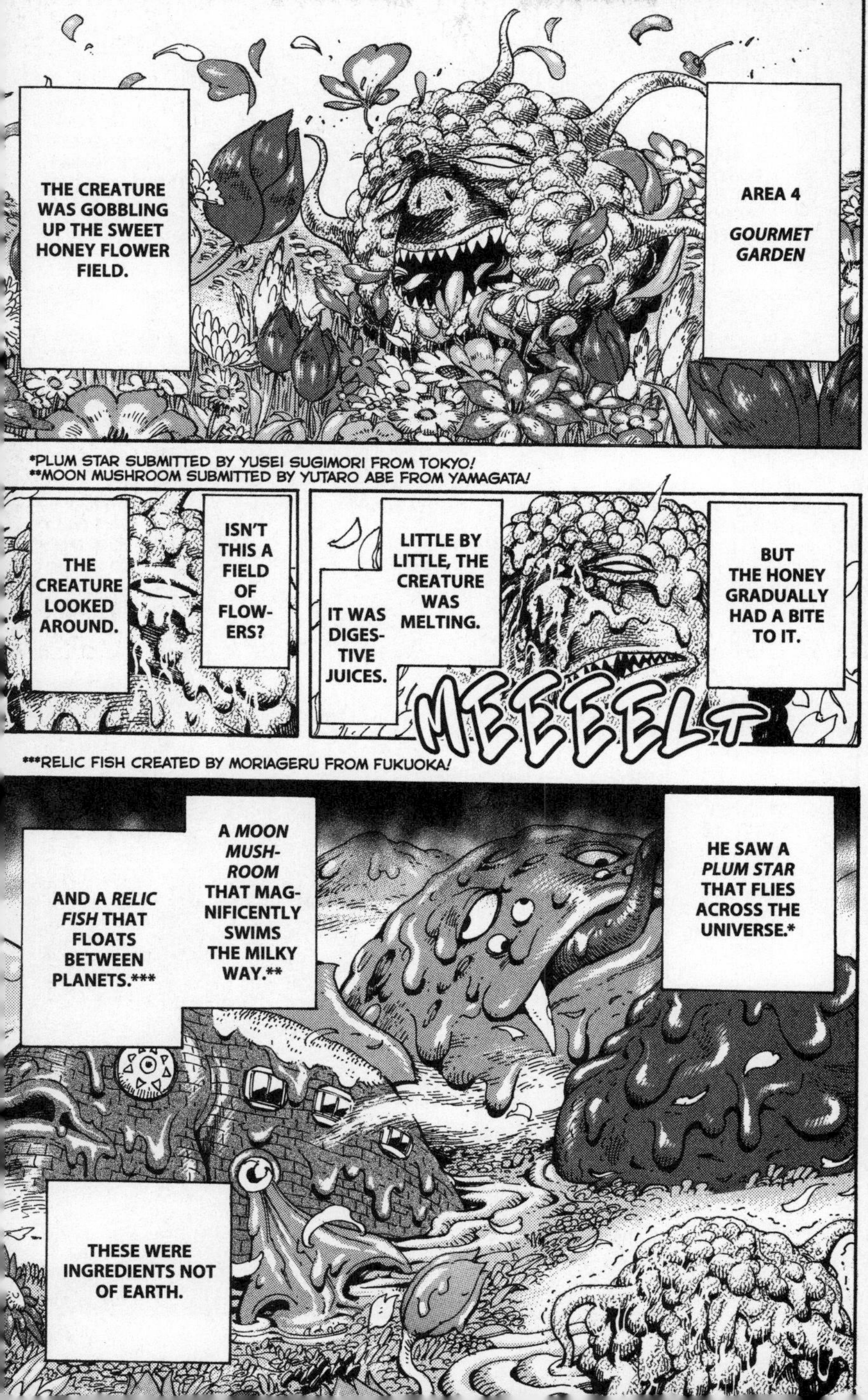
AREA 4 *GOURMET GARDEN*
THE CREATURE WAS GOBBLING UP THE SWEET HONEY FLOWER FIELD.
BUT THE HONEY GRADUALLY HAD A BITE TO IT.
LITTLE BY LITTLE, THE CREATURE WAS MELTING.
IT WAS DIGESTIVE JUICES.
MEEEEELT
ISN'T THIS A FIELD OF FLOWERS?
THE CREATURE LOOKED AROUND.
HE SAW A *PLUM STAR* THAT FLIES ACROSS THE UNIVERSE.*
A *MOON MUSHROOM* THAT MAGNIFICENTLY SWIMS THE MILKY WAY.**
AND A *RELIC FISH* THAT FLOATS BETWEEN PLANETS.***
THESE WERE INGREDIENTS NOT OF EARTH.

*PLUM STAR SUBMITTED BY YUSEI SUGIMORI FROM TOKYO!
**MOON MUSHROOM SUBMITTED BY YUTARO ABE FROM YAMAGATA!
***RELIC FISH CREATED BY MORIAGERU FROM FUKUOKA!

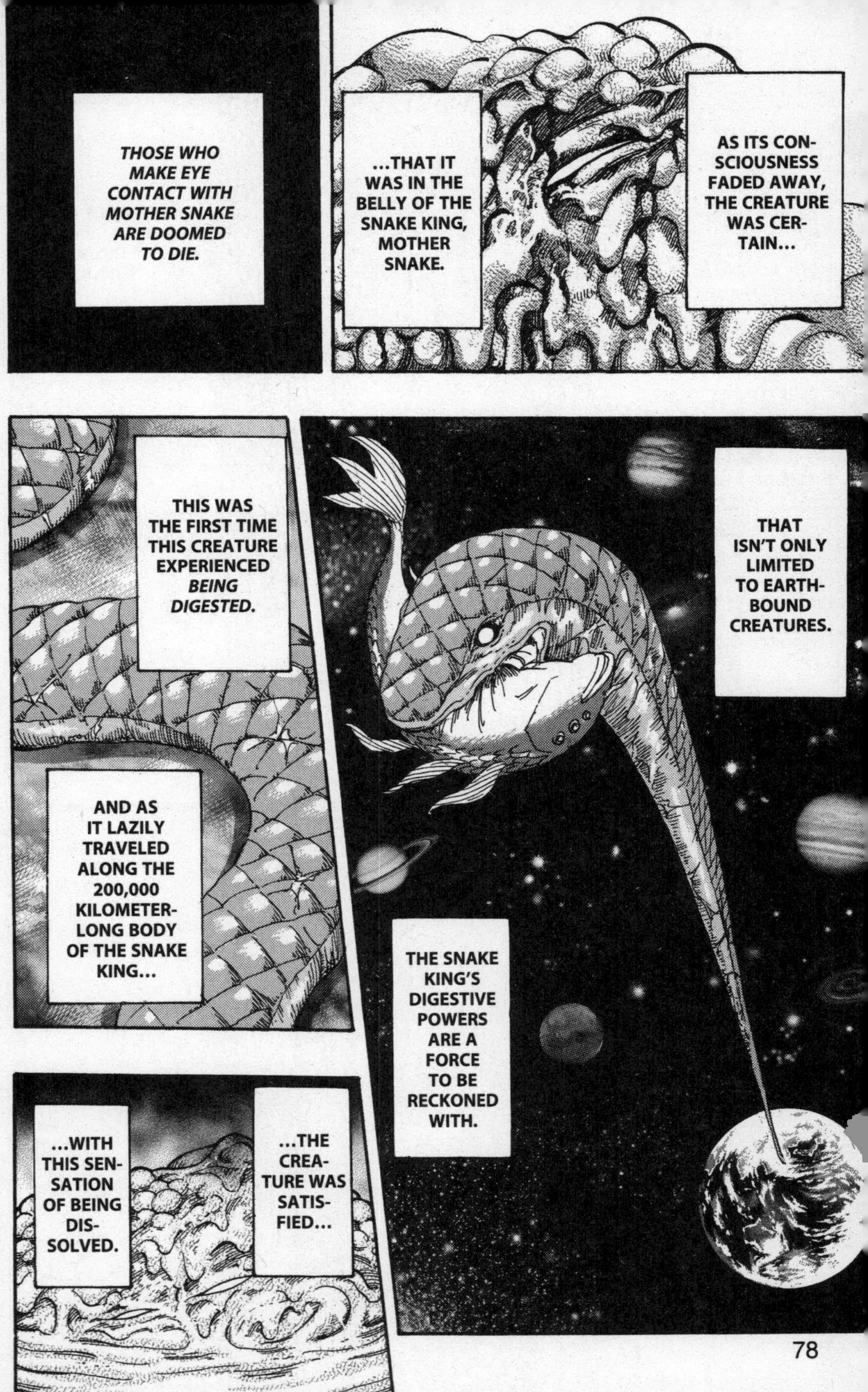
AS ITS CONSCIOUSNESS FADED AWAY, THE CREATURE WAS CERTAIN...
...THAT IT WAS IN THE BELLY OF THE SNAKE KING, MOTHER SNAKE.
THOSE WHO MAKE EYE CONTACT WITH MOTHER SNAKE ARE DOOMED TO DIE.
THAT ISN'T ONLY LIMITED TO EARTHBOUND CREATURES.
THE SNAKE KING'S DIGESTIVE POWERS ARE A FORCE TO BE RECKONED WITH.
THIS WAS THE FIRST TIME THIS CREATURE EXPERIENCED *BEING DIGESTED.*
AND AS IT LAZILY TRAVELED ALONG THE 200,000 KILOMETER-LONG BODY OF THE SNAKE KING...
...THE CREATURE WAS SATISFIED...
...WITH THIS SENSATION OF BEING DISSOLVED.

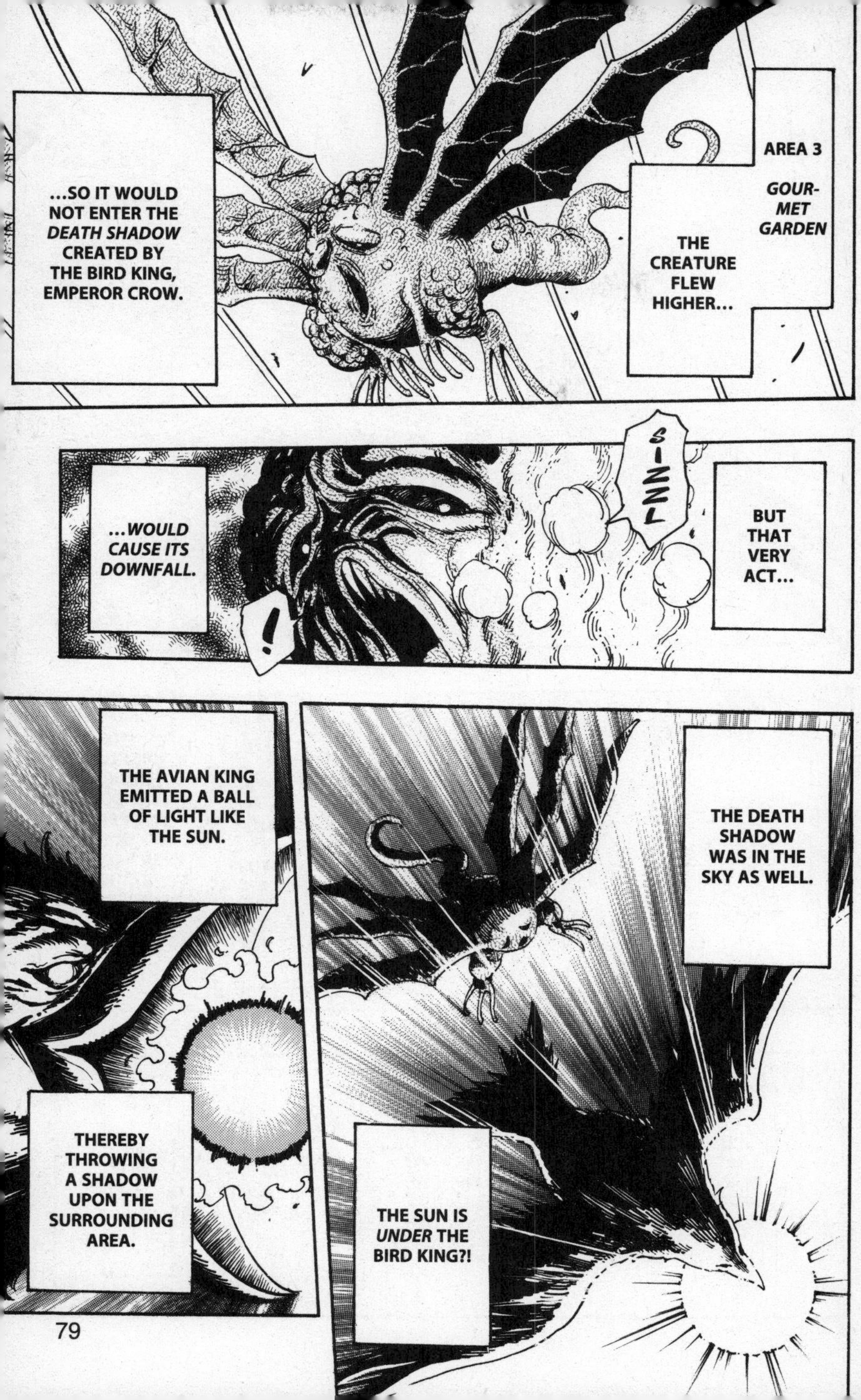
AREA 3
GOUR-
MET
GARDEN
THE CREATURE FLEW HIGHER...
...SO IT WOULD NOT ENTER THE *DEATH SHADOW* CREATED BY THE BIRD KING, EMPEROR CROW.
BUT THAT VERY ACT...
SIZZL
...*WOULD CAUSE ITS DOWNFALL.*
!
THE DEATH SHADOW WAS IN THE SKY AS WELL.
THE SUN IS *UNDER* THE BIRD KING?!
THE AVIAN KING EMITTED A BALL OF LIGHT LIKE THE SUN.
THEREBY THROWING A SHADOW UPON THE SURROUNDING AREA.

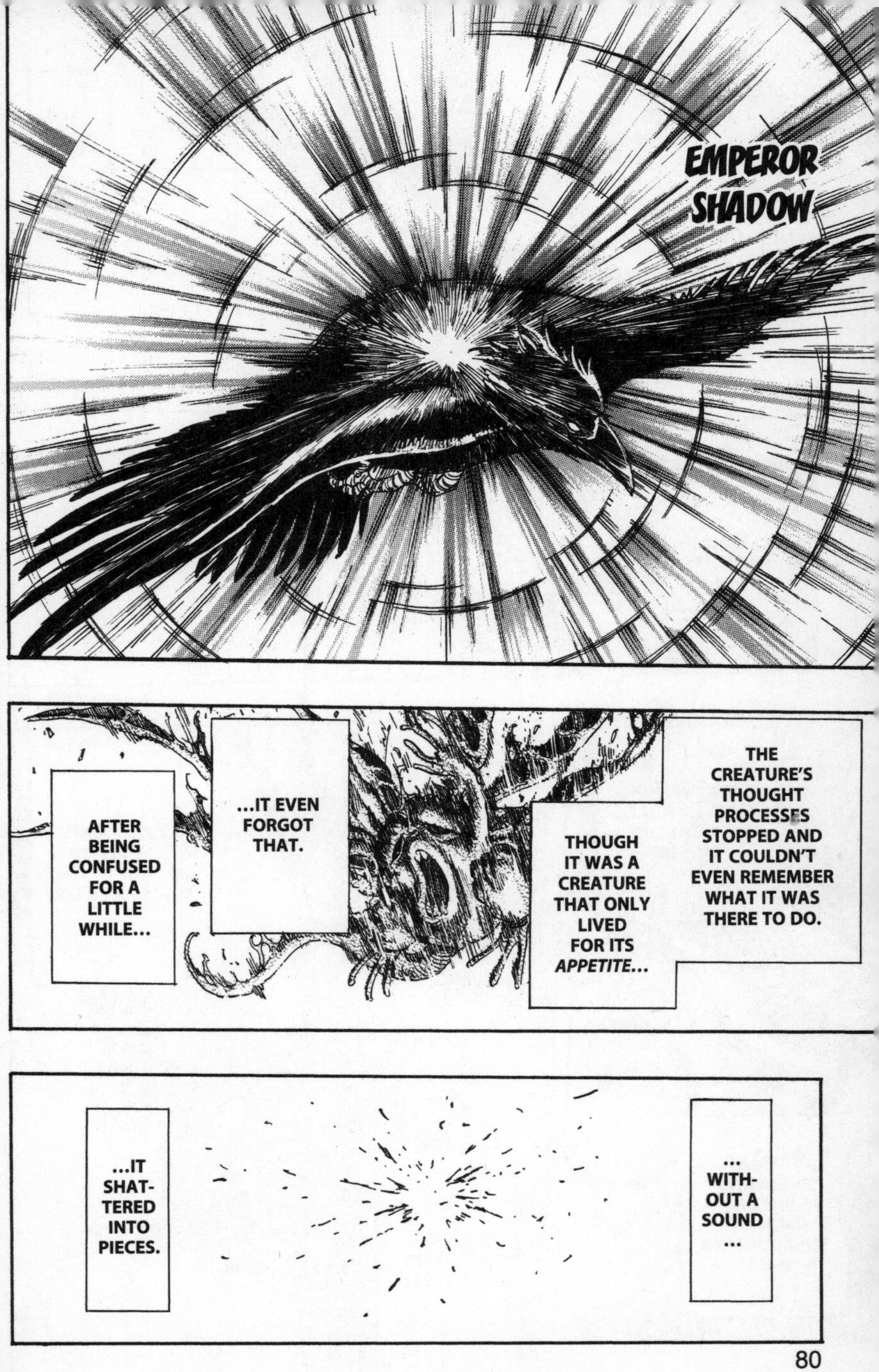
EMPEROR SHADOW
THE CREATURE'S THOUGHT PROCESSES STOPPED AND IT COULDN'T EVEN REMEMBER WHAT IT WAS THERE TO DO.
THOUGH IT WAS A CREATURE THAT ONLY LIVED FOR ITS *APPETITE*...
...IT EVEN FORGOT THAT.
AFTER BEING CONFUSED FOR A LITTLE WHILE...
...WITH-OUT A SOUND...
...IT SHAT-TERED INTO PIECES.

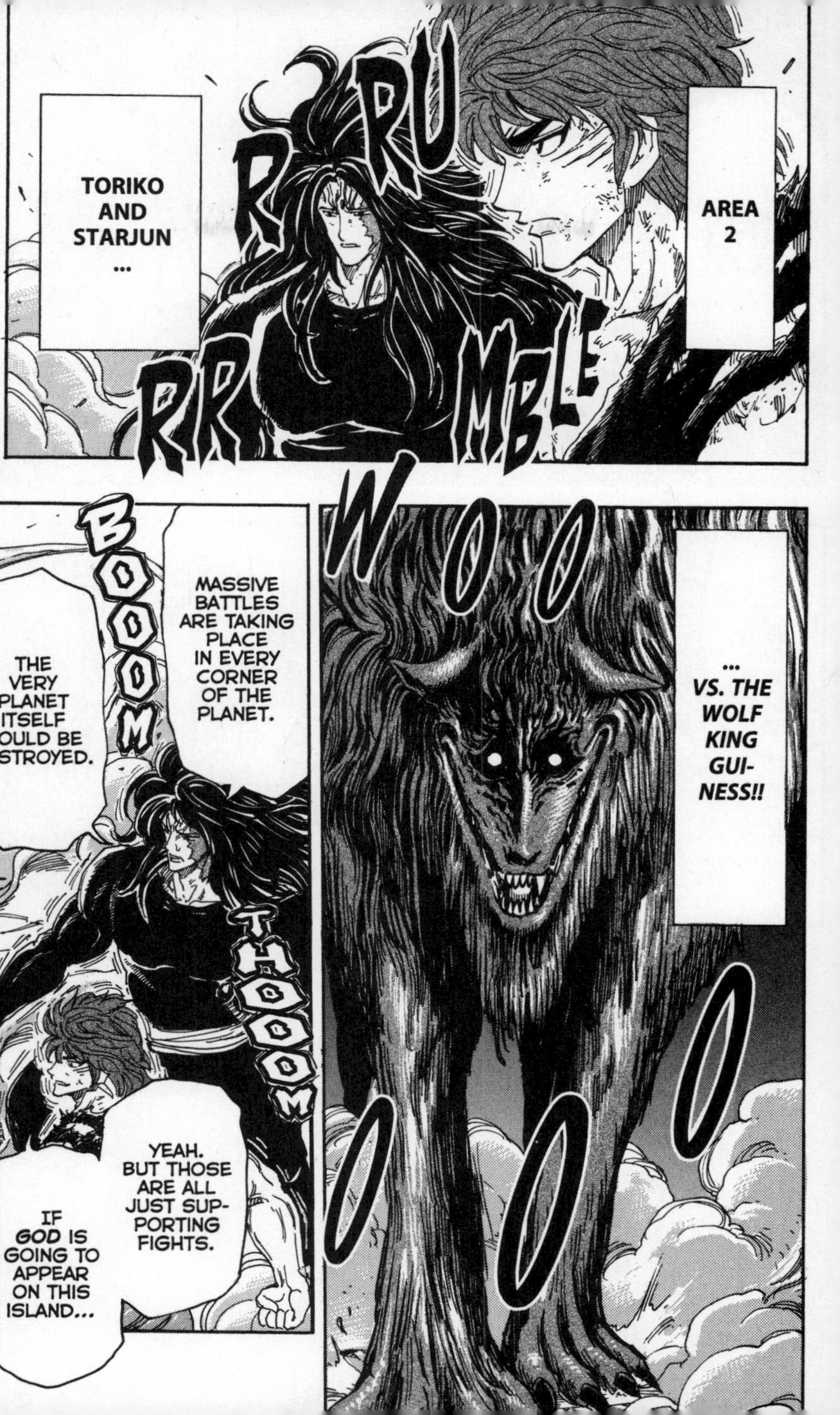
AREA 2
R RU
TORIKO AND STARJUN ...
RR MBLE
... VS. THE WOLF KING GUI-NESS!!
WOOO
OOOO
MASSIVE BATTLES ARE TAKING PLACE IN EVERY CORNER OF THE PLANET.
BOOOM
THE VERY PLANET ITSELF COULD BE DESTROYED.
THOOOM
YEAH. BUT THOSE ARE ALL JUST SUP-PORTING FIGHTS.
IF *GOD* IS GOING TO APPEAR ON THIS ISLAND...

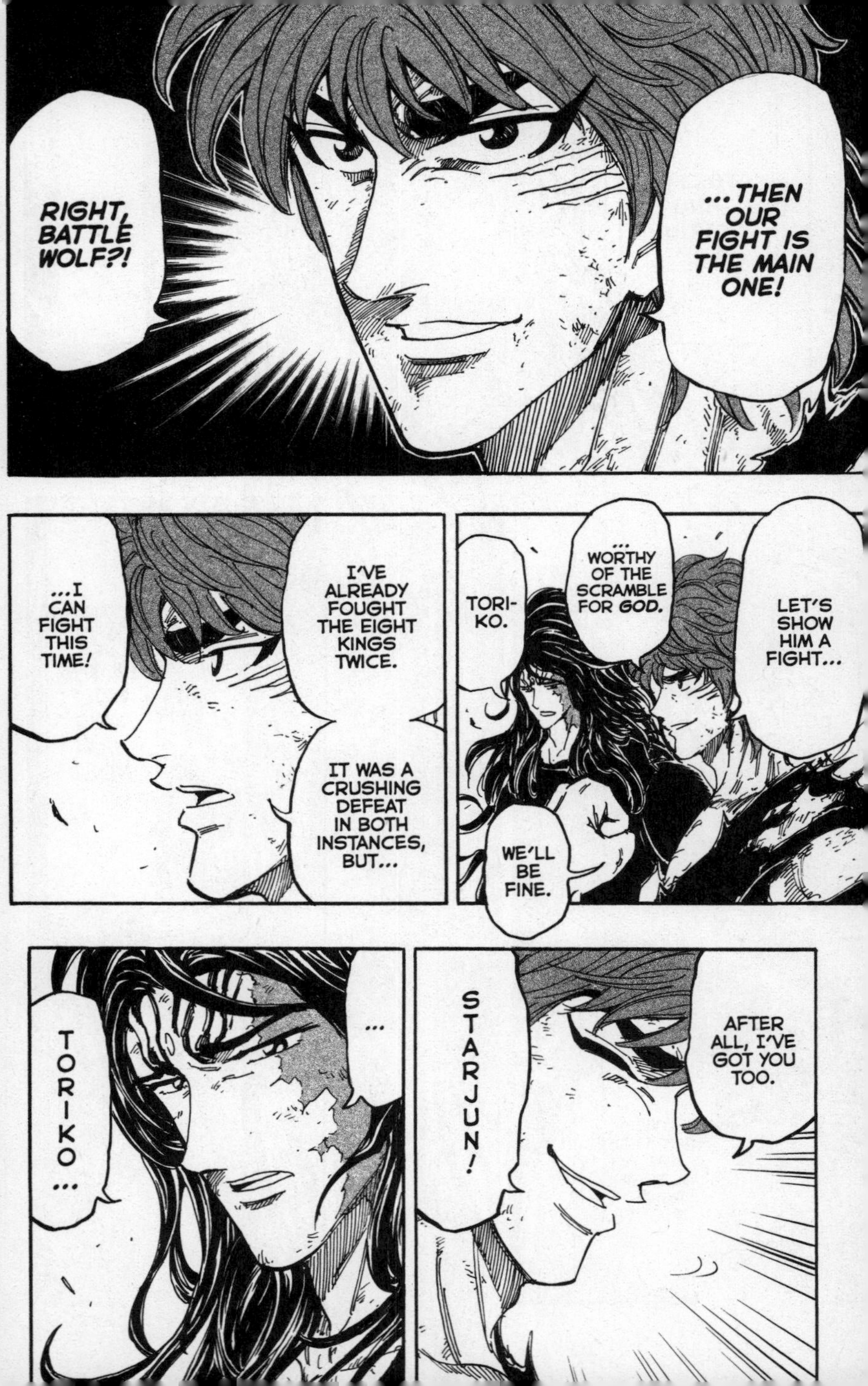
...THEN OUR FIGHT IS THE MAIN ONE!
RIGHT, BATTLE WOLF?!
LET'S SHOW HIM A FIGHT...
...WORTHY OF THE SCRAMBLE FOR *GOD*.
TORI-KO.
WE'LL BE FINE.
I'VE ALREADY FOUGHT THE EIGHT KINGS TWICE.
IT WAS A CRUSHING DEFEAT IN BOTH INSTANCES, BUT...
...I CAN FIGHT THIS TIME!
AFTER ALL, I'VE GOT YOU TOO.
STARJUN!
...
TORIKO...

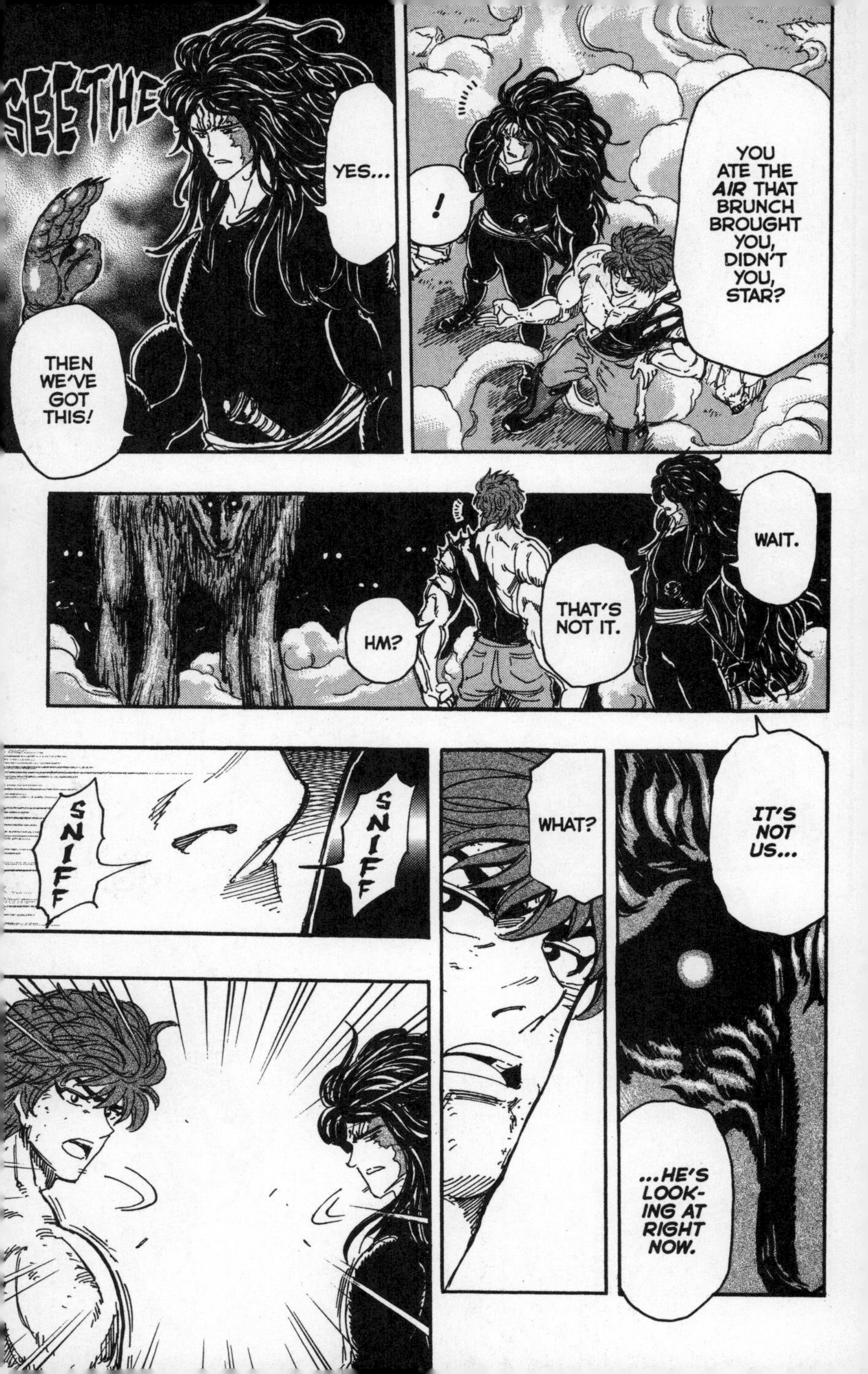
YOU ATE THE *AIR* THAT BRUNCH BROUGHT YOU, DIDN'T YOU, STAR?
!
SEETHE
YES...
THEN WE'VE GOT THIS!
WAIT.
THAT'S NOT IT.
HM?
IT'S NOT US...
...HE'S LOOKING AT RIGHT NOW.
WHAT?
SNIFF
SNIFF

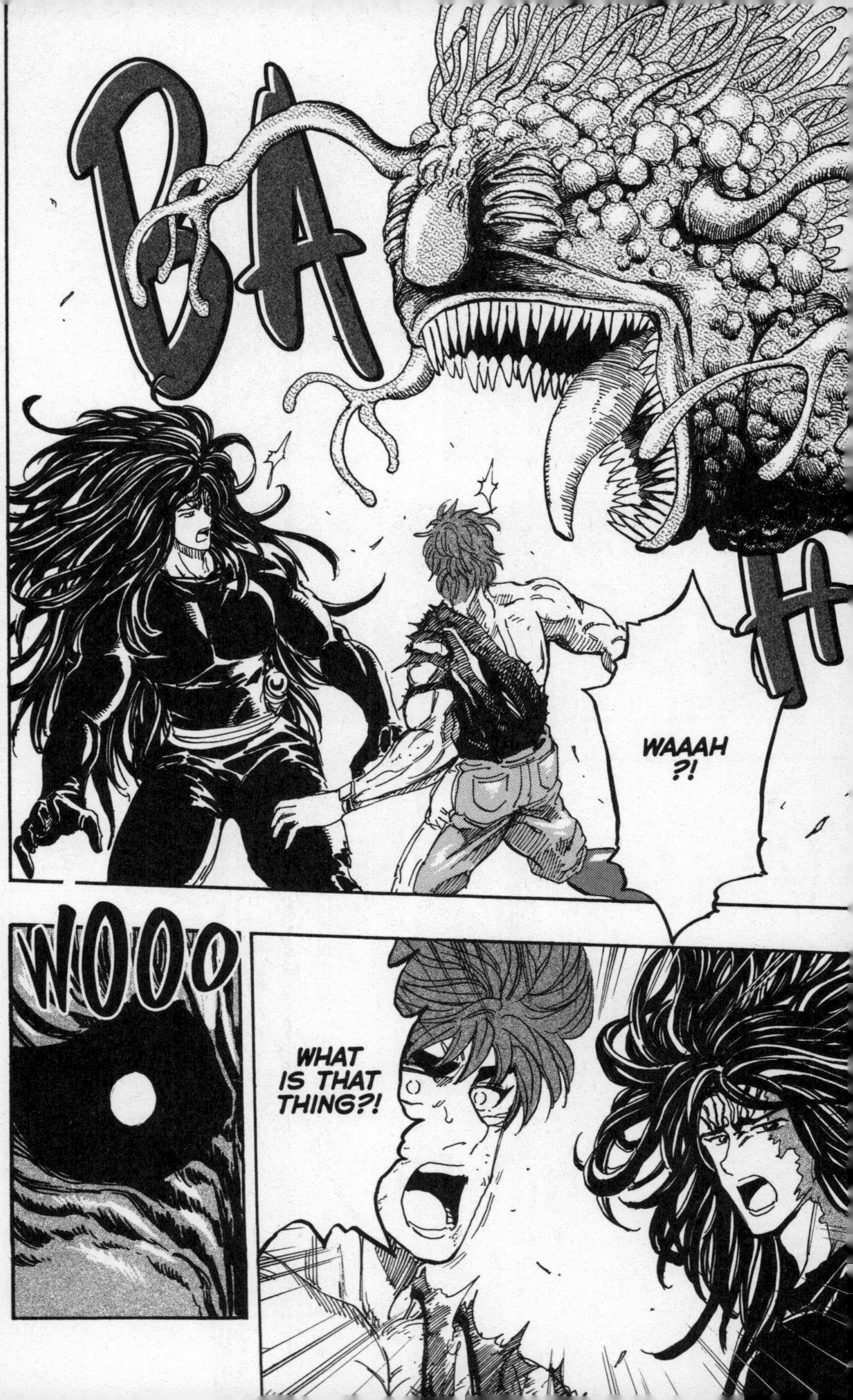
BA
H
WAAAH ?!
WHAT IS THAT THING?!
WOOO

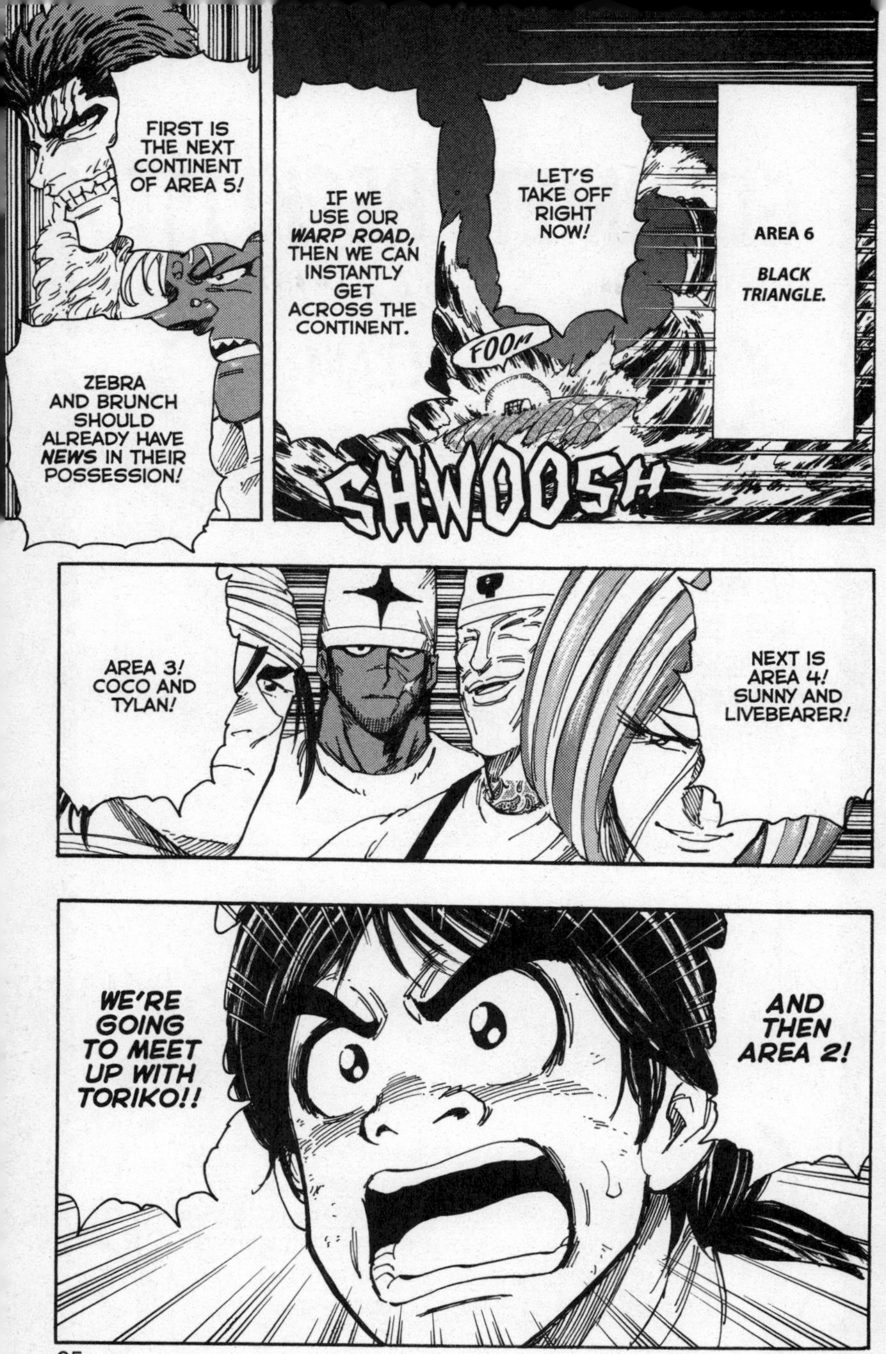
AREA 6
BLACK TRIANGLE.
LET'S TAKE OFF RIGHT NOW!
IF WE USE OUR WARP ROAD, THEN WE CAN INSTANTLY GET ACROSS THE CONTINENT.
FOOM
SHWOOSH
FIRST IS THE NEXT CONTINENT OF AREA 5!
ZEBRA AND BRUNCH SHOULD ALREADY HAVE NEWS IN THEIR POSSESSION!
NEXT IS AREA 4! SUNNY AND LIVEBEARER!
AREA 3! COCO AND TYLAN!
AND THEN AREA 2!
WE'RE GOING TO MEET UP WITH TORIKO!!

GOURMET CHECKLIST

Vol.384

MAGNETICLAM
(MOLLUSK)

CAPTURE LEVEL: 1,000
HABITAT: GOURMET
WORLD'S AREA 6
SIZE: 900 M
HEIGHT: 350 M
WEIGHT: 500,000 TONS
PRICE: 9,000 YEN PER 100
GRAMS OF MEAT

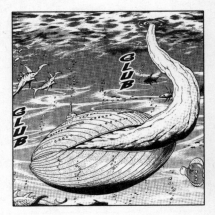

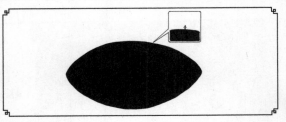

SCALE

A CAMPING MONSTER THAT EMITS A UNIQUE MAGNETIC FIELD, THEREBY TURNING ITS SURROUNDING AREA INTO A SAFE ZONE. THE GOLDEN CHEF, JIJI, USES THIS GIANT CLAM AS HIS HOME AWAY FROM HOME. ITS INSIDES ARE A STORAGE SPACE FOR HIS FOOD. IT CAN ALSO SUMMON DIFFERENT CAMPING MONSTERS TO FLOCK TO IT. IT'S FULLY EQUIPPED AND SO ARMED TO THE BRIM THAT IT'S MORE LIKE A MILITARY BASE THAN A VACATION HOME FOR A WANDERING NITRO.

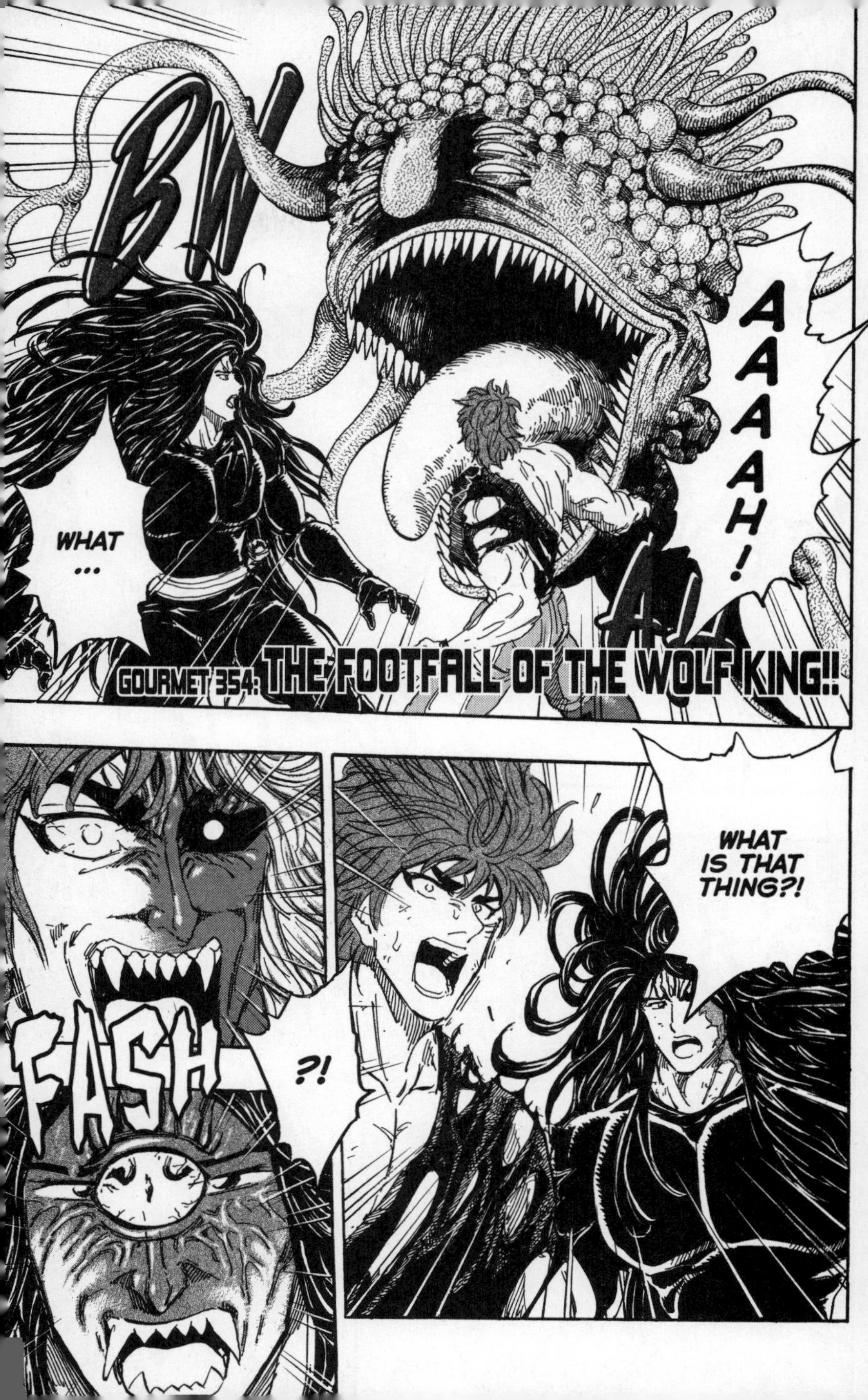
AAAAH!
AH
BWN
WHAT...
GOURMET 354: THE FOOTFALL OF THE WOLF KING!!
WHAT IS THAT THING?!
?!
FASH

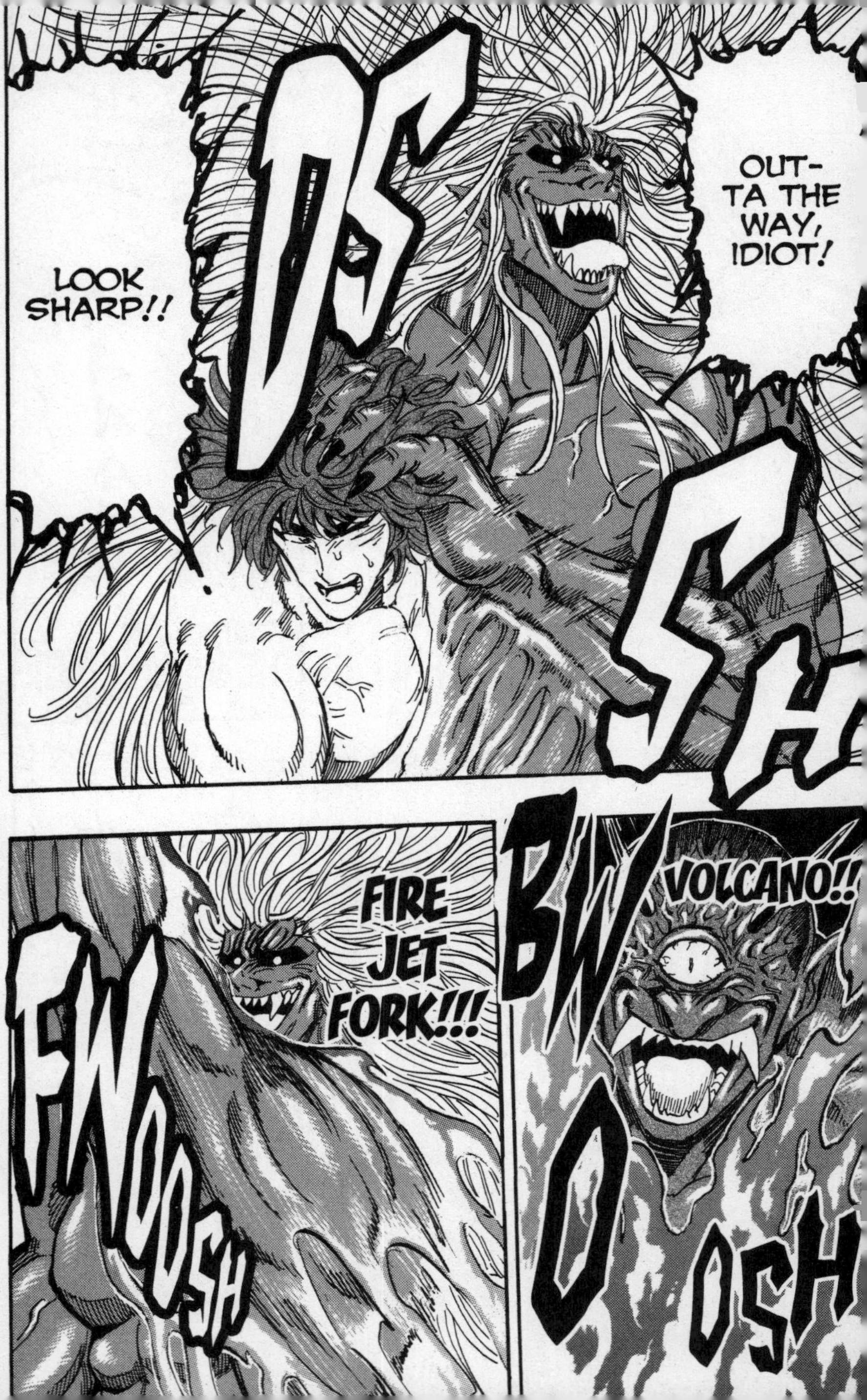
OUT-TA THE WAY, IDIOT!
DS
LOOK SHARP!!
SH
VOLCANO!!
BWOOSH
FIRE JET FORK!!!
FWOOSH

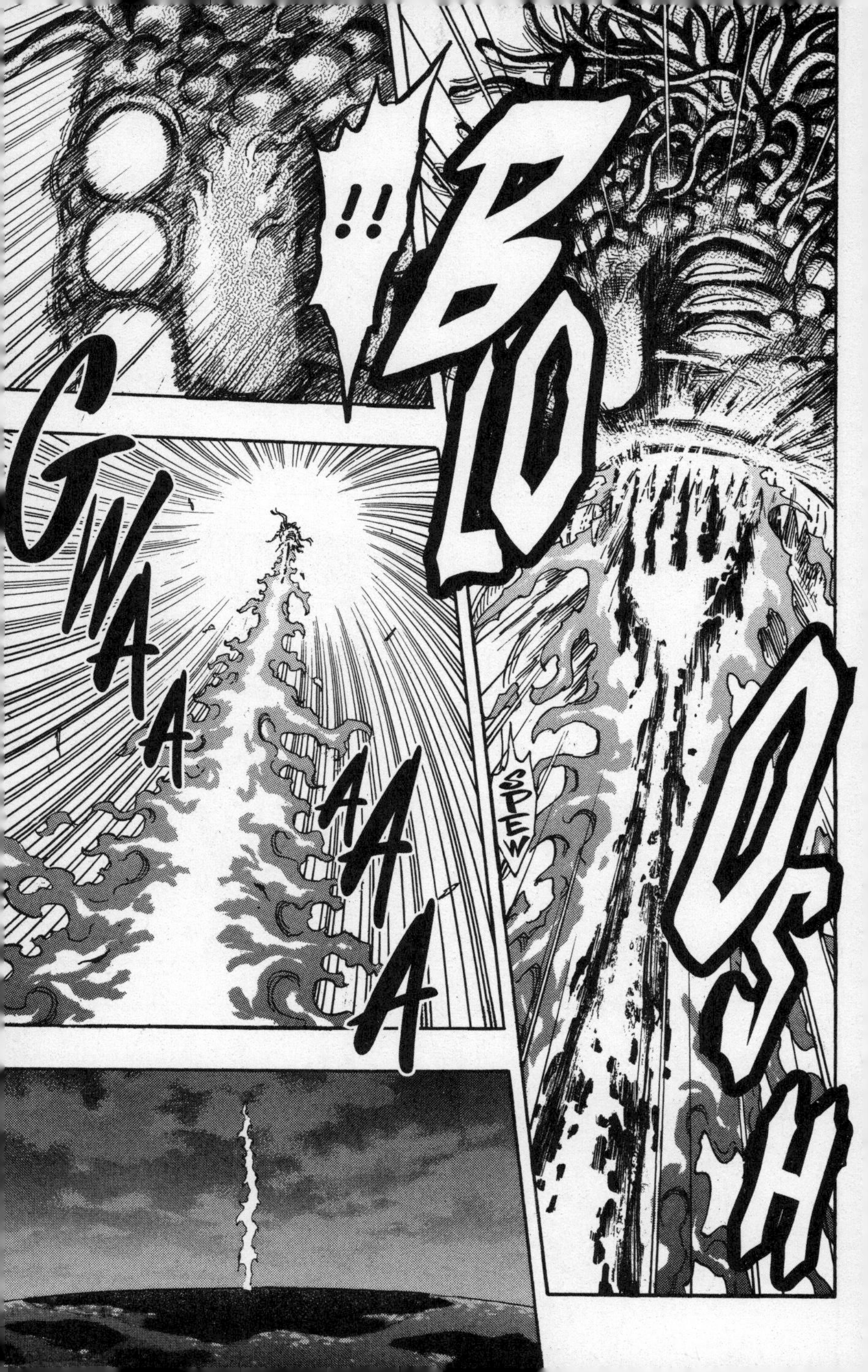
!!
B-LO
GWAAAAA
SPEW
OSCHA

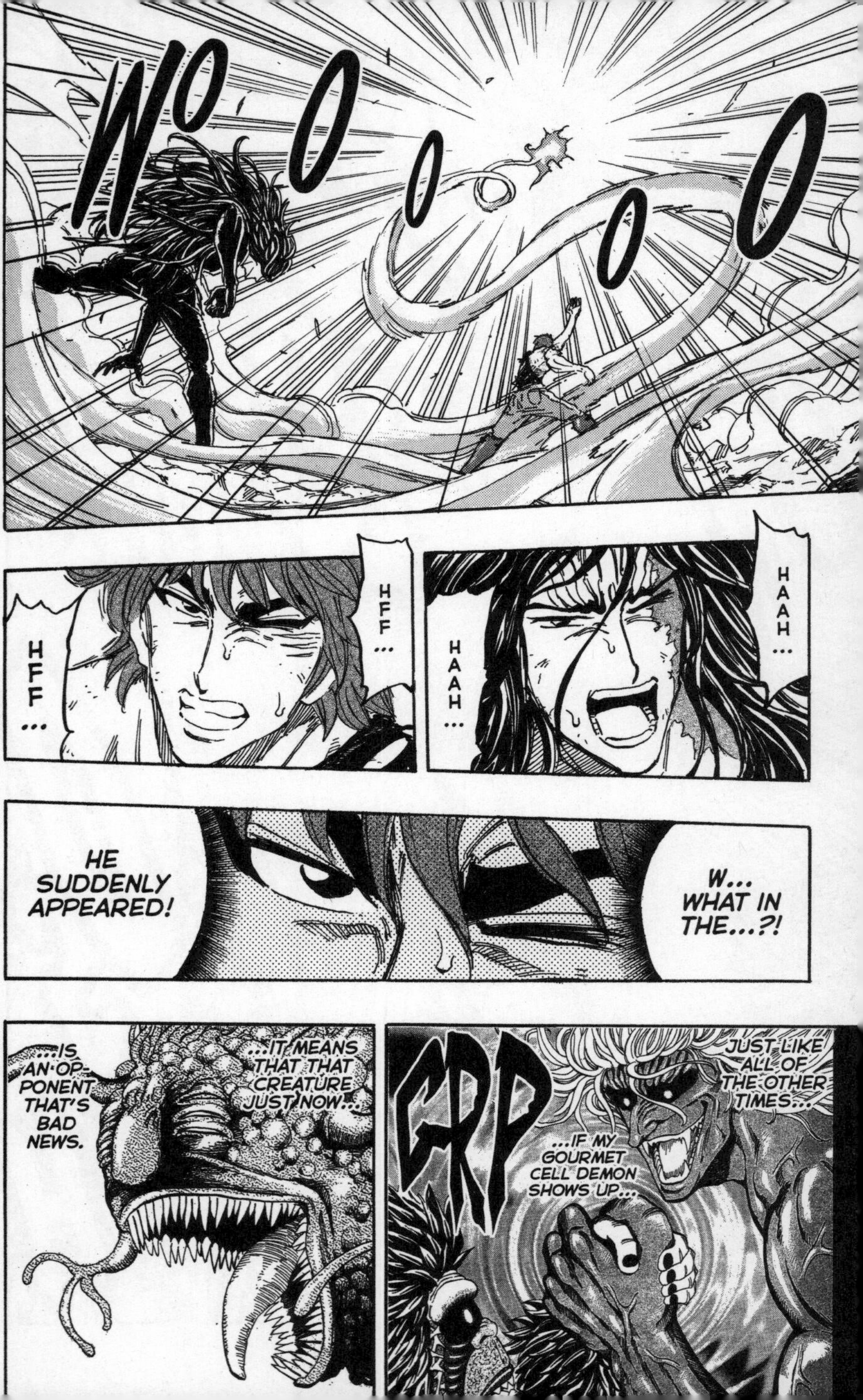
WOOOOOOO
HAAH...
HAAH...
HFF...
HFF...
W... WHAT IN THE...?!
HE SUDDENLY APPEARED!
GRP
JUST LIKE ALL OF THE OTHER TIMES...
...IF MY GOURMET CELL DEMON SHOWS UP...
...IT MEANS THAT THAT CREATURE JUST NOW...
...IS AN OP-PONENT THAT'S BAD NEWS.

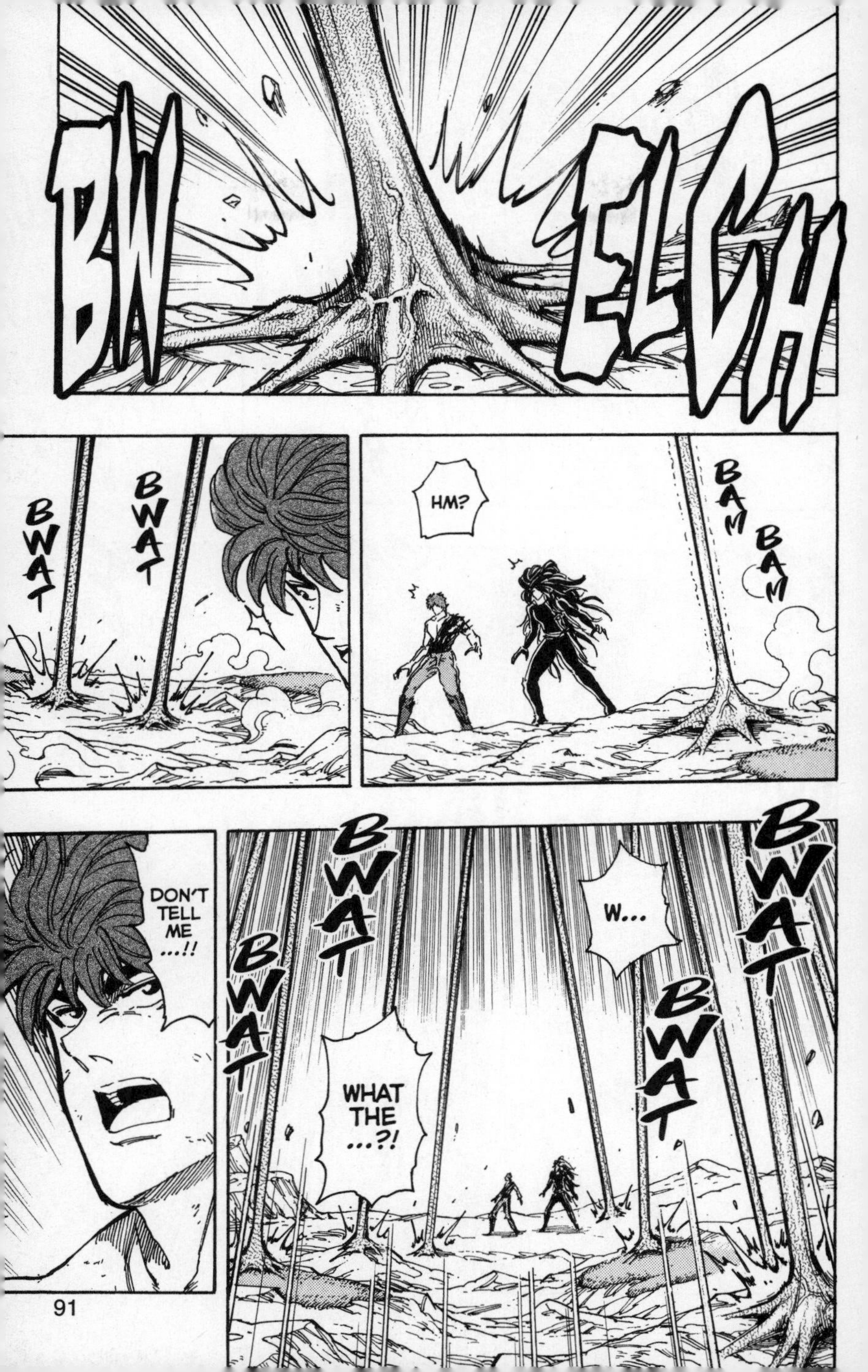
BW
ELCH
BAM
BAM
HM?
BWAT
BWAT
BWAT
W...
BWAT
BWAT
WHAT THE ...?!
BWAT
DON'T TELL ME ...!!

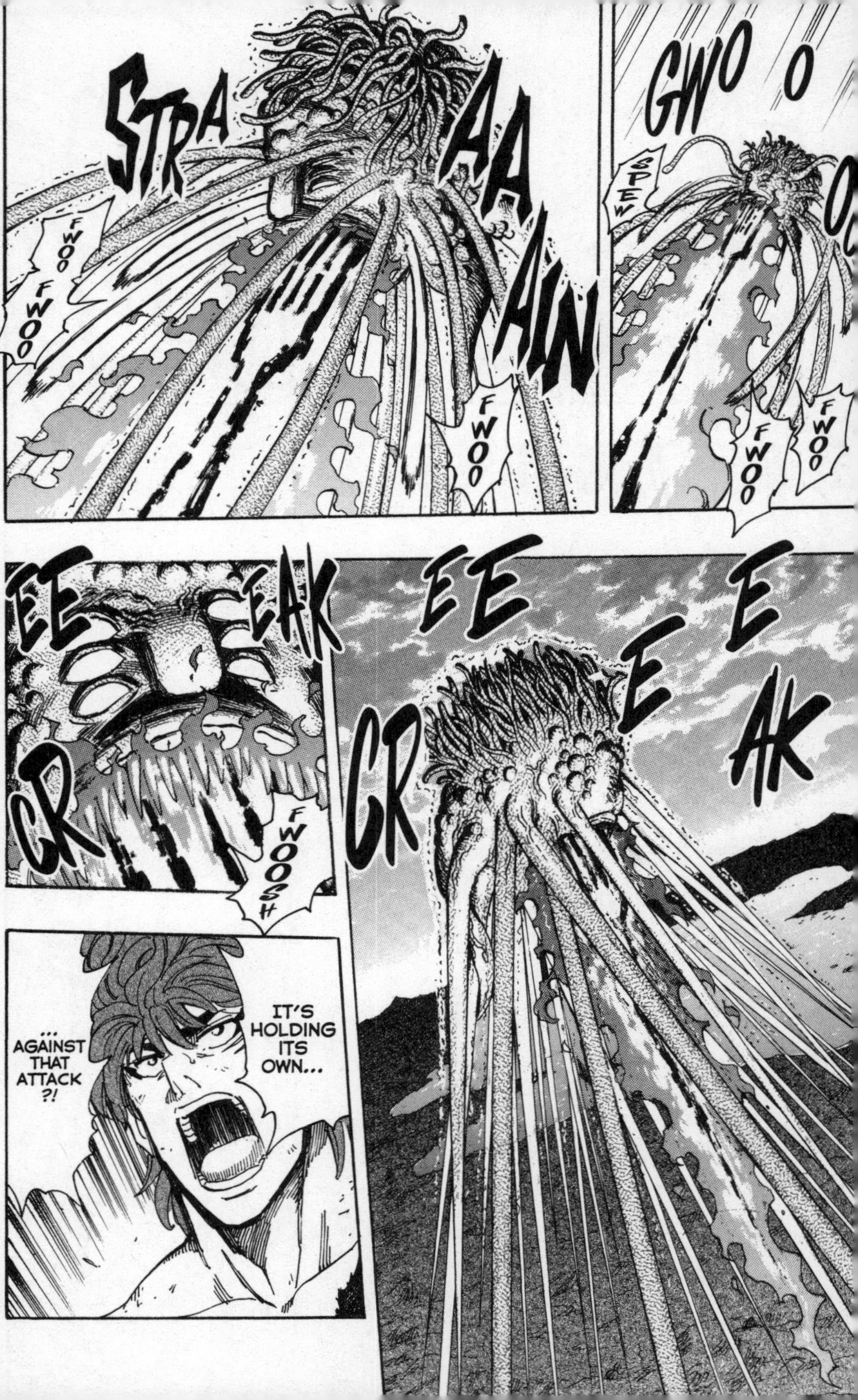
GWO O O
SPEW
FWOO
FWOO
STRAAAAIN
FWOO FWOO FWOO
FWOO
CREEEEEAK
EE EAK
CR
FWOOOSH
IT'S HOLDING ITS OWN...
...AGAINST THAT ATTACK ?!

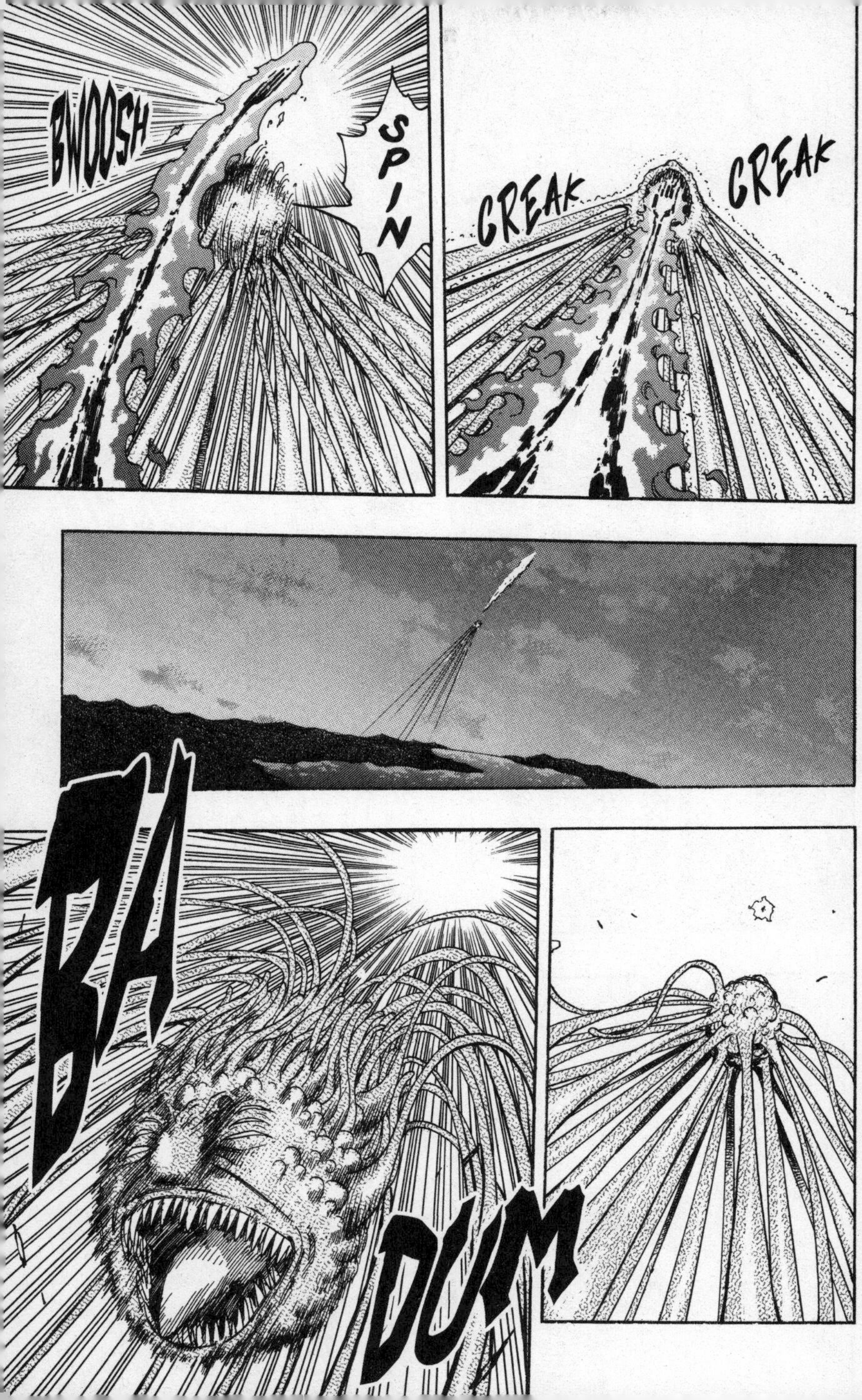
CREAK
CREAK
SPIN
BWOOSH
BA
DUM

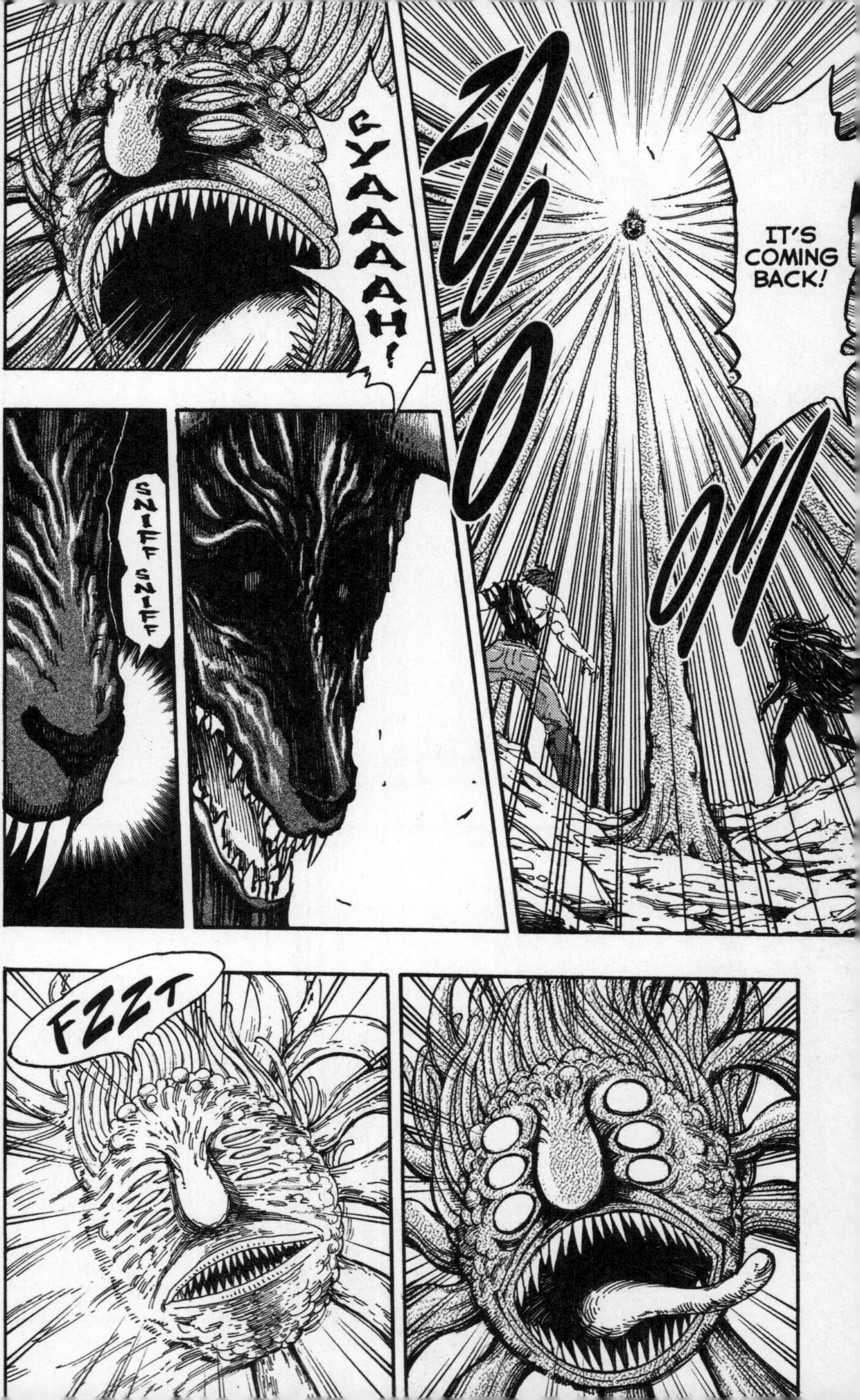
IT'S COMING BACK!
GYAAAAH!
SNIFF SNIFF
FZZT

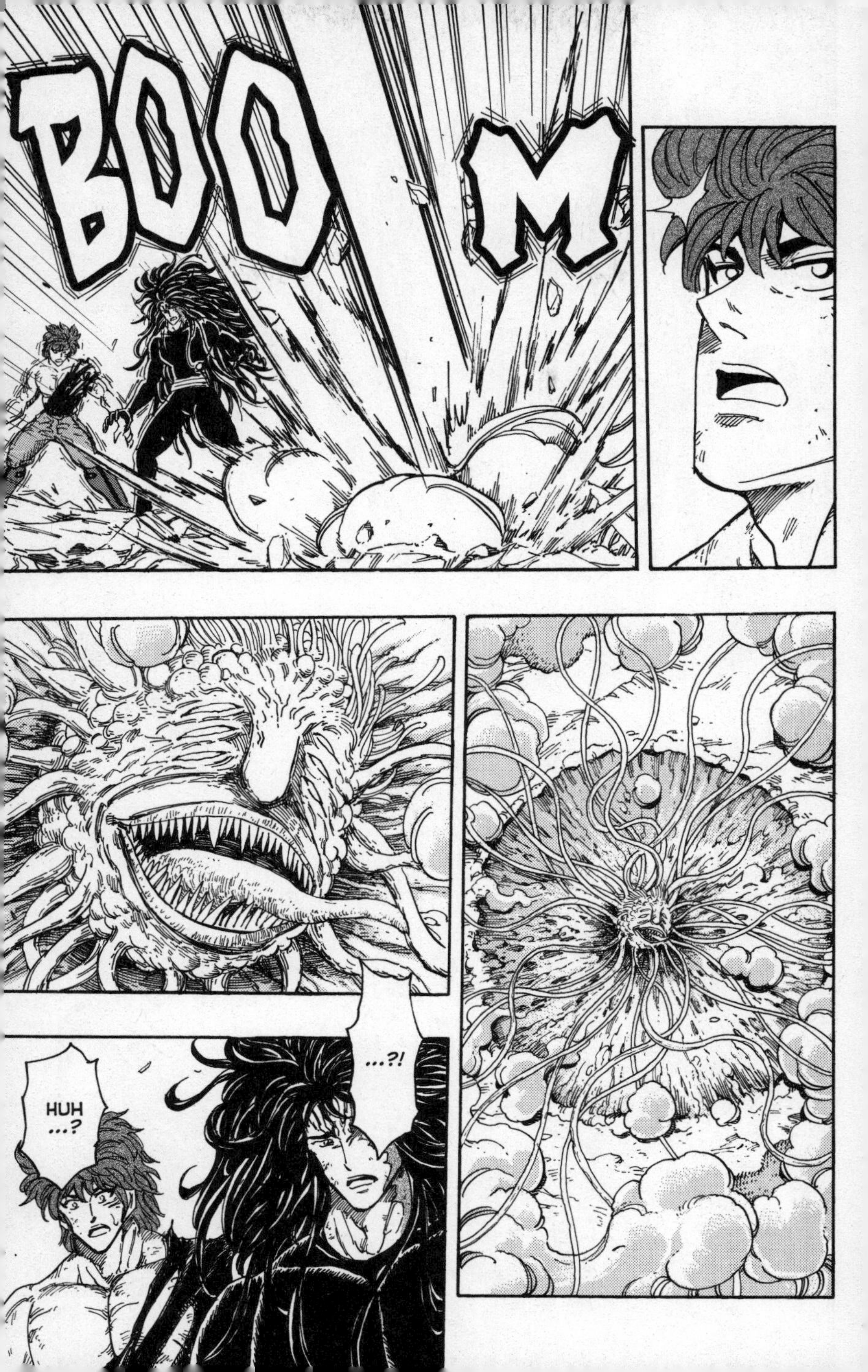
BOOM
...?!
HUH ...?

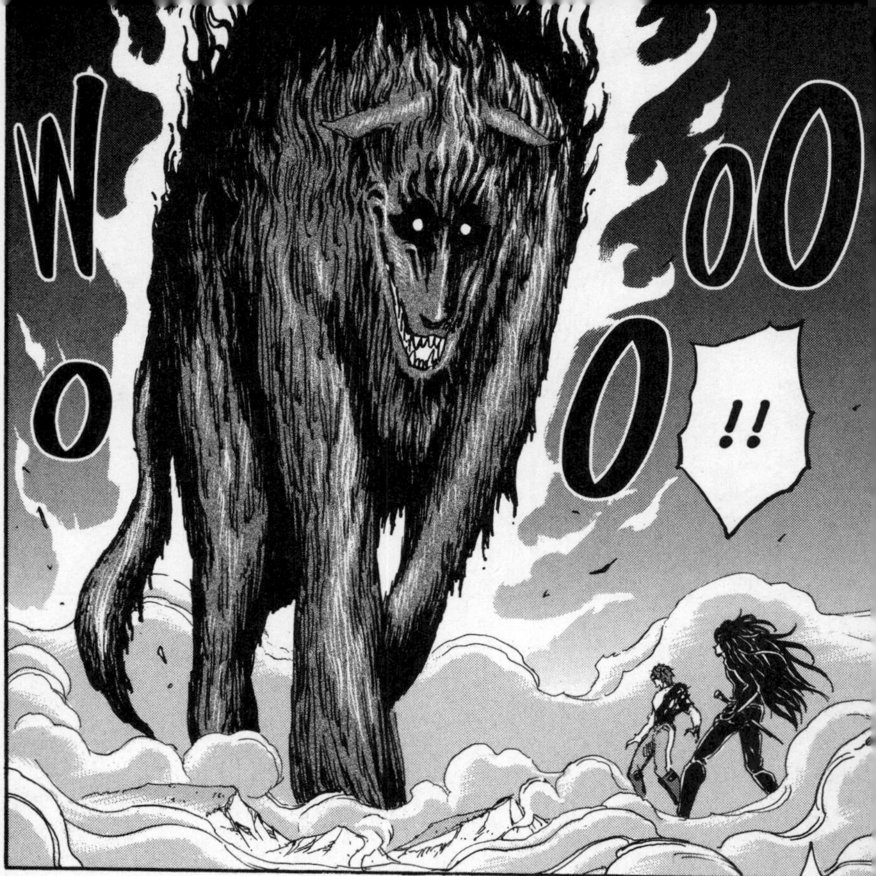
WOOOOO
!!
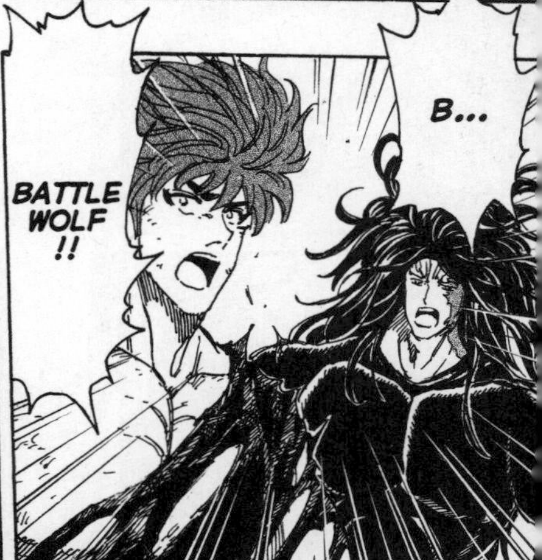
B...
BATTLE WOLF !!
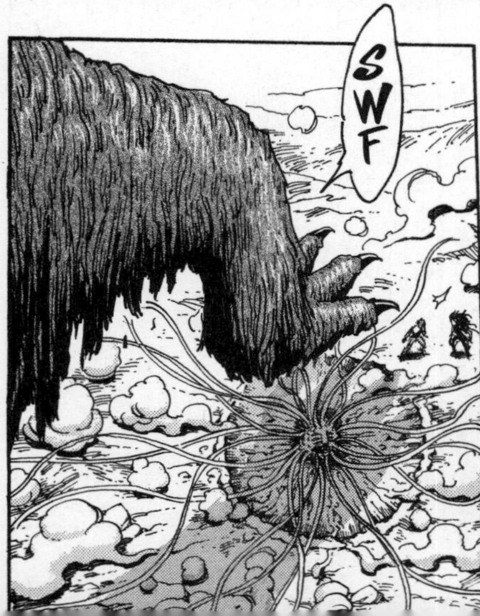
SWF

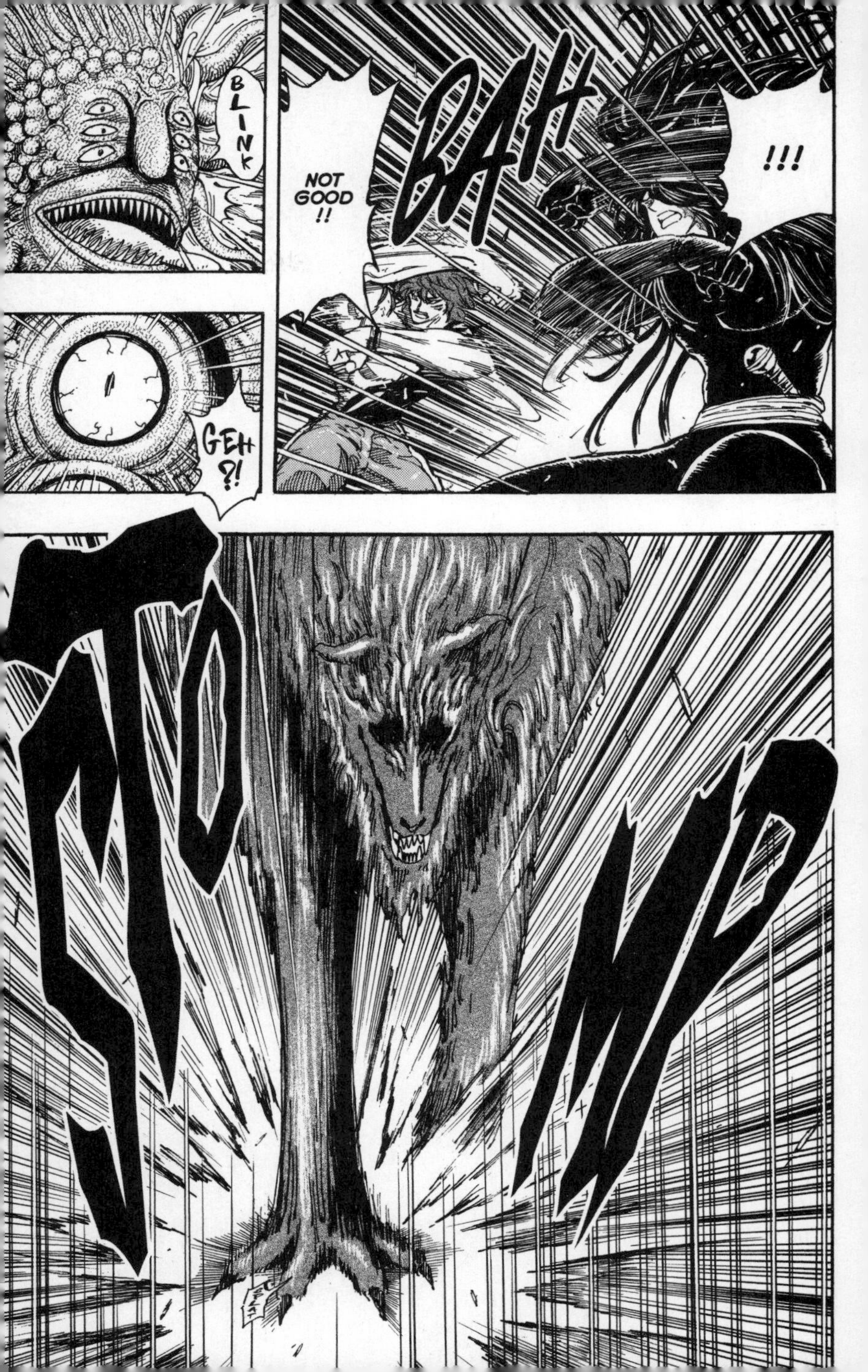
BAM
!!!
NOT GOOD !!
BLINK
GEH ?!

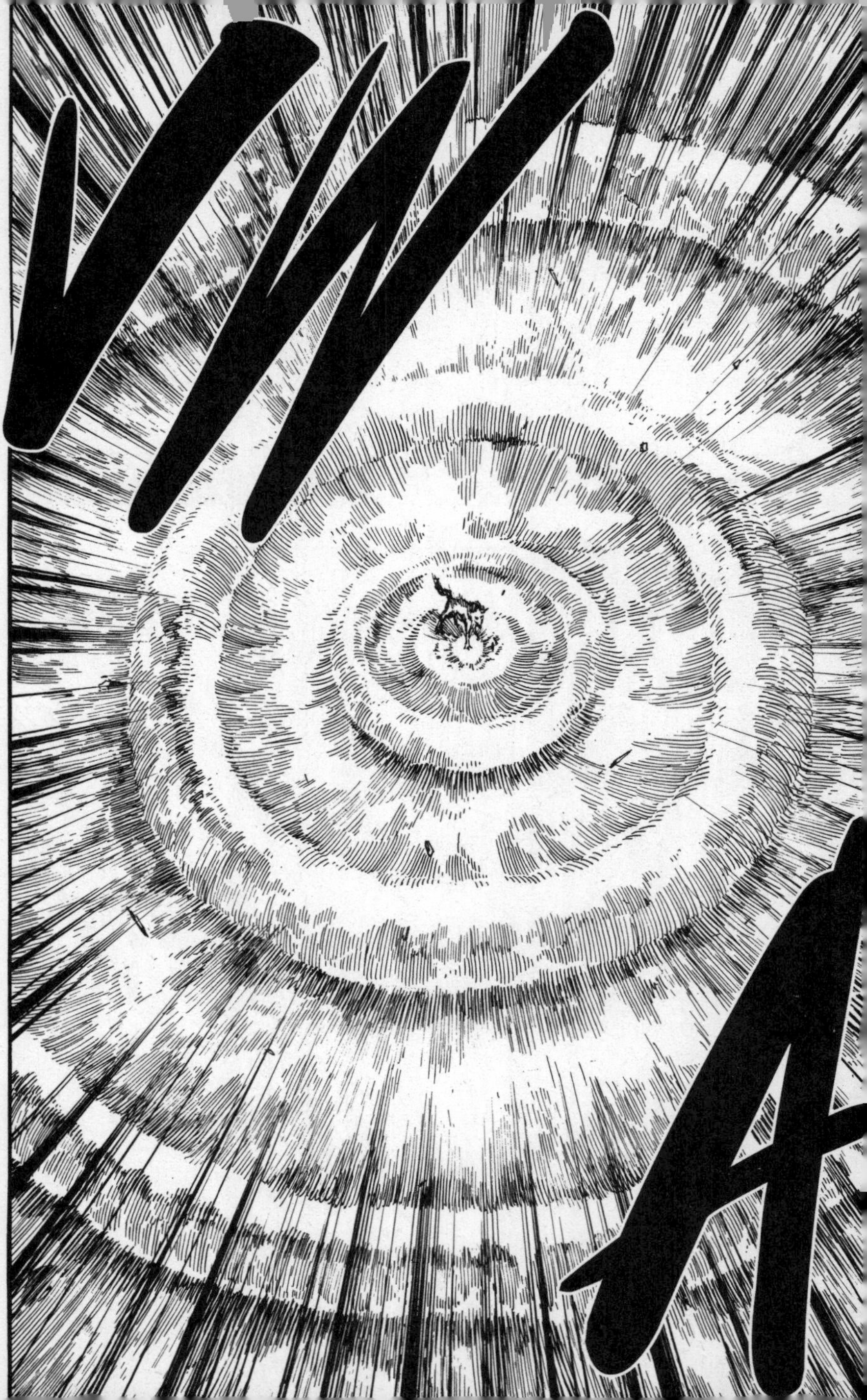

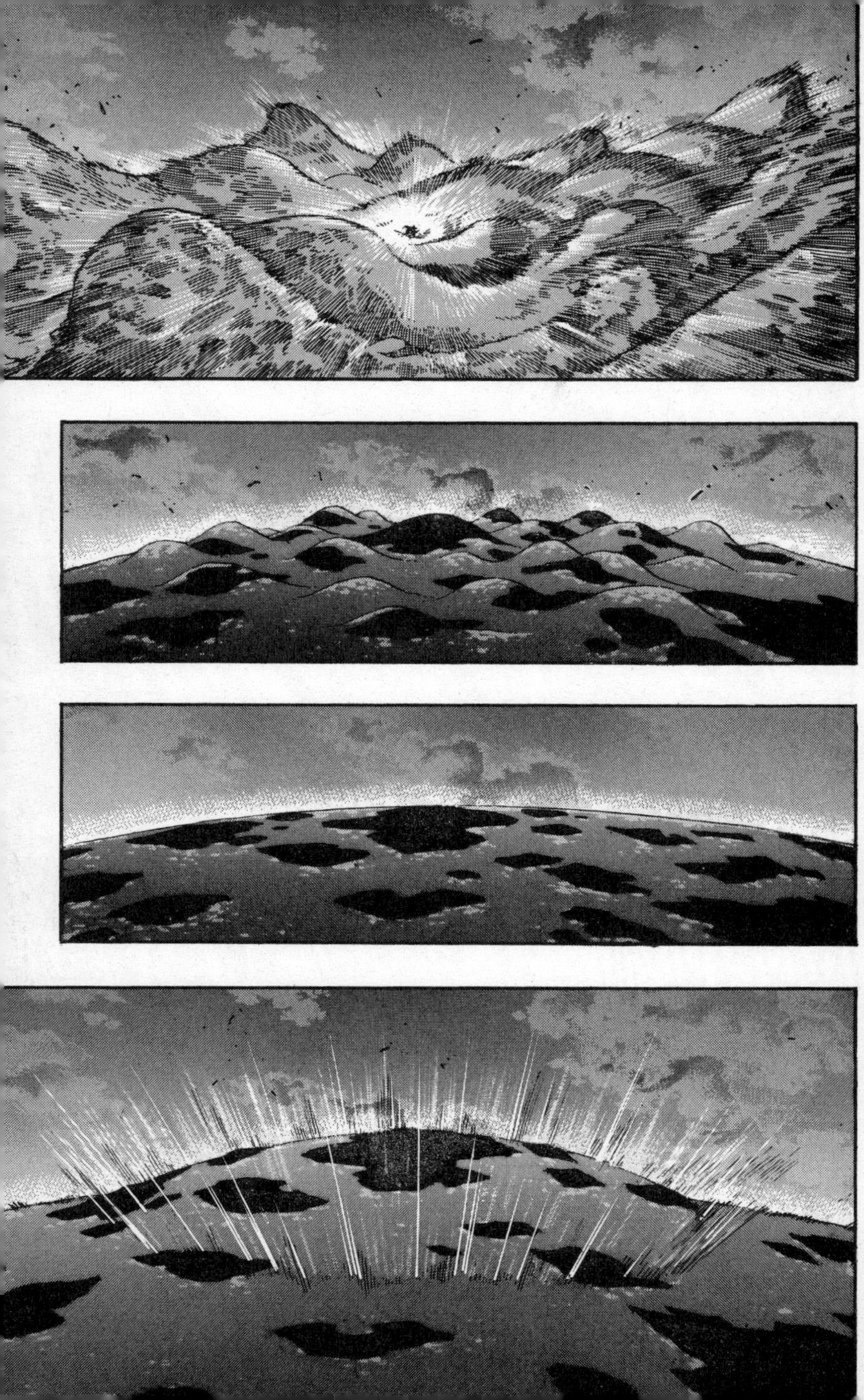

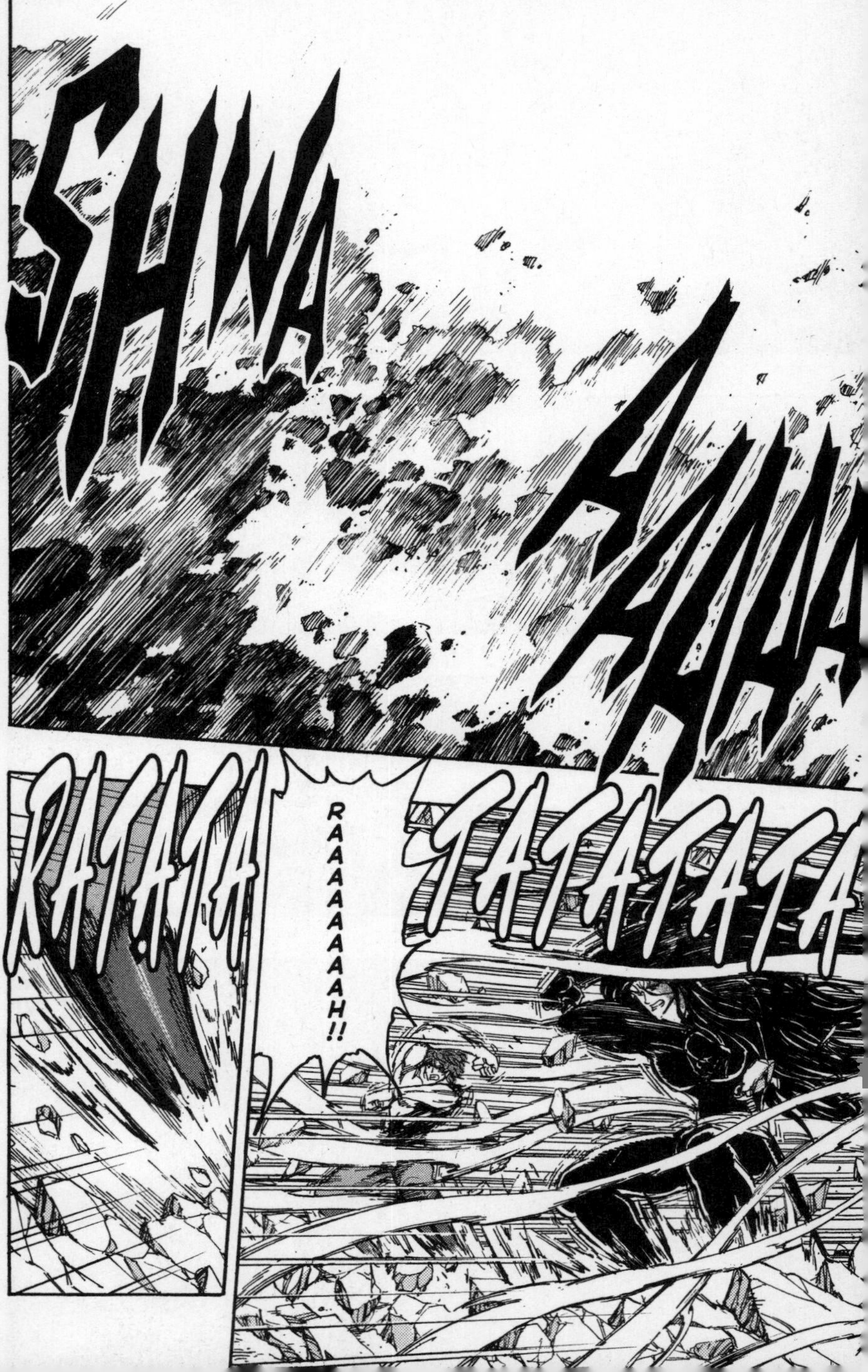
SHWAAAAA
TATATATA
RAAAAAAAAAAH!!
RATATA

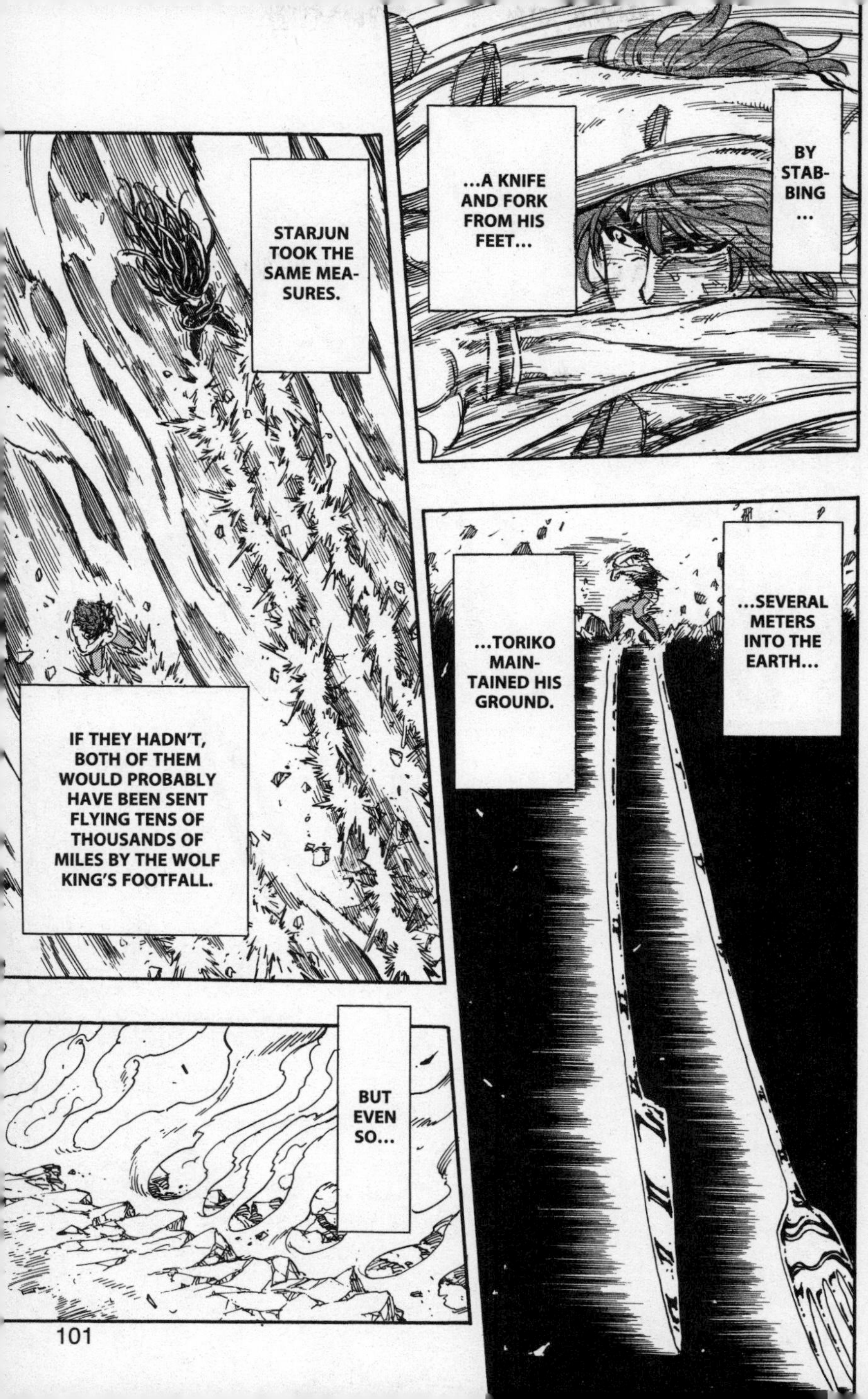
BY STAB-BING...
...A KNIFE AND FORK FROM HIS FEET...
...SEVERAL METERS INTO THE EARTH...
...TORIKO MAIN-TAINED HIS GROUND.
STARJUN TOOK THE SAME MEA-SURES.
IF THEY HADN'T, BOTH OF THEM WOULD PROBABLY HAVE BEEN SENT FLYING TENS OF THOUSANDS OF MILES BY THE WOLF KING'S FOOTFALL.
BUT EVEN SO...

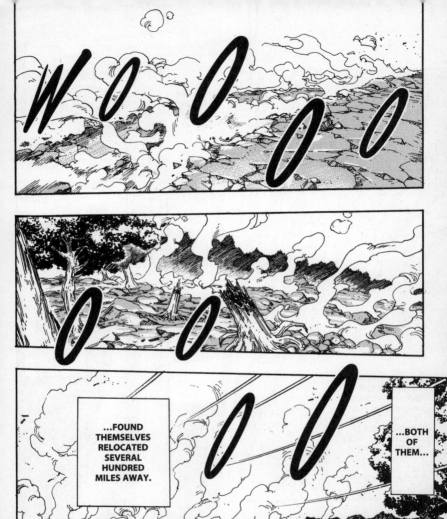

...FOUND THEMSELVES RELOCATED SEVERAL HUNDRED MILES AWAY.

...BOTH OF THEM...

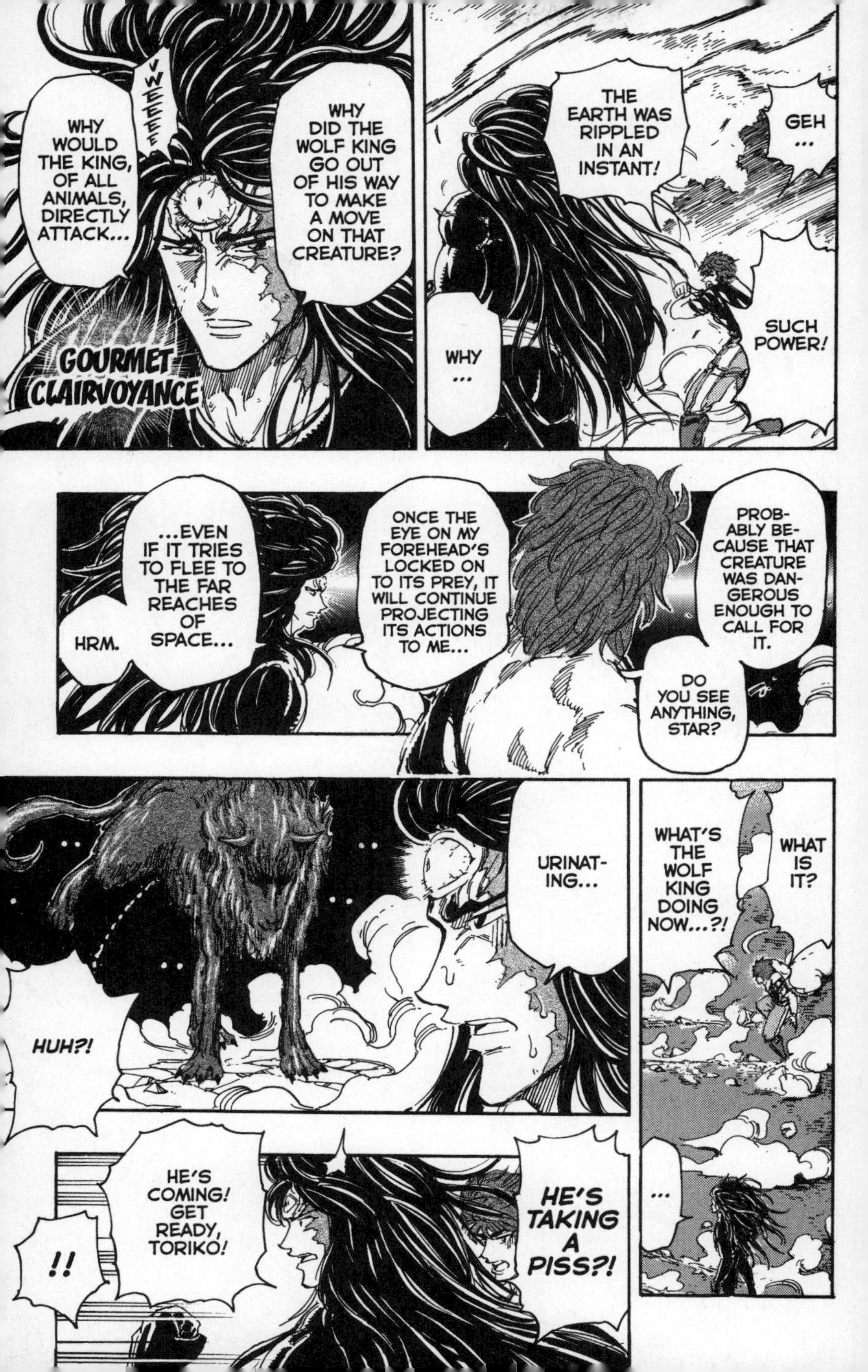
GEH...
THE EARTH WAS RIPPLED IN AN INSTANT!
SUCH POWER!
WHY...
WHY DID THE WOLF KING GO OUT OF HIS WAY TO MAKE A MOVE ON THAT CREATURE?
VWEEEE
WHY WOULD THE KING, OF ALL ANIMALS, DIRECTLY ATTACK...
GOURMET CLAIRVOYANCE
PROBABLY BECAUSE THAT CREATURE WAS DANGEROUS ENOUGH TO CALL FOR IT.
DO YOU SEE ANYTHING, STAR?
ONCE THE EYE ON MY FOREHEAD'S LOCKED ON TO ITS PREY, IT WILL CONTINUE PROJECTING ITS ACTIONS TO ME...
...EVEN IF IT TRIES TO FLEE TO THE FAR REACHES OF SPACE...
HRM.
WHAT IS IT?
WHAT'S THE WOLF KING DOING NOW...?!
...
URINATING...
HUH?!
HE'S TAKING A PISS?!
HE'S COMING! GET READY, TORIKO!
!!

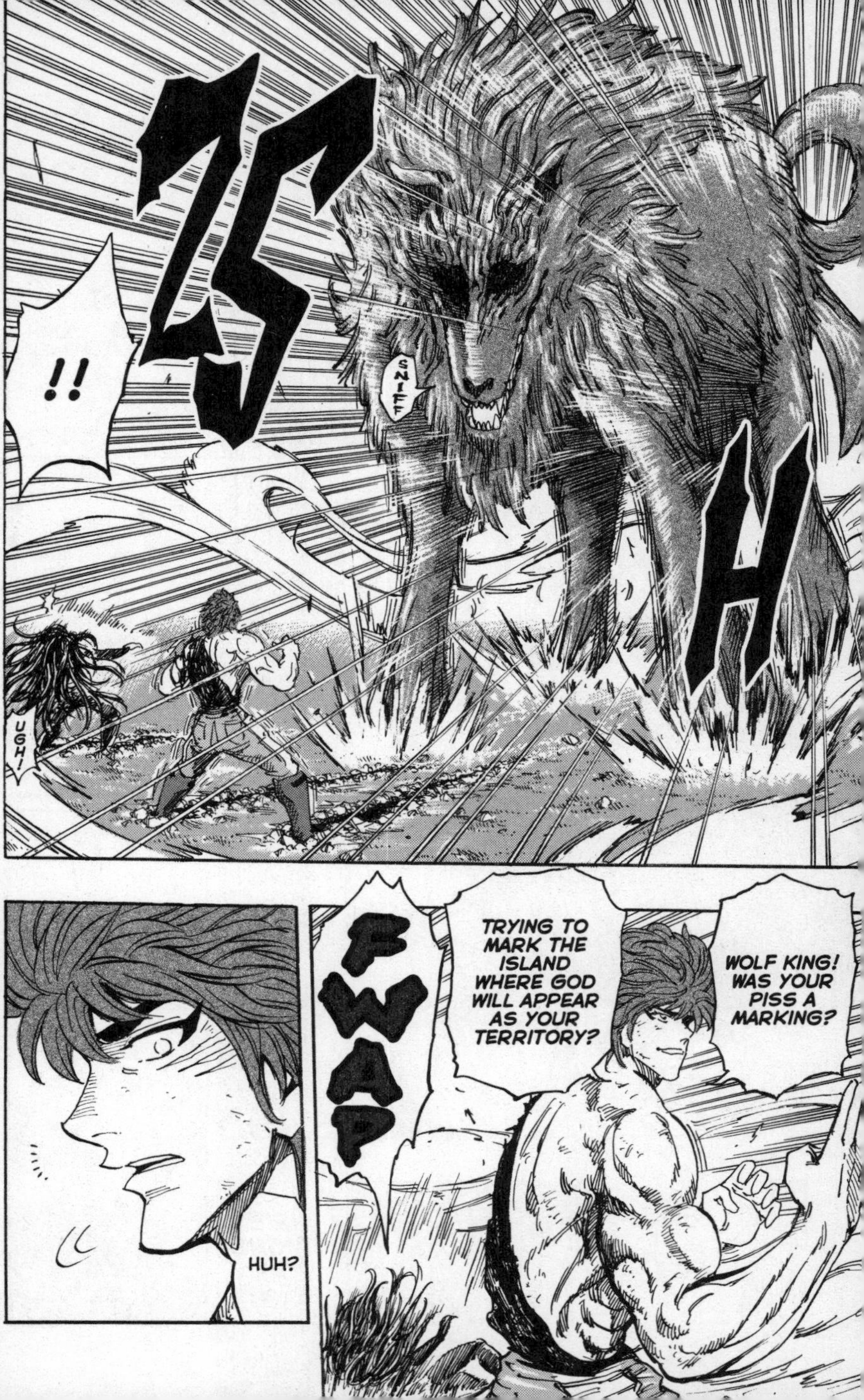
ZSH
SNIFF
!!
UGH!
WOLF KING! WAS YOUR PISS A MARKING?
TRYING TO MARK THE ISLAND WHERE GOD WILL APPEAR AS YOUR TERRITORY?
FWAP
HUH?

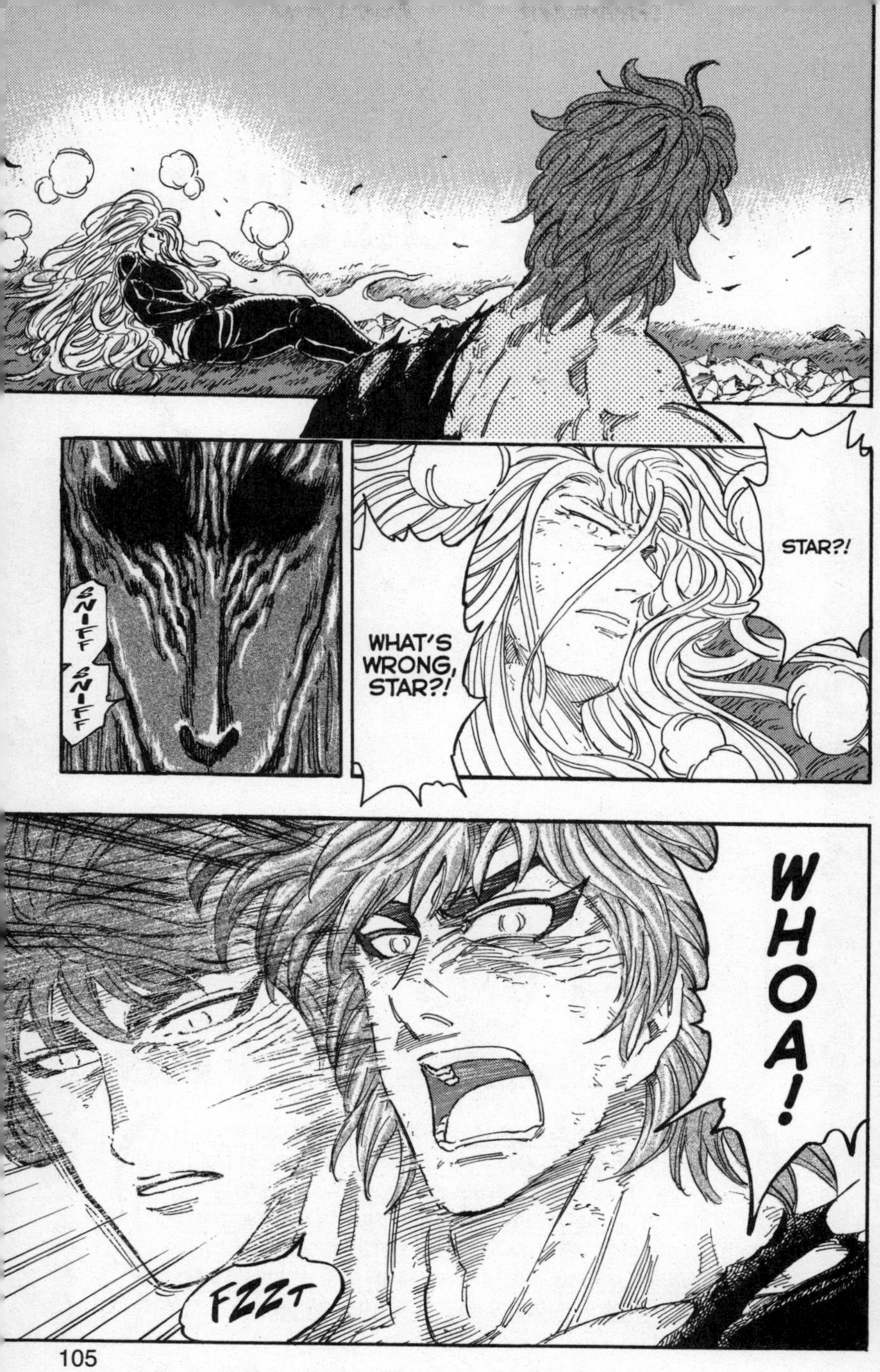
STAR?!
WHAT'S WRONG, STAR?!
SNIFF SNIFF
WHOA!
FZZT

TORIKO

GOURMET CHECKLIST

Vol. 385

PUZZLE PLANKTON
(MICROBE)

CAPTURE LEVEL: 1-4,000

HABITAT: GOURMET WORLD'S AREA 6

SIZE: 0.1 MM

HEIGHT: ---

WEIGHT: ---

PRICE: 100 YEN PER PIECE

IT'S A PLANKTON SHAPED LIKE A 0.1 MILLIMETER-WIDE PUZZLE PIECE.
WHEN COMBINED, THE DIFFERENT PUZZLE SHAPES CREATE AN INFINITE VARIETY OF FLAVORS. THERE'S USUALLY SEVERAL HUNDRED TRILLION PLANKTON IN A SINGLE SWARM.

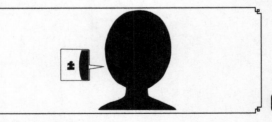

SCALE

A PLANKTON SHAPED LIKE A 0.1 MILLIMETER-WIDE PUZZLE PIECE. THE DIFFERENT PUZZLE SHAPES CAN BE COMBINED TO CREATE AN INFINITE VARIETY OF TASTES. EACH SWARM OF PLANKTON USUALLY CONTAINS SEVERAL HUNDRED TRILLION PIECES THAT CAN COME TOGETHER TO CREATE GIANT PATTERNS. THIS MAKES IT AN INGREDIENT THAT REQUIRES SPECIAL PREPARATION. ONLY AN INCREDIBLY SKILLED CHEF CAN CREATE A PUZZLE THAT BRINGS OUT THE BEST FLAVORS! IT'S A VERY TRICKY INGREDIENT TO WORK WITH, BUT IT'S A PIECE OF CAKE FOR A CHEF LIKE THE GOLDEN CHEF, JIJI!

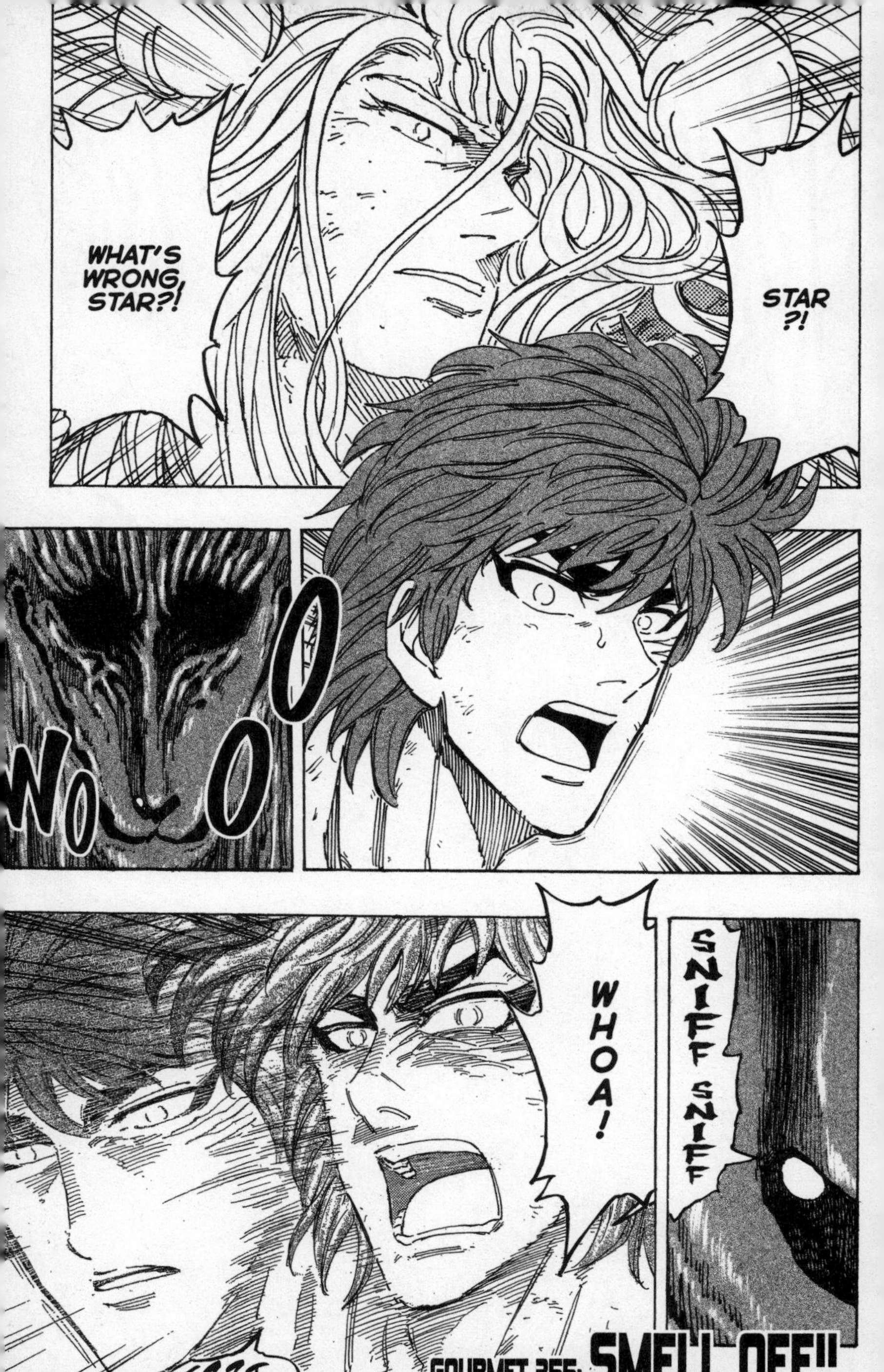
STAR ?!
WHAT'S WRONG, STAR?!
WOOOO
SNIFF SNIFF
WHOA!
FZZT

GOURMET 355: SMELL OFF!!

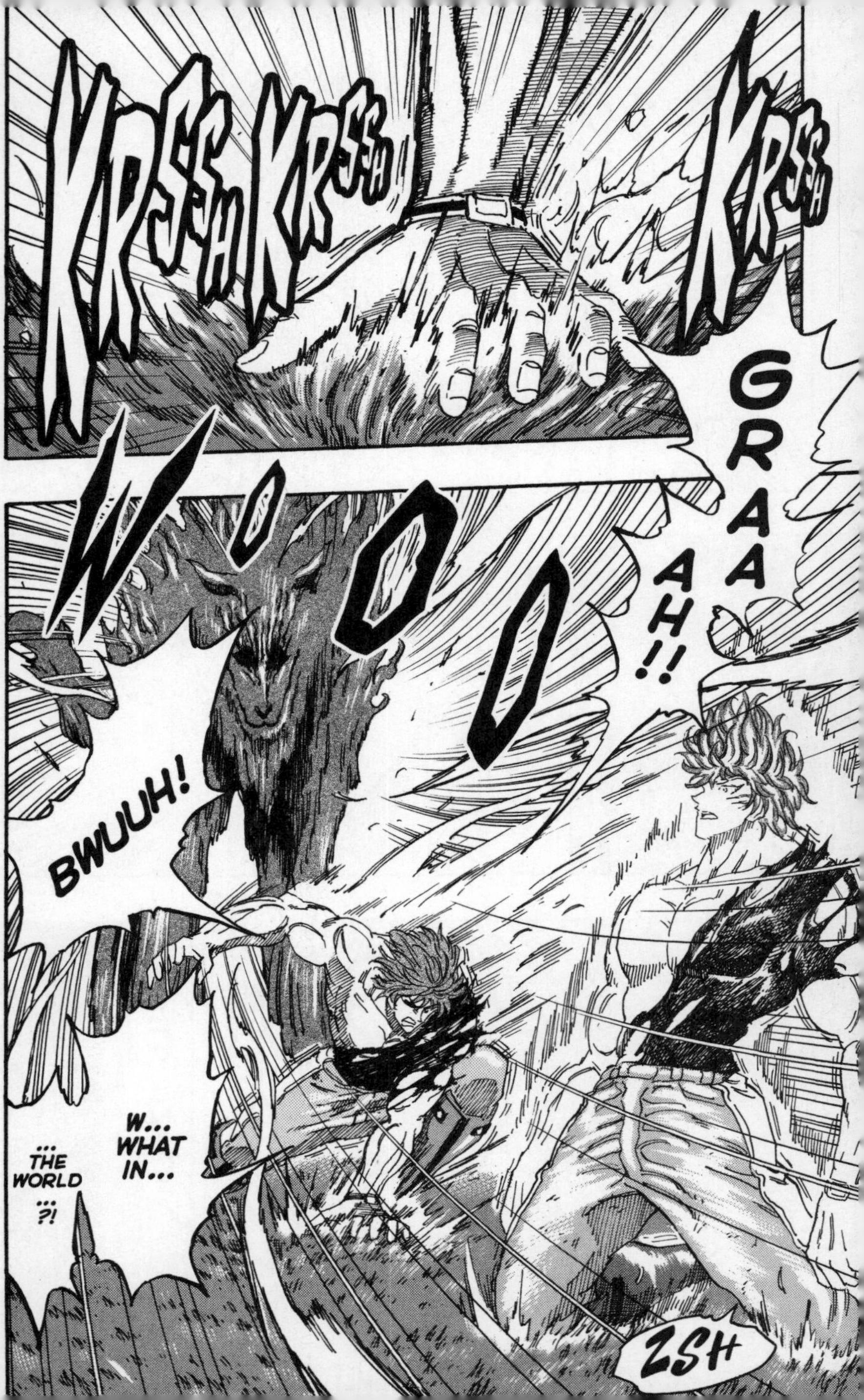
KRSSH
KRSSH KRSSH
GRAAAAH!!
WOOO
BWUUH!
W... WHAT IN...
...THE WORLD ...?!
ZSH

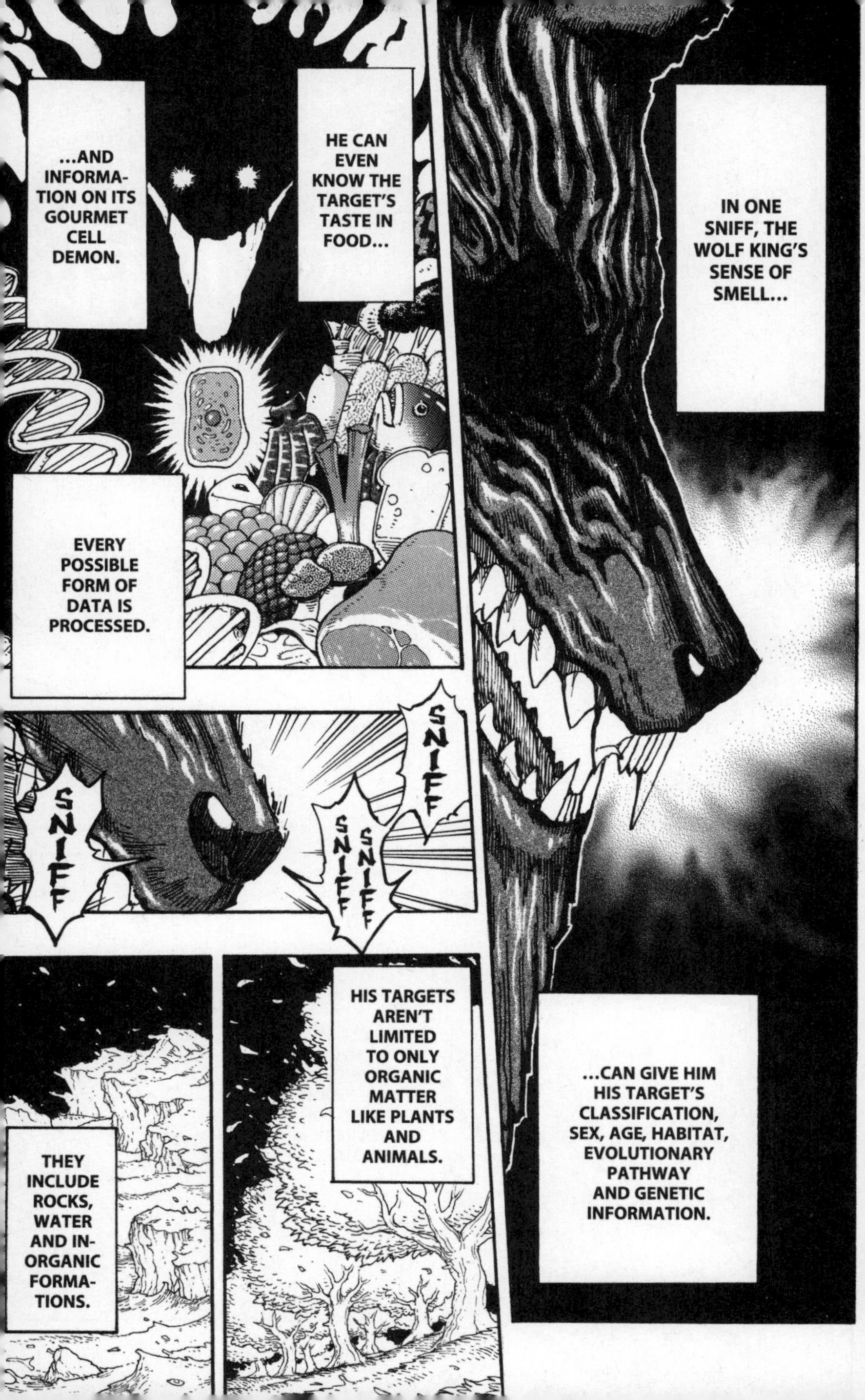
IN ONE SNIFF, THE WOLF KING'S SENSE OF SMELL...
...CAN GIVE HIM HIS TARGET'S CLASSIFICATION, SEX, AGE, HABITAT, EVOLUTIONARY PATHWAY AND GENETIC INFORMATION.
HE CAN EVEN KNOW THE TARGET'S TASTE IN FOOD...
...AND INFORMATION ON ITS GOURMET CELL DEMON.
EVERY POSSIBLE FORM OF DATA IS PROCESSED.
SNIFF
SNIFF
SNIFF
SNIFF
HIS TARGETS AREN'T LIMITED TO ONLY ORGANIC MATTER LIKE PLANTS AND ANIMALS.
THEY INCLUDE ROCKS, WATER AND IN-ORGANIC FORMA-TIONS.

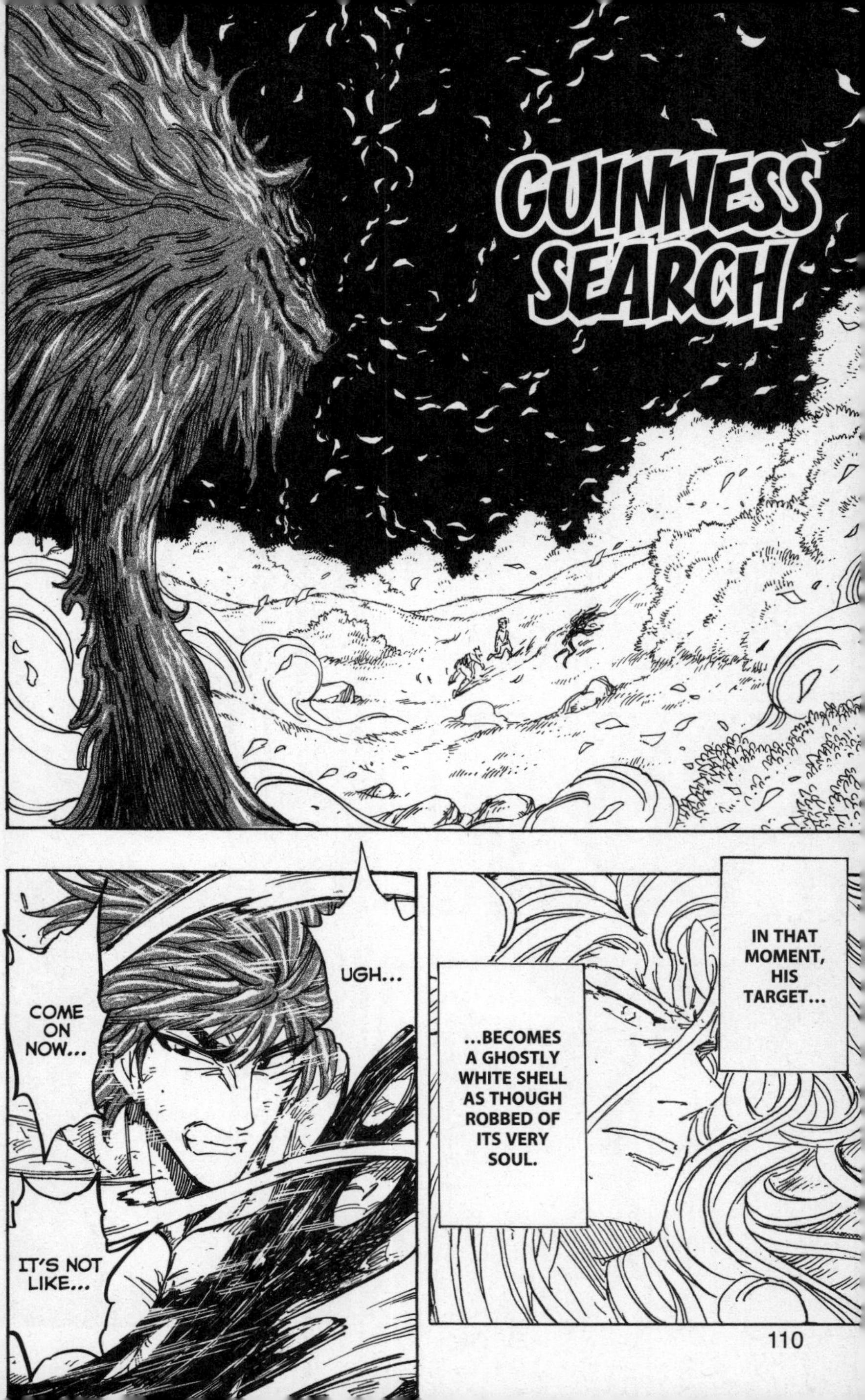
GUINNESS SEARCH
IN THAT MOMENT, HIS TARGET...
...BECOMES A GHOSTLY WHITE SHELL AS THOUGH ROBBED OF ITS VERY SOUL.
UGH...
COME ON NOW...
IT'S NOT LIKE...

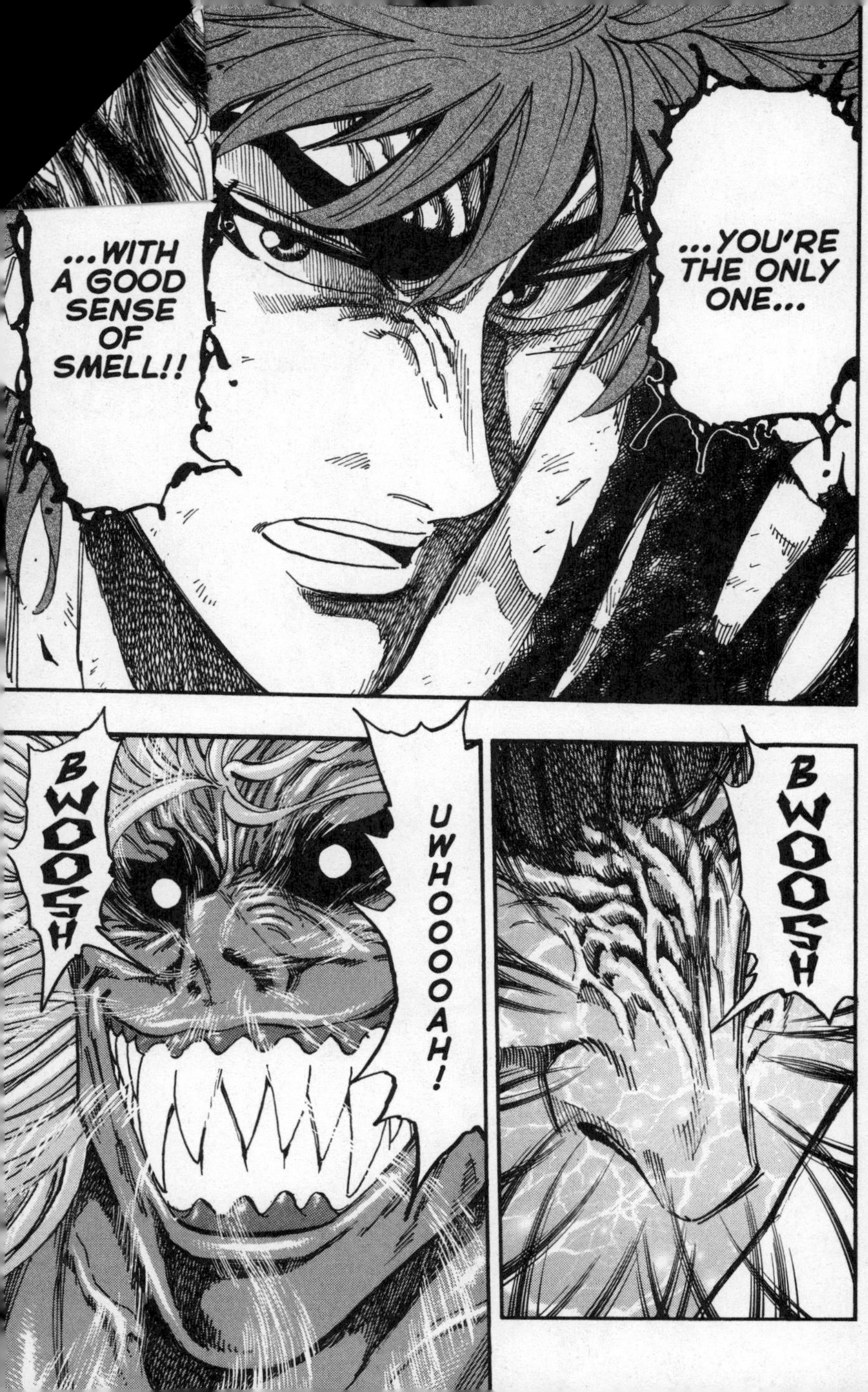
...YOU'RE THE ONLY ONE...
...WITH A GOOD SENSE OF SMELL!!
BWOOSH
UWHOOOOOAH!
BWOOSH

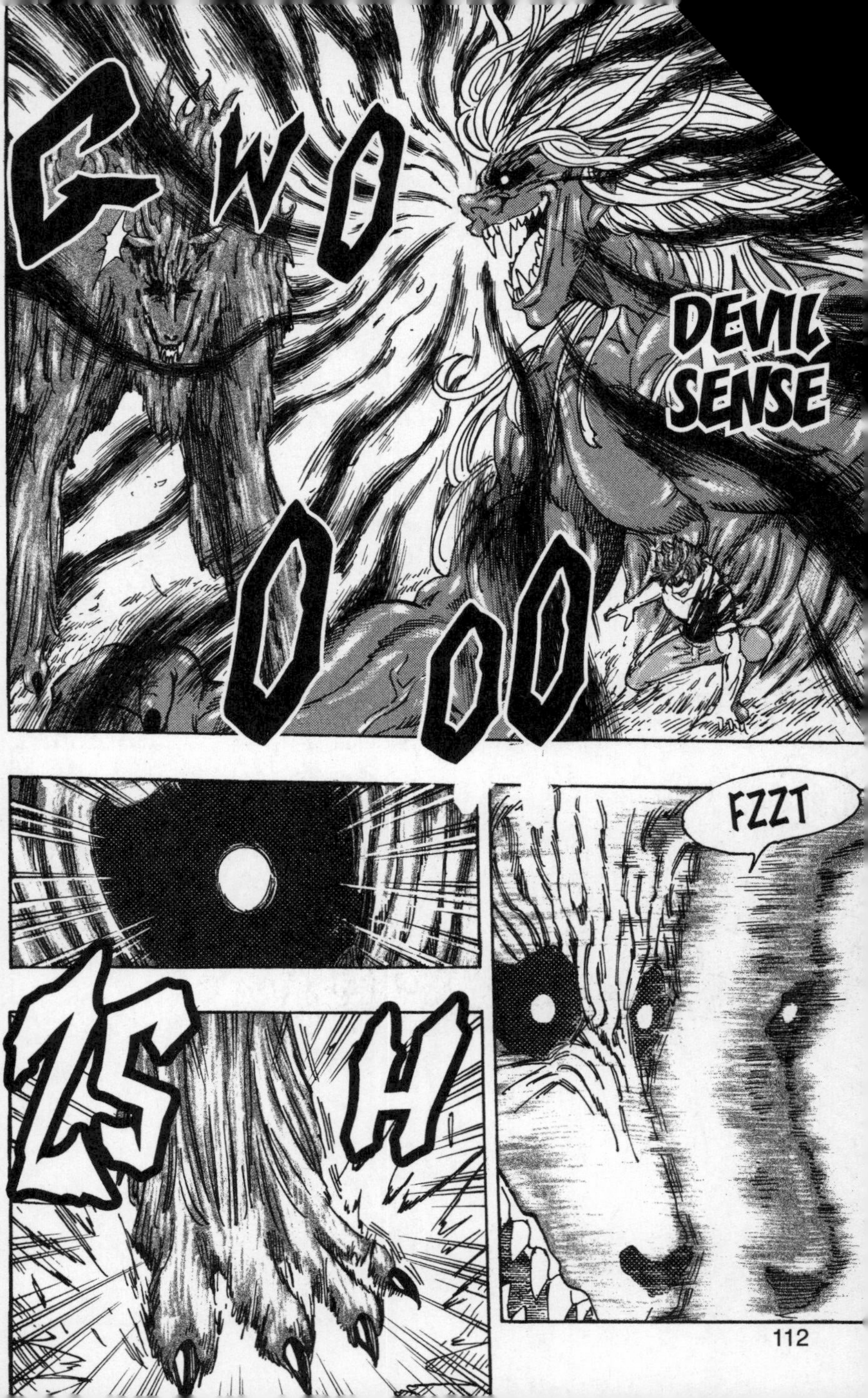
DEVIL SENSE
GWOOOO
FZZT
ZSH

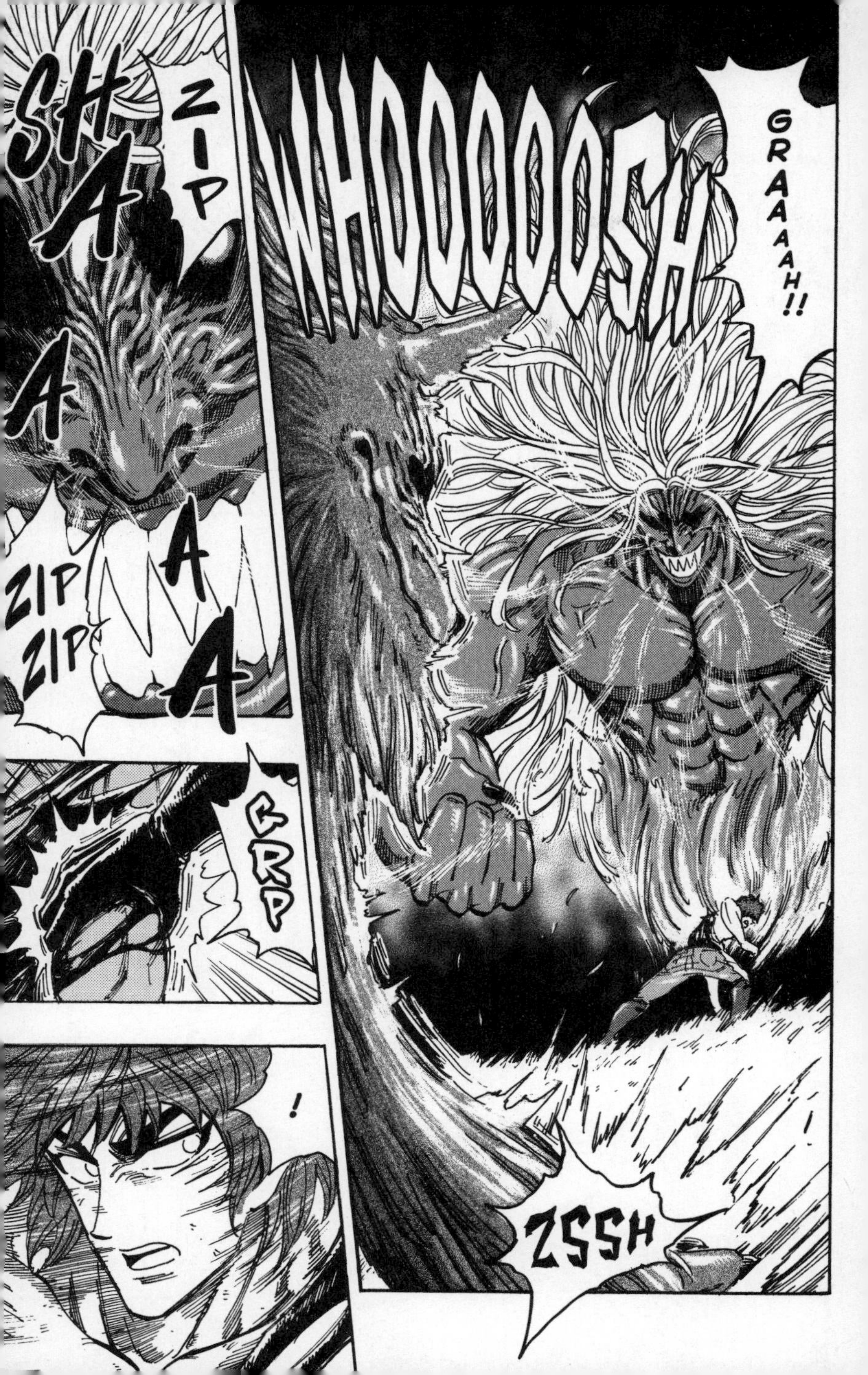
WHOOOOOSH
GRAAAAAH!!
!
ZSSH
SHAAAAA
ZIP
ZIP
ZIP
GRRP
!

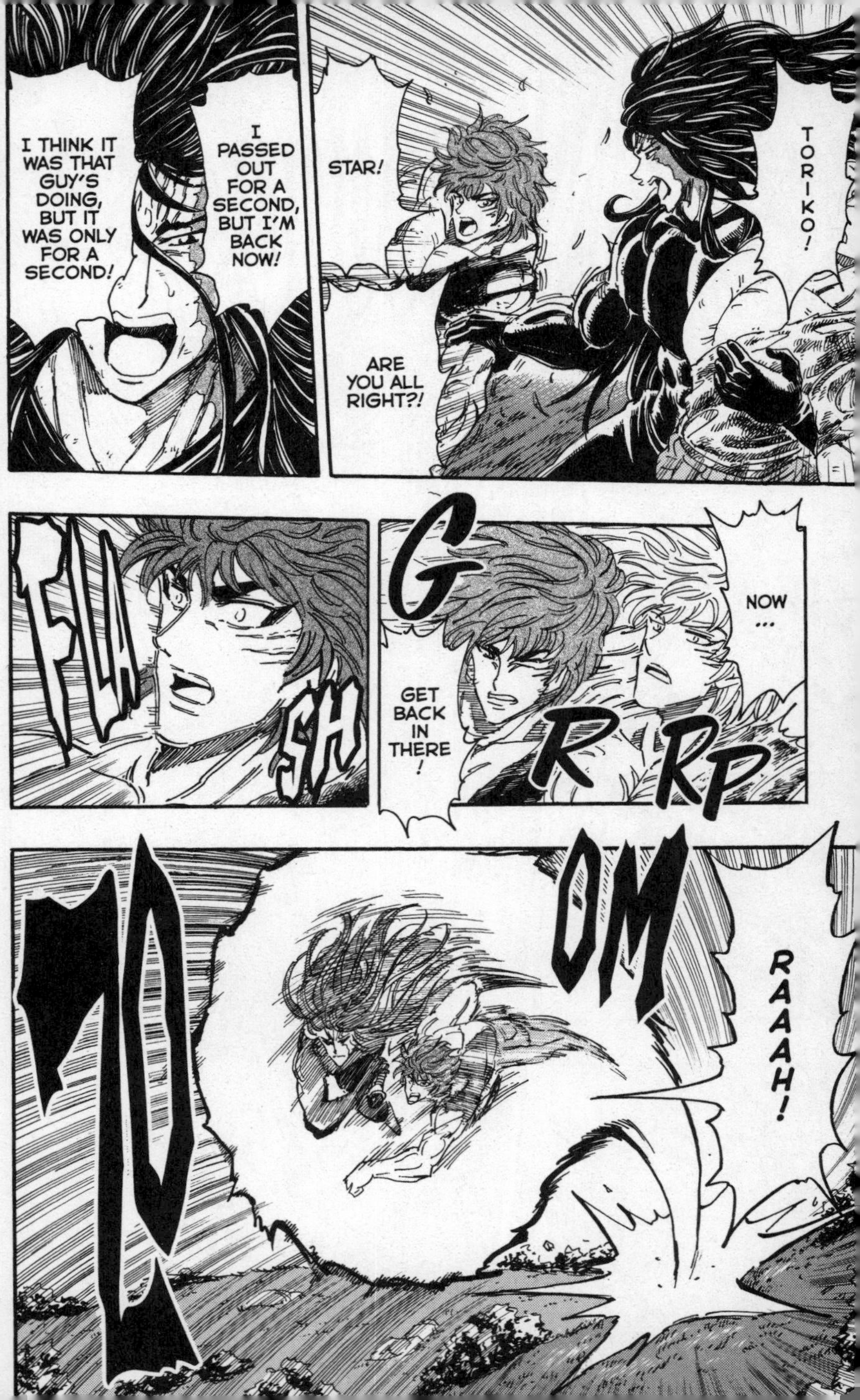

TORIKO!
STAR!
ARE YOU ALL RIGHT?!
I PASSED OUT FOR A SECOND, BUT I'M BACK NOW!
I THINK IT WAS THAT GUY'S DOING, BUT IT WAS ONLY FOR A SECOND!
NOW...
GET BACK IN THERE!
GRRP
FLASH
RAAAH!
OM
TO

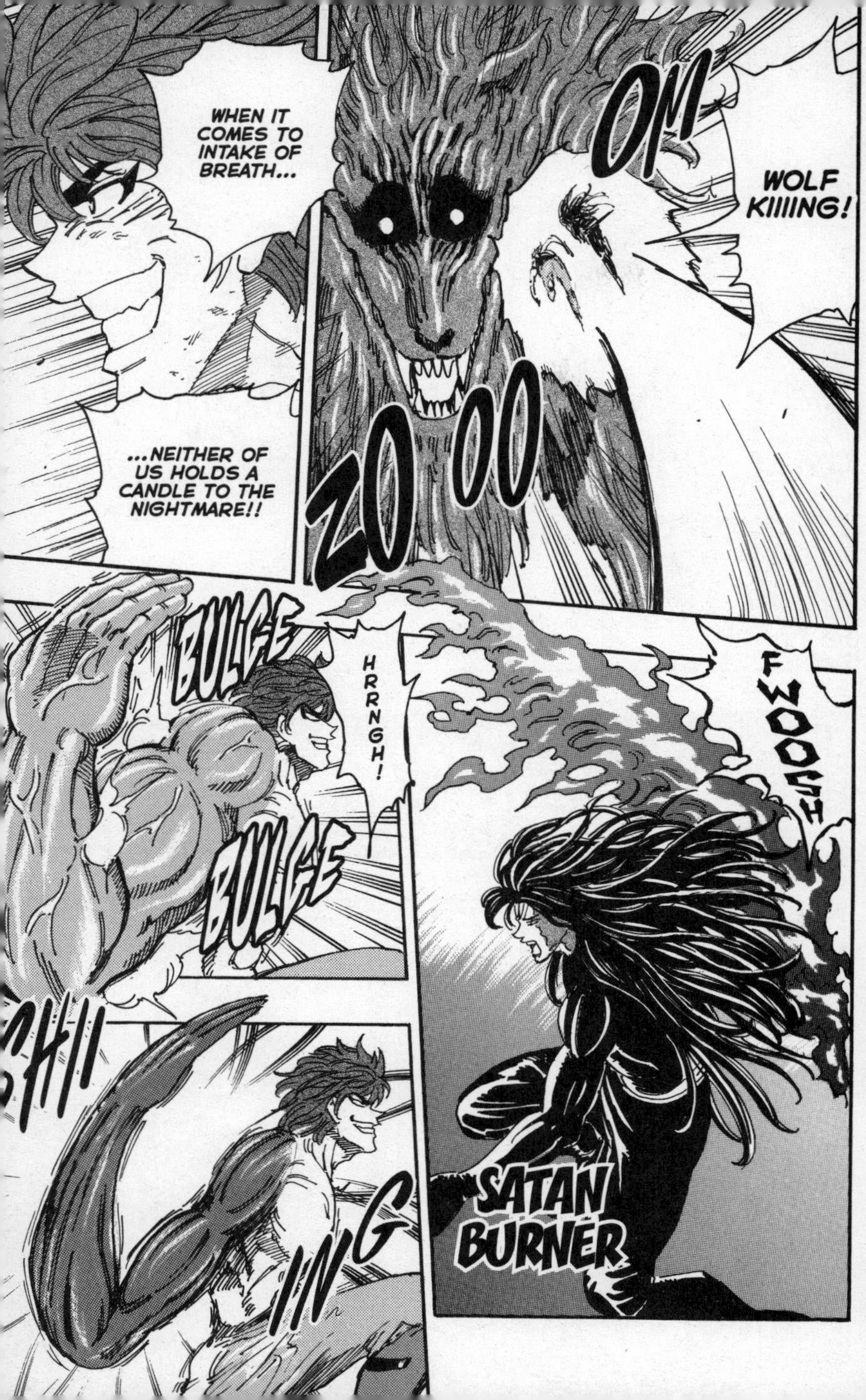
WOLF KIIIING!
ZOOOOM!
WHEN IT COMES TO INTAKE OF BREATH...
...NEITHER OF US HOLDS A CANDLE TO THE NIGHTMARE!!
FWOOOSH
SATAN BURNER
HRRNGH!
BULGE
BULGE
SHII
ING

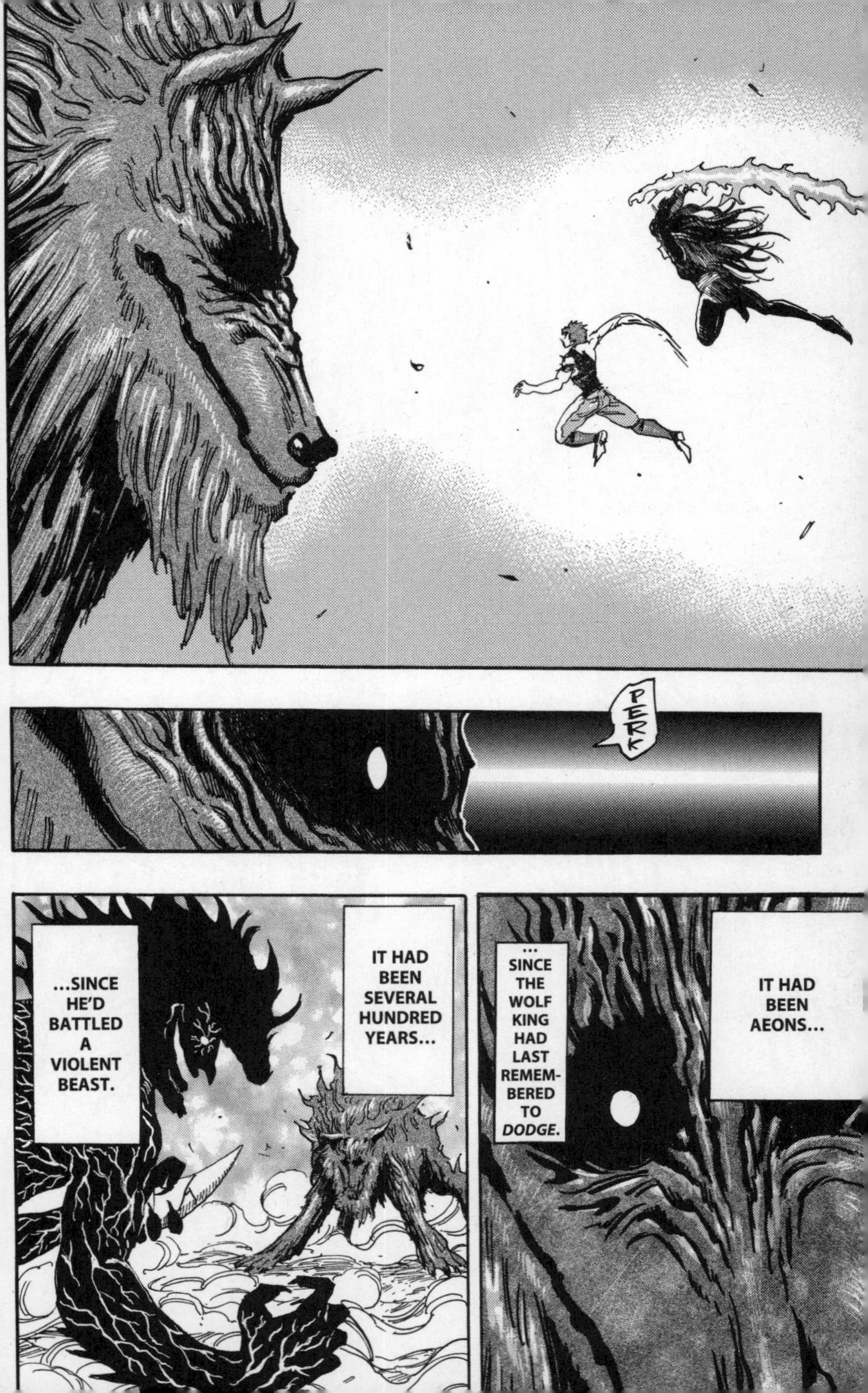
PERK
IT HAD BEEN AEONS...
...SINCE THE WOLF KING HAD LAST REMEMBERED TO *DODGE*.
IT HAD BEEN SEVERAL HUNDRED YEARS...
...SINCE HE'D BATTLED A VIOLENT BEAST.

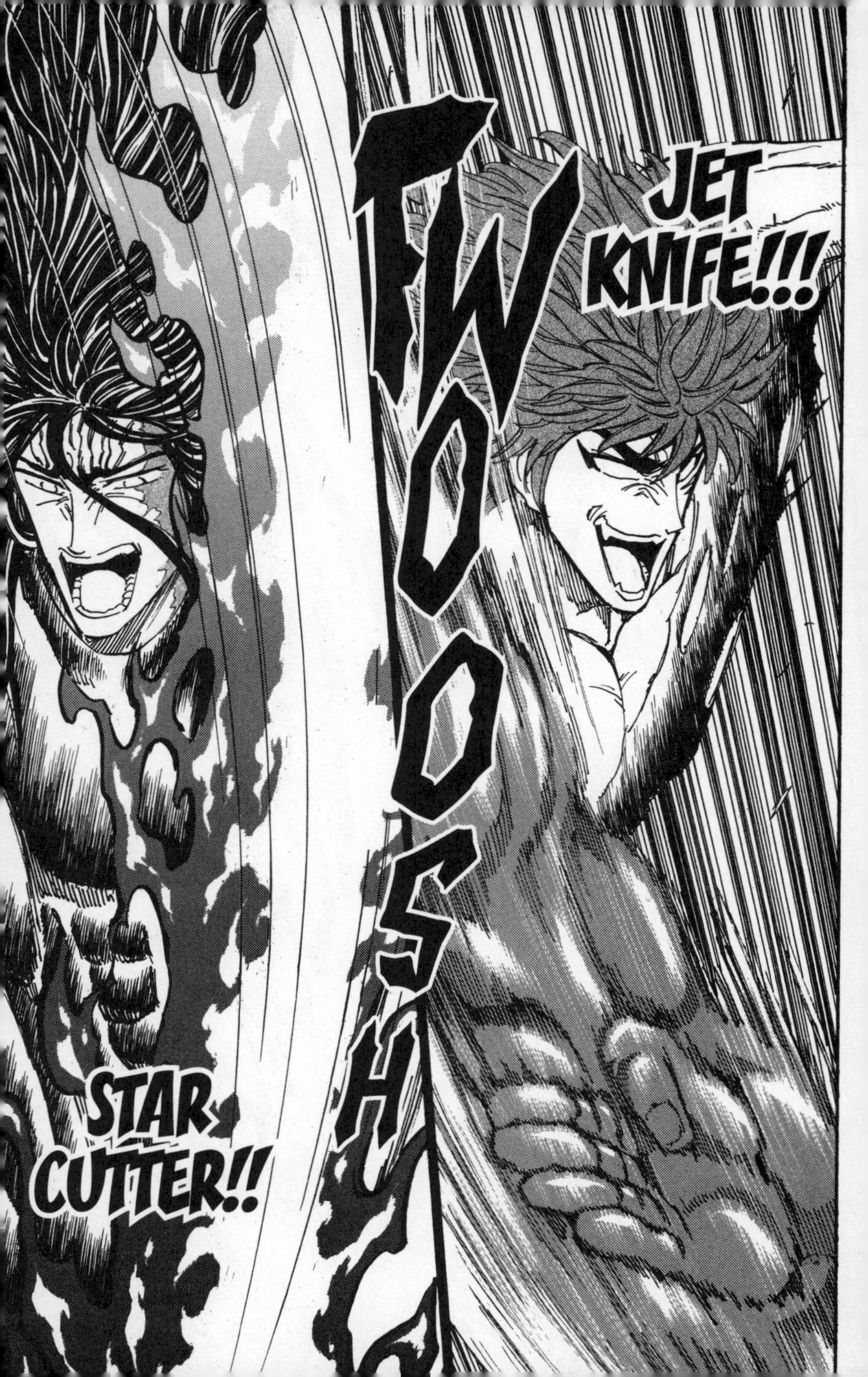
JET KNIFE!!!
FWOOSH
STAR CUTTER!!

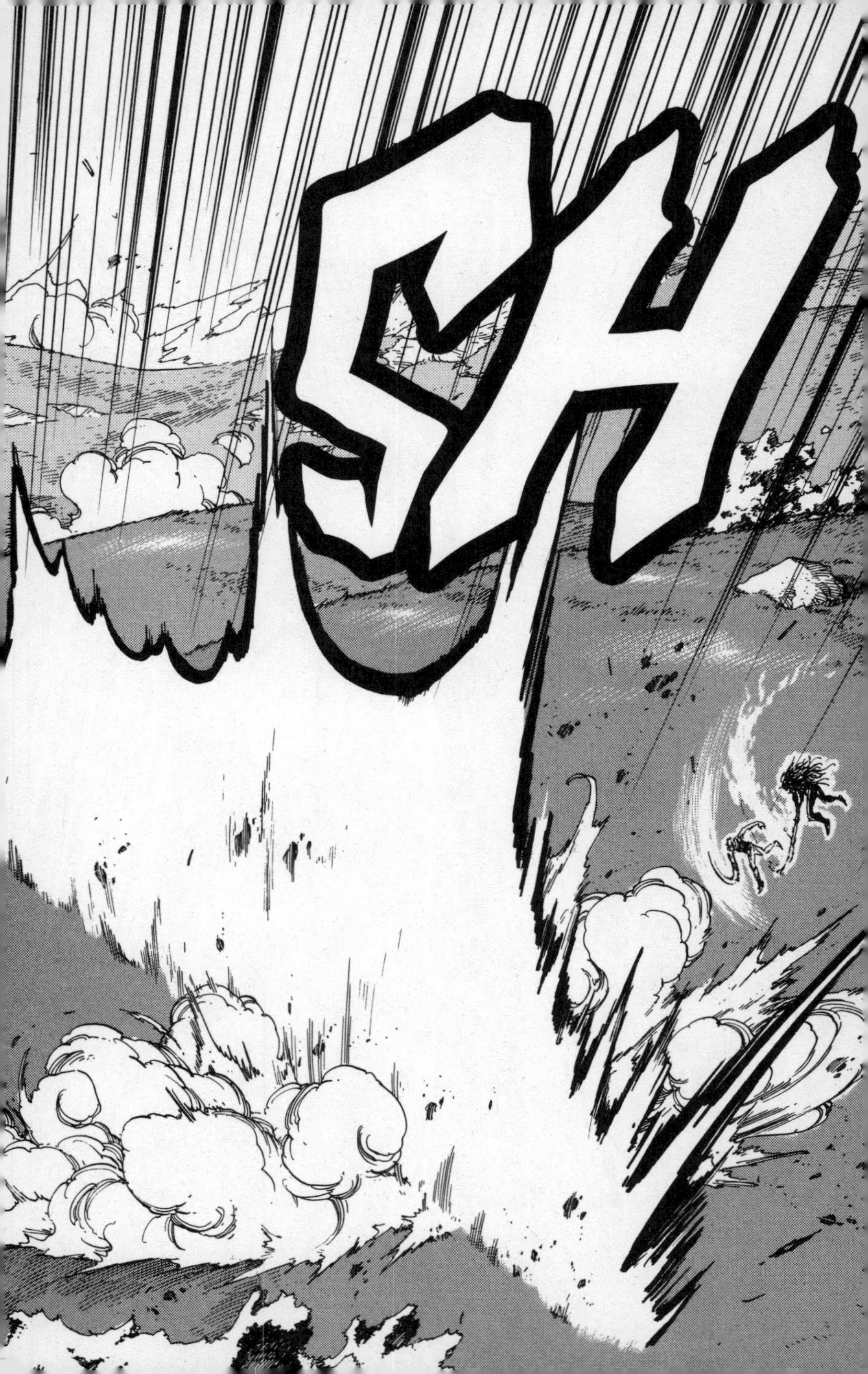

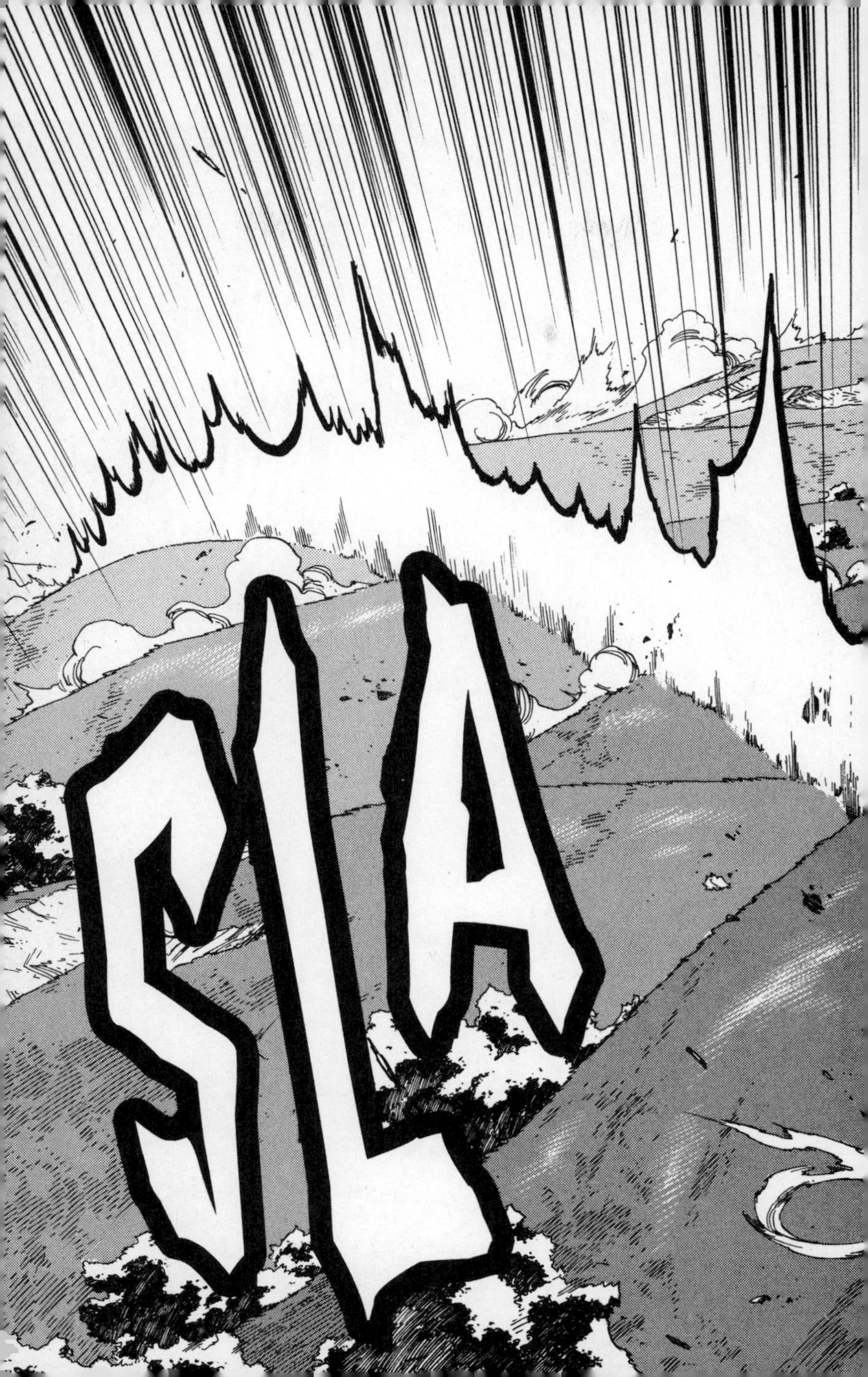
SLA

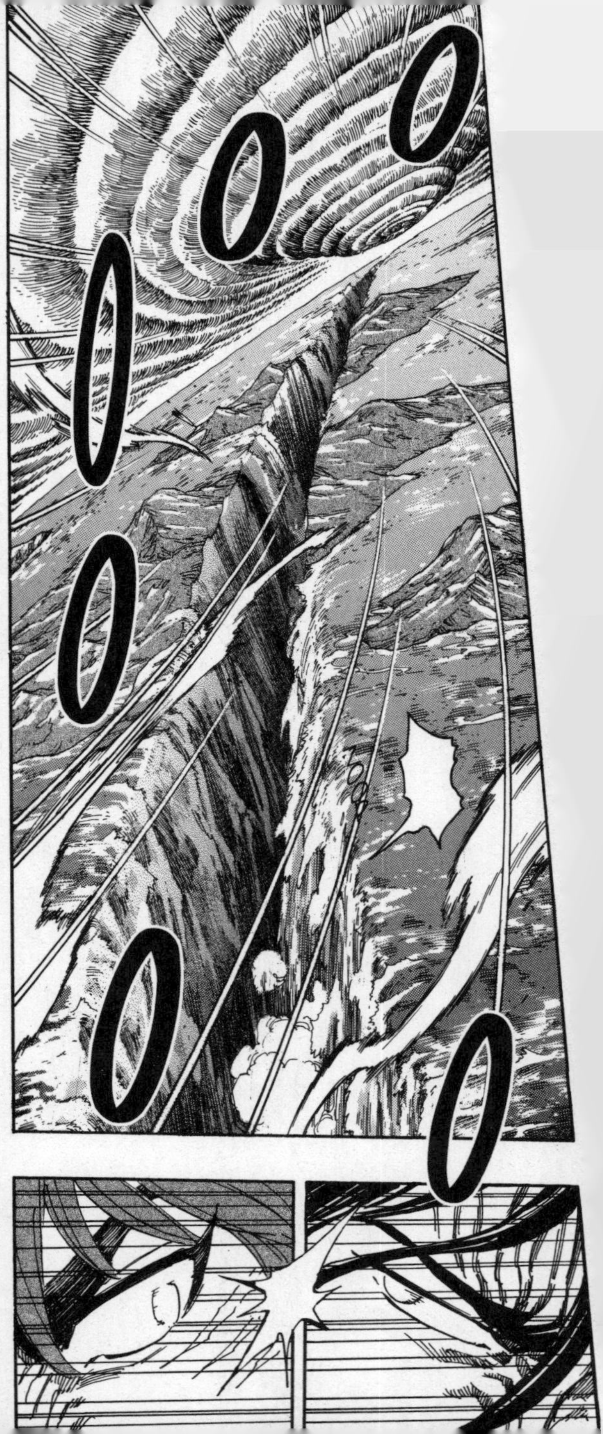

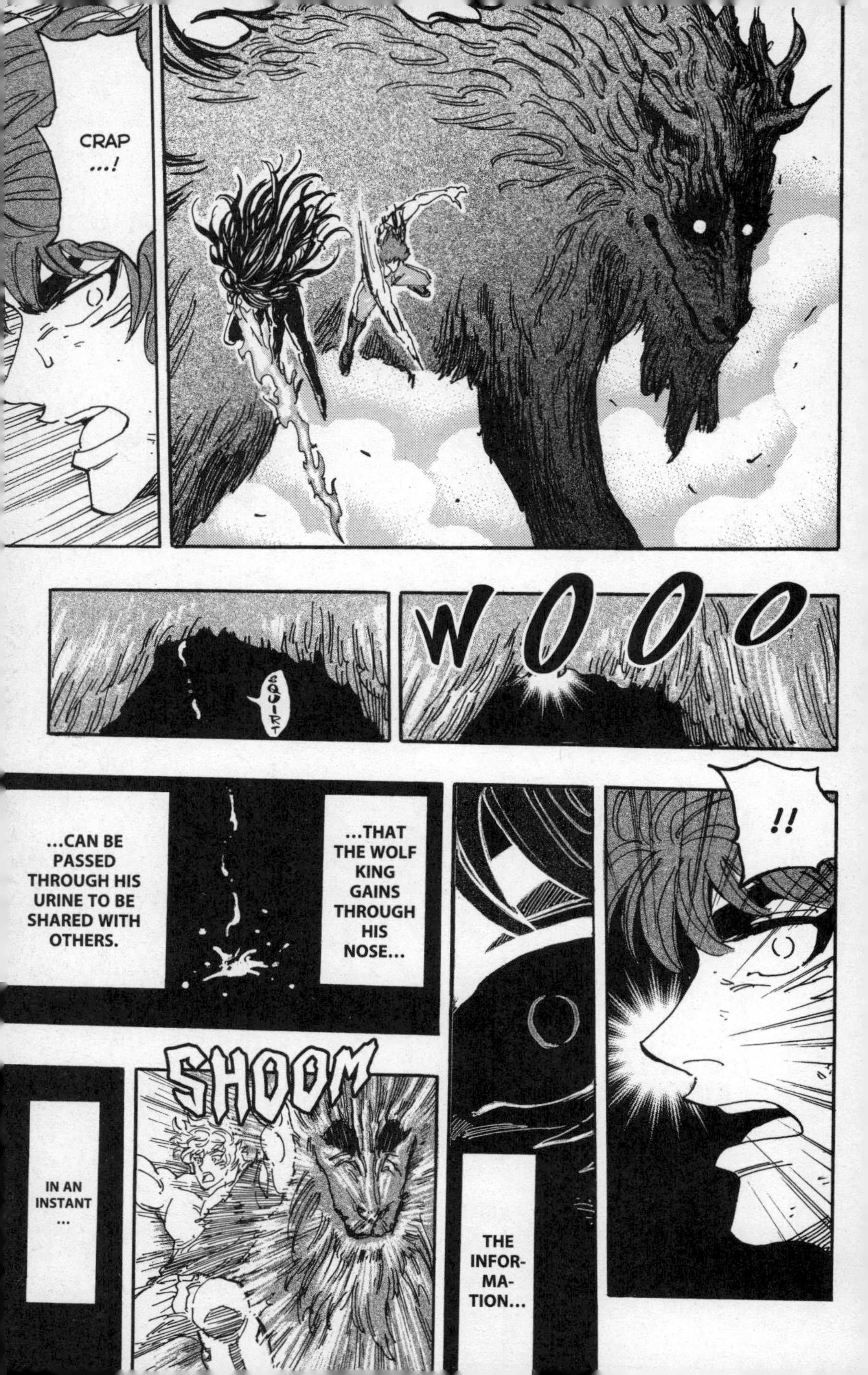
CRAP ...!
WOOO
SQUIRT
!!
THE INFORMATION...
...THAT THE WOLF KING GAINS THROUGH HIS NOSE...
...CAN BE PASSED THROUGH HIS URINE TO BE SHARED WITH OTHERS.
SHOOM
IN AN INSTANT ...

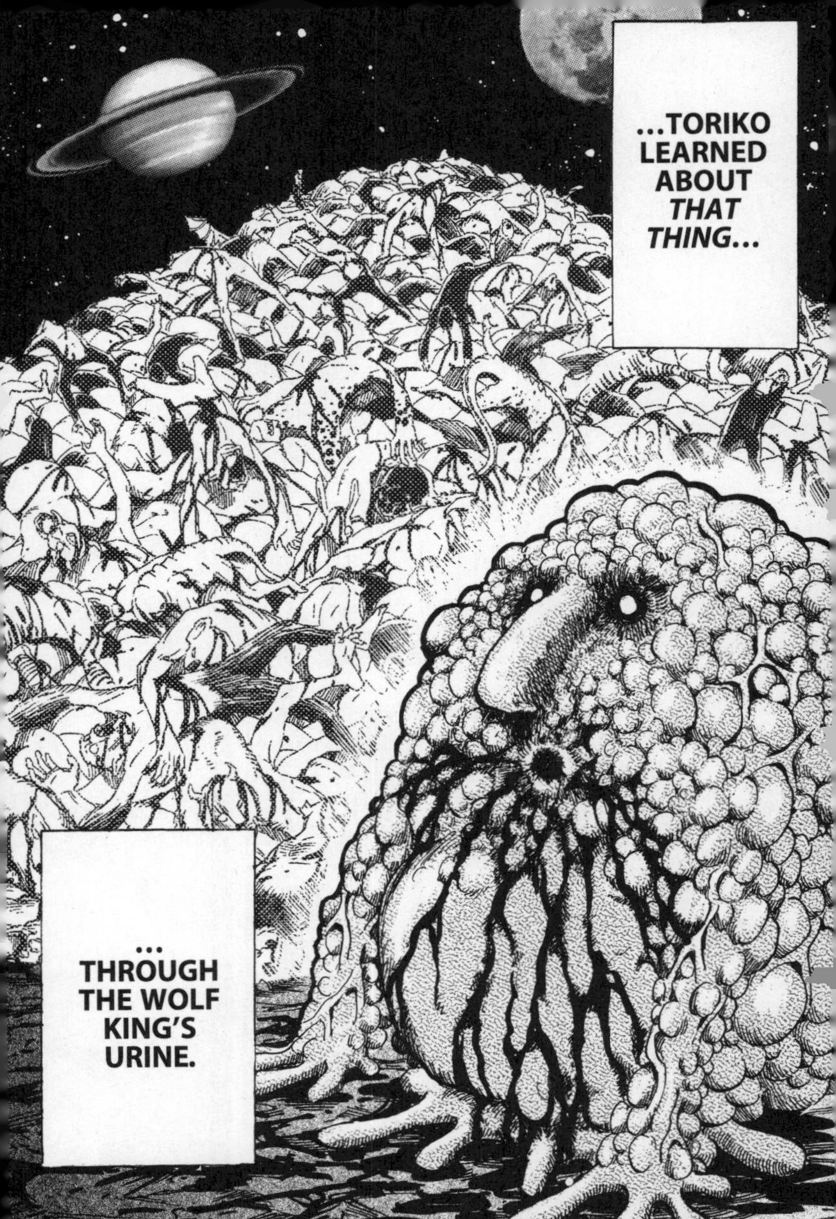
...TORIKO LEARNED ABOUT *THAT THING*...
... THROUGH THE WOLF KING'S URINE.

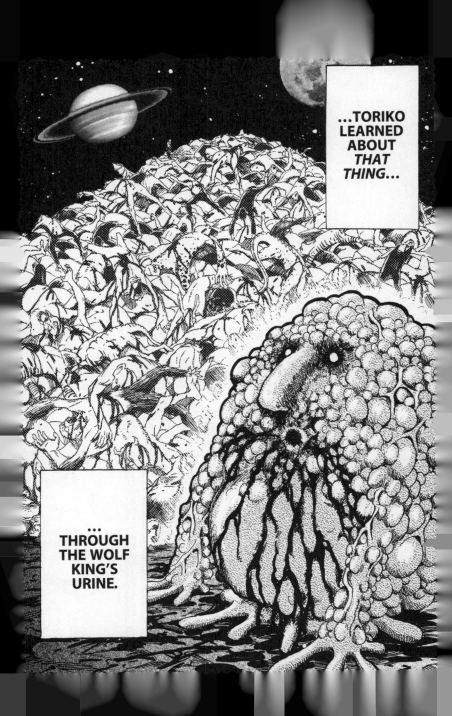

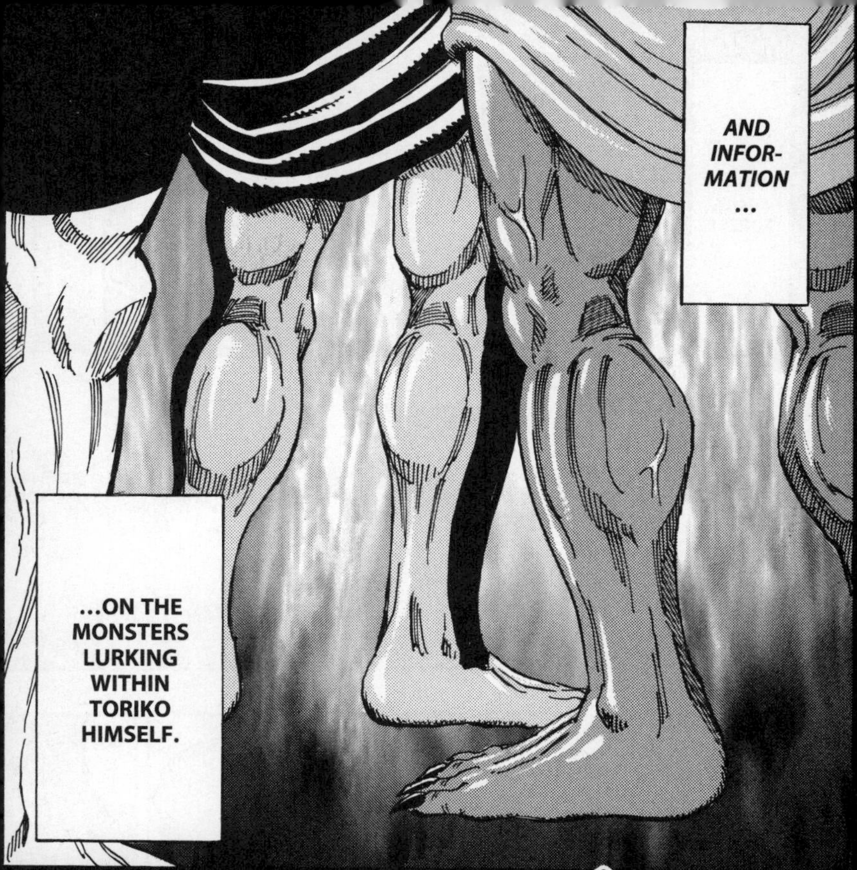
AND INFORMATION ...
...ON THE MONSTERS LURKING WITHIN TORIKO HIMSELF.
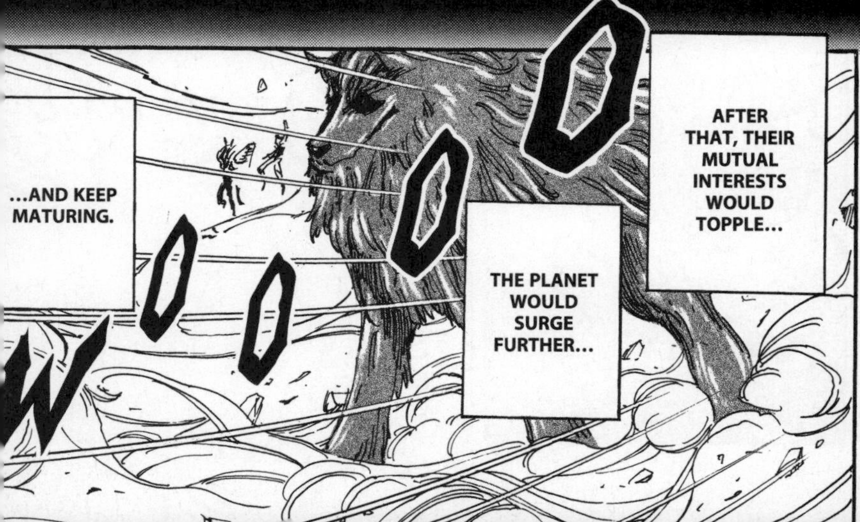
AFTER THAT, THEIR MUTUAL INTERESTS WOULD TOPPLE...
THE PLANET WOULD SURGE FURTHER...
...AND KEEP MATURING.
WOOOO

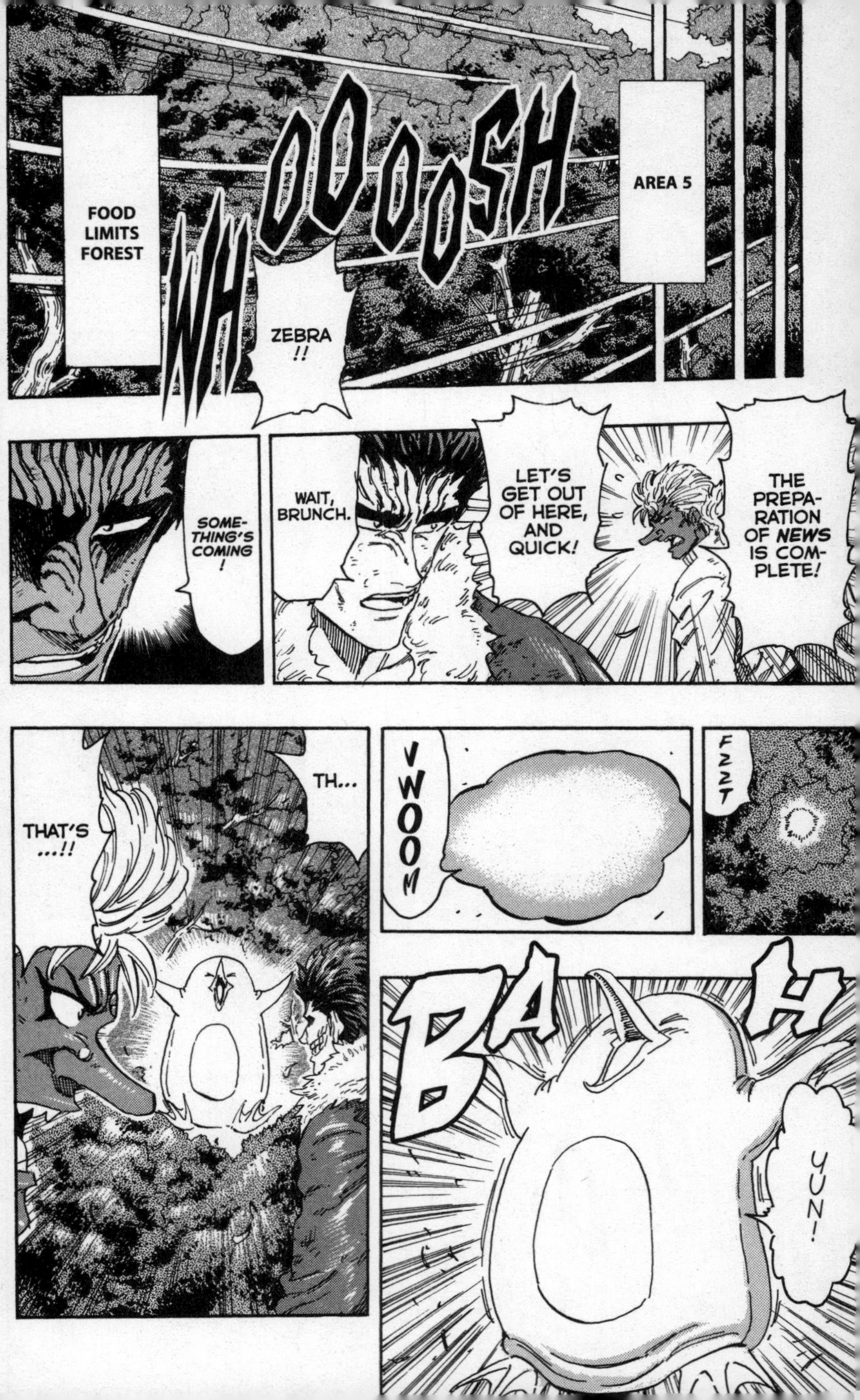
AREA 5
FOOD LIMITS FOREST
WHOOOOSH
ZEBRA!!
THE PREPARATION OF NEWS IS COMPLETE!
LET'S GET OUT OF HERE, AND QUICK!
WAIT, BRUNCH.
SOMETHING'S COMING!
FZZT
VWOOOM
BAH
YUN!
TH...
THAT'S...!!

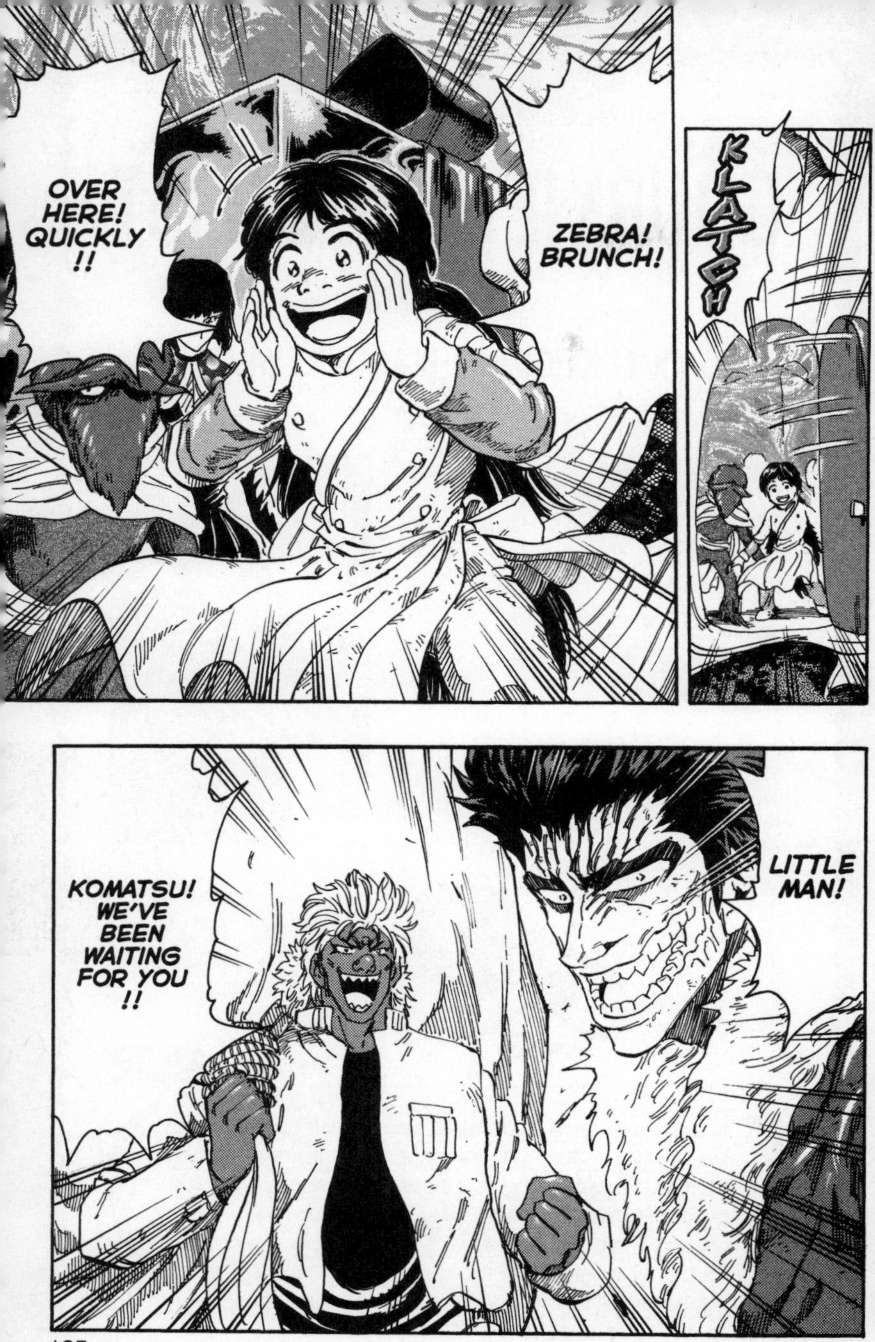
KLATCH
ZEBRA! BRUNCH!
OVER HERE! QUICKLY!!
LITTLE MAN!
KOMATSU! WE'VE BEEN WAITING FOR YOU!!

GOURMET CHECKLIST

Vol. 386

WHALE KING MOON: BLACK HOLE WHALE
(MAMMAL)

CAPTURE LEVEL: 6,600
HABITAT: GOURMET WORLD'S AREA 6
SIZE: 10,000 M
HEIGHT: 2,500 M
WEIGHT: 1.5 TRILLION TONS
PRICE: UNKNOWN

THE KING OF THE OCEAN WHO RESIDES IN THE PITCH-BLACK TRIANGULAR ZONE, BLACK TRIANGLE...
...IS A WHALE THAT SUCKS IN ALL MATTER AND LIGHT--THE WHALE KING MOON*! ALSO KNOWN AS THE BLACK HOLE WHALE.
THE WHALE KING'S STRENGTH ALONE IS SAID TO BE THE GREATEST OF ALL THE EIGHT KINGS, AND THAT'S WHAT MAKES THIS AREA'S LEVEL SO HIGH.
NOW I'LL DELEGATE WHICH OF THE REST OF YOU WILL GO TO THE OTHER AREAS.

SCALE

THE WHALE KING THAT LIVES IN THE BLACK TRIANGLE WITHIN THE SEAS OF THE GOURMET WORLD'S AREA 6. THIS WHALE CAN ABSORB ALL MATTER AND LIGHT, EARNING IT ITS NICKNAME--THE BLACK HOLE WHALE. IT IS ALSO KNOWN AS THE WHALE KING BECAUSE IT IS CONSIDERED TO BE THE MOST POWERFUL OF ALL THE EIGHT KINGS. EVEN THE WHALE KING ITSELF DOESN'T KNOW WHERE ITS STOMACH LEADS TO, AS THE GRAVITATIONAL PULL OF ITS STOMACH WILL ABSORB EVERYTHING INCLUDING LIGHT. THE REASON WHY THE BLACK TRIANGLE LOCATION IS ALWAYS SHROUDED IN DARKNESS IS BECAUSE OF THE WHALE KING, AND IT'S CERTAINLY FAIR TO SAY THAT THIS THING IS A DEMON WHO CONSUMES ANYTHING AND EVERYTHING IN THIS WORLD.

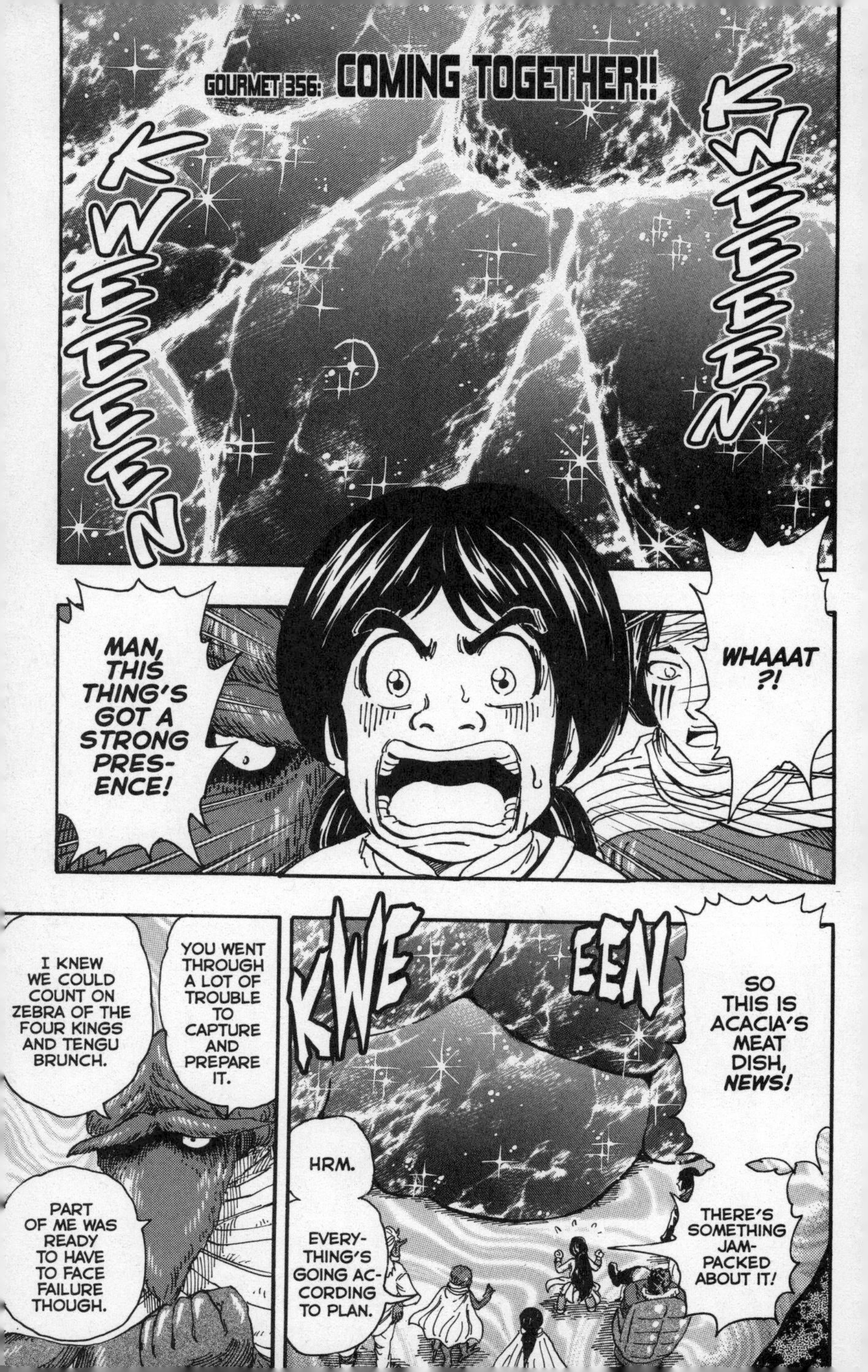
GOURMET 356: COMING TOGETHER!!
KWEEEEEN
KWEEEEEN
WHAAAT?!
MAN, THIS THING'S GOT A STRONG PRESENCE!
SO THIS IS ACACIA'S MEAT DISH, NEWS!
KWE
EEN
THERE'S SOMETHING JAM-PACKED ABOUT IT!
HRM.
EVERYTHING'S GOING ACCORDING TO PLAN.
YOU WENT THROUGH A LOT OF TROUBLE TO CAPTURE AND PREPARE IT.
I KNEW WE COULD COUNT ON ZEBRA OF THE FOUR KINGS AND TENGU BRUNCH.
PART OF ME WAS READY TO HAVE TO FACE FAILURE THOUGH.

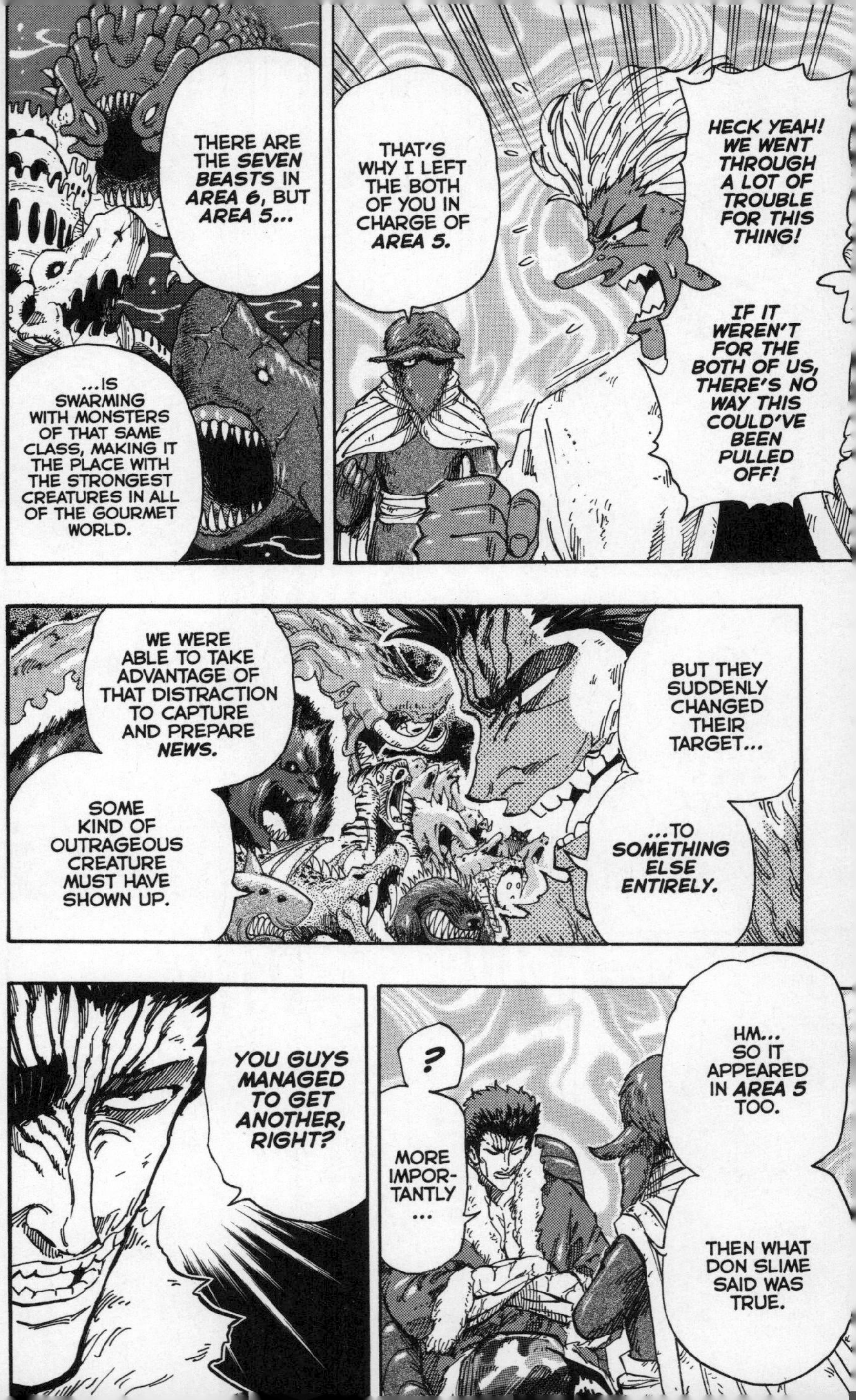
THAT'S WHY I LEFT THE BOTH OF YOU IN CHARGE OF AREA 5.
HECK YEAH! WE WENT THROUGH A LOT OF TROUBLE FOR THIS THING!
IF IT WEREN'T FOR THE BOTH OF US, THERE'S NO WAY THIS COULD'VE BEEN PULLED OFF!
THERE ARE THE SEVEN BEASTS IN AREA 6, BUT AREA 5...
...IS SWARMING WITH MONSTERS OF THAT SAME CLASS, MAKING IT THE PLACE WITH THE STRONGEST CREATURES IN ALL OF THE GOURMET WORLD.
BUT THEY SUDDENLY CHANGED THEIR TARGET...
...TO SOMETHING ELSE ENTIRELY.
WE WERE ABLE TO TAKE ADVANTAGE OF THAT DISTRACTION TO CAPTURE AND PREPARE NEWS.
SOME KIND OF OUTRAGEOUS CREATURE MUST HAVE SHOWN UP.
HM... SO IT APPEARED IN AREA 5 TOO.
THEN WHAT DON SLIME SAID WAS TRUE.
?
MORE IMPORTANTLY...
YOU GUYS MANAGED TO GET ANOTHER, RIGHT?

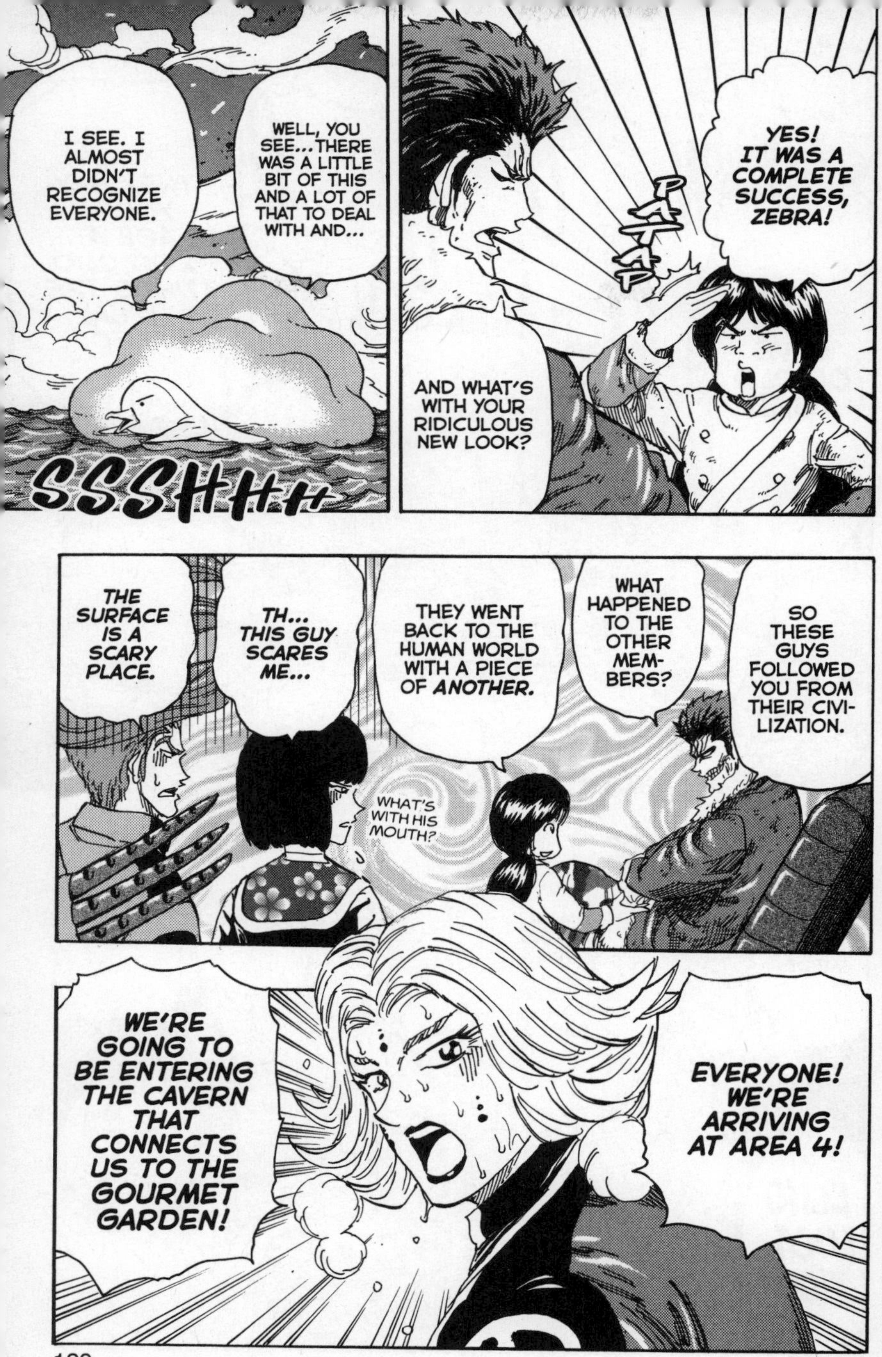
YES! IT WAS A COMPLETE SUCCESS, ZEBRA!
PATAP
AND WHAT'S WITH YOUR RIDICULOUS NEW LOOK?
WELL, YOU SEE... THERE WAS A LITTLE BIT OF THIS AND A LOT OF THAT TO DEAL WITH AND...
I SEE. I ALMOST DIDN'T RECOGNIZE EVERYONE.
SSSHHHH
SO THESE GUYS FOLLOWED YOU FROM THEIR CIVILIZATION.
WHAT HAPPENED TO THE OTHER MEMBERS?
THEY WENT BACK TO THE HUMAN WORLD WITH A PIECE OF *ANOTHER*.
WHAT'S WITH HIS MOUTH?
TH... THIS GUY SCARES ME...
THE SURFACE IS A SCARY PLACE.
EVERYONE! WE'RE ARRIVING AT AREA 4!
WE'RE GOING TO BE ENTERING THE CAVERN THAT CONNECTS US TO THE GOURMET GARDEN!

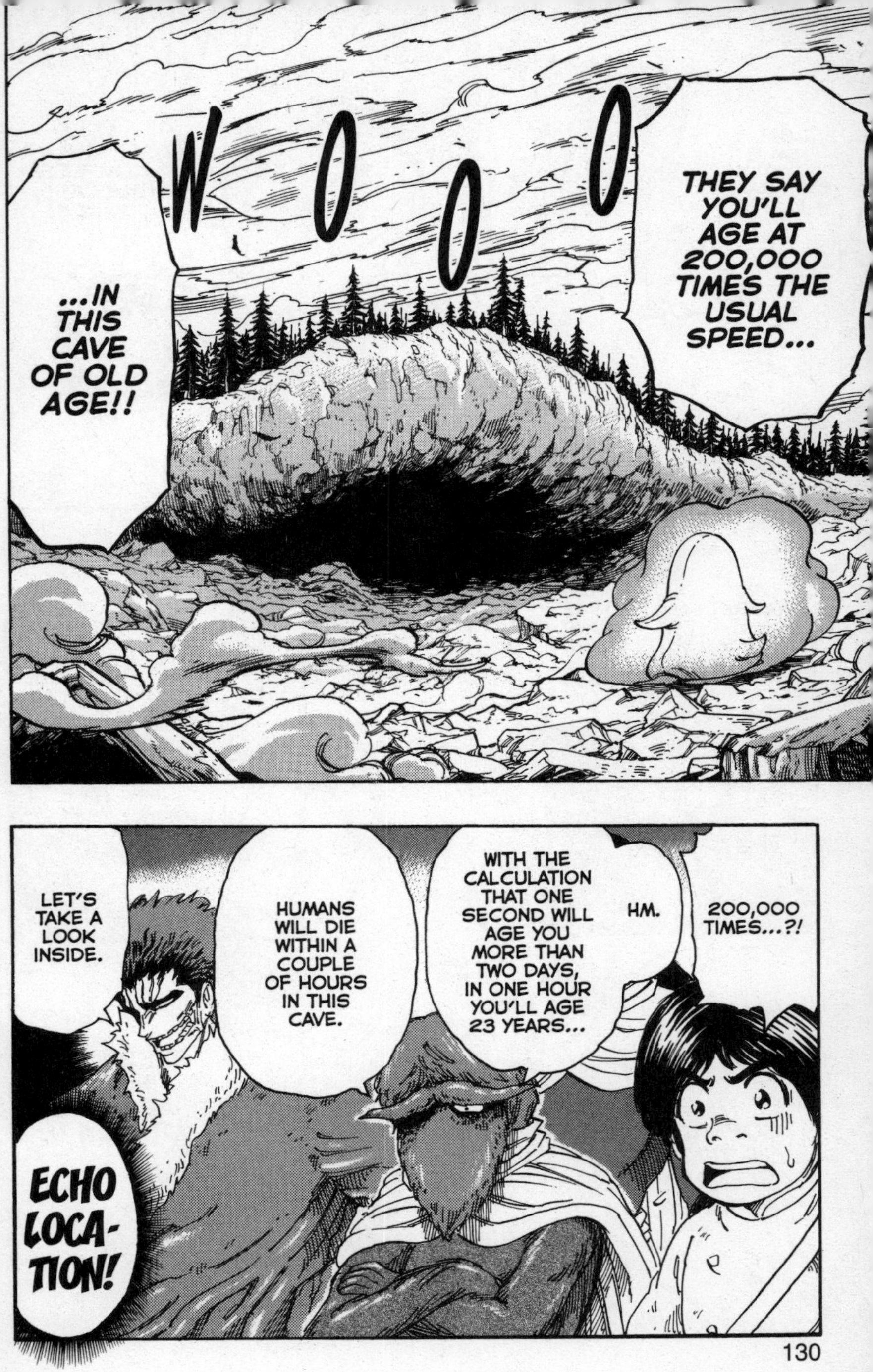
THEY SAY YOU'LL AGE AT 200,000 TIMES THE USUAL SPEED...
WOOOO
...IN THIS CAVE OF OLD AGE!!
200,000 TIMES...?!
HM.
WITH THE CALCULATION THAT ONE SECOND WILL AGE YOU MORE THAN TWO DAYS, IN ONE HOUR YOU'LL AGE 23 YEARS...
HUMANS WILL DIE WITHIN A COUPLE OF HOURS IN THIS CAVE.
LET'S TAKE A LOOK INSIDE.
ECHO LOCATION!

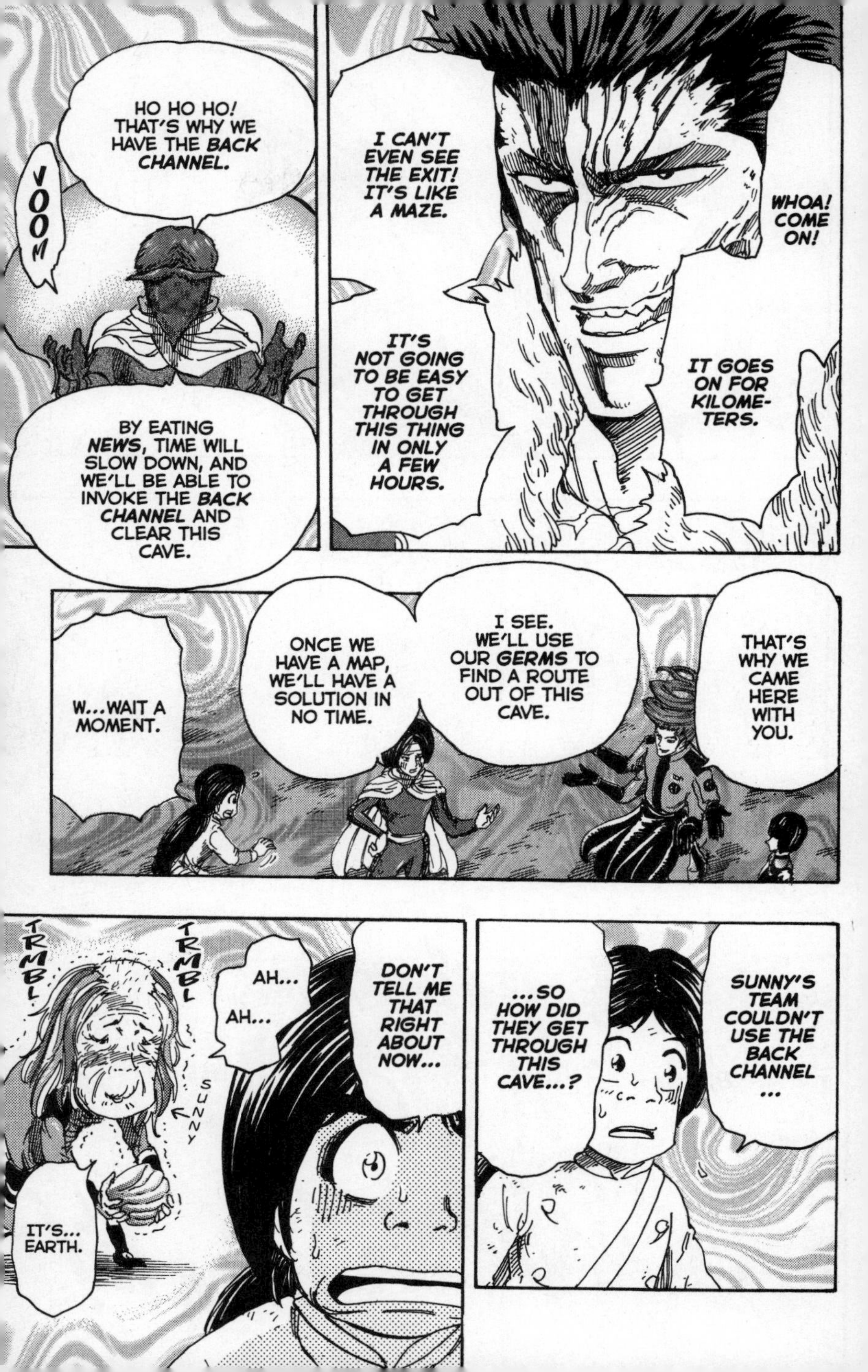
WHOA! COME ON!
I CAN'T EVEN SEE THE EXIT! IT'S LIKE A MAZE.
IT GOES ON FOR KILOMETERS.
IT'S NOT GOING TO BE EASY TO GET THROUGH THIS THING IN ONLY A FEW HOURS.
HO HO HO! THAT'S WHY WE HAVE THE BACK CHANNEL.
VOOM
BY EATING NEWS, TIME WILL SLOW DOWN, AND WE'LL BE ABLE TO INVOKE THE BACK CHANNEL AND CLEAR THIS CAVE.
THAT'S WHY WE CAME HERE WITH YOU.
I SEE. WE'LL USE OUR GERMS TO FIND A ROUTE OUT OF THIS CAVE.
ONCE WE HAVE A MAP, WE'LL HAVE A SOLUTION IN NO TIME.
W...WAIT A MOMENT.
SUNNY'S TEAM COULDN'T USE THE BACK CHANNEL ...
...SO HOW DID THEY GET THROUGH THIS CAVE...?
DON'T TELL ME THAT RIGHT ABOUT NOW...
AH...
AH...
TRMBL
TRMBL
SUNNY
IT'S... EARTH.

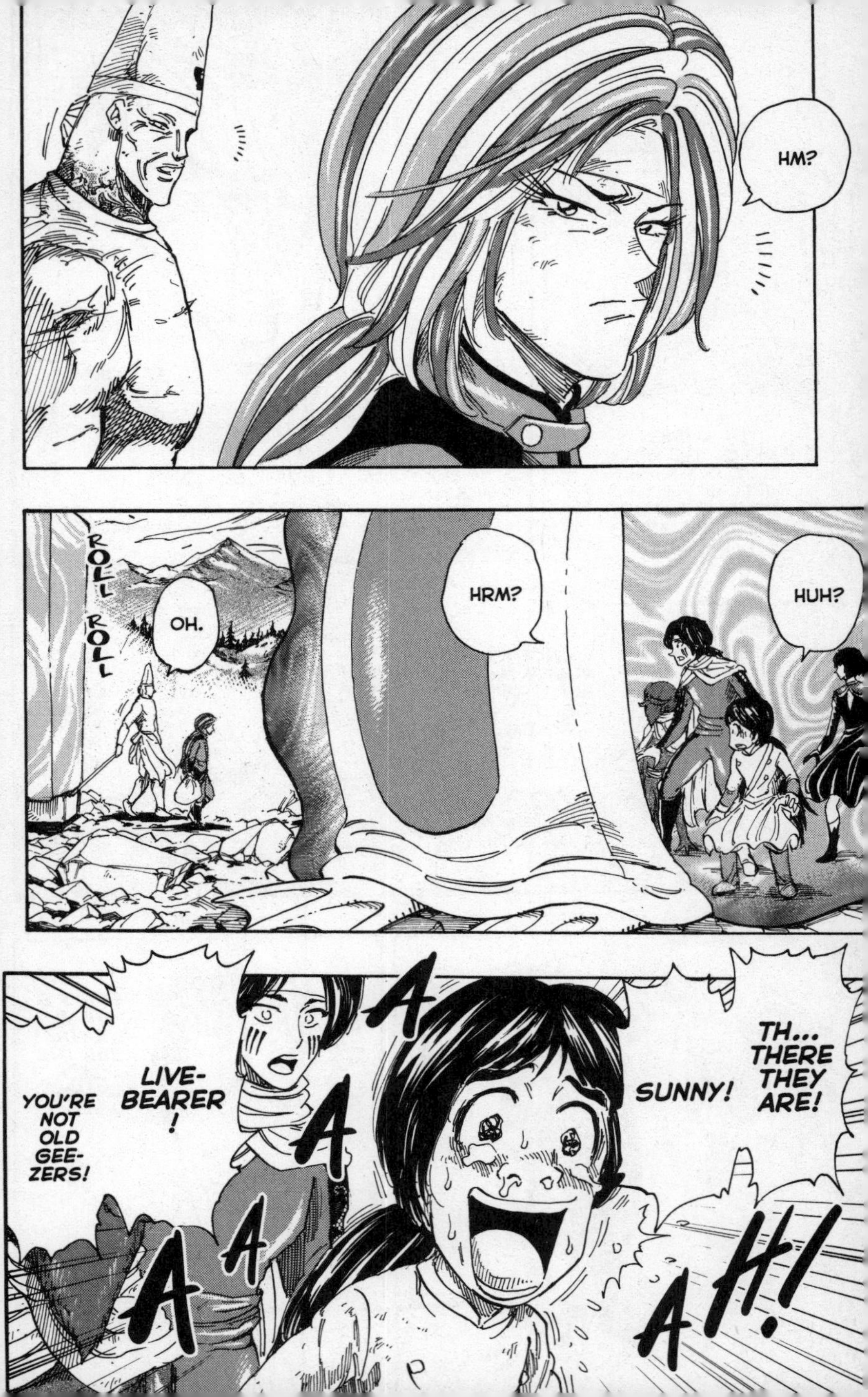
HM?
HUH?
HRM?
OH.
ROLL ROLL
TH... THERE THEY ARE!
SUNNY!
LIVE-BEARER!
YOU'RE NOT OLD GEE-ZERS!
AAAAAAH!

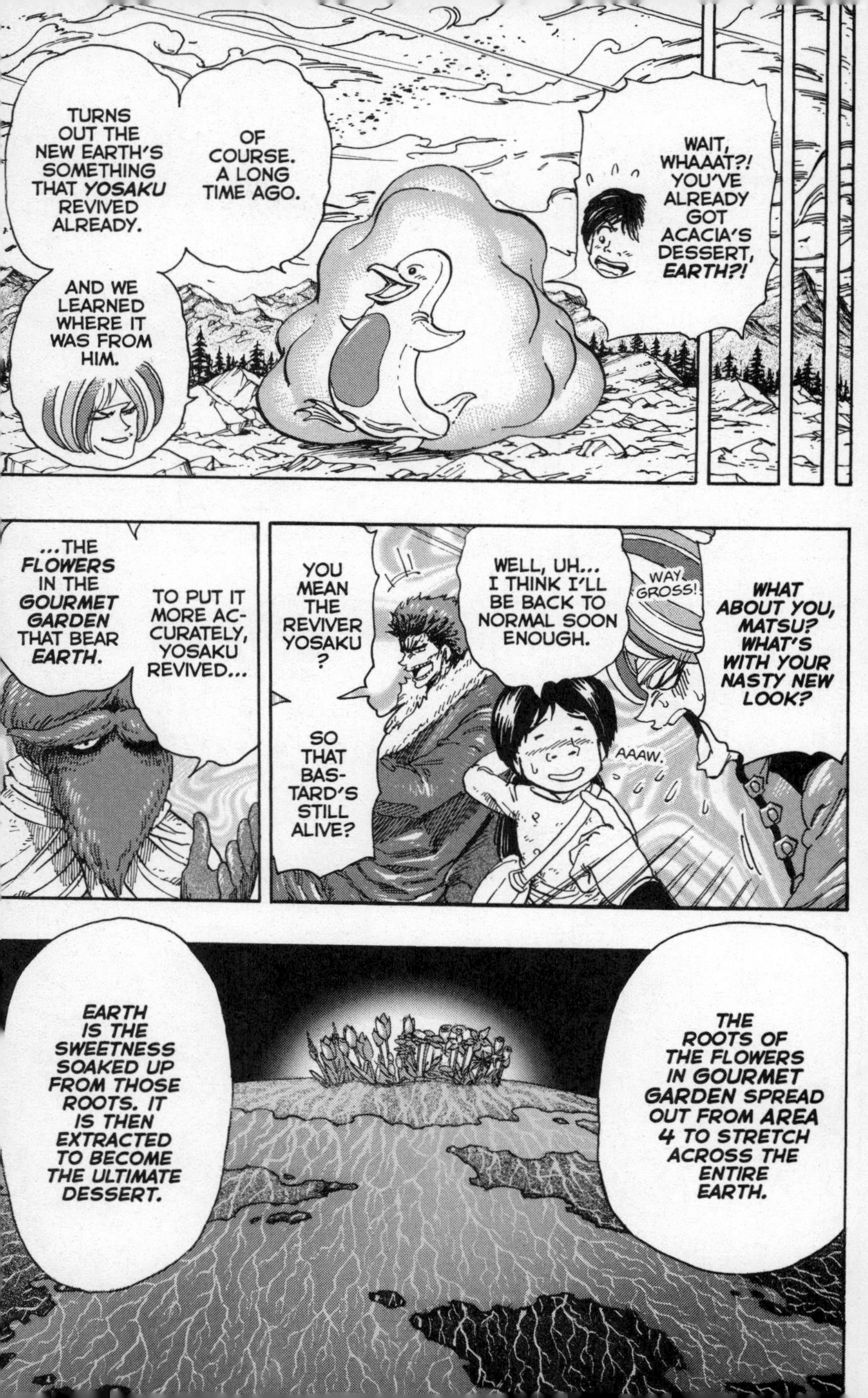
WAIT, WHAAAT?! YOU'VE ALREADY GOT ACACIA'S DESSERT, EARTH?!
OF COURSE. A LONG TIME AGO.
TURNS OUT THE NEW EARTH'S SOMETHING THAT YOSAKU REVIVED ALREADY.
AND WE LEARNED WHERE IT WAS FROM HIM.
WHAT ABOUT YOU, MATSU? WHAT'S WITH YOUR NASTY NEW LOOK?
WAY GROSS!
WELL, UH... I THINK I'LL BE BACK TO NORMAL SOON ENOUGH.
AAAW.
YOU MEAN THE REVIVER YOSAKU?
SO THAT BASTARD'S STILL ALIVE?
TO PUT IT MORE ACCURATELY, YOSAKU REVIVED...
...THE FLOWERS IN THE GOURMET GARDEN THAT BEAR EARTH.
THE ROOTS OF THE FLOWERS IN GOURMET GARDEN SPREAD OUT FROM AREA 4 TO STRETCH ACROSS THE ENTIRE EARTH.
EARTH IS THE SWEETNESS SOAKED UP FROM THOSE ROOTS. IT IS THEN EXTRACTED TO BECOME THE ULTIMATE DESSERT.

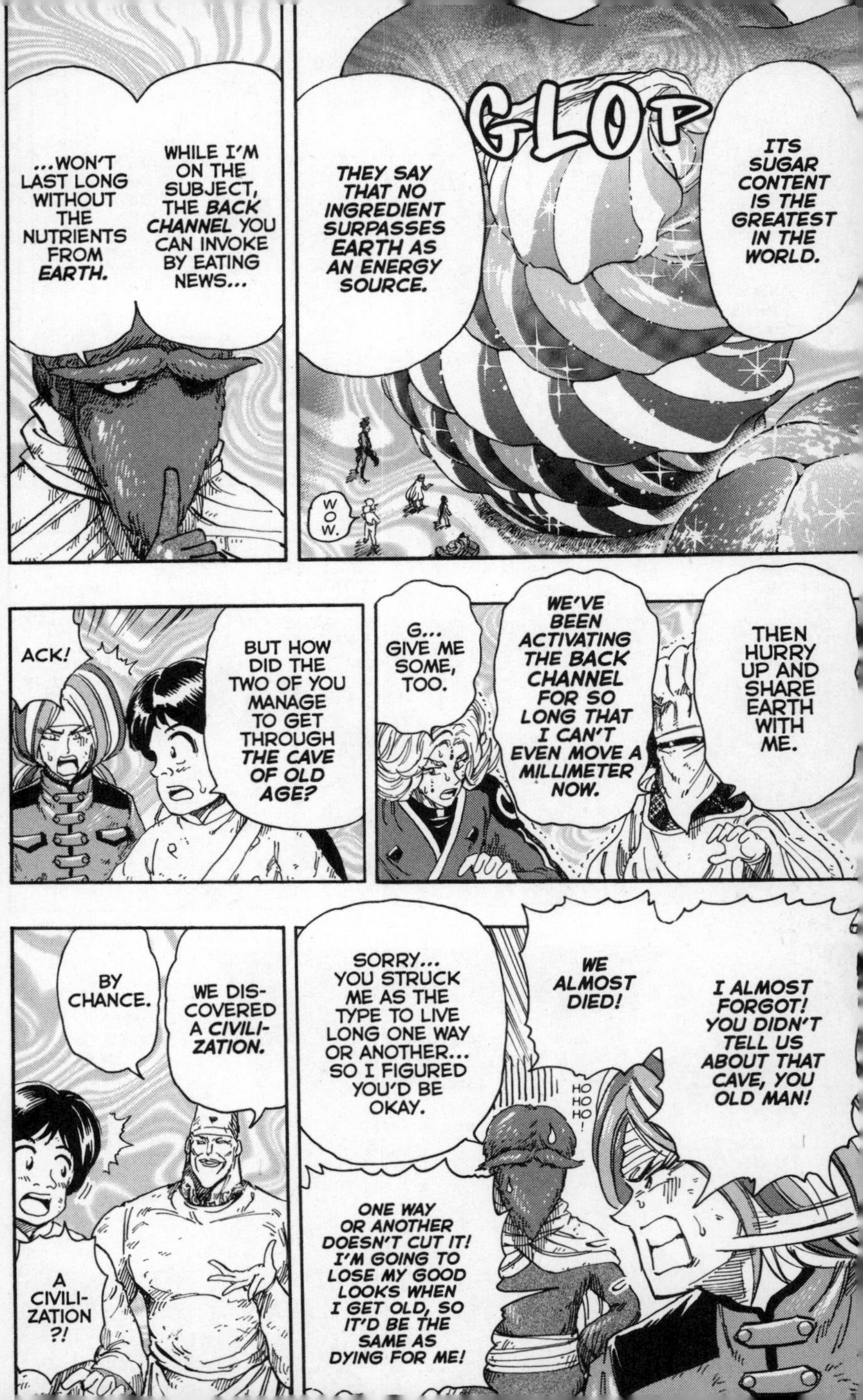
ITS SUGAR CONTENT IS THE GREATEST IN THE WORLD.
GLOP
THEY SAY THAT NO INGREDIENT SURPASSES EARTH AS AN ENERGY SOURCE.
WOW.
WHILE I'M ON THE SUBJECT, THE *BACK CHANNEL* YOU CAN INVOKE BY EATING NEWS...
...WON'T LAST LONG WITHOUT THE NUTRIENTS FROM *EARTH*.
THEN HURRY UP AND SHARE EARTH WITH ME.
WE'VE BEEN ACTIVATING THE BACK CHANNEL FOR SO LONG THAT I CAN'T EVEN MOVE A MILLIMETER NOW.
G... GIVE ME SOME, TOO.
BUT HOW DID THE TWO OF YOU MANAGE TO GET THROUGH *THE CAVE OF OLD AGE?*
ACK!
I ALMOST FORGOT! YOU DIDN'T TELL US ABOUT THAT CAVE, YOU OLD MAN!
WE ALMOST DIED!
HO HO HO!
SORRY... YOU STRUCK ME AS THE TYPE TO LIVE LONG ONE WAY OR ANOTHER... SO I FIGURED YOU'D BE OKAY.
ONE WAY OR ANOTHER DOESN'T CUT IT! I'M GOING TO LOSE MY GOOD LOOKS WHEN I GET OLD, SO IT'D BE THE SAME AS DYING FOR ME!
WE DIS-COVERED A *CIVILI-ZATION*.
BY CHANCE.
A CIVILI-ZATION ?!

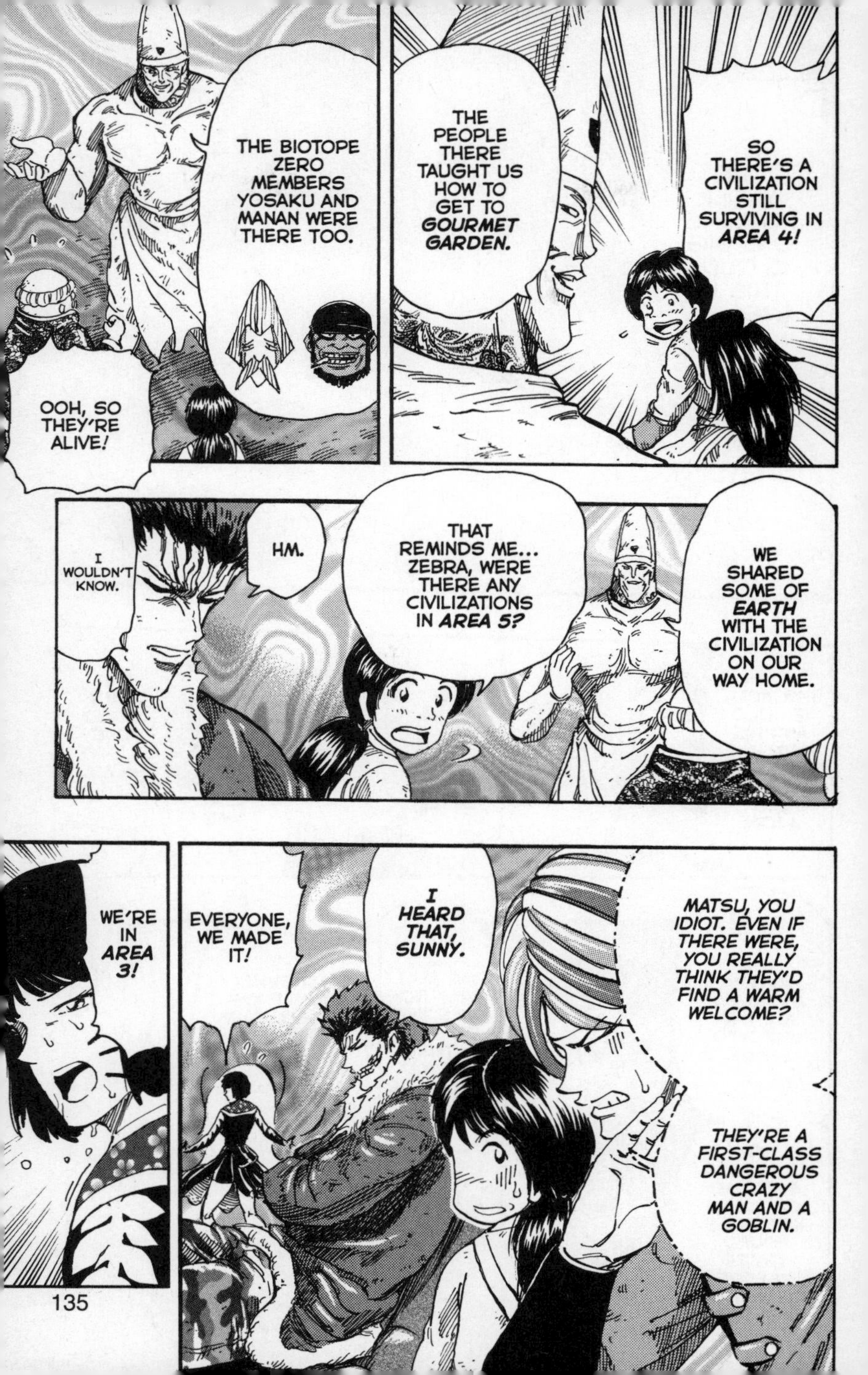

SO THERE'S A CIVILIZATION STILL SURVIVING IN *AREA 4!*
THE PEOPLE THERE TAUGHT US HOW TO GET TO *GOURMET GARDEN.*
THE BIOTOPE ZERO MEMBERS YOSAKU AND MANAN WERE THERE TOO.
OOH, SO THEY'RE ALIVE!
WE SHARED SOME OF *EARTH* WITH THE CIVILIZATION ON OUR WAY HOME.
THAT REMINDS ME... ZEBRA, WERE THERE ANY CIVILIZATIONS IN *AREA 5?*
HM.
I WOULDN'T KNOW.
MATSU, YOU IDIOT. EVEN IF THERE WERE, YOU REALLY THINK THEY'D FIND A WARM WELCOME?
THEY'RE A FIRST-CLASS DANGEROUS CRAZY MAN AND A GOBLIN.
I *HEARD* THAT, SUNNY.
EVERYONE, WE MADE IT!
WE'RE IN *AREA 3!*

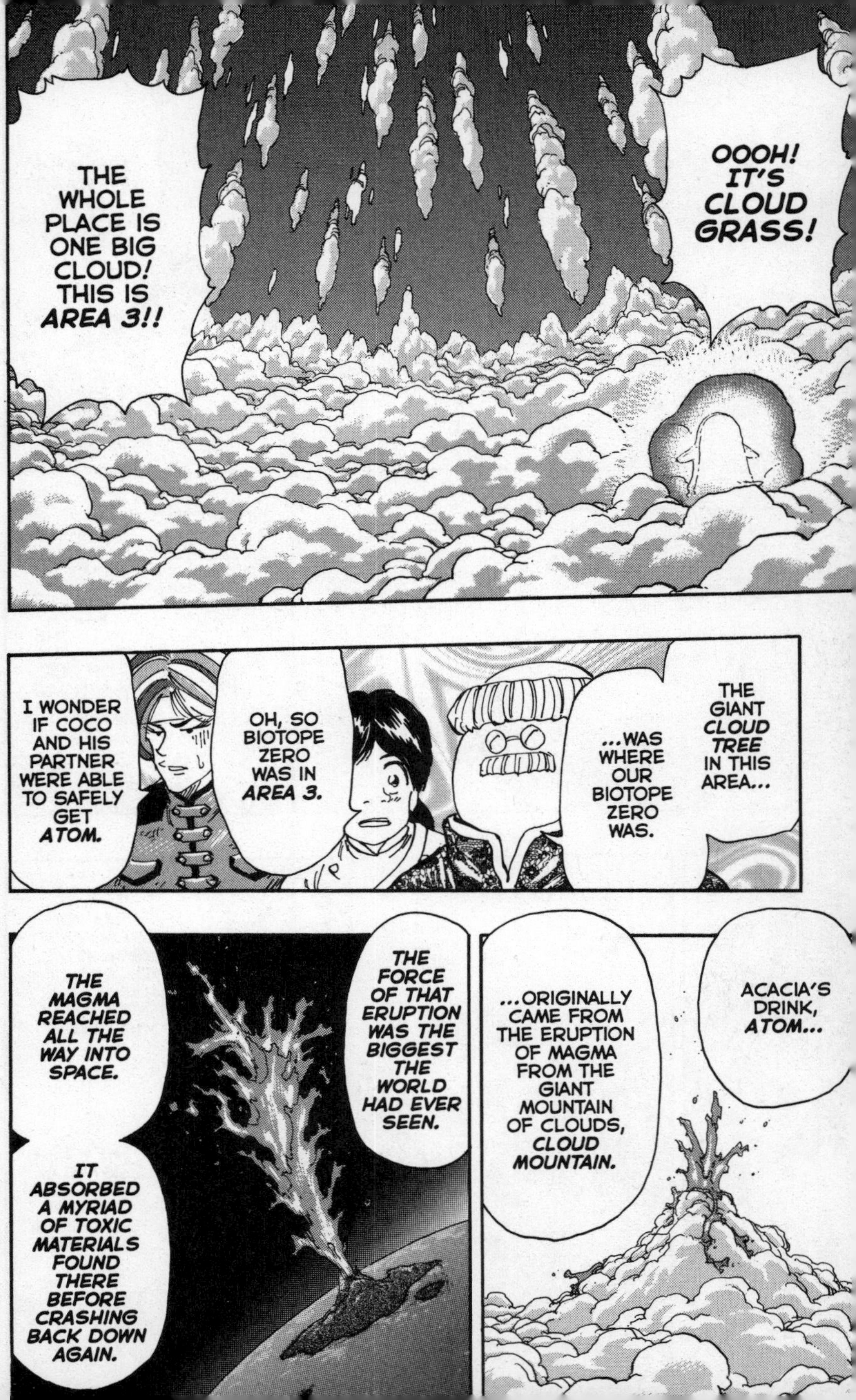
OOOH! IT'S CLOUD GRASS!
THE WHOLE PLACE IS ONE BIG CLOUD! THIS IS *AREA 3!!*
THE GIANT *CLOUD TREE* IN THIS AREA...
...WAS WHERE OUR BIOTOPE ZERO WAS.
OH, SO BIOTOPE ZERO WAS IN *AREA 3.*
I WONDER IF COCO AND HIS PARTNER WERE ABLE TO SAFELY GET *ATOM.*
ACACIA'S DRINK, *ATOM...*
...ORIGINALLY CAME FROM THE ERUPTION OF MAGMA FROM THE GIANT MOUNTAIN OF CLOUDS, *CLOUD MOUNTAIN.*
THE FORCE OF THAT ERUPTION WAS THE BIGGEST THE WORLD HAD EVER SEEN.
THE MAGMA REACHED ALL THE WAY INTO SPACE.
IT ABSORBED A MYRIAD OF TOXIC MATERIALS FOUND THERE BEFORE CRASHING BACK DOWN AGAIN.

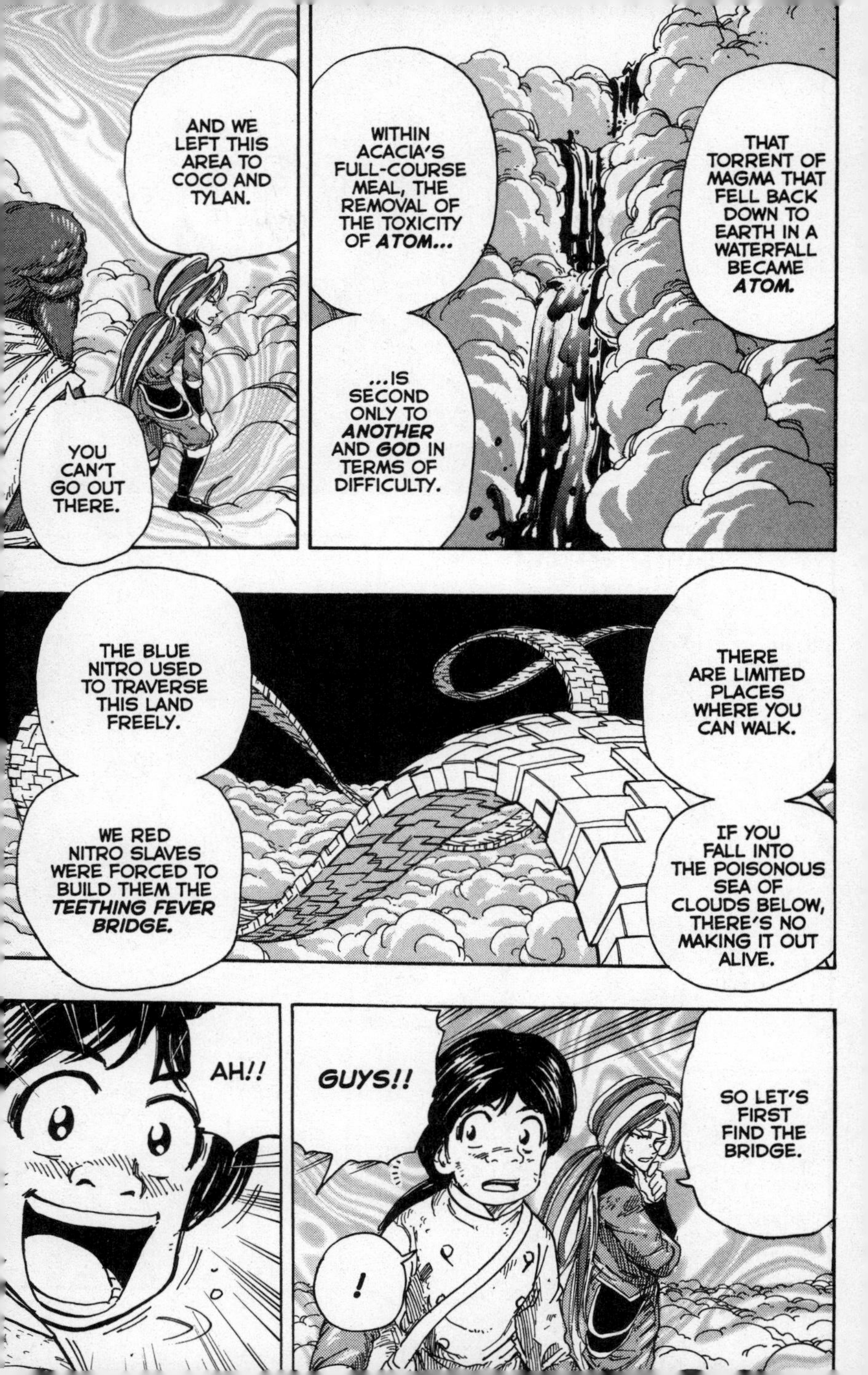
THAT TORRENT OF MAGMA THAT FELL BACK DOWN TO EARTH IN A WATERFALL BECAME ***ATOM.***
WITHIN ACACIA'S FULL-COURSE MEAL, THE REMOVAL OF THE TOXICITY OF ***ATOM...***
...IS SECOND ONLY TO ***ANOTHER*** AND ***GOD*** IN TERMS OF DIFFICULTY.
AND WE LEFT THIS AREA TO COCO AND TYLAN.
YOU CAN'T GO OUT THERE.
THERE ARE LIMITED PLACES WHERE YOU CAN WALK.
IF YOU FALL INTO THE POISONOUS SEA OF CLOUDS BELOW, THERE'S NO MAKING IT OUT ALIVE.
THE BLUE NITRO USED TO TRAVERSE THIS LAND FREELY.
WE RED NITRO SLAVES WERE FORCED TO BUILD THEM THE ***TEETHING FEVER BRIDGE.***
SO LET'S FIRST FIND THE BRIDGE.
GUYS!!
!
AH!!

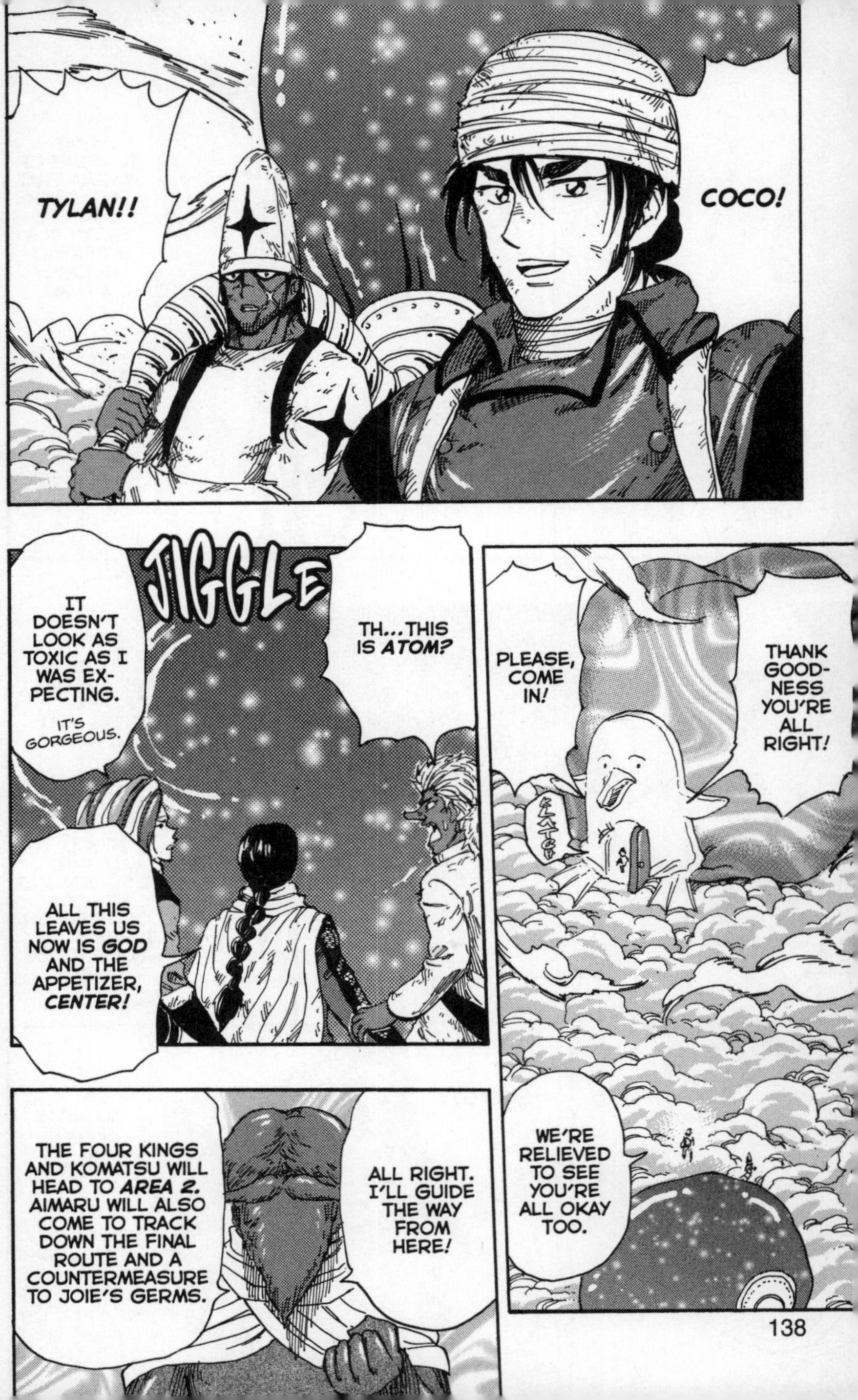
COCO!
TYLAN!!
THANK GOODNESS YOU'RE ALL RIGHT!
PLEASE, COME IN!
KLATCH
WE'RE RELIEVED TO SEE YOU'RE ALL OKAY TOO.
TH...THIS IS ATOM?
JIGGLE
IT DOESN'T LOOK AS TOXIC AS I WAS EXPECTING.
IT'S GORGEOUS.
ALL THIS LEAVES US NOW IS GOD AND THE APPETIZER, CENTER!
ALL RIGHT. I'LL GUIDE THE WAY FROM HERE!
THE FOUR KINGS AND KOMATSU WILL HEAD TO AREA 2. AIMARU WILL ALSO COME TO TRACK DOWN THE FINAL ROUTE AND A COUNTERMEASURE TO JOIE'S GERMS.

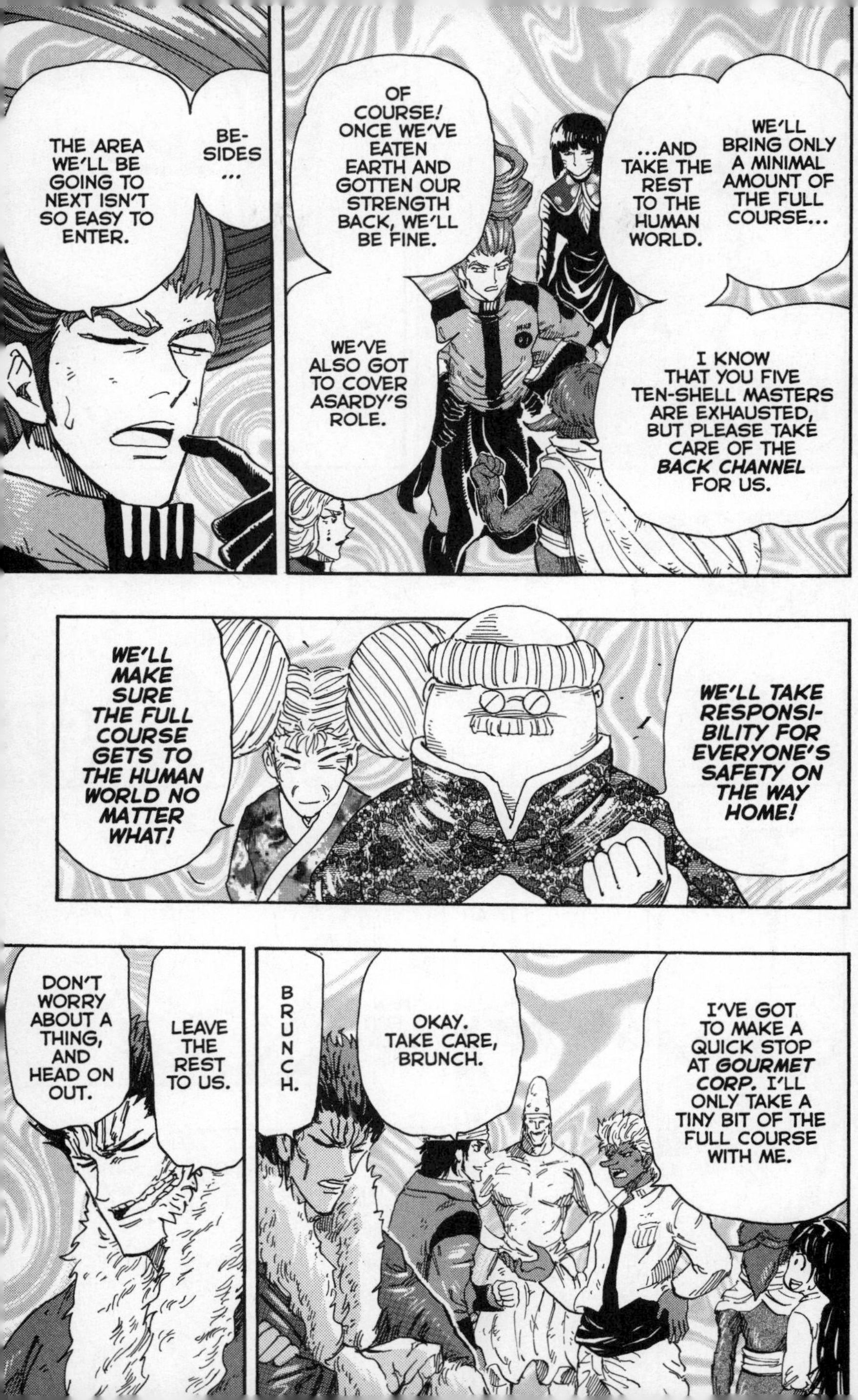
WE'LL BRING ONLY A MINIMAL AMOUNT OF THE FULL COURSE...
...AND TAKE THE REST TO THE HUMAN WORLD.
OF COURSE! ONCE WE'VE EATEN EARTH AND GOTTEN OUR STRENGTH BACK, WE'LL BE FINE.
I KNOW THAT YOU FIVE TEN-SHELL MASTERS ARE EXHAUSTED, BUT PLEASE TAKE CARE OF THE *BACK CHANNEL* FOR US.
WE'VE ALSO GOT TO COVER ASARDY'S ROLE.
BE-SIDES...
THE AREA WE'LL BE GOING TO NEXT ISN'T SO EASY TO ENTER.
WE'LL TAKE RESPONSI-BILITY FOR EVERYONE'S SAFETY ON THE WAY HOME!
WE'LL MAKE SURE THE FULL COURSE GETS TO THE HUMAN WORLD NO MATTER WHAT!
I'VE GOT TO MAKE A QUICK STOP AT *GOURMET CORP.* I'LL ONLY TAKE A TINY BIT OF THE FULL COURSE WITH ME.
OKAY. TAKE CARE, BRUNCH.
BRUNCH.
LEAVE THE REST TO US.
DON'T WORRY ABOUT A THING, AND HEAD ON OUT.

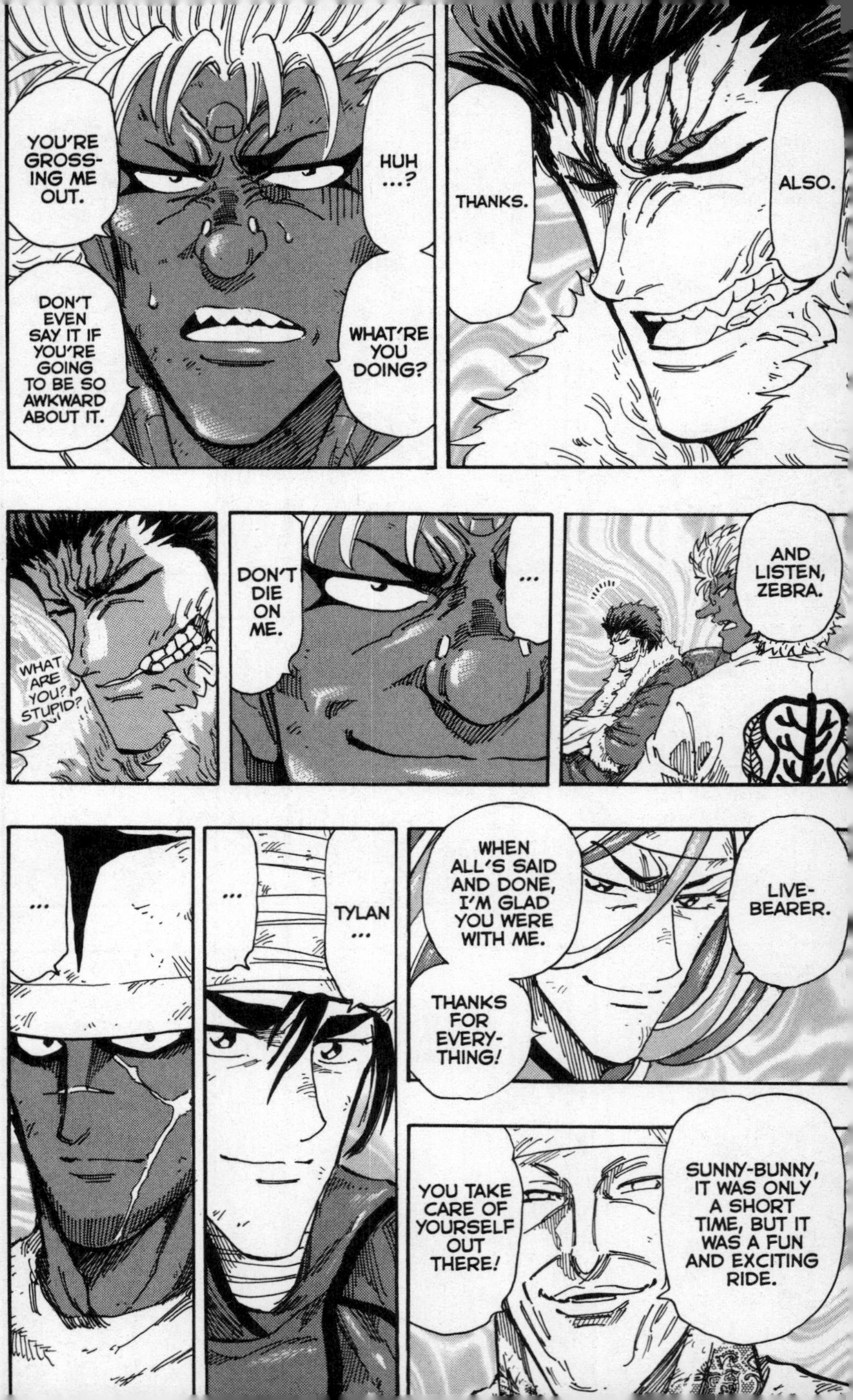
ALSO.
THANKS.
HUH ...?
WHAT'RE YOU DOING?
YOU'RE GROSSING ME OUT.
DON'T EVEN SAY IT IF YOU'RE GOING TO BE SO AWKWARD ABOUT IT.
AND LISTEN, ZEBRA.
...
DON'T DIE ON ME.
WHAT ARE YOU? STUPID?
LIVE-BEARER.
WHEN ALL'S SAID AND DONE, I'M GLAD YOU WERE WITH ME.
THANKS FOR EVERYTHING!
SUNNY-BUNNY, IT WAS ONLY A SHORT TIME, BUT IT WAS A FUN AND EXCITING RIDE.
YOU TAKE CARE OF YOURSELF OUT THERE!
TYLAN ...
...
...

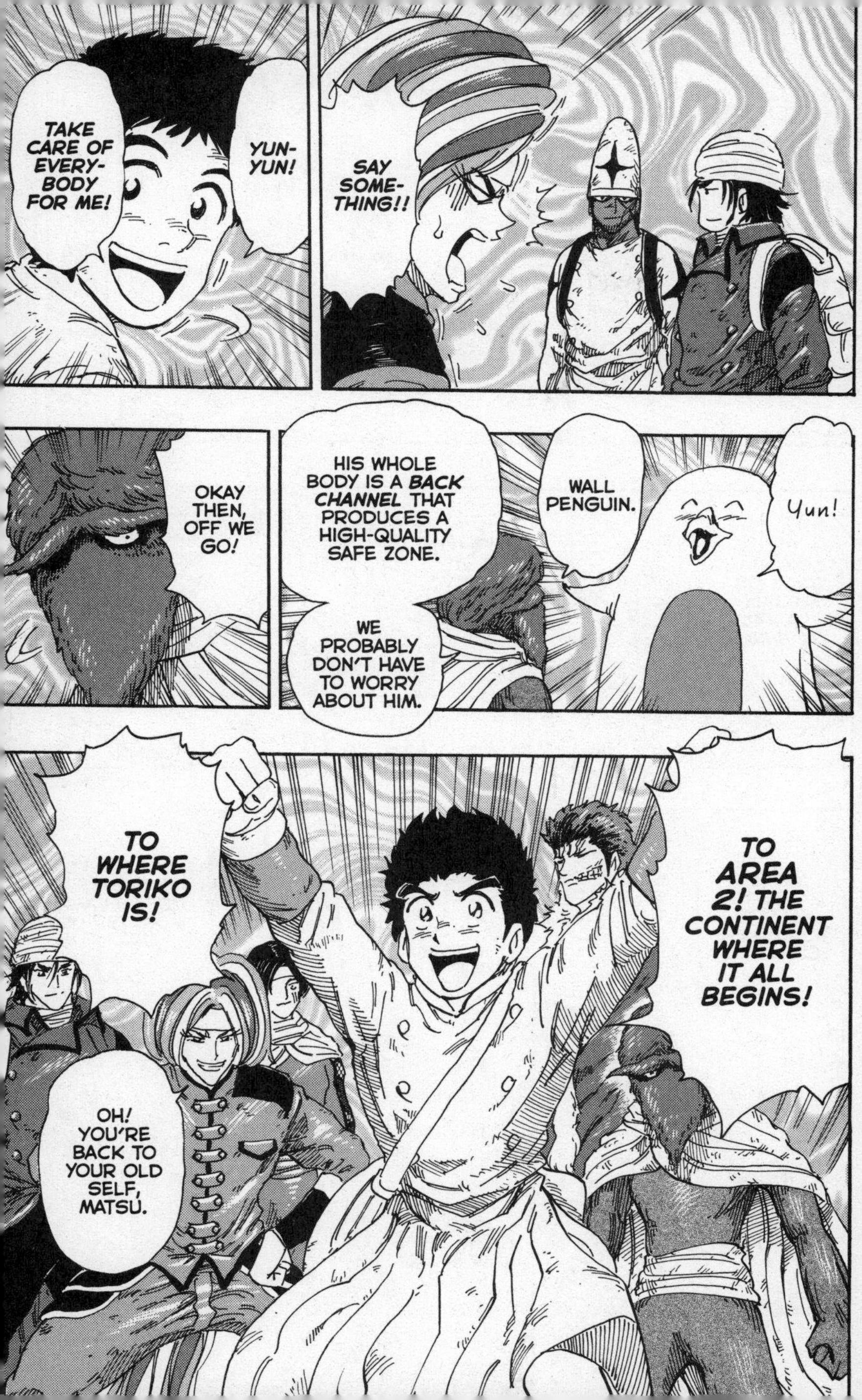
SAY SOMETHING!!
YUN-YUN!
TAKE CARE OF EVERYBODY FOR ME!
Yun!
WALL PENGUIN.
HIS WHOLE BODY IS A *BACK CHANNEL* THAT PRODUCES A HIGH-QUALITY SAFE ZONE.
WE PROBABLY DON'T HAVE TO WORRY ABOUT HIM.
OKAY THEN, OFF WE GO!
TO AREA 2! THE CONTINENT WHERE IT ALL BEGINS!
TO WHERE TORIKO IS!
OH! YOU'RE BACK TO YOUR OLD SELF, MATSU.

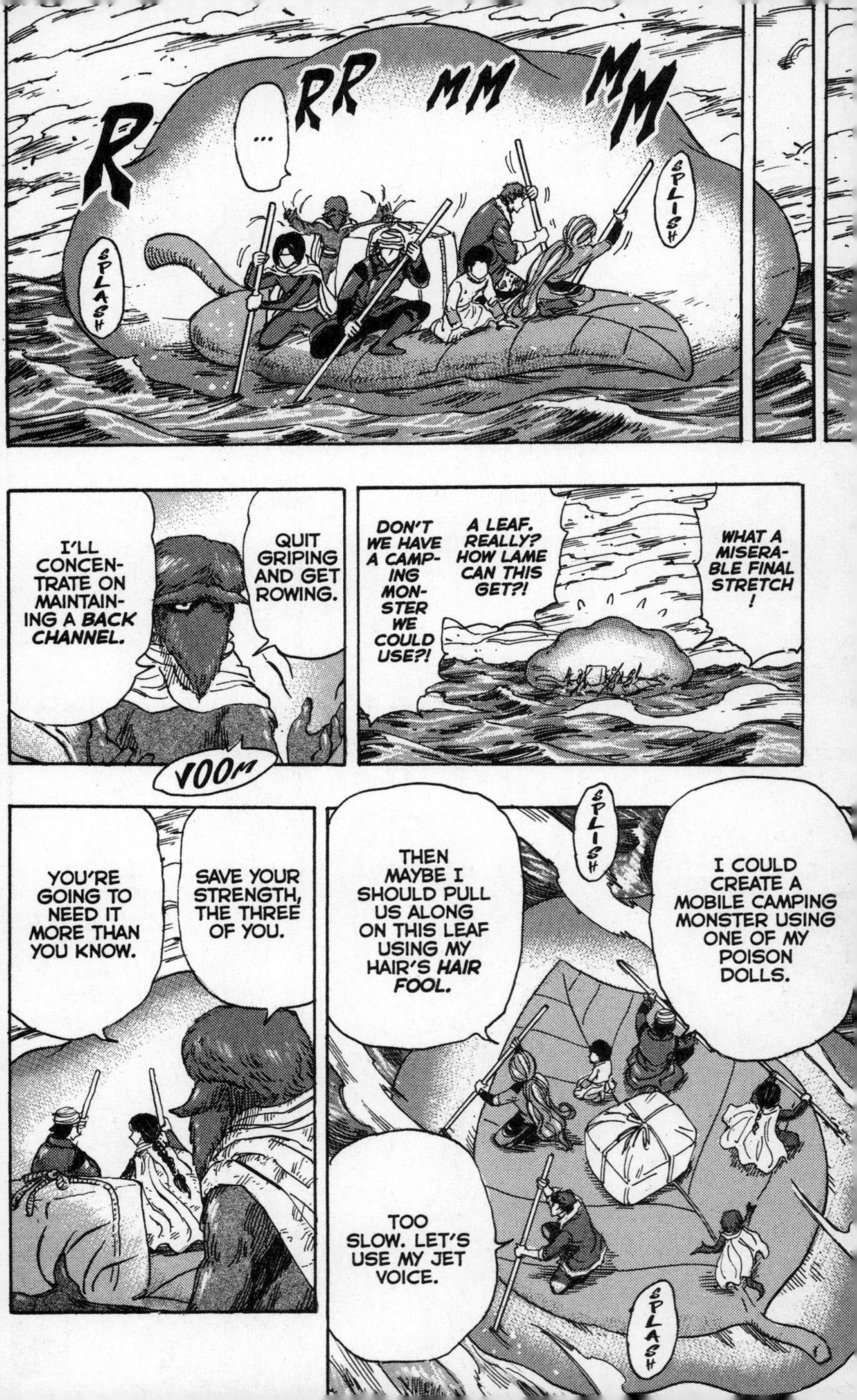
RRRMMMM
SPLISH
...
SPLASH
WHAT A MISERABLE FINAL STRETCH!
A LEAF. REALLY? HOW LAME CAN THIS GET?!
DON'T WE HAVE A CAMPING MONSTER WE COULD USE?!
QUIT GRIPING AND GET ROWING.
I'LL CONCENTRATE ON MAINTAINING A *BACK CHANNEL*.
VOOM
I COULD CREATE A MOBILE CAMPING MONSTER USING ONE OF MY POISON DOLLS.
SPLISH
THEN MAYBE I SHOULD PULL US ALONG ON THIS LEAF USING MY HAIR'S *HAIR FOOL*.
SPLASH
TOO SLOW. LET'S USE MY JET VOICE.
SAVE YOUR STRENGTH, THE THREE OF YOU.
YOU'RE GOING TO NEED IT MORE THAN YOU KNOW.

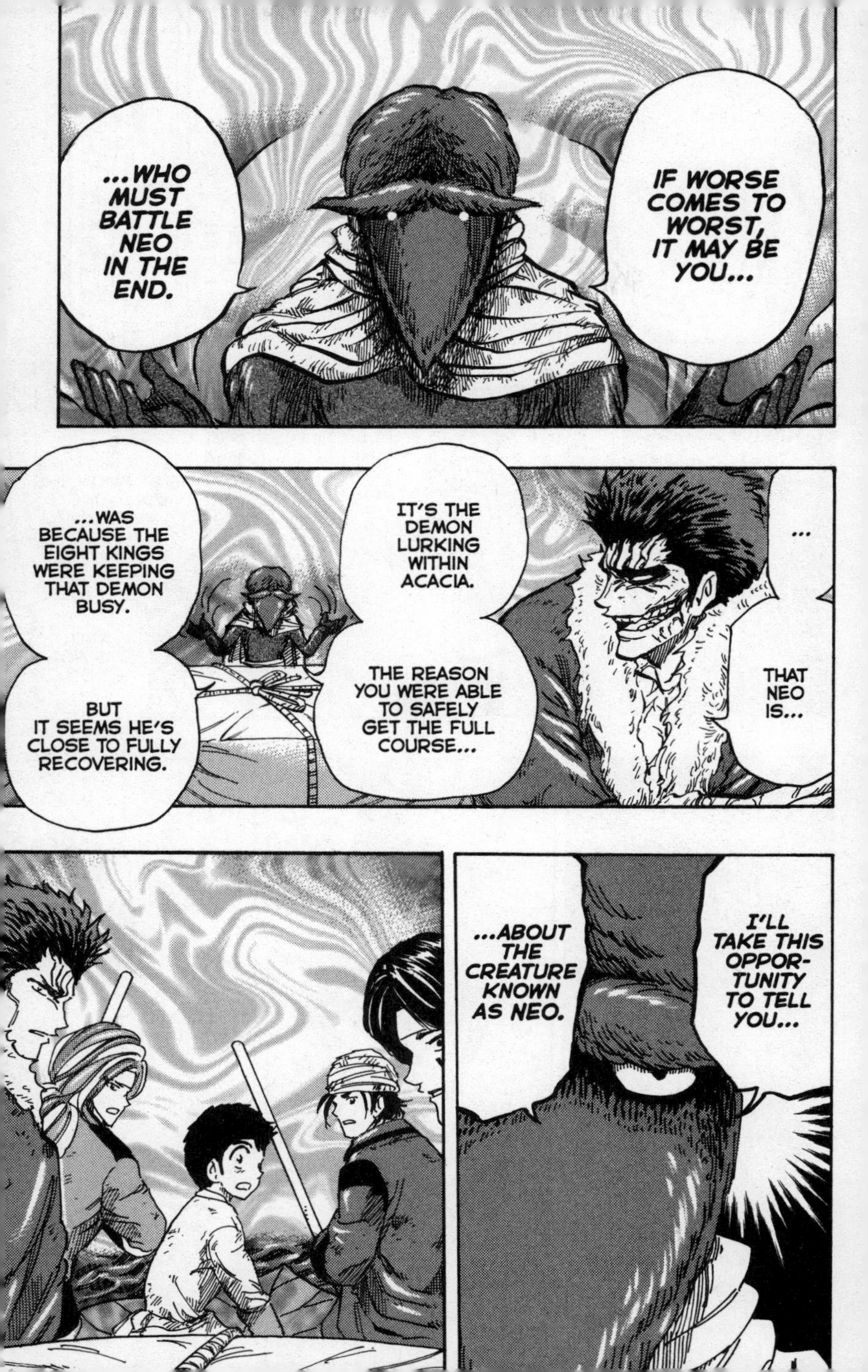
IF WORSE COMES TO WORST, IT MAY BE YOU...
...WHO MUST BATTLE NEO IN THE END.
...
THAT NEO IS...
IT'S THE DEMON LURKING WITHIN ACACIA.
THE REASON YOU WERE ABLE TO SAFELY GET THE FULL COURSE...
...WAS BECAUSE THE EIGHT KINGS WERE KEEPING THAT DEMON BUSY.
BUT IT SEEMS HE'S CLOSE TO FULLY RECOVERING.
I'LL TAKE THIS OPPORTUNITY TO TELL YOU...
...ABOUT THE CREATURE KNOWN AS NEO.

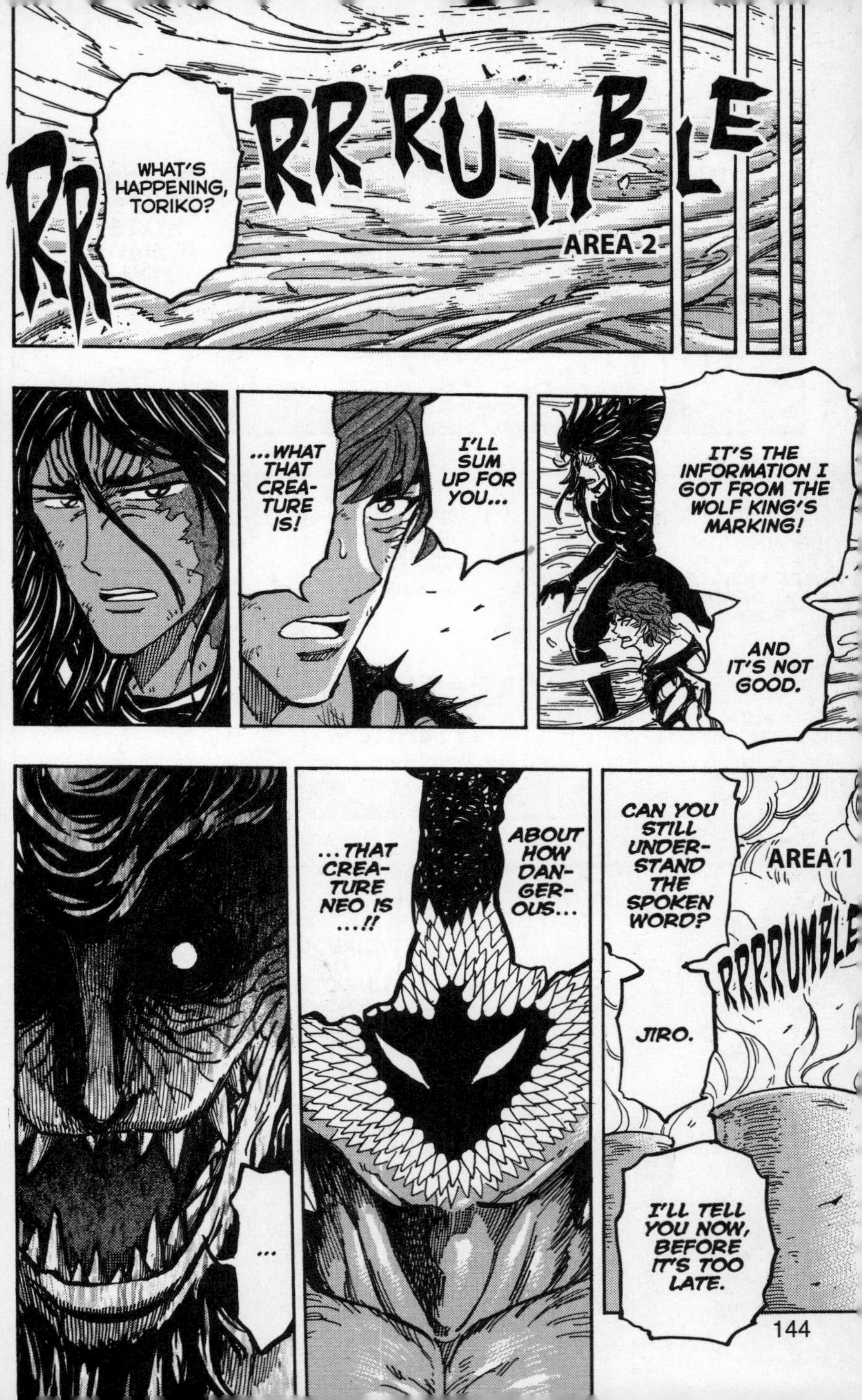

RRRRRUMBLE
WHAT'S HAPPENING, TORIKO?
AREA 2
IT'S THE INFORMATION I GOT FROM THE WOLF KING'S MARKING!
AND IT'S NOT GOOD.
I'LL SUM UP FOR YOU...
...WHAT THAT CREATURE IS!
AREA 1
RRRRUMBLE
CAN YOU STILL UNDERSTAND THE SPOKEN WORD?
JIRO.
I'LL TELL YOU NOW, BEFORE IT'S TOO LATE.
ABOUT HOW DANGEROUS...
...THAT CREATURE NEO IS...!!
...

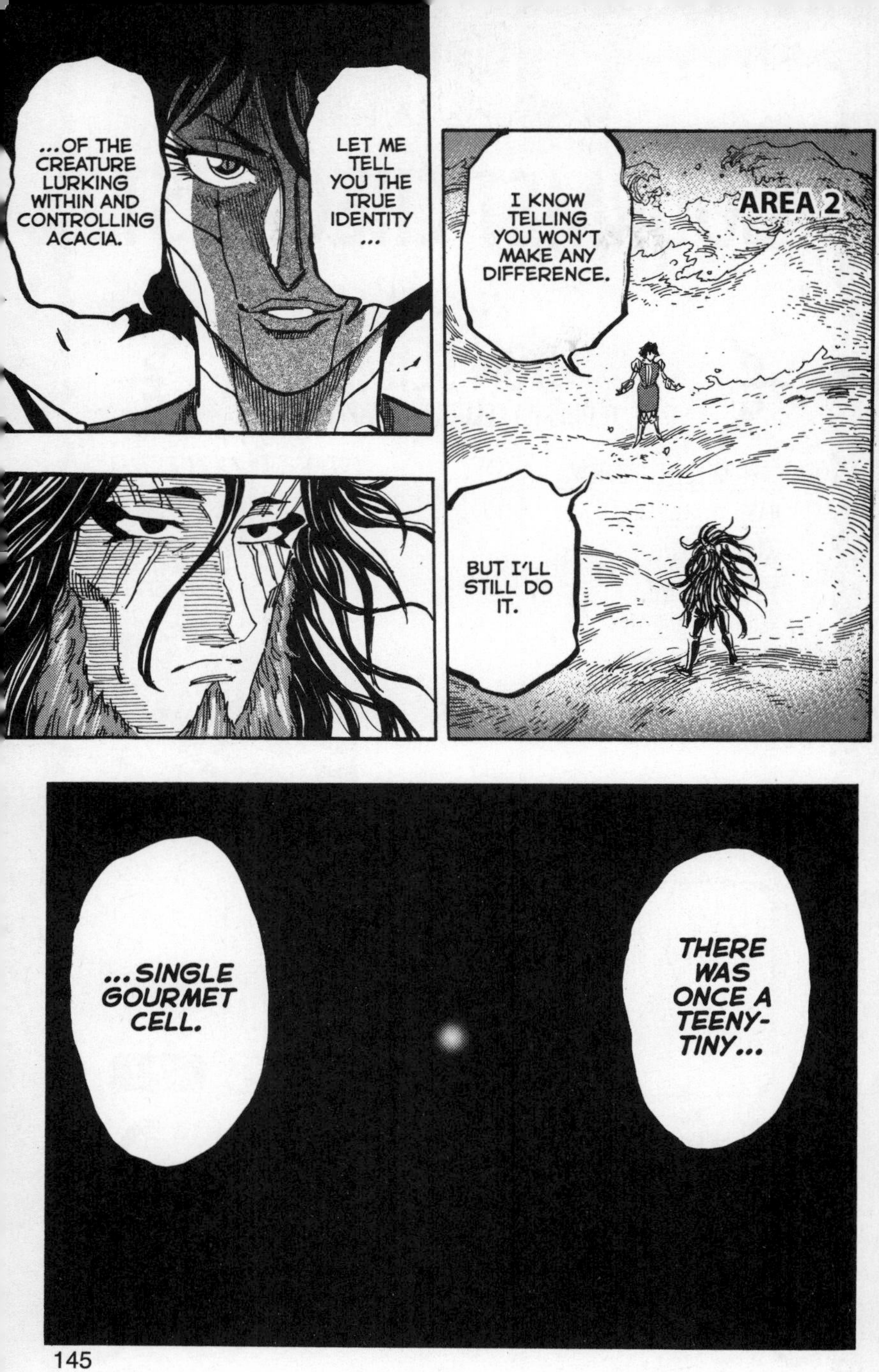
AREA 2
I KNOW TELLING YOU WON'T MAKE ANY DIFFERENCE.
BUT I'LL STILL DO IT.
LET ME TELL YOU THE TRUE IDENTITY ...
...OF THE CREATURE LURKING WITHIN AND CONTROLLING ACACIA.
THERE WAS ONCE A TEENY-TINY...
...SINGLE GOURMET CELL.

TORIKO

GOURMET CHECKLIST

Vol. 387

DON SLIME

(GOURMET CELL DEMON/APPETITE)

CAPTURE LEVEL: UNKNOWN
HABITAT: BLUE GRILL (CURRENTLY)
SIZE: UNKNOWN
HEIGHT: UNKNOWN
WEIGHT: UNKNOWN
PRICE: UNKNOWN

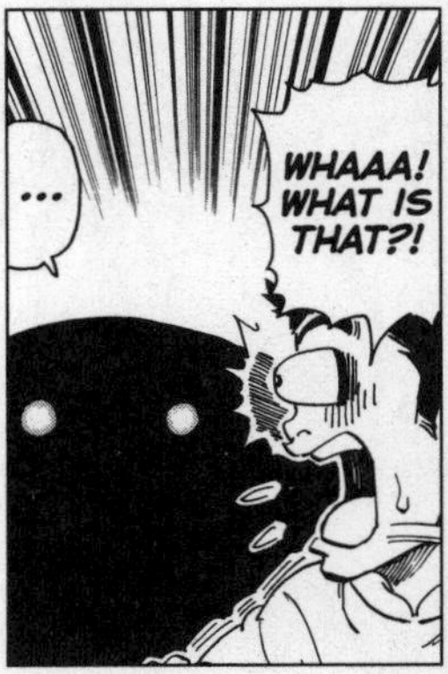
WHAAA! WHAT IS THAT?!
...

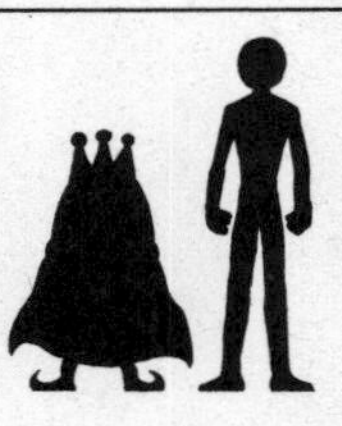

SCALE

THE KING OF THE DEEP-SEA GOURMET CIVILIZATION BLUE GRILL IN AREA 6, AND CURRENTLY A FOOD SPIRIT. THERE ARE MANY INHABITANTS WHO HAVE NEVER SEEN HIM, BUT HE IS UNDOUBTEDLY THE SYMBOL OF BLUE GRILL'S CIVILIZATION AND RECOGNIZED AS THE KING BY ALL HIS SUBJECTS. HE USED TO BE ICHIRYU'S GOURMET CELL DEMON, AND HE'S A TRANSCENDENT BEING WHO'S EVEN NICKNAMED HIMSELF A NATURAL DISASTER FULL OF EVIL INTENT. HIS SUPERIOR ABILITIES MAKE IT SO THAT HE'S SAID TO BE THE ONLY BEING ABLE TO CONTEND WITH A FULLY REVIVED ACACIA.

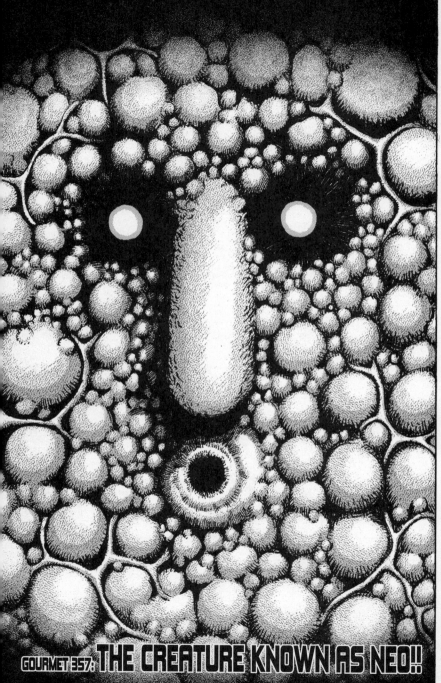

GOURMET 357: THE CREATURE KNOWN AS NEO!!

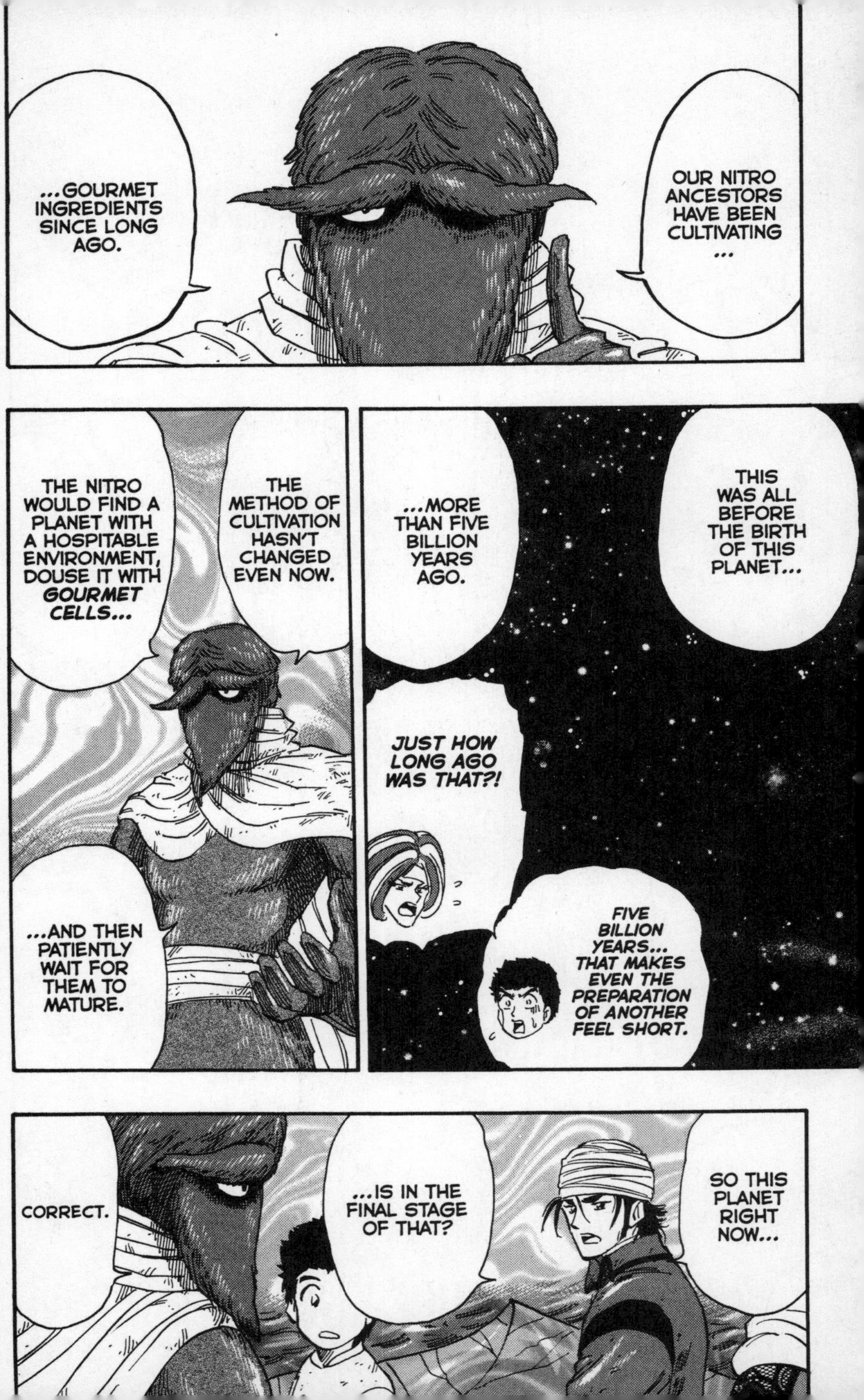
OUR NITRO ANCESTORS HAVE BEEN CULTIVATING ...
...GOURMET INGREDIENTS SINCE LONG AGO.
THIS WAS ALL BEFORE THE BIRTH OF THIS PLANET...
...MORE THAN FIVE BILLION YEARS AGO.
JUST HOW LONG AGO WAS THAT?!
FIVE BILLION YEARS... THAT MAKES EVEN THE PREPARATION OF ANOTHER FEEL SHORT.
THE METHOD OF CULTIVATION HASN'T CHANGED EVEN NOW.
THE NITRO WOULD FIND A PLANET WITH A HOSPITABLE ENVIRONMENT, DOUSE IT WITH *GOURMET CELLS...*
...AND THEN PATIENTLY WAIT FOR THEM TO MATURE.
SO THIS PLANET RIGHT NOW...
...IS IN THE FINAL STAGE OF THAT?
CORRECT.

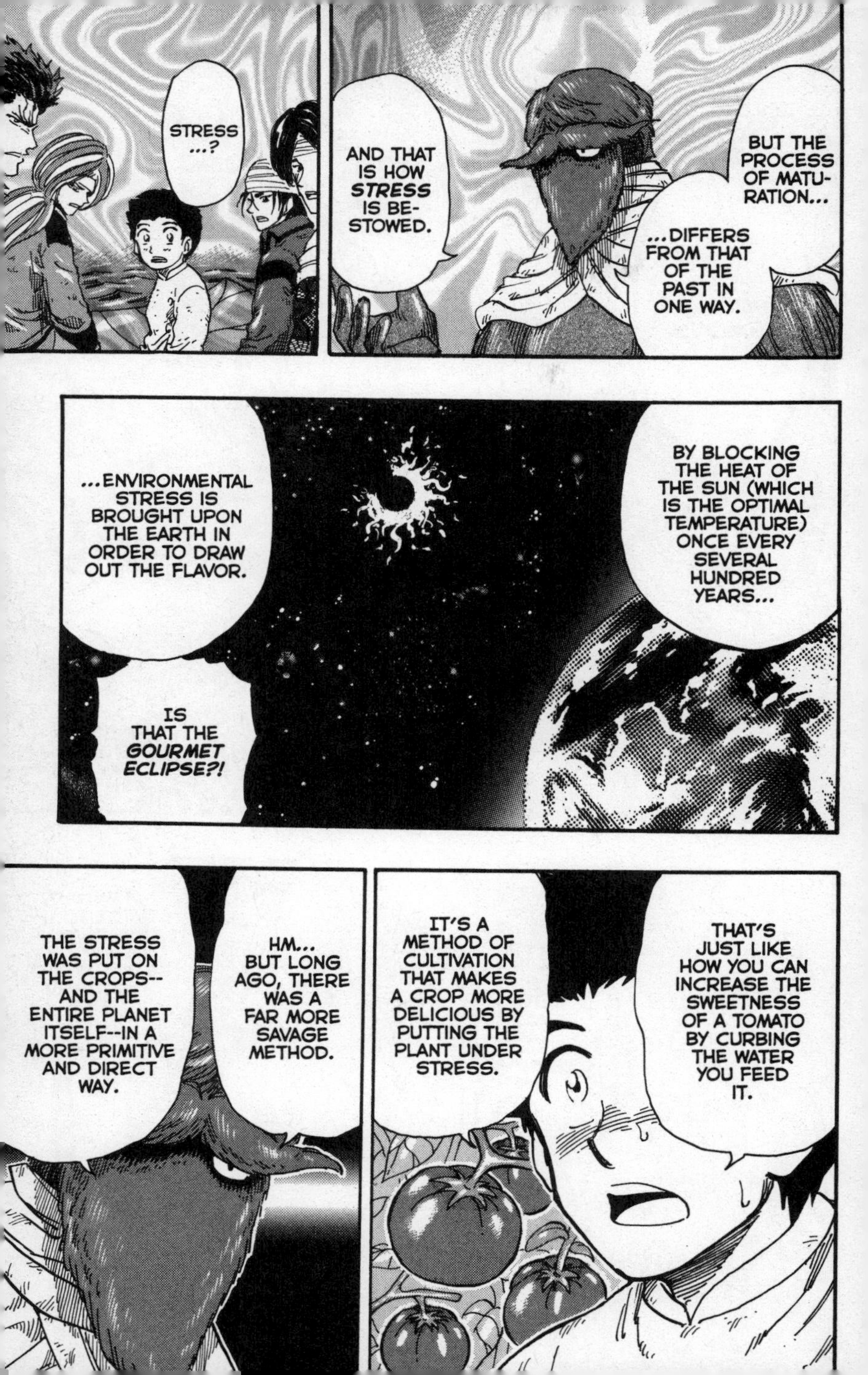
BUT THE PROCESS OF MATU- RATION...
...DIFFERS FROM THAT OF THE PAST IN ONE WAY.
AND THAT IS HOW *STRESS* IS BE- STOWED.
STRESS ...?
BY BLOCKING THE HEAT OF THE SUN (WHICH IS THE OPTIMAL TEMPERATURE) ONCE EVERY SEVERAL HUNDRED YEARS...
...ENVIRONMENTAL STRESS IS BROUGHT UPON THE EARTH IN ORDER TO DRAW OUT THE FLAVOR.
IS THAT THE *GOURMET ECLIPSE?!*
THAT'S JUST LIKE HOW YOU CAN INCREASE THE SWEETNESS OF A TOMATO BY CURBING THE WATER YOU FEED IT.
IT'S A METHOD OF CULTIVATION THAT MAKES A CROP MORE DELICIOUS BY PUTTING THE PLANT UNDER STRESS.
HM... BUT LONG AGO, THERE WAS A FAR MORE SAVAGE METHOD.
THE STRESS WAS PUT ON THE CROPS-- AND THE ENTIRE PLANET ITSELF--IN A MORE PRIMITIVE AND DIRECT WAY.

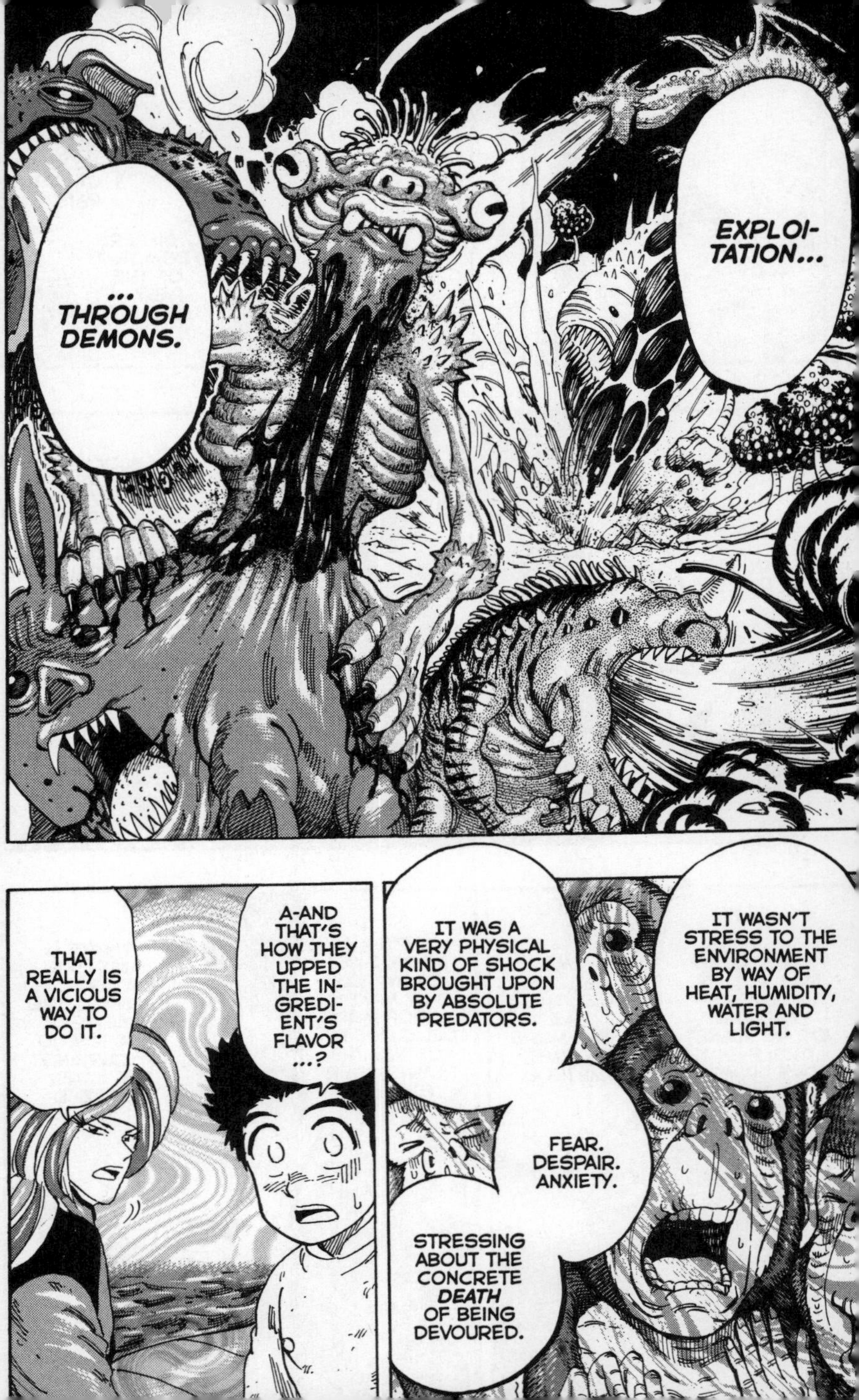
EXPLOITATION...
...THROUGH DEMONS.
IT WASN'T STRESS TO THE ENVIRONMENT BY WAY OF HEAT, HUMIDITY, WATER AND LIGHT.
IT WAS A VERY PHYSICAL KIND OF SHOCK BROUGHT UPON BY ABSOLUTE PREDATORS.
FEAR. DESPAIR. ANXIETY.
STRESSING ABOUT THE CONCRETE *DEATH* OF BEING DEVOURED.
A-AND THAT'S HOW THEY UPPED THE INGREDIENT'S FLAVOR ...?
THAT REALLY IS A VICIOUS WAY TO DO IT.

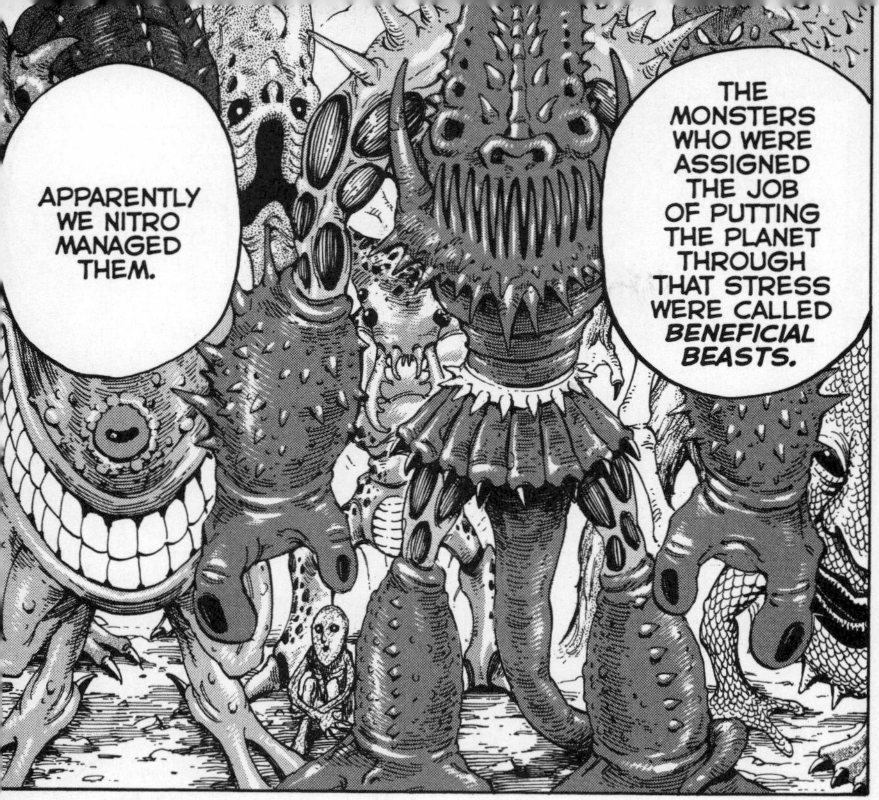
THE MONSTERS WHO WERE ASSIGNED THE JOB OF PUTTING THE PLANET THROUGH THAT STRESS WERE CALLED *BENEFICIAL BEASTS.*
APPARENTLY WE NITRO MANAGED THEM.

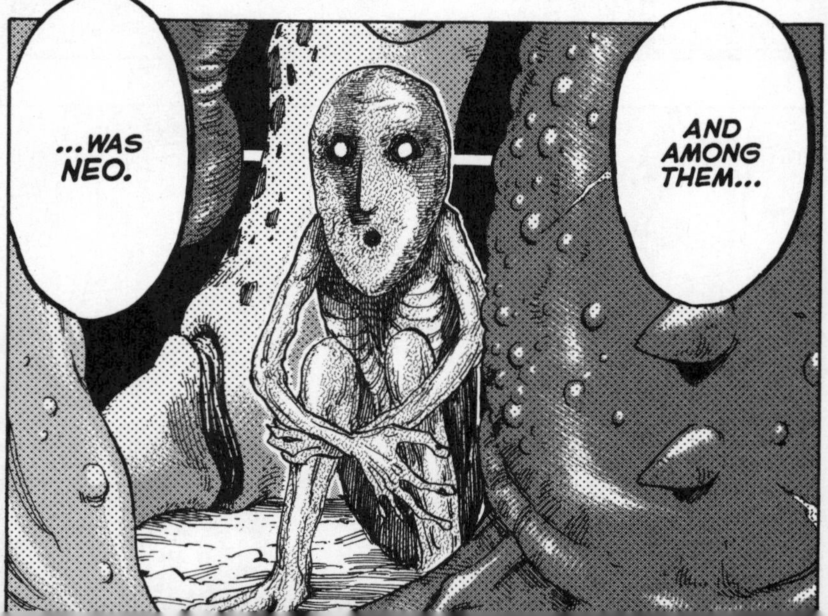
AND AMONG THEM...
...WAS NEO.

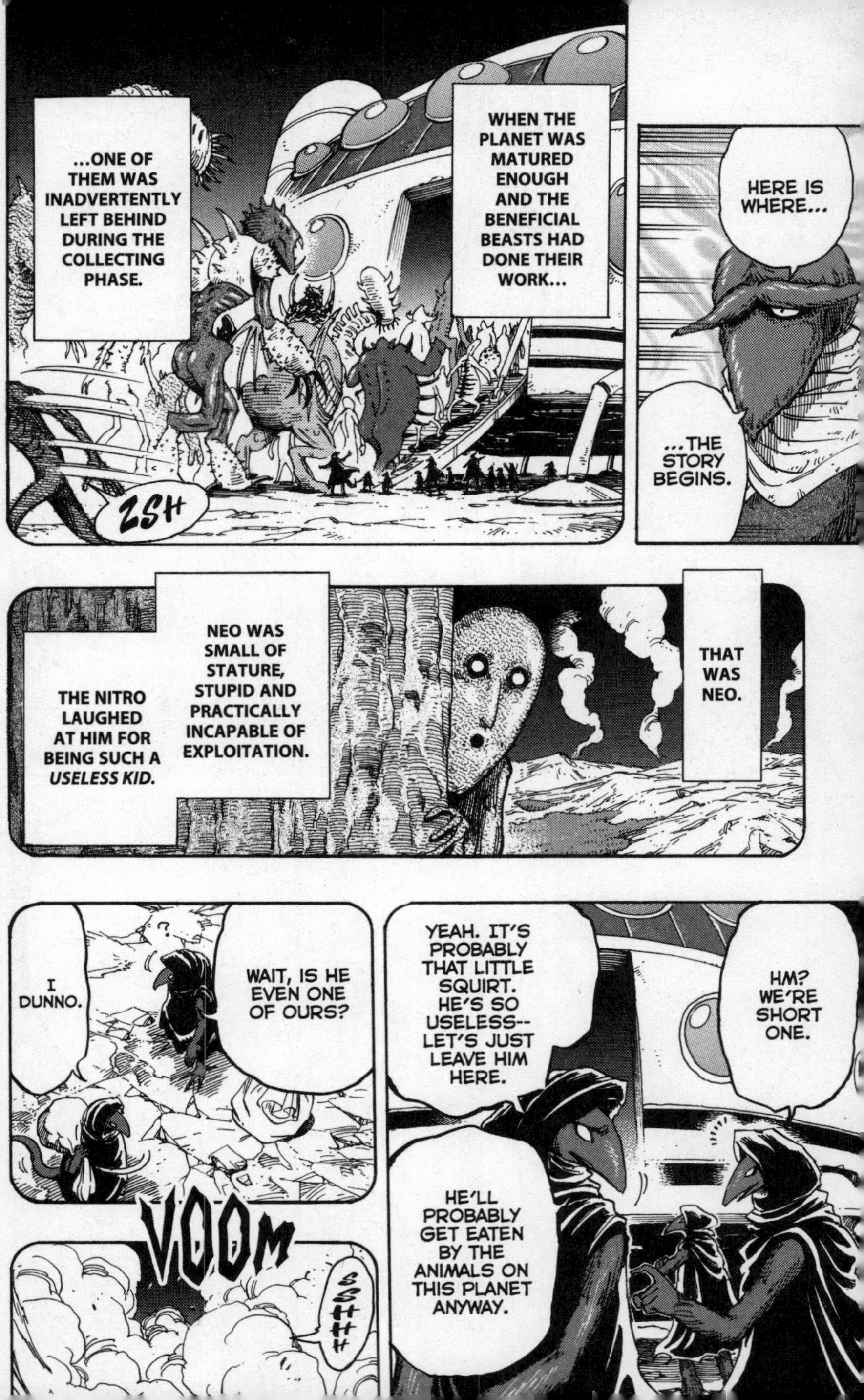
HERE IS WHERE...
...THE STORY BEGINS.
WHEN THE PLANET WAS MATURED ENOUGH AND THE BENEFICIAL BEASTS HAD DONE THEIR WORK...
...ONE OF THEM WAS INADVERTENTLY LEFT BEHIND DURING THE COLLECTING PHASE.
ZSH
THAT WAS NEO.
NEO WAS SMALL OF STATURE, STUPID AND PRACTICALLY INCAPABLE OF EXPLOITATION.
THE NITRO LAUGHED AT HIM FOR BEING SUCH A *USELESS KID.*
HM? WE'RE SHORT ONE.
YEAH. IT'S PROBABLY THAT LITTLE SQUIRT. HE'S SO USELESS-- LET'S JUST LEAVE HIM HERE.
HE'LL PROBABLY GET EATEN BY THE ANIMALS ON THIS PLANET ANYWAY.
WAIT, IS HE EVEN ONE OF OURS?
I DUNNO.
VOOM
SSHHH

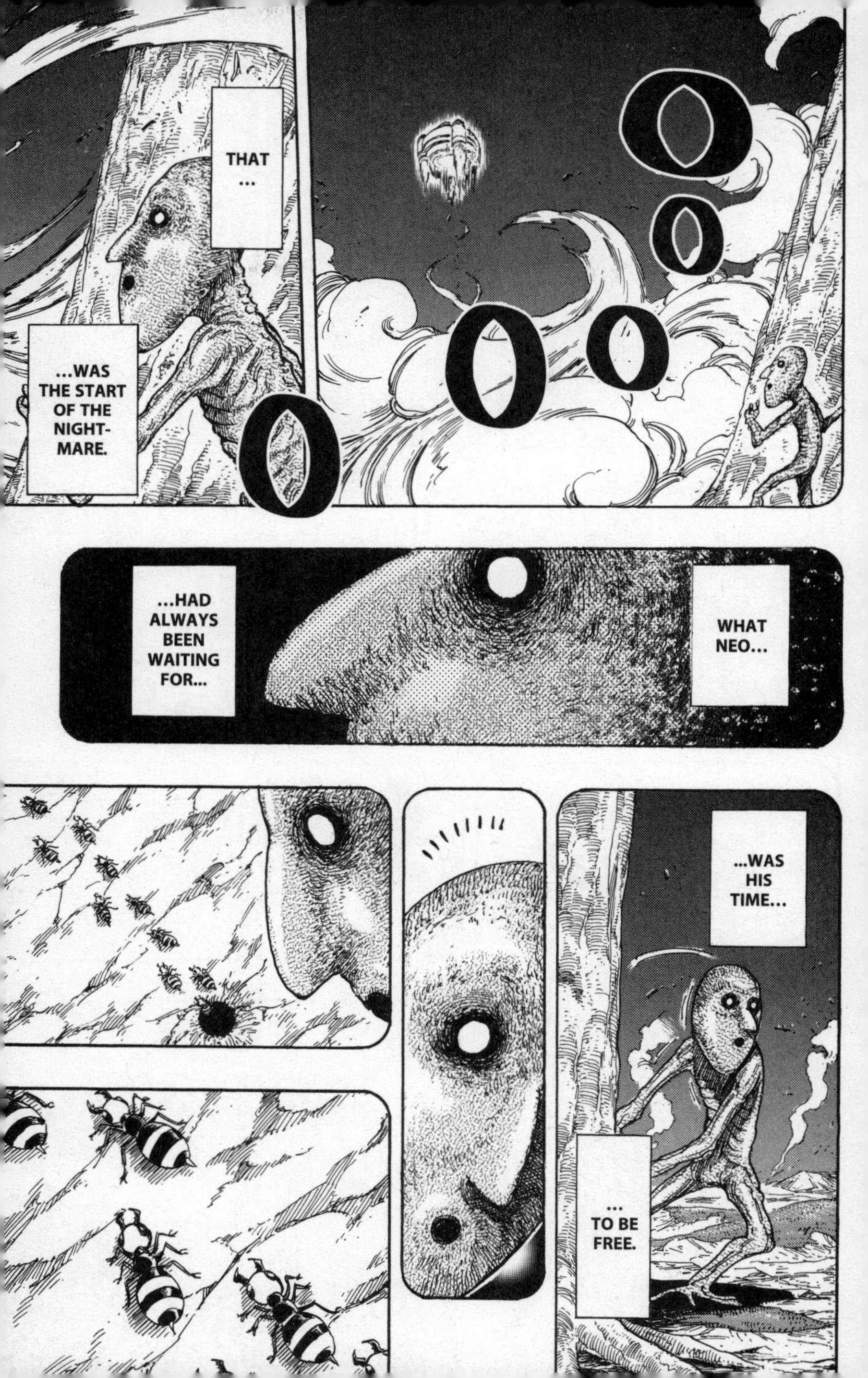
THAT ...
...WAS THE START OF THE NIGHT-MARE.
WHAT NEO...
...HAD ALWAYS BEEN WAITING FOR...
...WAS HIS TIME...
... TO BE FREE.

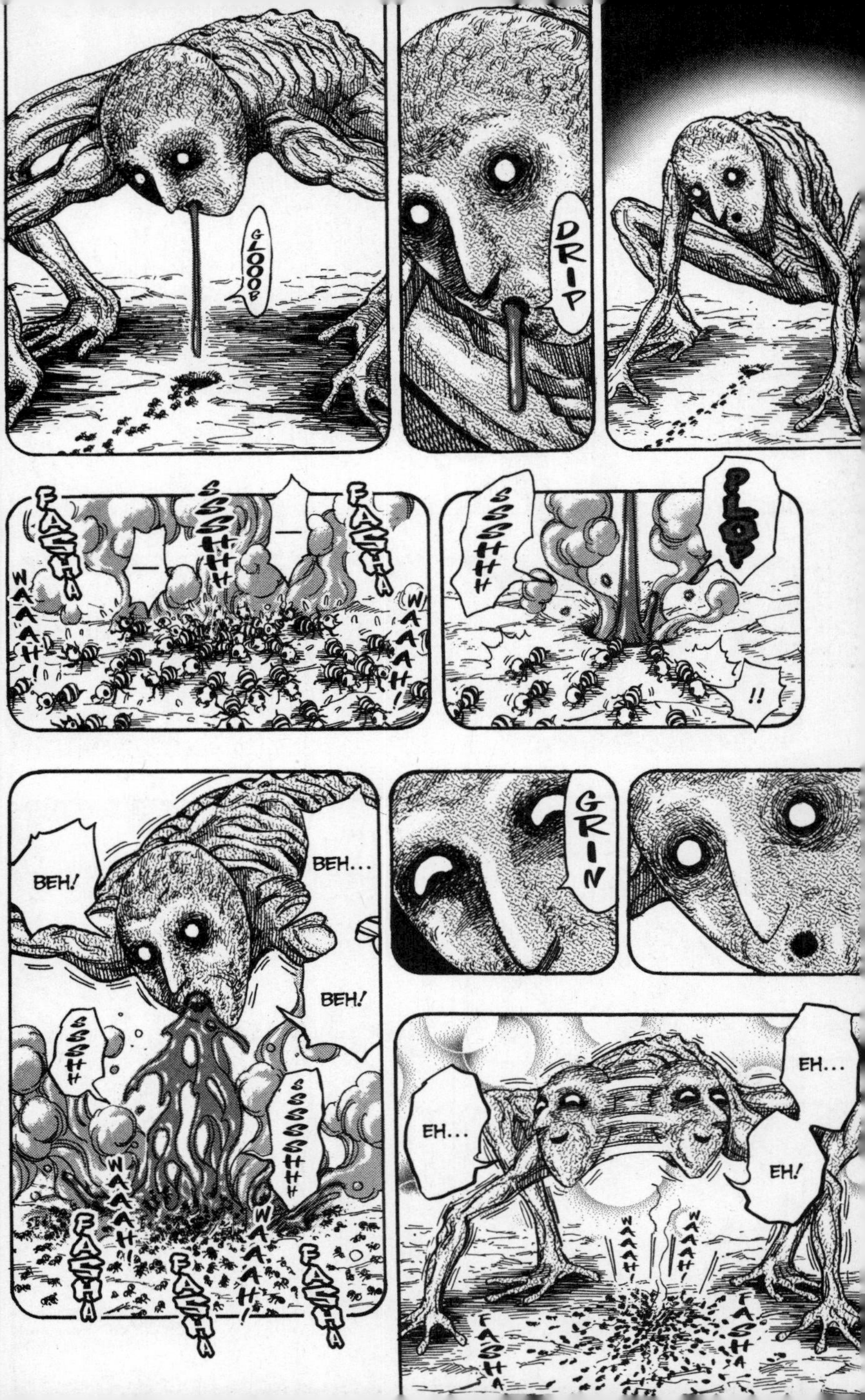
DRIP
GLOOOB
PLOP
SSSHHH
!!
FASHA
SSSHHH
WAAAAH!
FASHA
WAAAAH!
GRIN
EH...
EH!
EH...
WAAAAH!
WAAAAH!
FASHA
FASHA
BEH...
BEH!
BEH!
SSSSSHHH
SSSHH
WAAAAH!
FASHA
FASHA
WAAAAH!
FASHA

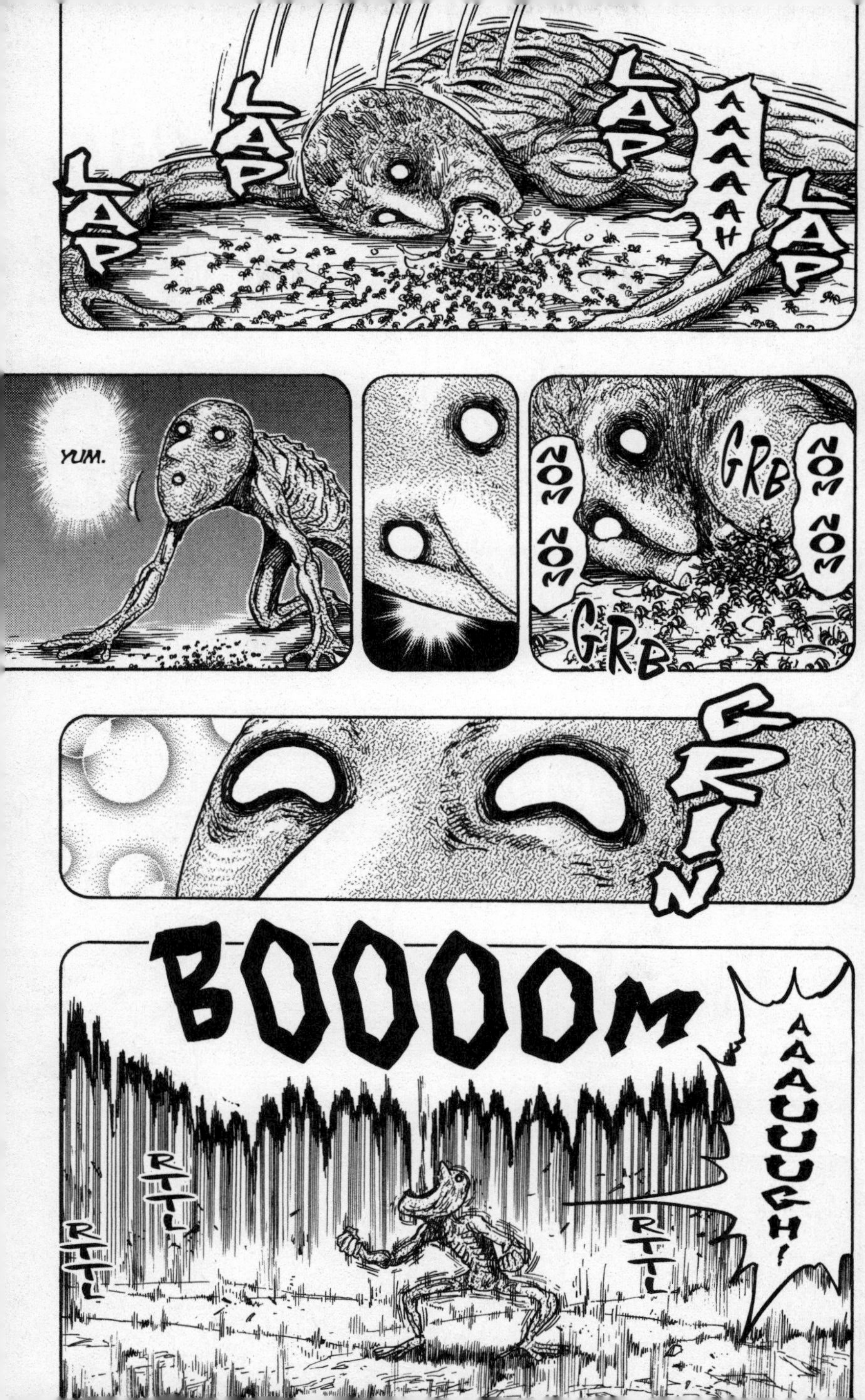
LAP
AAAAAAH
LAP
LAP
LAP
NOM NOM
GRB
NOM NOM
GRB
YUM.
GRIN
BOOOOM
AAAUUUGH!
RTTL
RTTL
RTTL

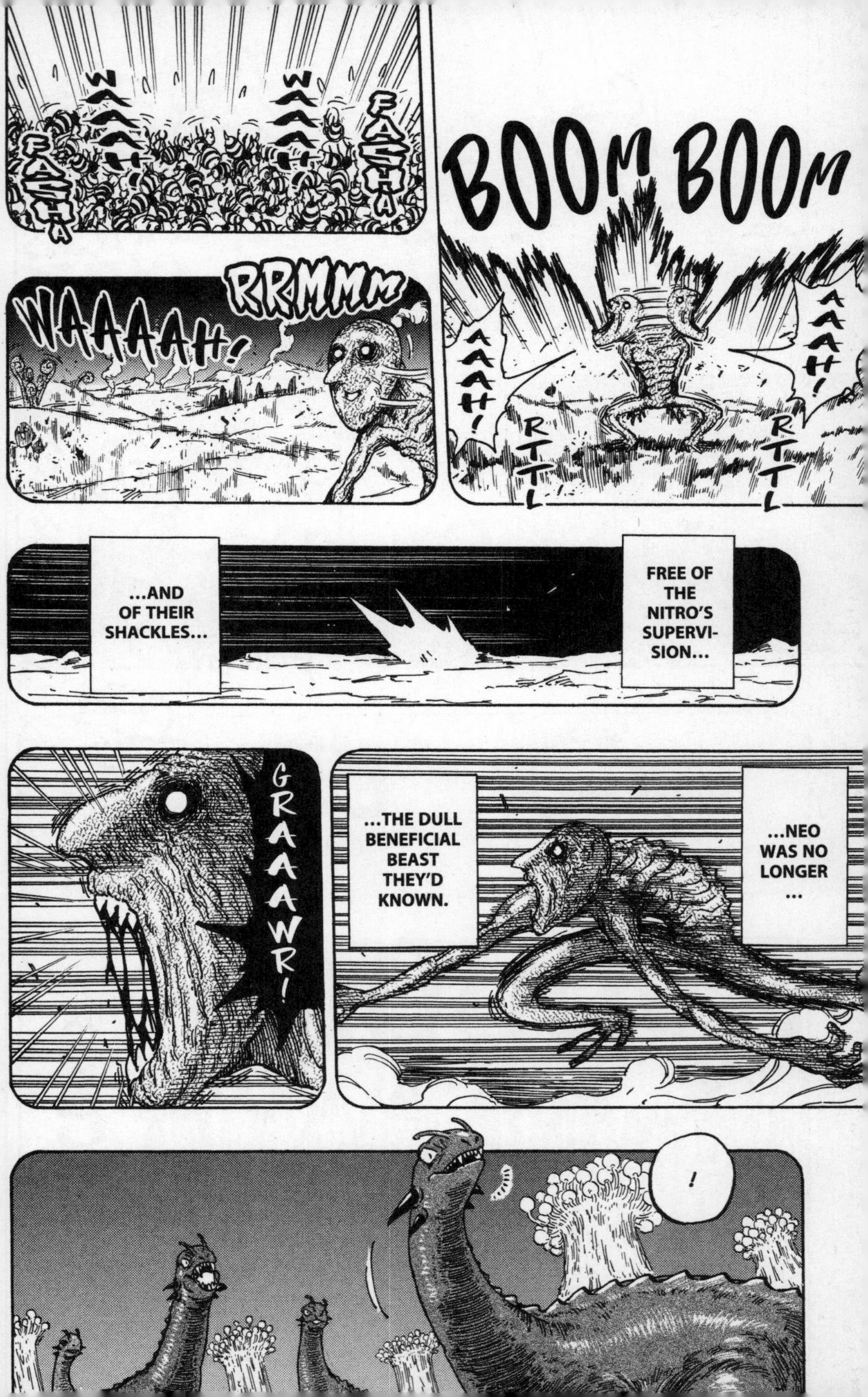
BOOM BOOM
AAAAH!
RTTL
AAAAH!
RTTL
FASHA
WAAAH
WAAAH
FASHA
RRMMM
WAAAAAH!
FREE OF THE NITRO'S SUPERVI-SION...
...AND OF THEIR SHACKLES...
...NEO WAS NO LONGER ...
...THE DULL BENEFICIAL BEAST THEY'D KNOWN.
GRAAAAWR!
!

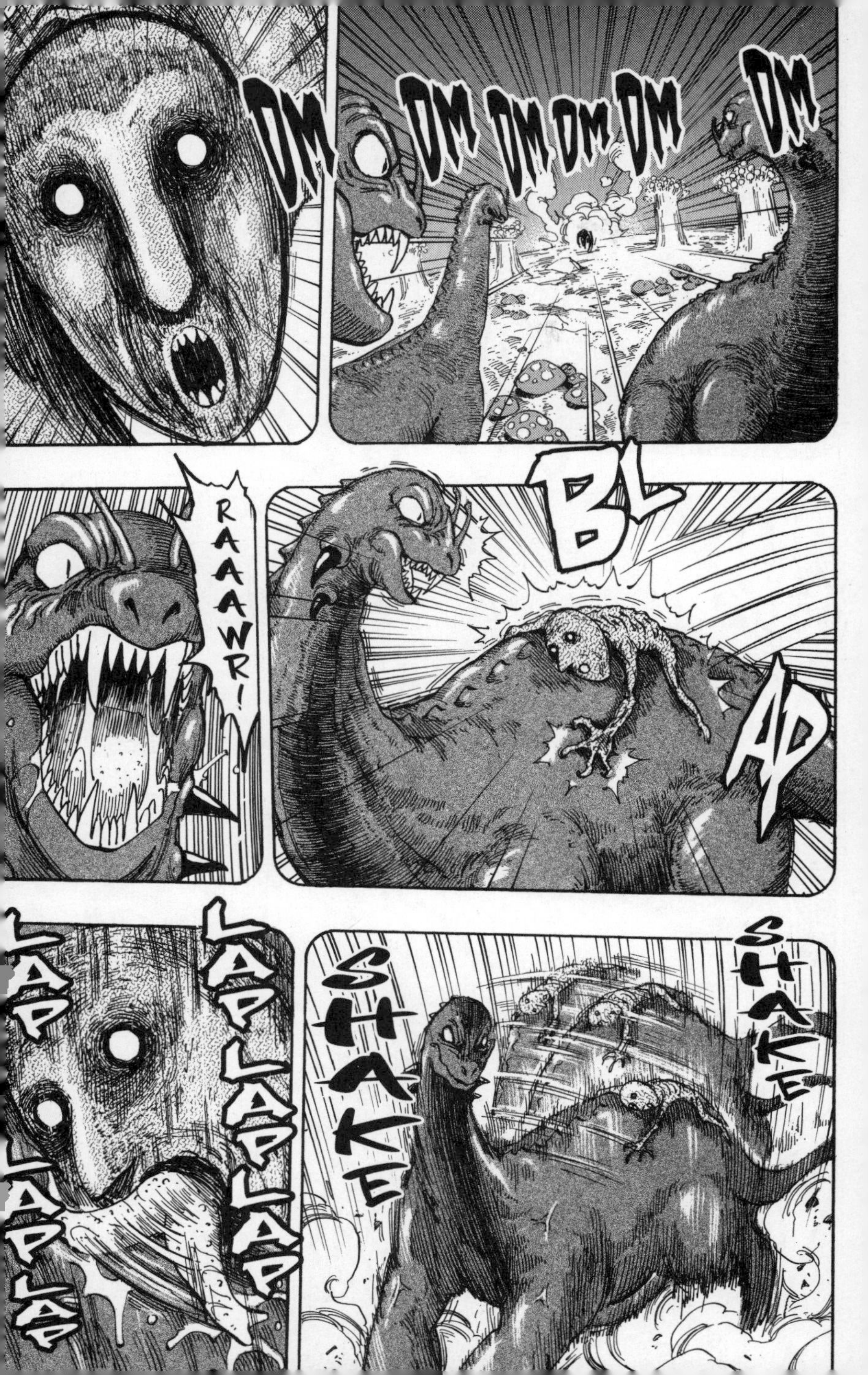
DM DM DM DM DM DM
DM
BL
AP
RAAAAWR!
SHAKE
SHAKE
LAPLAPLAPLAP

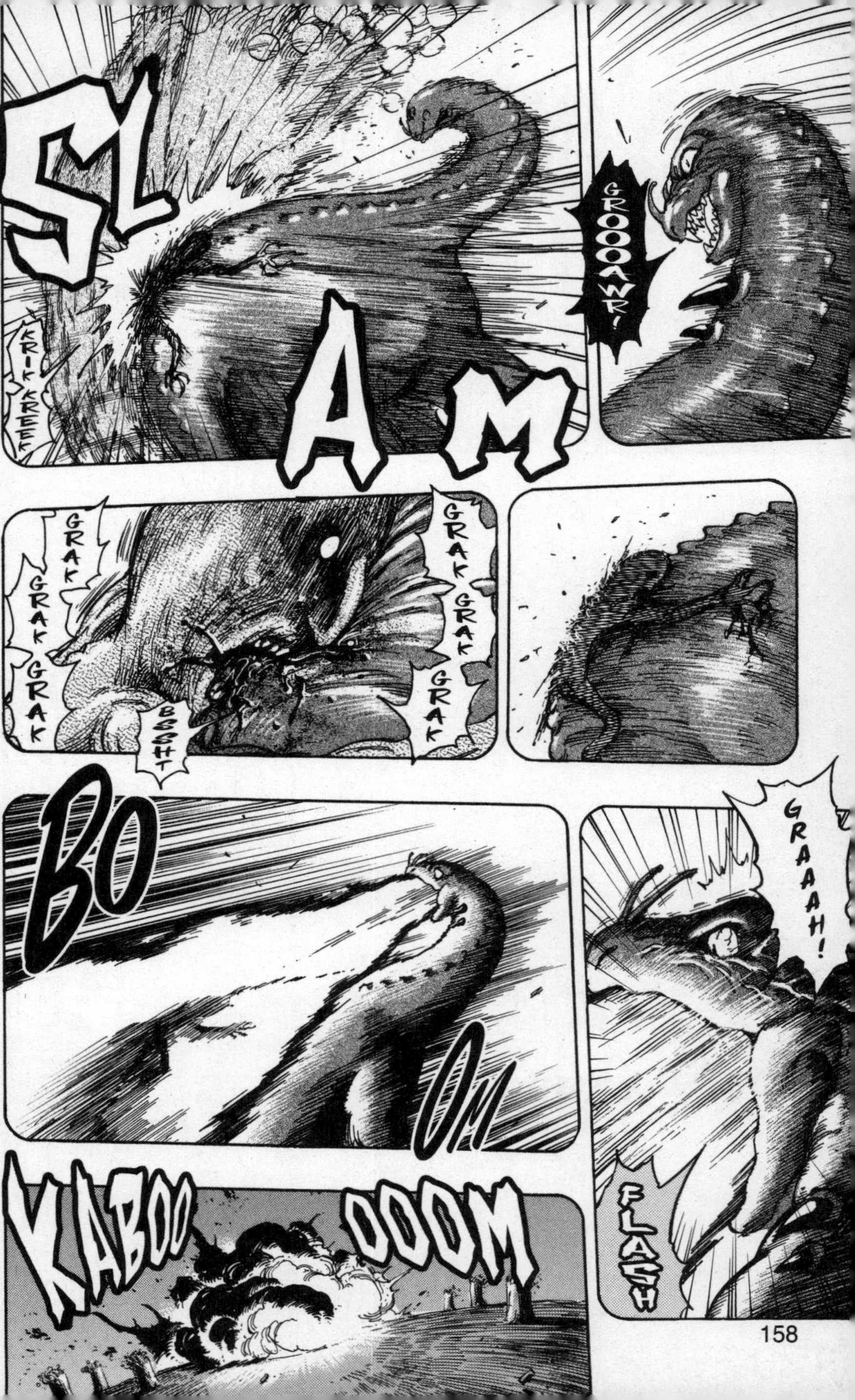
GROOOAWR!
SLAM
KRIK KREEK
GRAK GRAK GRAK
BSSHT
GRAK GRAK GRAK
GRAAAAH!
FLASH
BOOM
KABOOOOOM

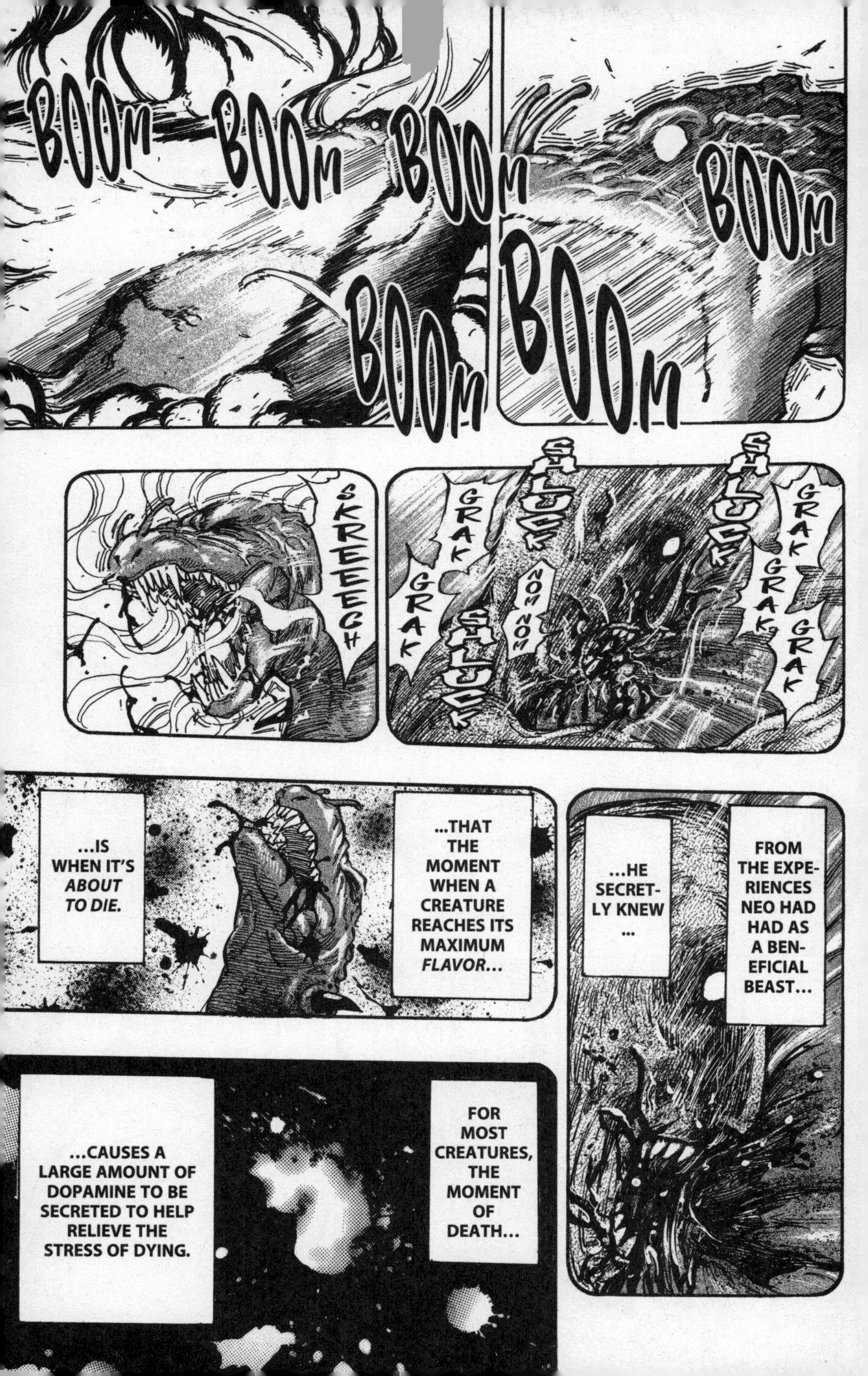
BOOM
BOOM
BOOM
BOOM
BOOM
BOOM
SHLUCK
GRAK GRAK
SHLUCK
GRAK GRAK GRAK
NOM NOM
SHLUCK
GRAK GRAK
SKREEEECH
FROM THE EXPE-RIENCES NEO HAD HAD AS A BEN-EFICIAL BEAST...
...HE SECRET-LY KNEW...
...THAT THE MOMENT WHEN A CREATURE REACHES ITS MAXIMUM *FLAVOR*...
...IS WHEN IT'S *ABOUT TO DIE.*
FOR MOST CREATURES, THE MOMENT OF DEATH...
...CAUSES A LARGE AMOUNT OF DOPAMINE TO BE SECRETED TO HELP RELIEVE THE STRESS OF DYING.

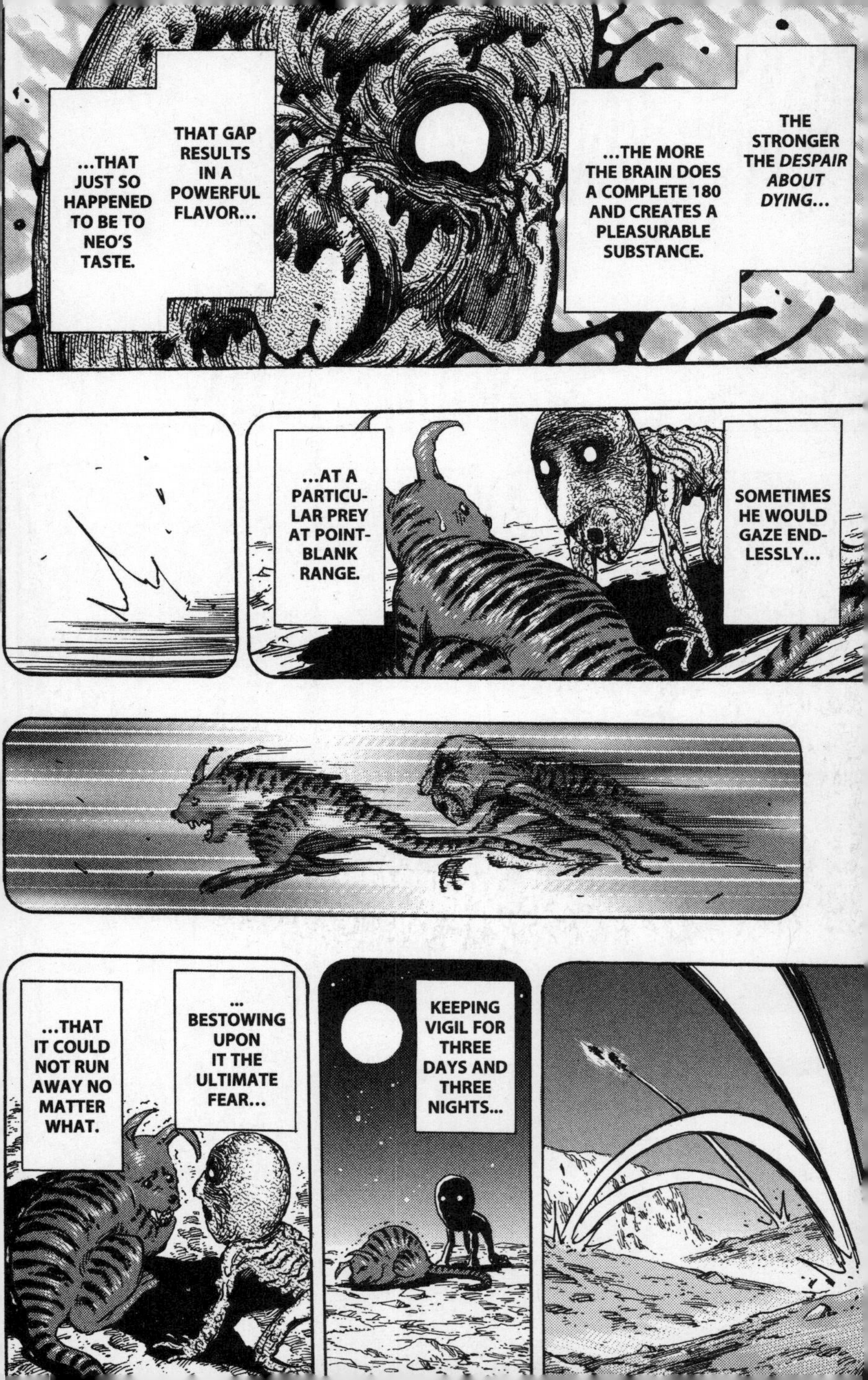
THE STRONGER THE *DESPAIR ABOUT DYING*...
...THE MORE THE BRAIN DOES A COMPLETE 180 AND CREATES A PLEASURABLE SUBSTANCE.
THAT GAP RESULTS IN A POWERFUL FLAVOR...
...THAT JUST SO HAPPENED TO BE TO NEO'S TASTE.
SOMETIMES HE WOULD GAZE ENDLESSLY...
...AT A PARTICULAR PREY AT POINT-BLANK RANGE.
KEEPING VIGIL FOR THREE DAYS AND THREE NIGHTS...
... BESTOWING UPON IT THE ULTIMATE FEAR...
...THAT IT COULD NOT RUN AWAY NO MATTER WHAT.

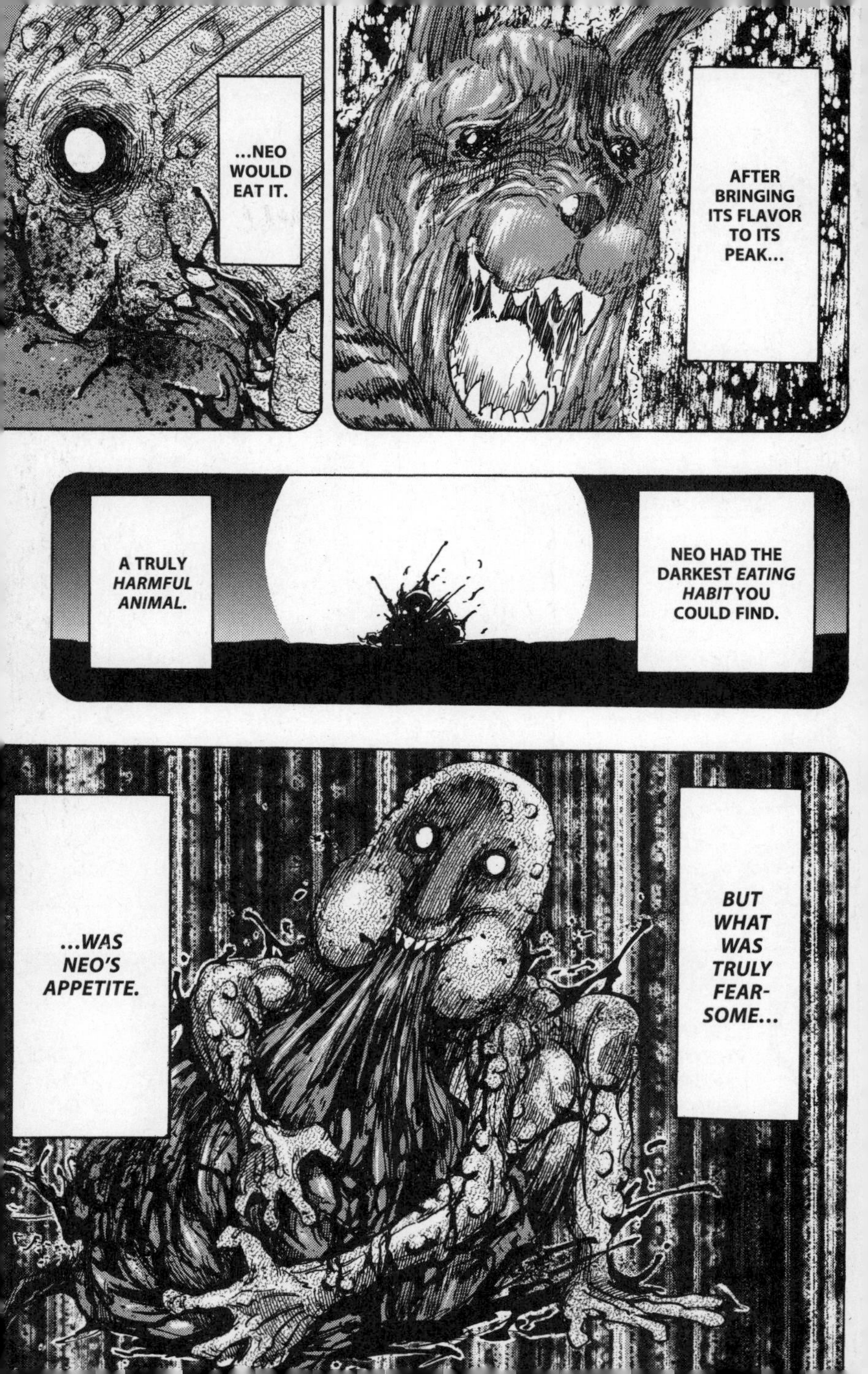
AFTER BRINGING ITS FLAVOR TO ITS PEAK...
...NEO WOULD EAT IT.
NEO HAD THE DARKEST *EATING HABIT* YOU COULD FIND.
A TRULY *HARMFUL ANIMAL.*
BUT WHAT WAS TRULY FEAR-SOME...
...WAS NEO'S APPETITE.

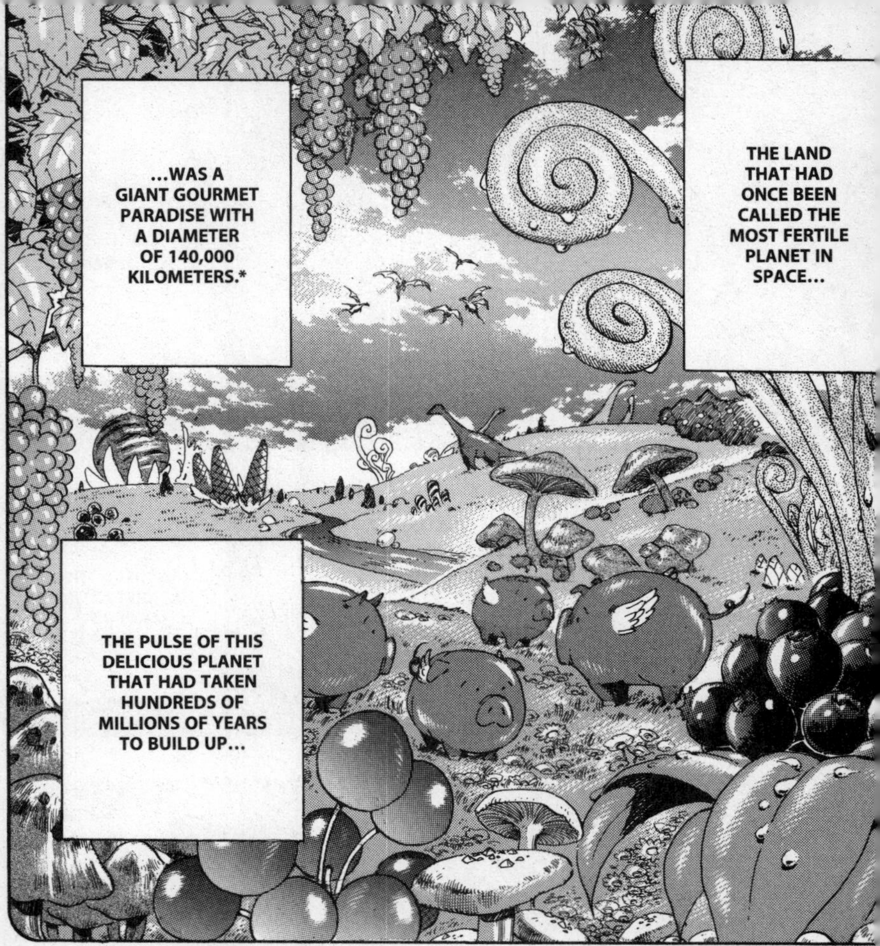
THE LAND THAT HAD ONCE BEEN CALLED THE MOST FERTILE PLANET IN SPACE...
...WAS A GIANT GOURMET PARADISE WITH A DIAMETER OF 140,000 KILOMETERS.*
THE PULSE OF THIS DELICIOUS PLANET THAT HAD TAKEN HUNDREDS OF MILLIONS OF YEARS TO BUILD UP...

*ALMOST THE SAME SIZE AS JUPITER.

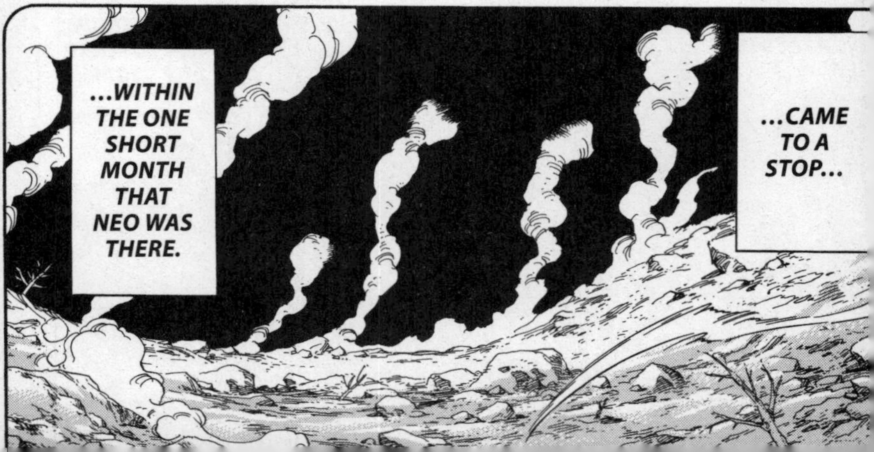
...CAME TO A STOP...
...WITHIN THE ONE SHORT MONTH THAT NEO WAS THERE.

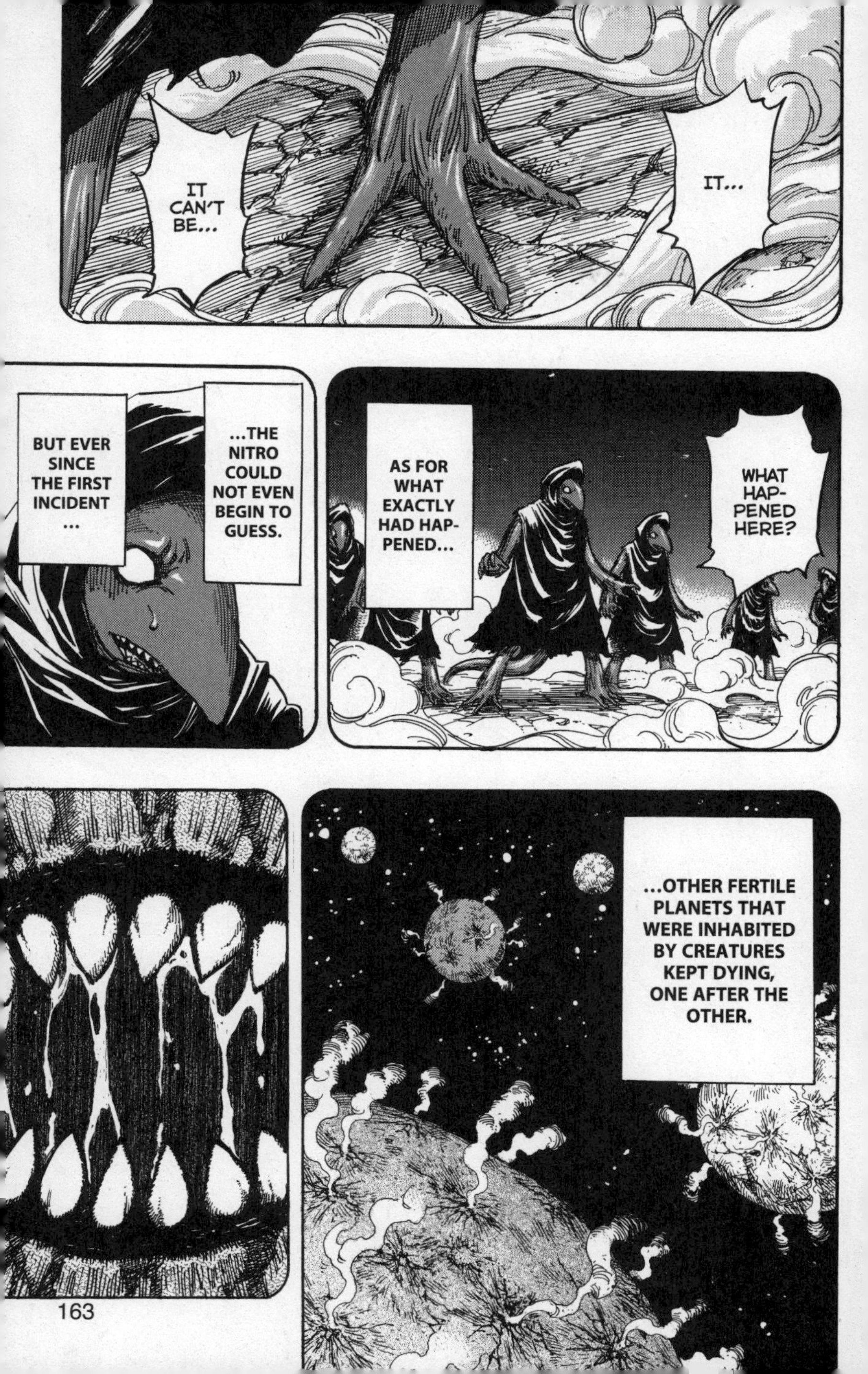
IT...
IT CAN'T BE...
WHAT HAP-PENED HERE?
AS FOR WHAT EXACTLY HAD HAP-PENED...
...THE NITRO COULD NOT EVEN BEGIN TO GUESS.
BUT EVER SINCE THE FIRST INCIDENT ...
...OTHER FERTILE PLANETS THAT WERE INHABITED BY CREATURES KEPT DYING, ONE AFTER THE OTHER.

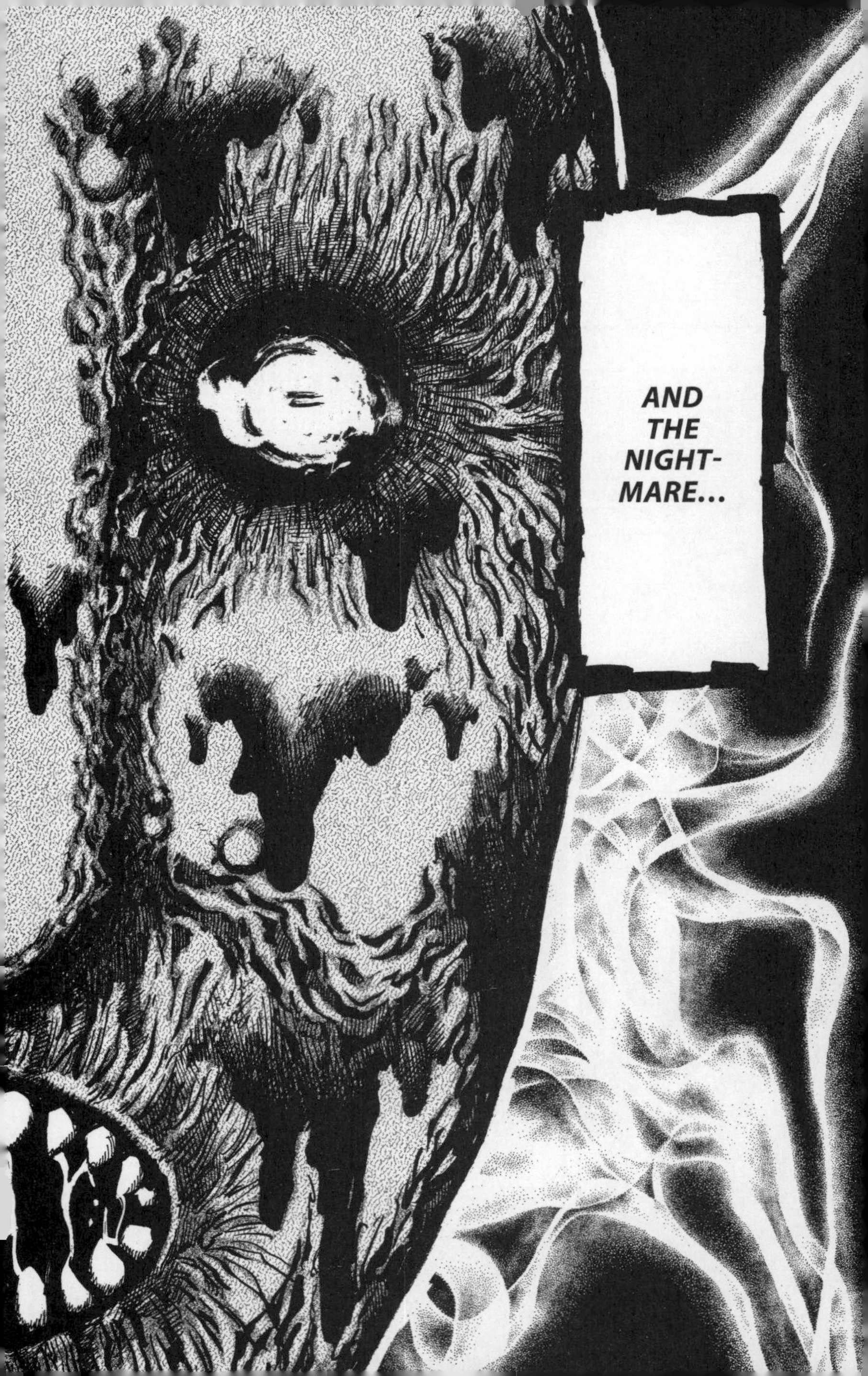
AND THE NIGHT-MARE...

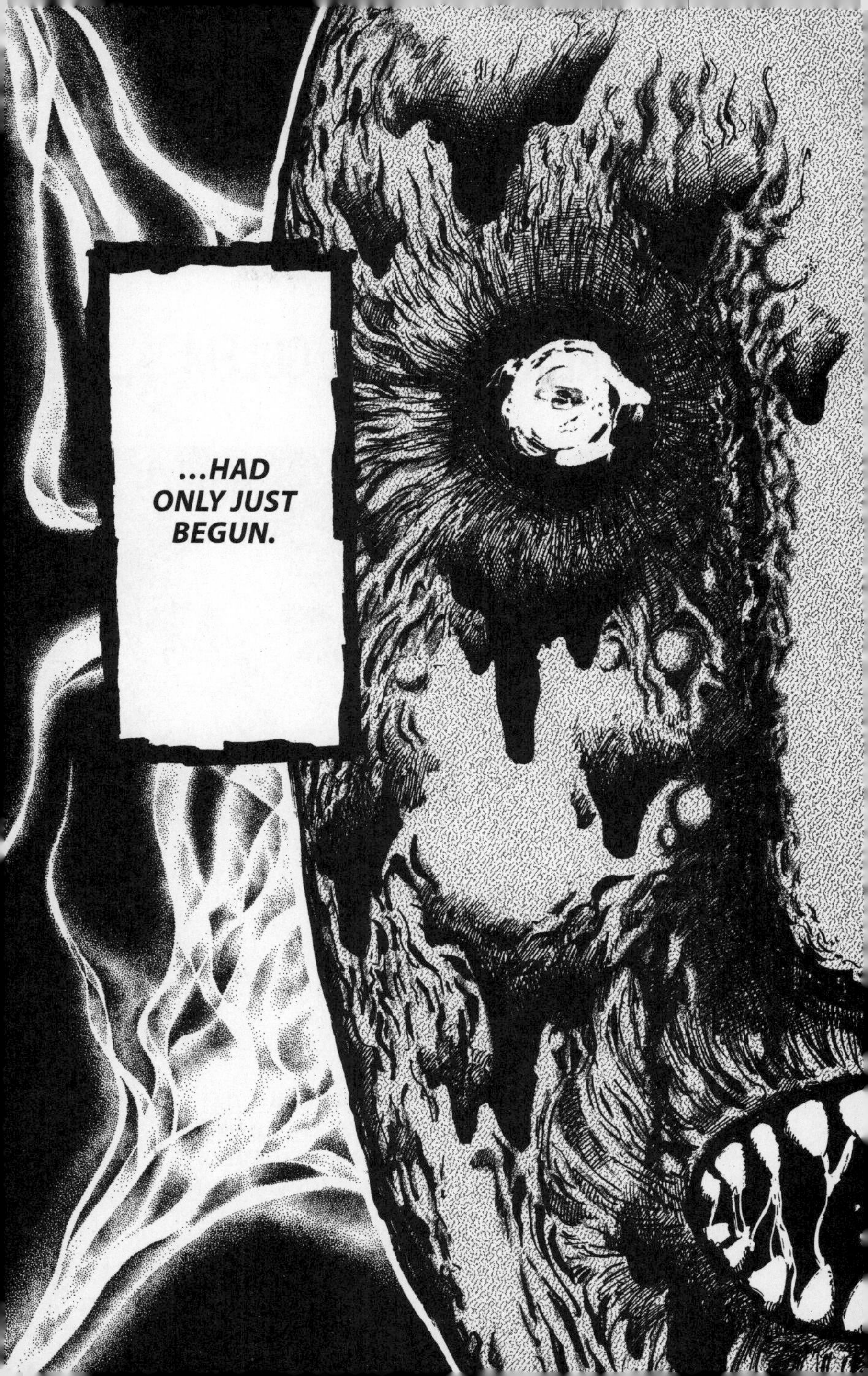
...HAD ONLY JUST BEGUN.

TORIKO

GOURMET CHECKLIST

Vol. 388

CORAL KING: CORAL GOLEM
(CORAL MONSTER)

CAPTURE LEVEL: 4,500
HABITAT: GOURMET WORLD'S AREA 6
SIZE: 20,000 M
HEIGHT: ---
WEIGHT: ---
PRICE: INEDIBLE

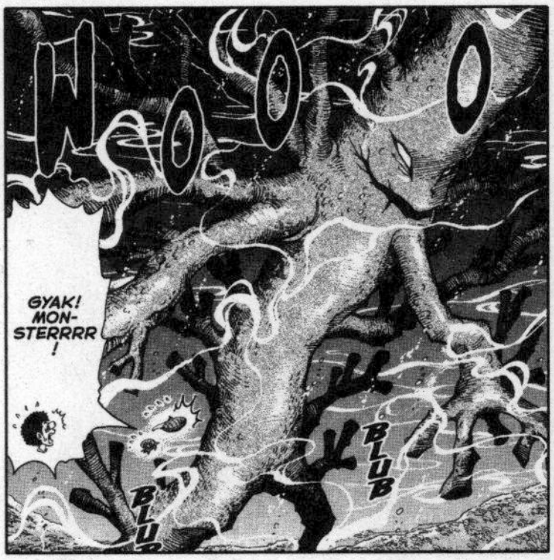
WOOO
GYAK! MON-STERRRR!
BLUB

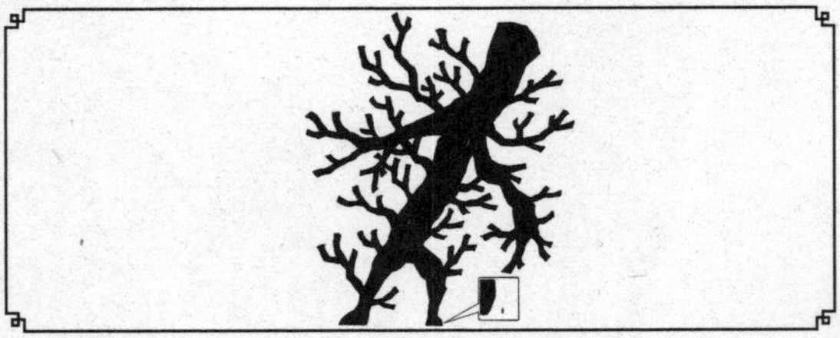

SCALE

IN ADDITION TO THE WHALE KING MOON, IN AREA 6 THERE ARE SEVEN KINGS THAT YOU MUST AVOID AT ALL COSTS—THE SEVEN BEASTS. THEY ARE POWERFUL MONSTERS WITH CAPTURE LEVELS EASILY OVER 4,000 EACH. ONE OF THEM IS THE CORAL KING! WHILE ITS CAPTURE LEVEL ALONE MAKES IT STAND OUT, ITS BODY CAN ALSO BE USED TO MAKE GOLDEN COOKWARE, WHICH IS NEEDED TO PREPARE ANOTHER, THE FISH DISH IN ACACIA'S FULL-COURSE MEAL. THE MATERIALS ARE USED TO MAKE THE CUTTING BOARD.

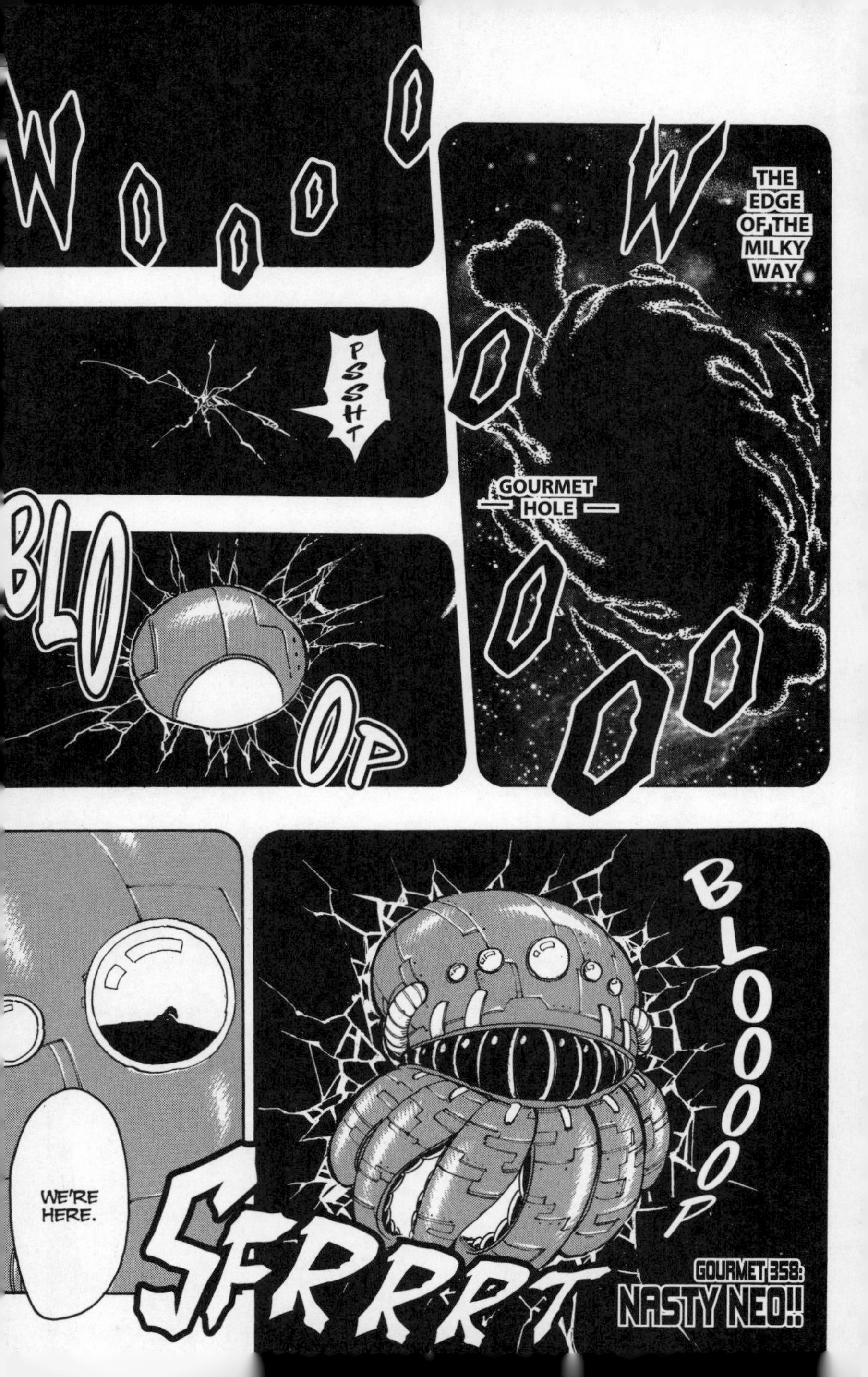
WOOOOOW
THE EDGE OF THE MILKY WAY
GOURMET HOLE
WOOOO
PSSHT
BLOOP
BLOOOOOP
GOURMET 358: NASTY NEO!!
SFRRRT
WE'RE HERE.

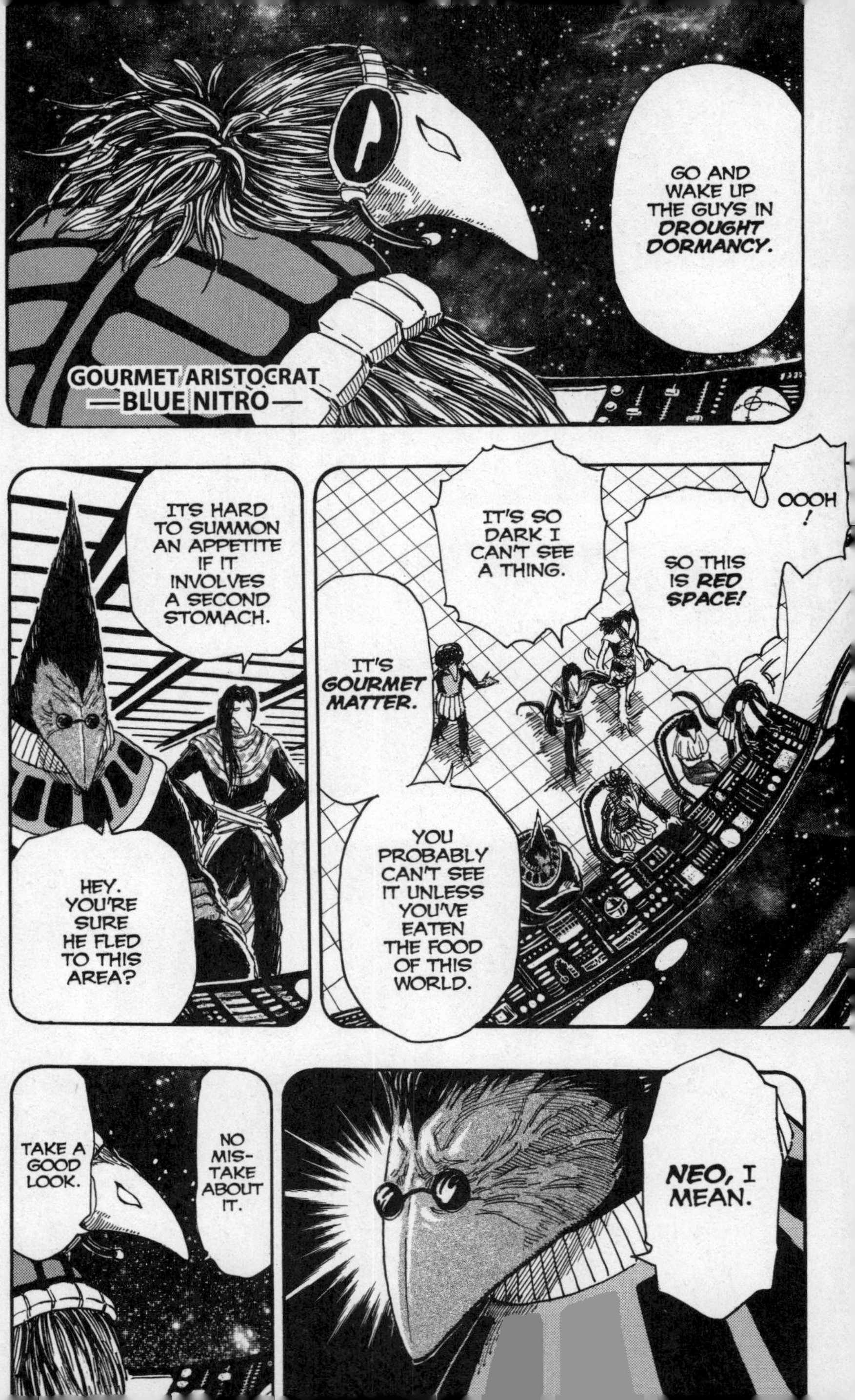
GO AND WAKE UP THE GUYS IN DROUGHT DORMANCY.
GOURMET ARISTOCRAT —BLUE NITRO—
OOOH!
SO THIS IS RED SPACE!
IT'S SO DARK I CAN'T SEE A THING.
IT'S GOURMET MATTER.
YOU PROBABLY CAN'T SEE IT UNLESS YOU'VE EATEN THE FOOD OF THIS WORLD.
IT'S HARD TO SUMMON AN APPETITE IF IT INVOLVES A SECOND STOMACH.
HEY. YOU'RE SURE HE FLED TO THIS AREA?
NEO, I MEAN.
NO MIS-TAKE ABOUT IT.
TAKE A GOOD LOOK.

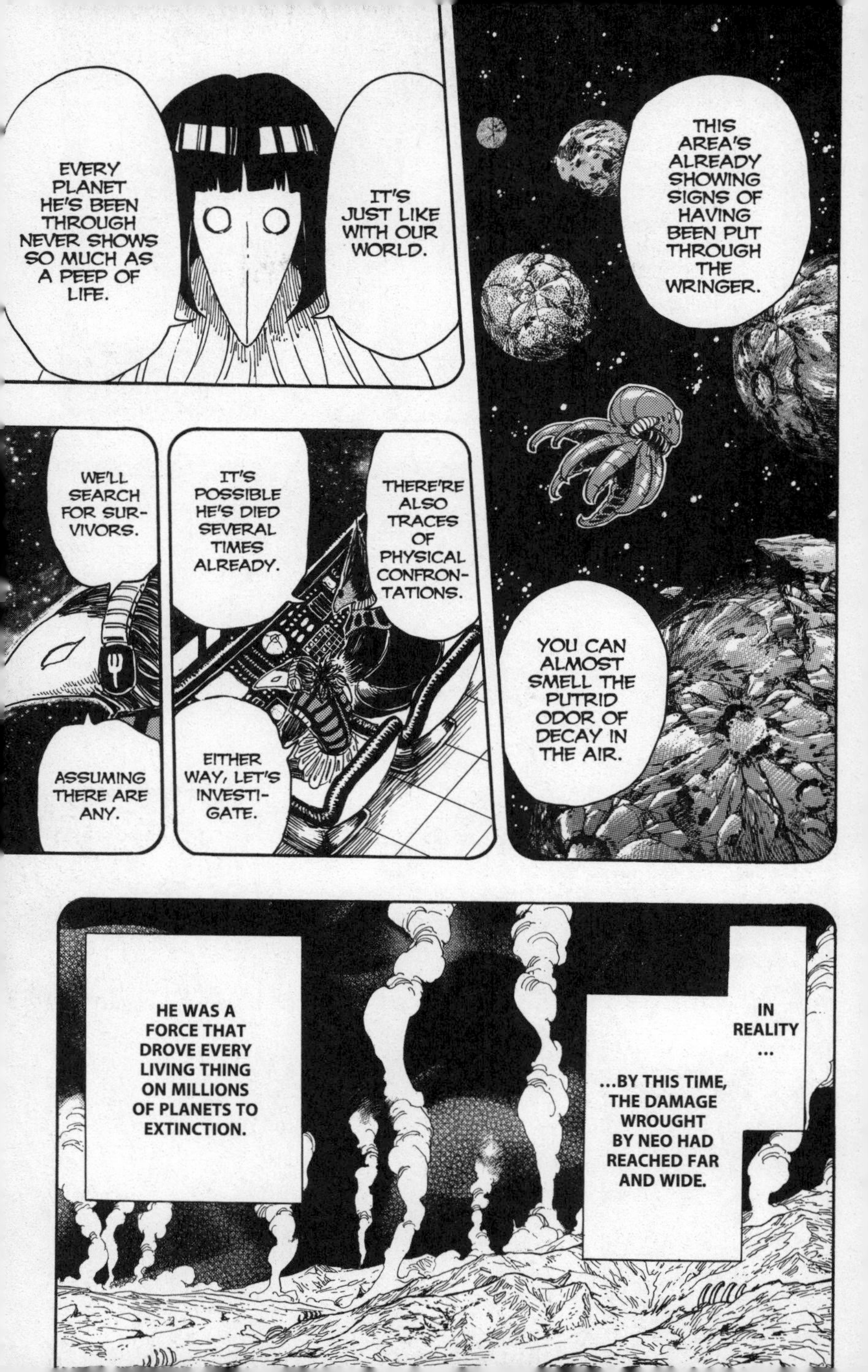
THIS AREA'S ALREADY SHOWING SIGNS OF HAVING BEEN PUT THROUGH THE WRINGER.
YOU CAN ALMOST SMELL THE PUTRID ODOR OF DECAY IN THE AIR.
IT'S JUST LIKE WITH OUR WORLD.
EVERY PLANET HE'S BEEN THROUGH NEVER SHOWS SO MUCH AS A PEEP OF LIFE.
THERE'RE ALSO TRACES OF PHYSICAL CONFRON-TATIONS.
IT'S POSSIBLE HE'S DIED SEVERAL TIMES ALREADY.
WE'LL SEARCH FOR SUR-VIVORS.
EITHER WAY, LET'S INVESTI-GATE.
ASSUMING THERE ARE ANY.
IN REALITY ...
...BY THIS TIME, THE DAMAGE WROUGHT BY NEO HAD REACHED FAR AND WIDE.
HE WAS A FORCE THAT DROVE EVERY LIVING THING ON MILLIONS OF PLANETS TO EXTINCTION.

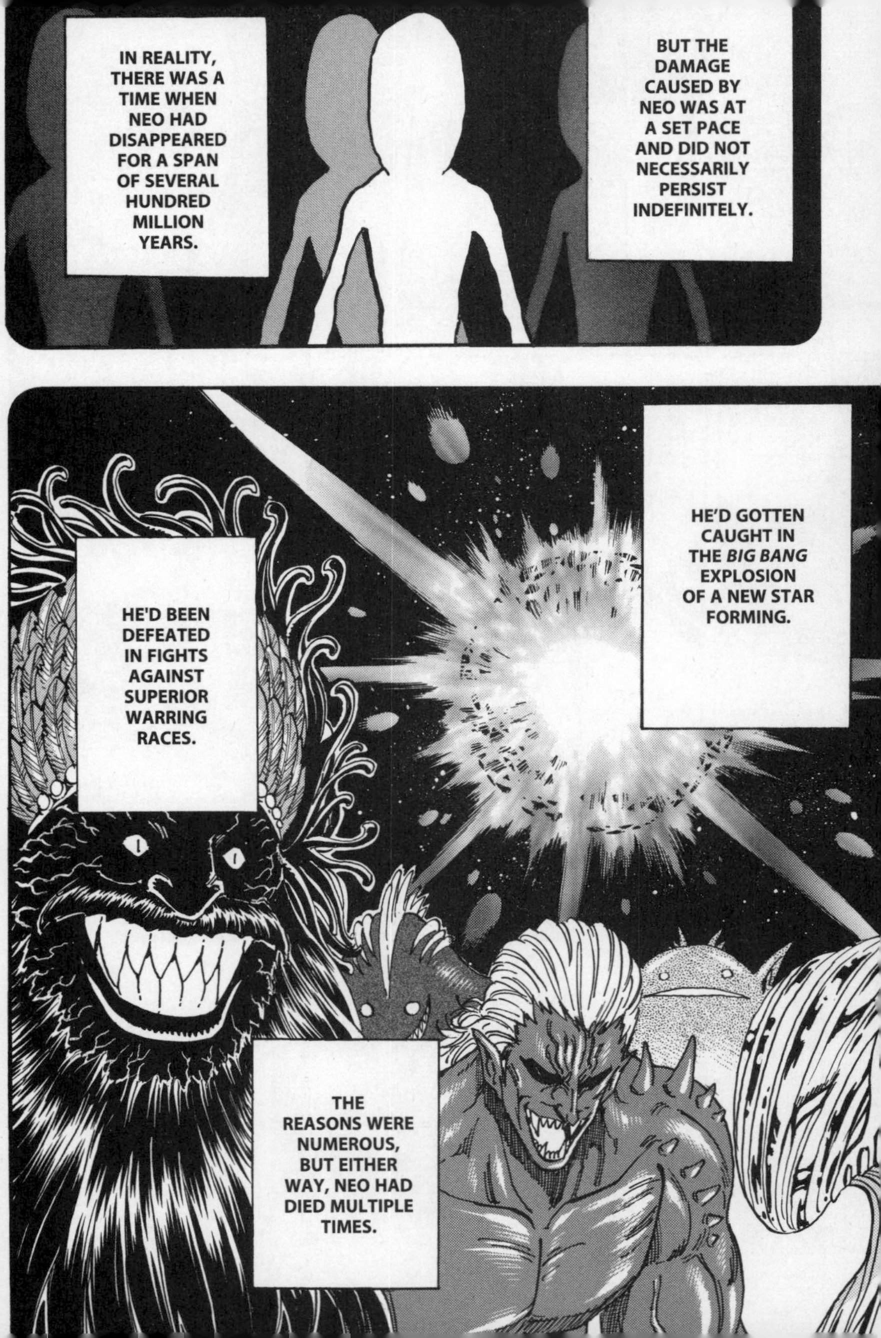
BUT THE DAMAGE CAUSED BY NEO WAS AT A SET PACE AND DID NOT NECESSARILY PERSIST INDEFINITELY.
IN REALITY, THERE WAS A TIME WHEN NEO HAD DISAPPEARED FOR A SPAN OF SEVERAL HUNDRED MILLION YEARS.
HE'D GOTTEN CAUGHT IN THE *BIG BANG* EXPLOSION OF A NEW STAR FORMING.
HE'D BEEN DEFEATED IN FIGHTS AGAINST SUPERIOR WARRING RACES.
THE REASONS WERE NUMEROUS, BUT EITHER WAY, NEO HAD DIED MULTIPLE TIMES.

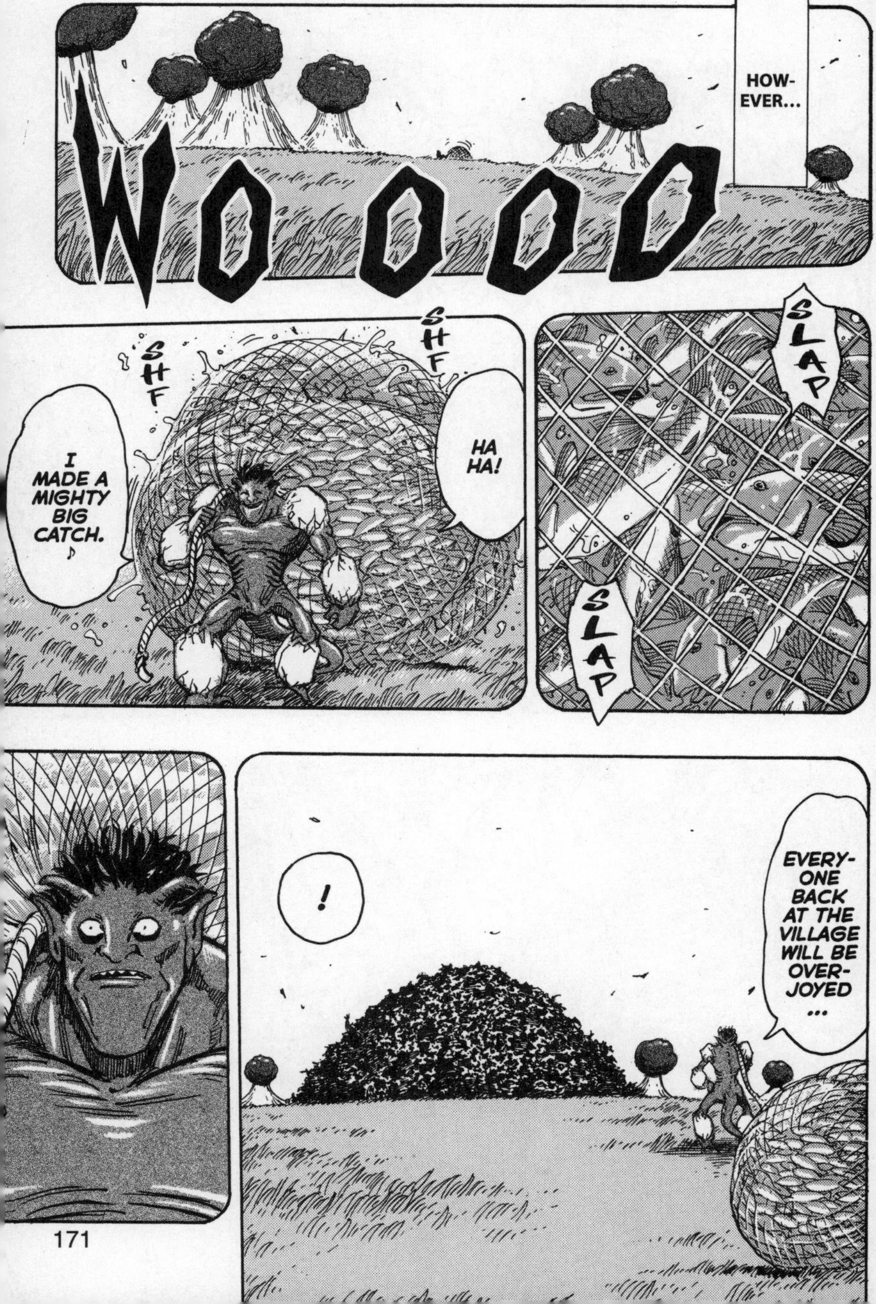
HOW-EVER...
WOOOD
SLAP
SLAP
SHF
HA HA!
SHF
I MADE A MIGHTY BIG CATCH. ♪
EVERY-ONE BACK AT THE VILLAGE WILL BE OVER-JOYED ...
!

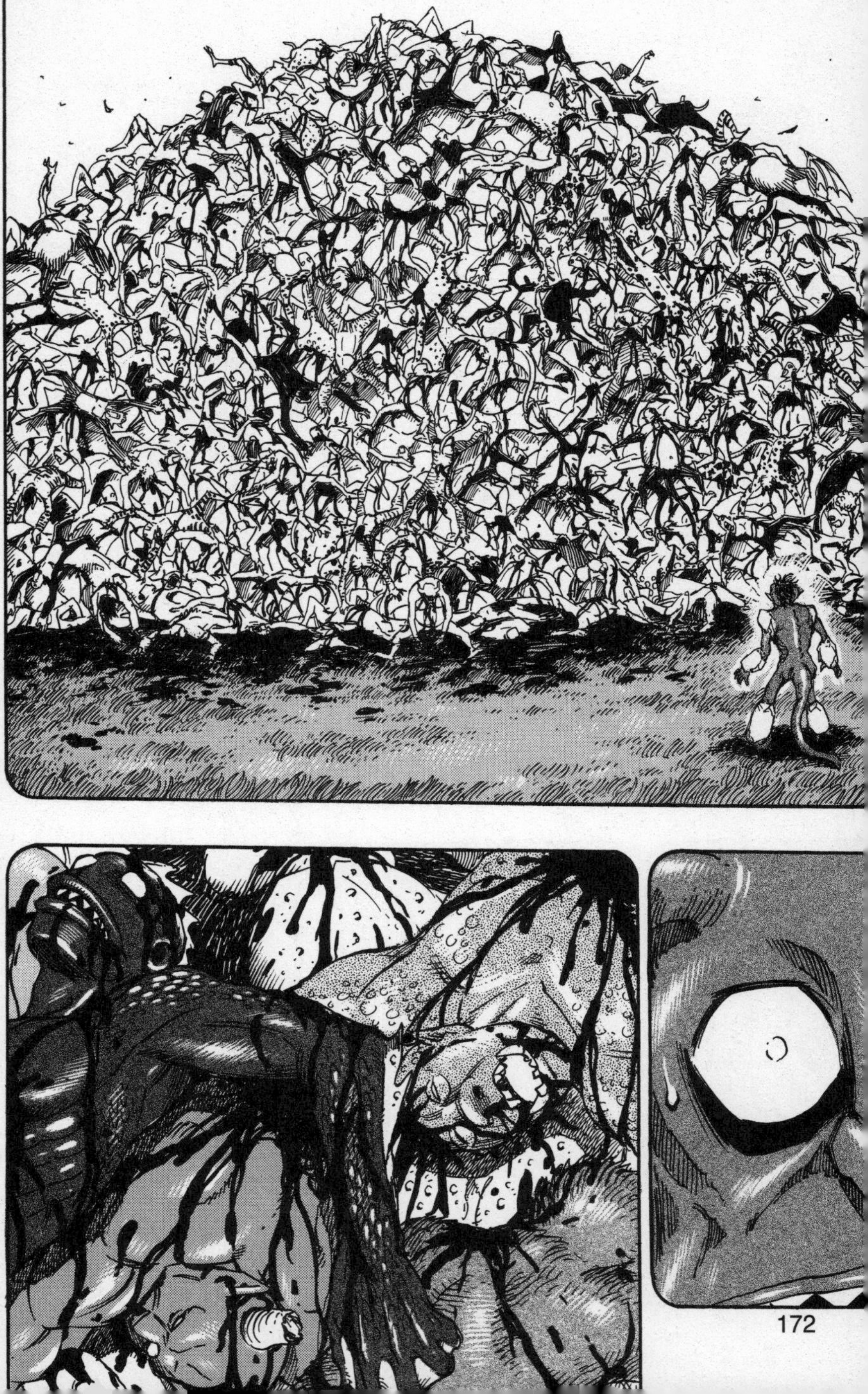

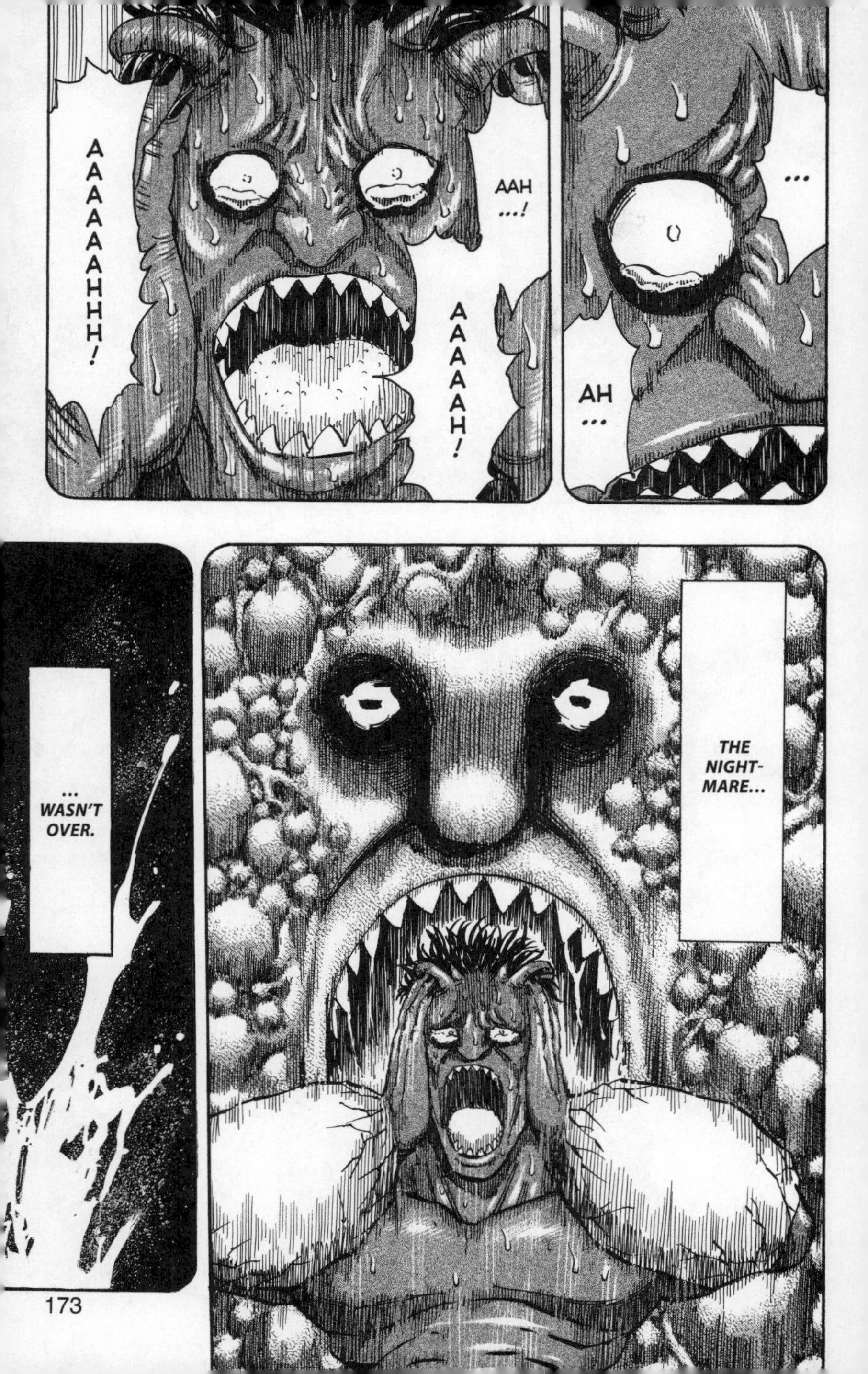
...
AH ...
AAH ...!
AAAAAH!
AAAAAAHHH!
THE NIGHT-MARE...
... WASN'T OVER.

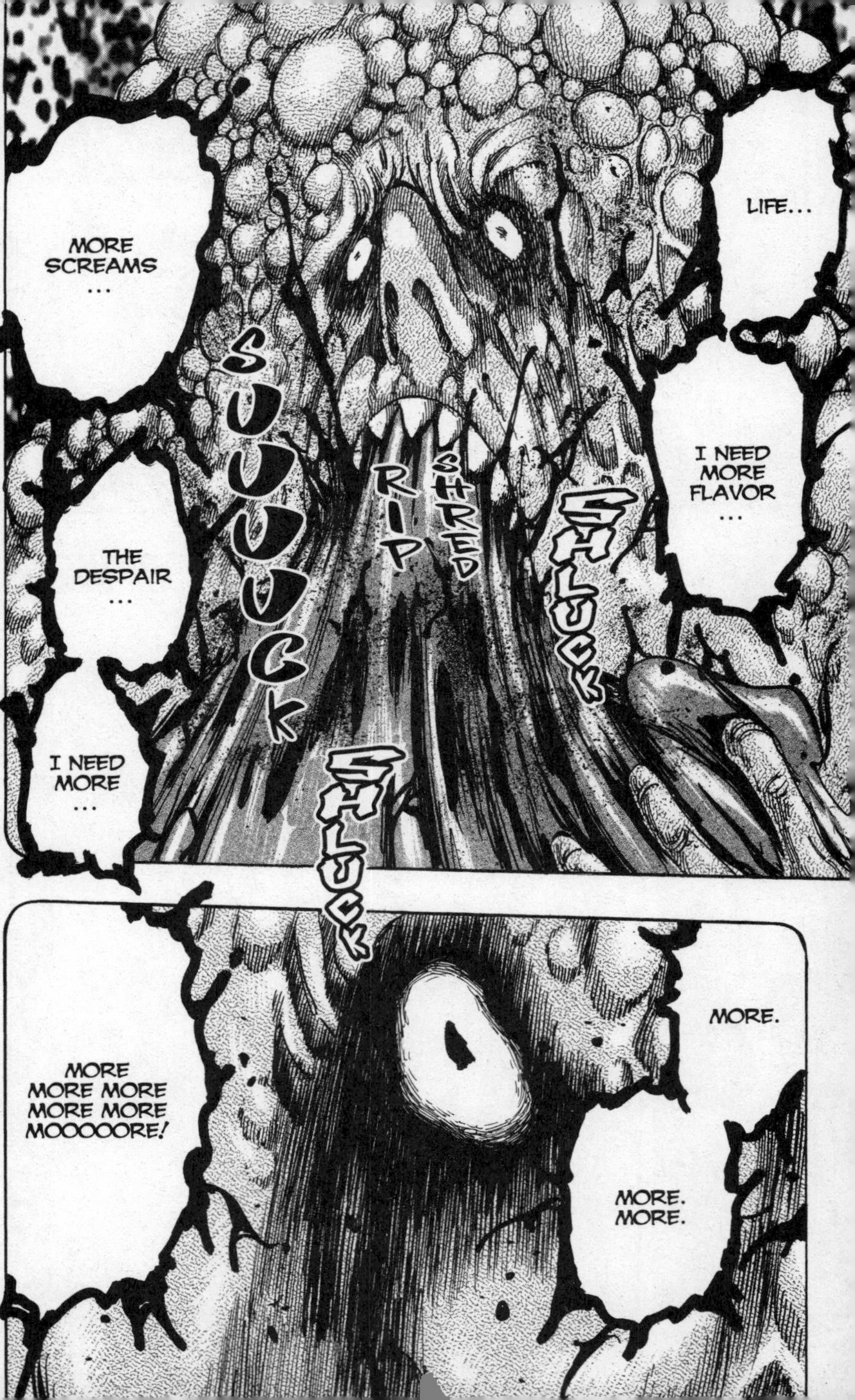
LIFE…
I NEED MORE FLAVOR…
SHLUCK
SHRED
RIP
SUUUUCK
MORE SCREAMS…
THE DESPAIR…
I NEED MORE…
SHLUCK
MORE.
MORE. MORE.
MORE MORE MORE MORE MORE MOOOOORE!

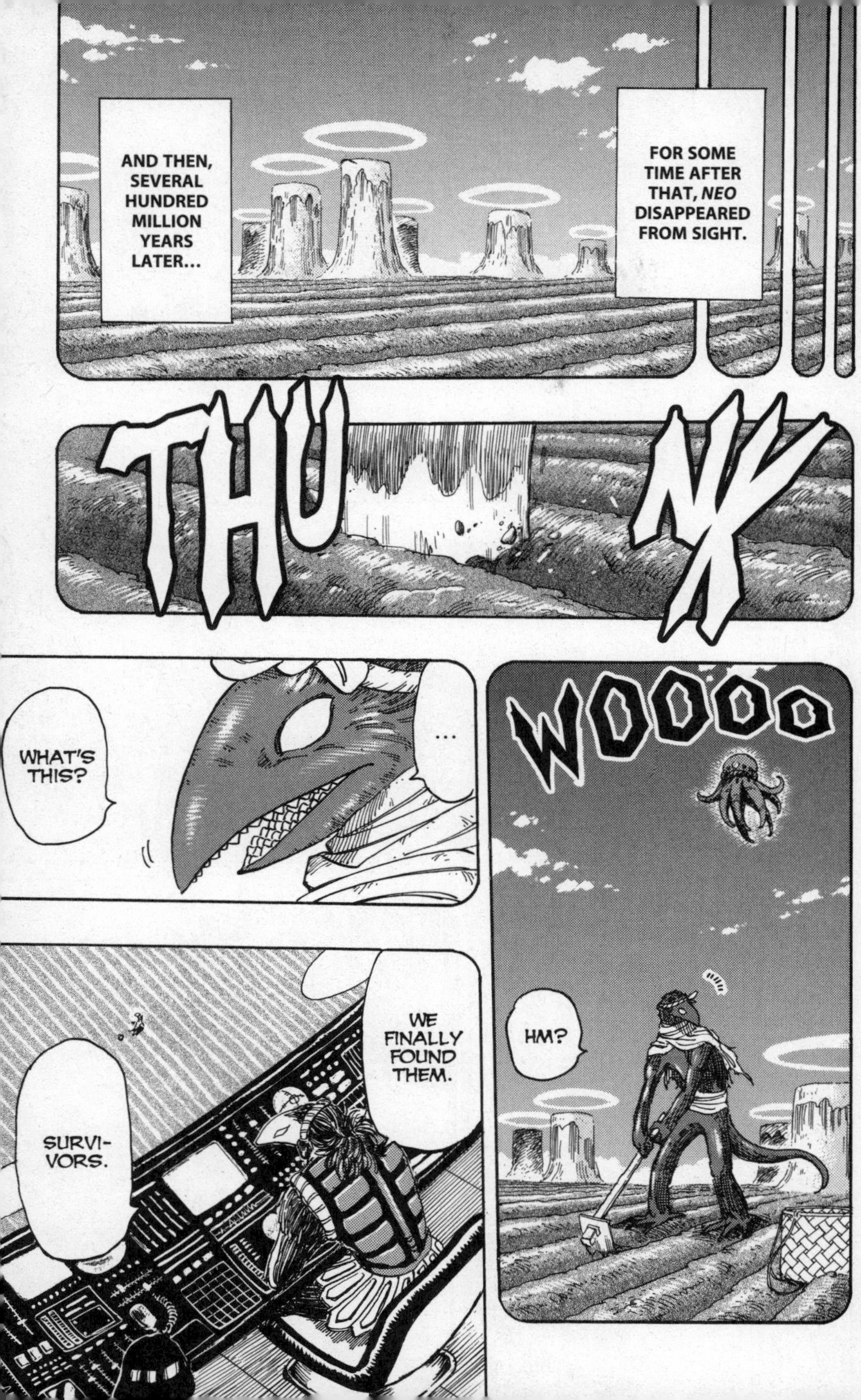
FOR SOME TIME AFTER THAT, *NEO* DISAPPEARED FROM SIGHT.
AND THEN, SEVERAL HUNDRED MILLION YEARS LATER…
THUNK
WOOOO
HM?
…
WHAT'S THIS?
WE FINALLY FOUND THEM.
SURVIVORS.

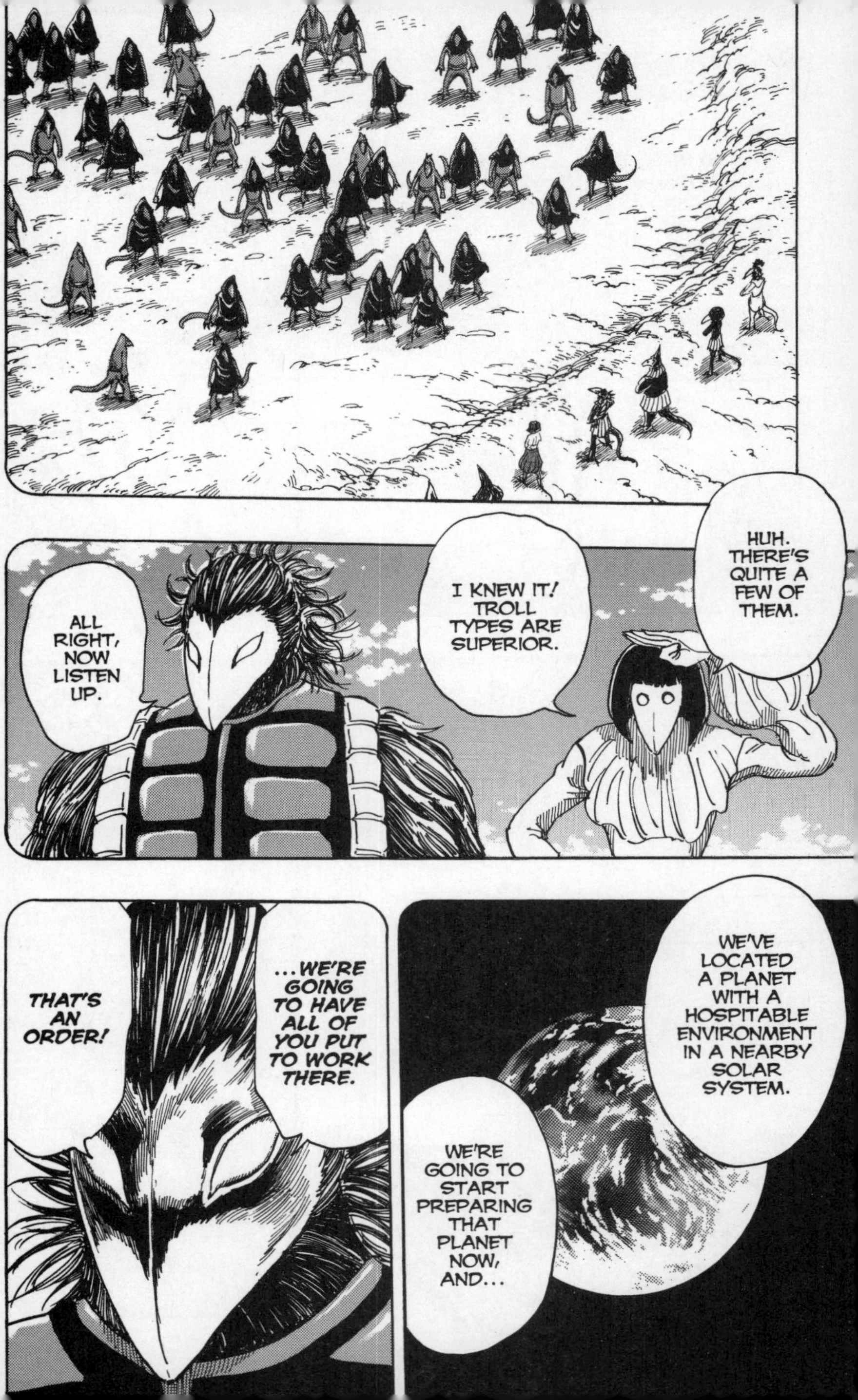
HUH. THERE'S QUITE A FEW OF THEM.
I KNEW IT! TROLL TYPES ARE SUPERIOR.
ALL RIGHT, NOW LISTEN UP.
WE'VE LOCATED A PLANET WITH A HOSPITABLE ENVIRONMENT IN A NEARBY SOLAR SYSTEM.
WE'RE GOING TO START PREPARING THAT PLANET NOW, AND...
...WE'RE GOING TO HAVE ALL OF YOU PUT TO WORK THERE.
THAT'S AN ORDER!

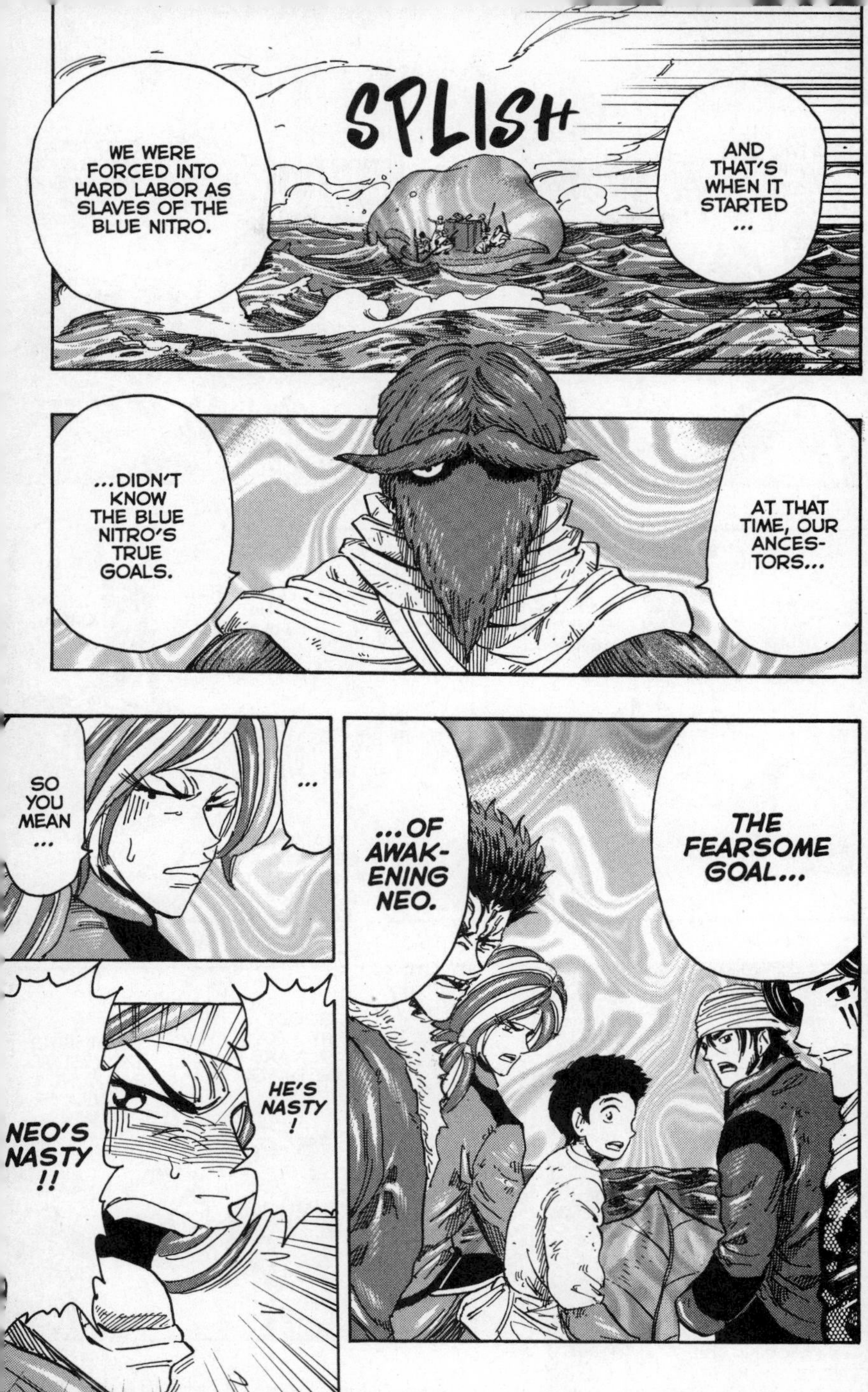
AND THAT'S WHEN IT STARTED ...
SPLISH
WE WERE FORCED INTO HARD LABOR AS SLAVES OF THE BLUE NITRO.
AT THAT TIME, OUR ANCES-TORS...
...DIDN'T KNOW THE BLUE NITRO'S TRUE GOALS.
THE FEARSOME GOAL...
...OF AWAK-ENING NEO.
...
SO YOU MEAN ...
HE'S NASTY!
NEO'S NASTY!!

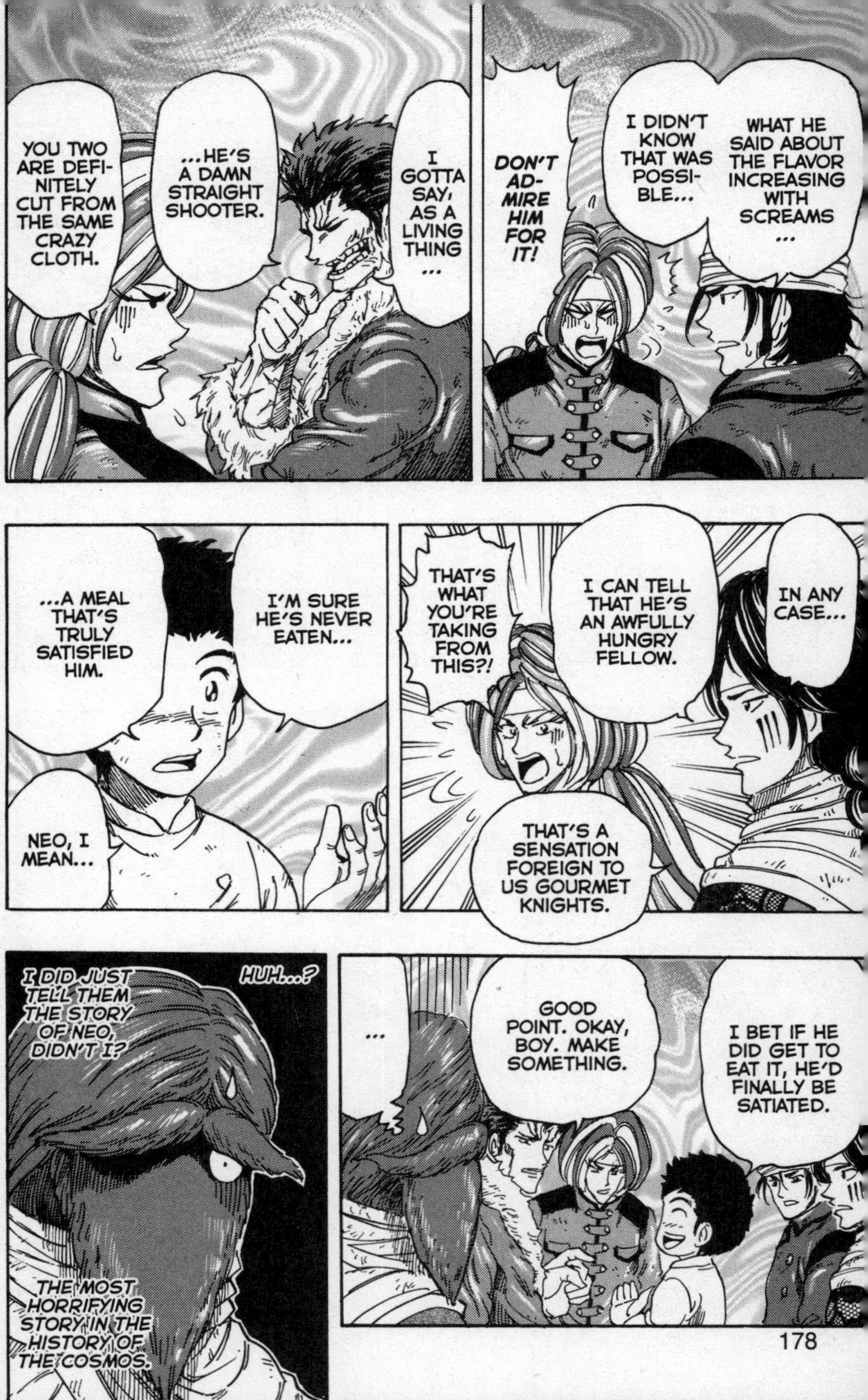
WHAT HE SAID ABOUT THE FLAVOR INCREASING WITH SCREAMS ...
I DIDN'T KNOW THAT WAS POSSIBLE...
DON'T ADMIRE HIM FOR IT!
I GOTTA SAY, AS A LIVING THING ...
...HE'S A DAMN STRAIGHT SHOOTER.
YOU TWO ARE DEFINITELY CUT FROM THE SAME CRAZY CLOTH.
IN ANY CASE...
I CAN TELL THAT HE'S AN AWFULLY HUNGRY FELLOW.
THAT'S WHAT YOU'RE TAKING FROM THIS?!
THAT'S A SENSATION FOREIGN TO US GOURMET KNIGHTS.
I'M SURE HE'S NEVER EATEN...
...A MEAL THAT'S TRULY SATISFIED HIM.
NEO, I MEAN...
I BET IF HE DID GET TO EAT IT, HE'D FINALLY BE SATIATED.
GOOD POINT. OKAY, BOY. MAKE SOMETHING.
...
HUH...?
I DID JUST TELL THEM THE STORY OF NEO, DIDN'T I?
THE MOST HORRIFYING STORY IN THE HISTORY OF THE COSMOS.

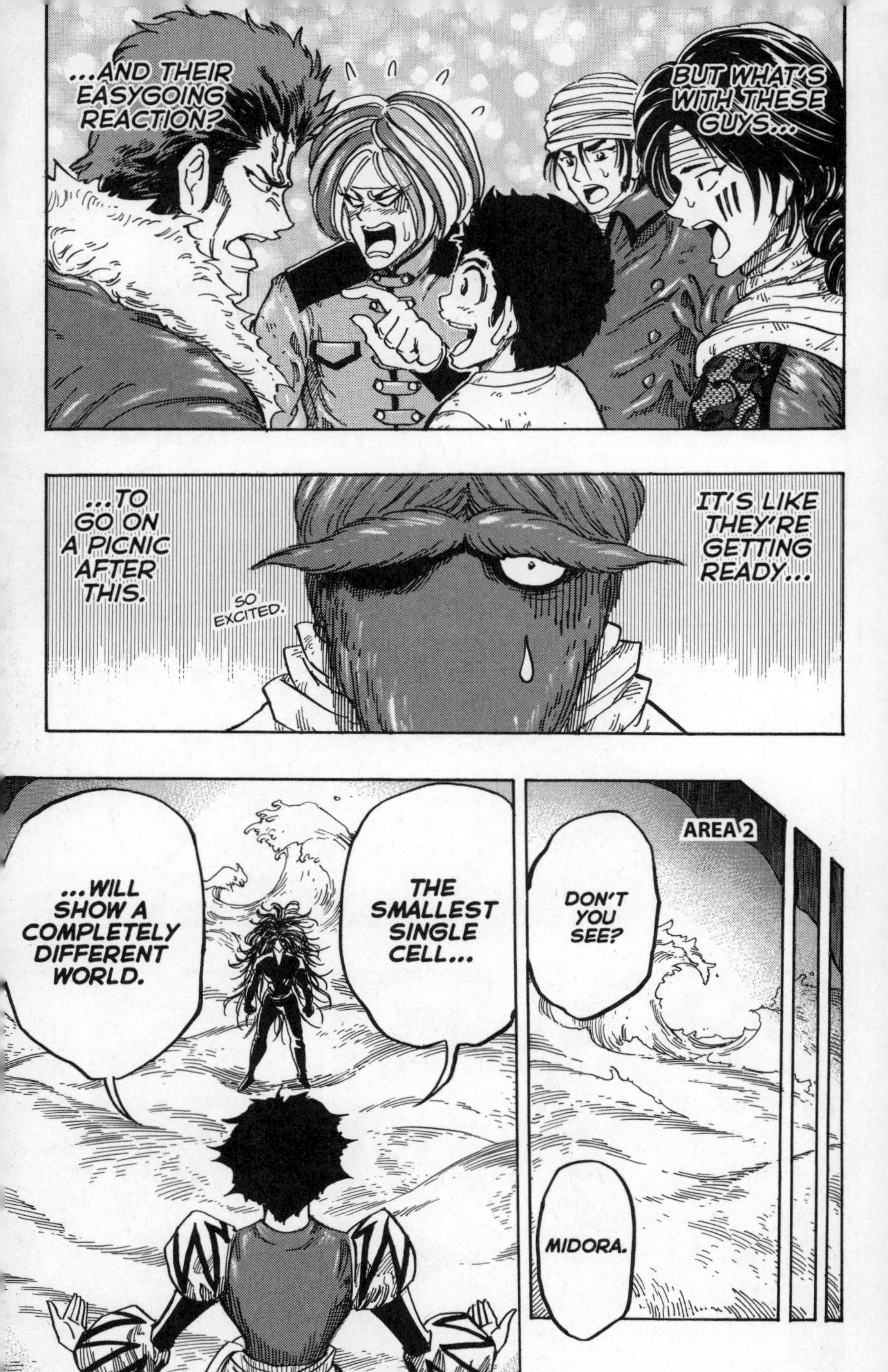
BUT WHAT'S WITH THESE GUYS...
...AND THEIR EASYGOING REACTION?
IT'S LIKE THEY'RE GETTING READY...
...TO GO ON A PICNIC AFTER THIS.
SO EXCITED.
AREA 2
DON'T YOU SEE?
MIDORA.
THE SMALLEST SINGLE CELL...
...WILL SHOW A COMPLETELY DIFFERENT WORLD.

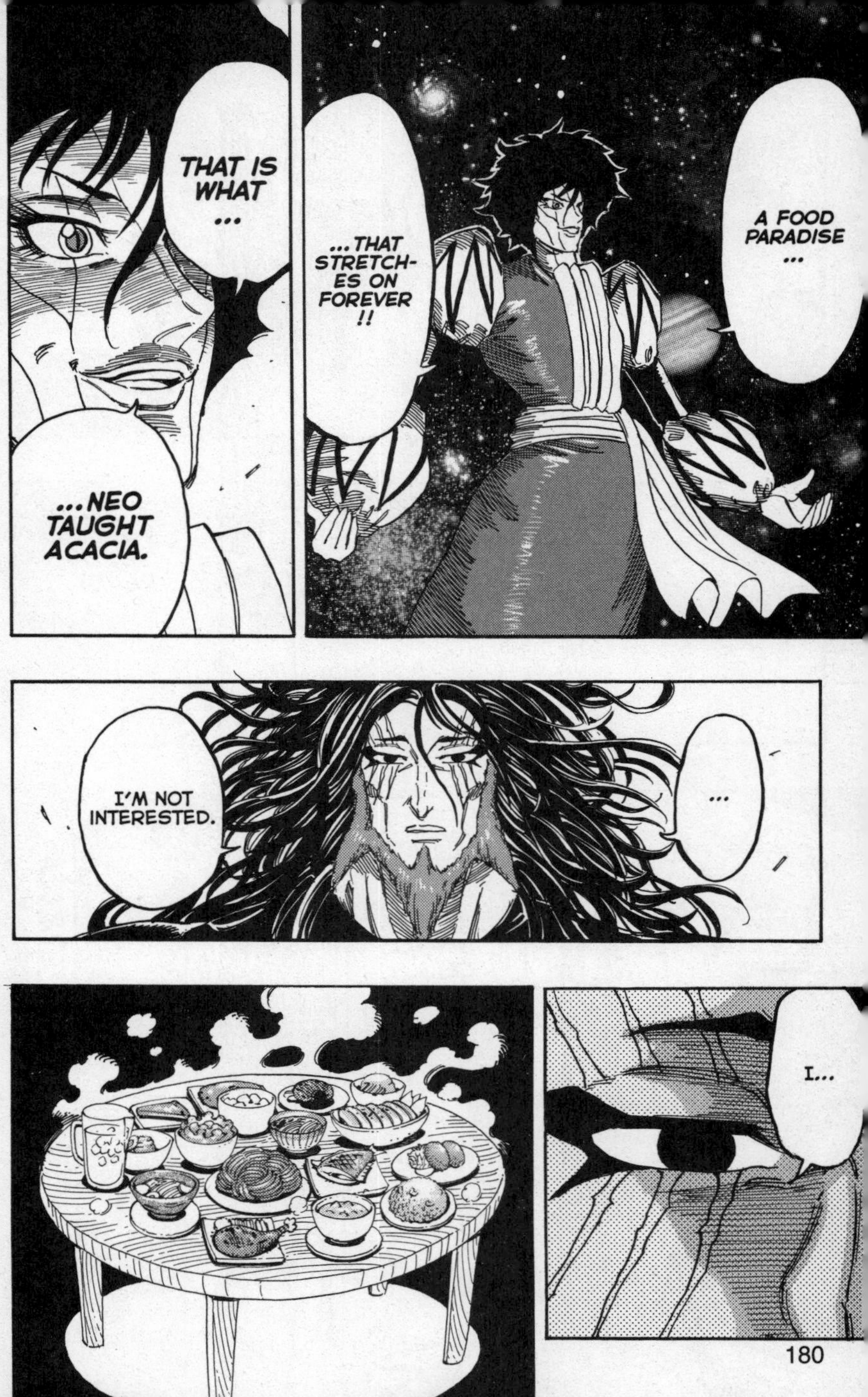
A FOOD PARADISE ...
...THAT STRETCH-ES ON FOREVER !!
THAT IS WHAT ...
...NEO TAUGHT ACACIA.
...
I'M NOT INTERESTED.
I...

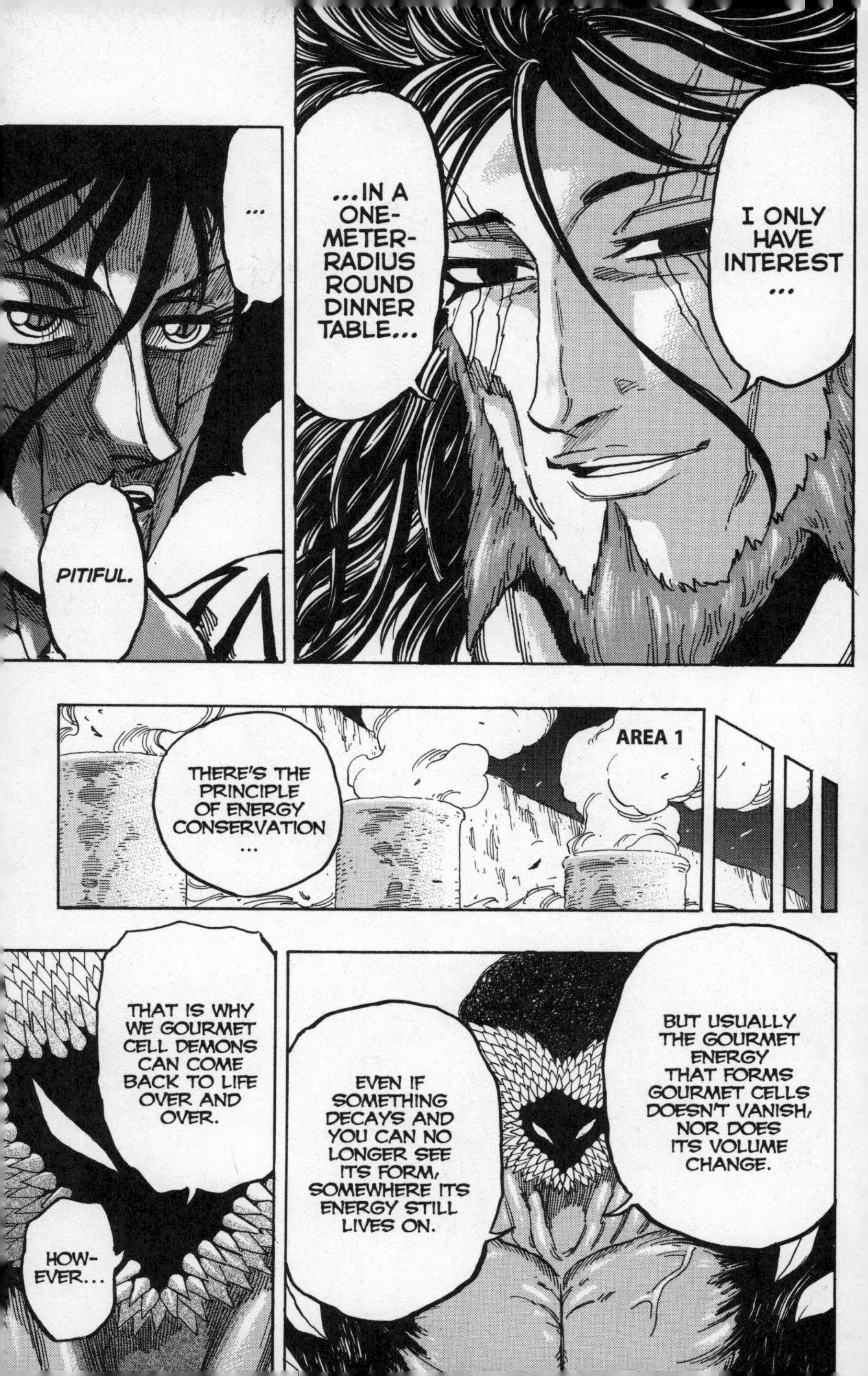
I ONLY HAVE INTEREST ...
...IN A ONE-METER-RADIUS ROUND DINNER TABLE...
...
PITIFUL.
AREA 1
THERE'S THE PRINCIPLE OF ENERGY CONSERVATION ...
BUT USUALLY THE GOURMET ENERGY THAT FORMS GOURMET CELLS DOESN'T VANISH, NOR DOES ITS VOLUME CHANGE.
EVEN IF SOMETHING DECAYS AND YOU CAN NO LONGER SEE ITS FORM, SOMEWHERE ITS ENERGY STILL LIVES ON.
THAT IS WHY WE GOURMET CELL DEMONS CAN COME BACK TO LIFE OVER AND OVER.
HOW-EVER...

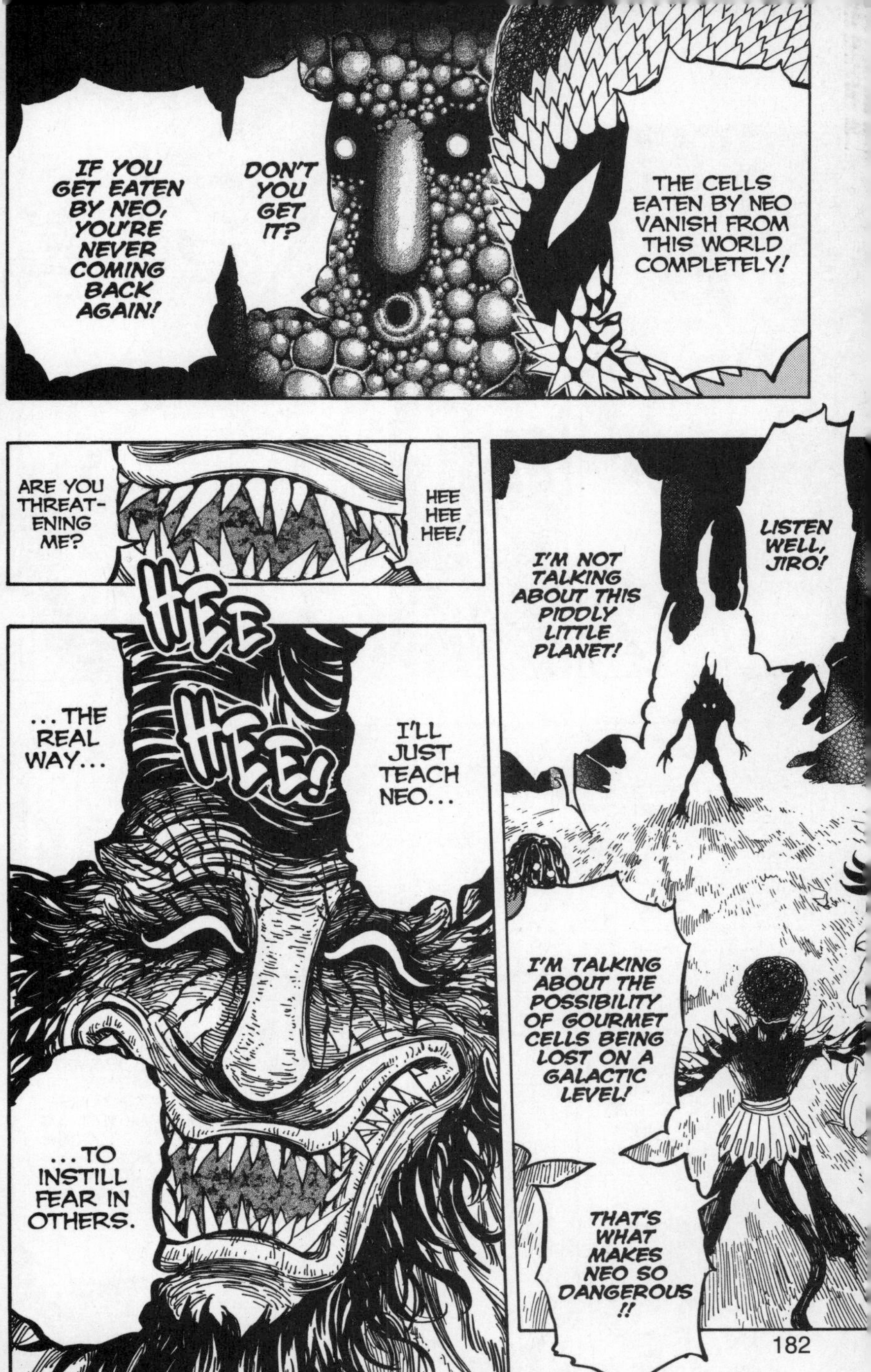
THE CELLS EATEN BY NEO VANISH FROM THIS WORLD COMPLETELY!
DON'T YOU GET IT?
IF YOU GET EATEN BY NEO, YOU'RE NEVER COMING BACK AGAIN!
LISTEN WELL, JIRO!
I'M NOT TALKING ABOUT THIS PIDDLY LITTLE PLANET!
I'M TALKING ABOUT THE POSSIBILITY OF GOURMET CELLS BEING LOST ON A GALACTIC LEVEL!
THAT'S WHAT MAKES NEO SO DANGEROUS!!
HEE HEE HEE!
ARE YOU THREAT-ENING ME?
HEE HEE!
I'LL JUST TEACH NEO...
...THE REAL WAY...
...TO INSTILL FEAR IN OTHERS.

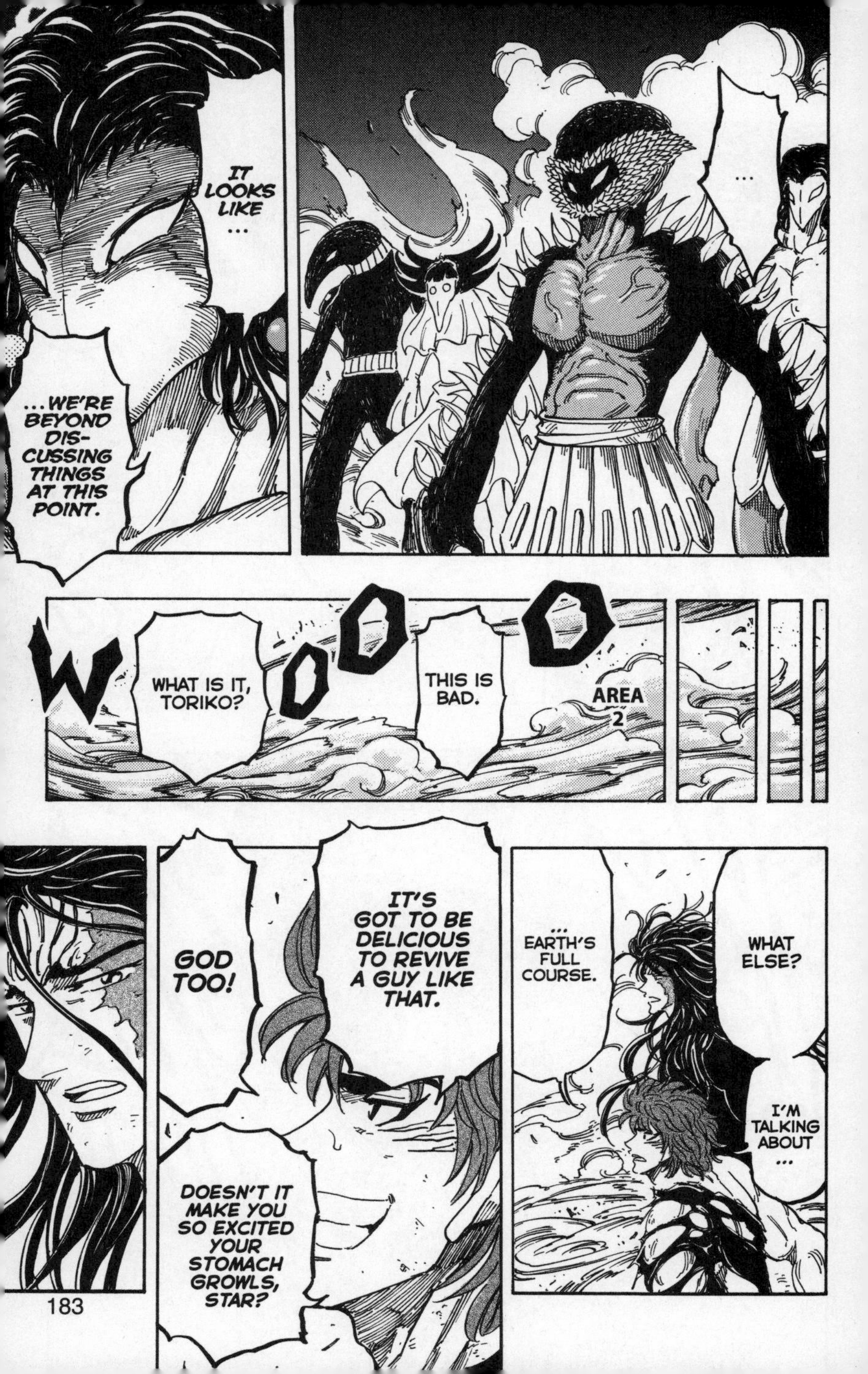
...
IT LOOKS LIKE ...
...WE'RE BEYOND DIS-CUSSING THINGS AT THIS POINT.
AREA 2
THIS IS BAD.
WHAT IS IT, TORIKO?
WOOO
WHAT ELSE?
I'M TALKING ABOUT ...
... EARTH'S FULL COURSE.
IT'S GOT TO BE DELICIOUS TO REVIVE A GUY LIKE THAT.
GOD TOO!
DOESN'T IT MAKE YOU SO EXCITED YOUR STOMACH GROWLS, STAR?

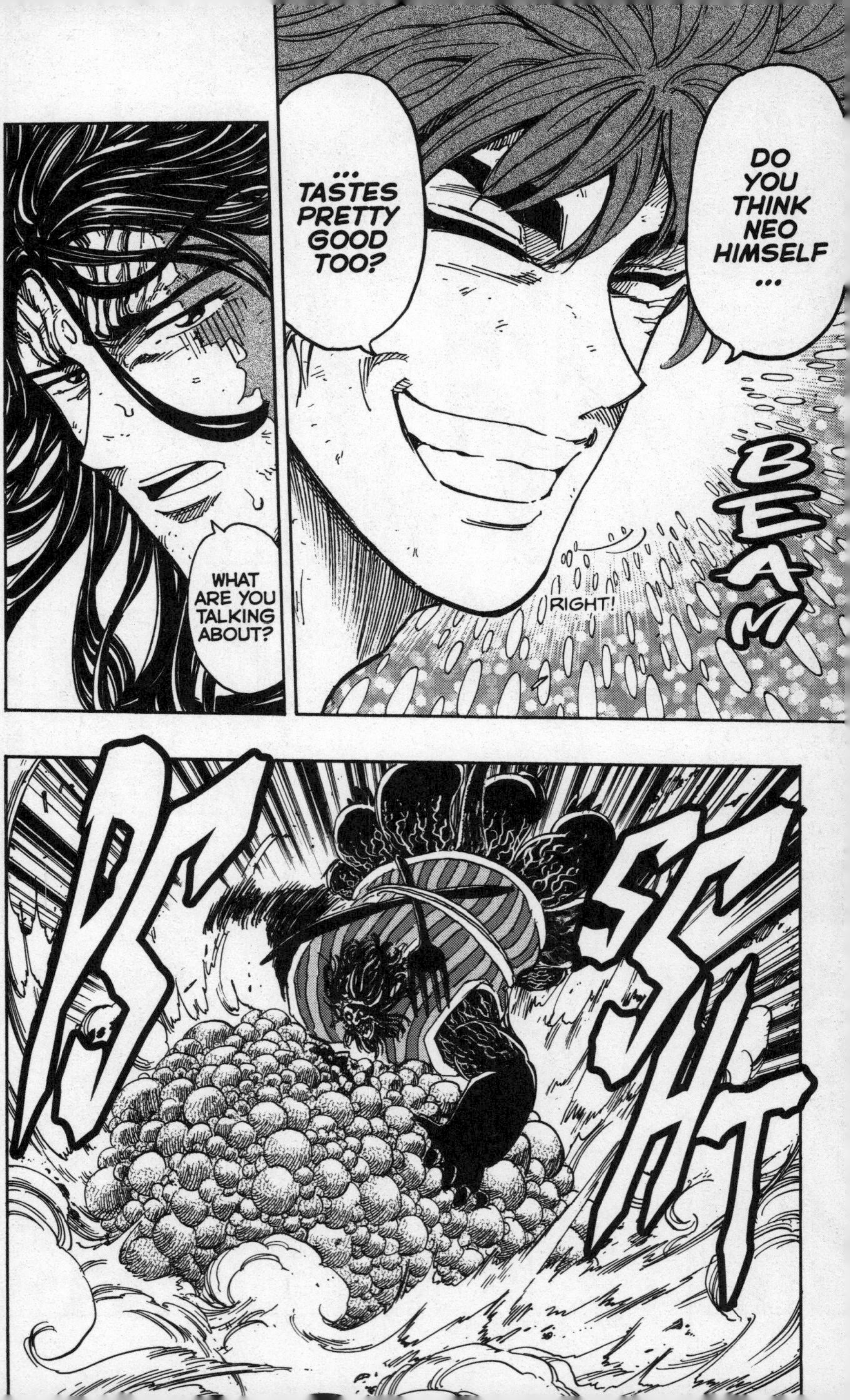
DO YOU THINK NEO HIMSELF ...
... TASTES PRETTY GOOD TOO?
BEAM
RIGHT!
WHAT ARE YOU TALKING ABOUT?

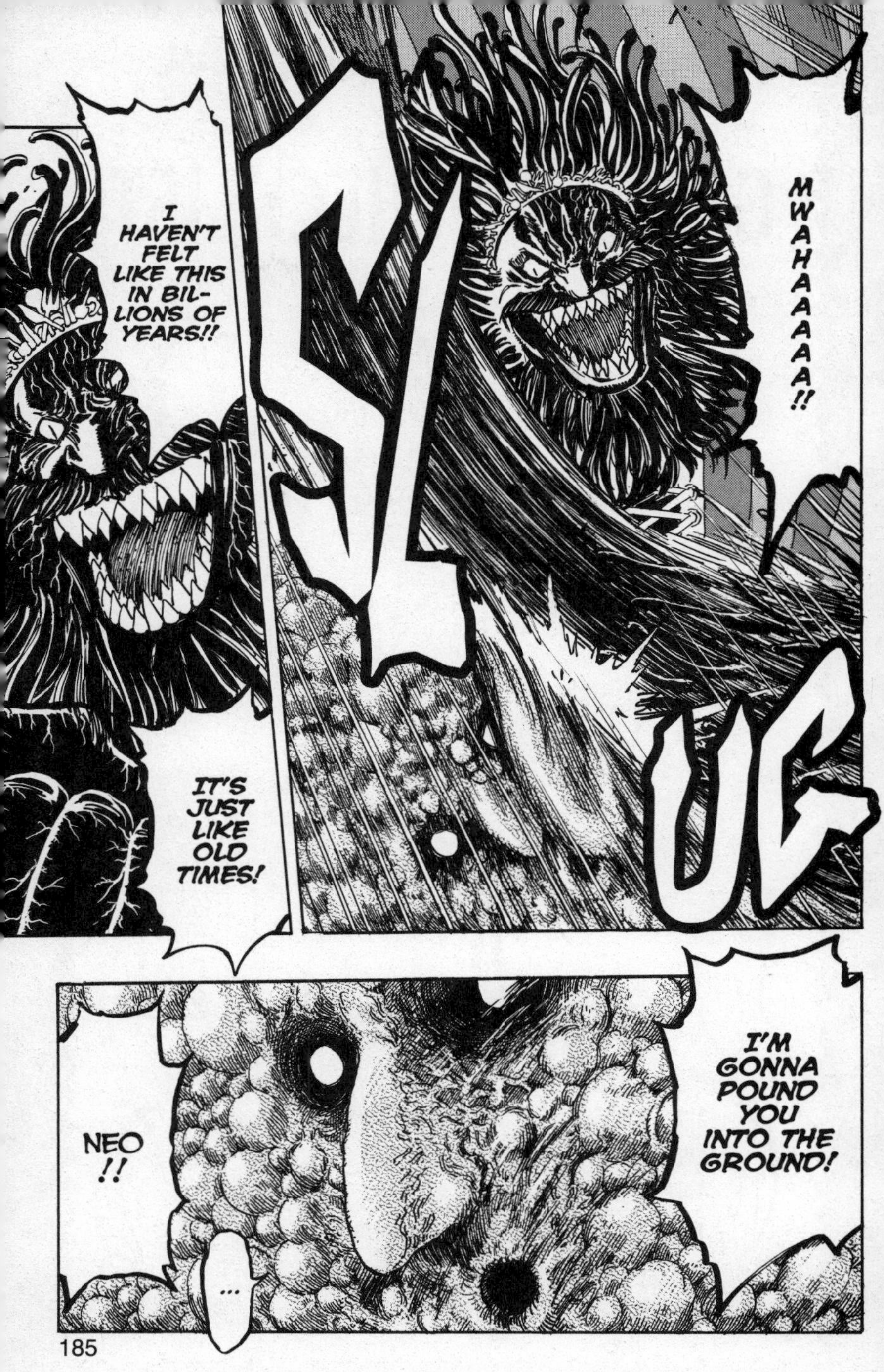
MWAHAAAAAA!!
I HAVEN'T FELT LIKE THIS IN BIL-LIONS OF YEARS!!
IT'S JUST LIKE OLD TIMES!
UG
I'M GONNA POUND YOU INTO THE GROUND!
NEO !!
...

GOURMET CHECKLIST

Vol. 389

UNIRA
(TALISMAN INGREDIENT)

CAPTURE LEVEL: 3
HABITAT: BLUE GRILL IN GOURMET WORLD'S AREA 6
SIZE: 10 CM
HEIGHT: ---
WEIGHT: 100 G
PRICE: 100,000 YEN PER TALISMAN

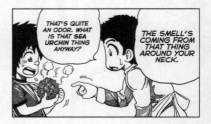

THE SMELL'S COMING FROM THAT THING AROUND YOUR NECK.
THAT'S QUITE AN ODOR. WHAT IS THAT SEA URCHIN THING ANYWAY?

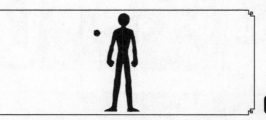

SCALE

THE STRONG SMELL OF THIS INGREDIENT WARDS OFF FOOD SPIRITS THAT HAVE ACCUMULATED IN BLUE GRILL. IF YOU PREPARE IT JUST RIGHT, IT CAN ALSO BE USED AS A COOKING INGREDIENT. HOWEVER, DUE TO ITS HIGH PRICE AND ITS USE IN PERSONAL SAFETY, THERE ARE RELATIVELY FEW PEOPLE WHO ACTUALLY EAT IT.

GOURMET 359: DON SLIME'S THE NAME!!

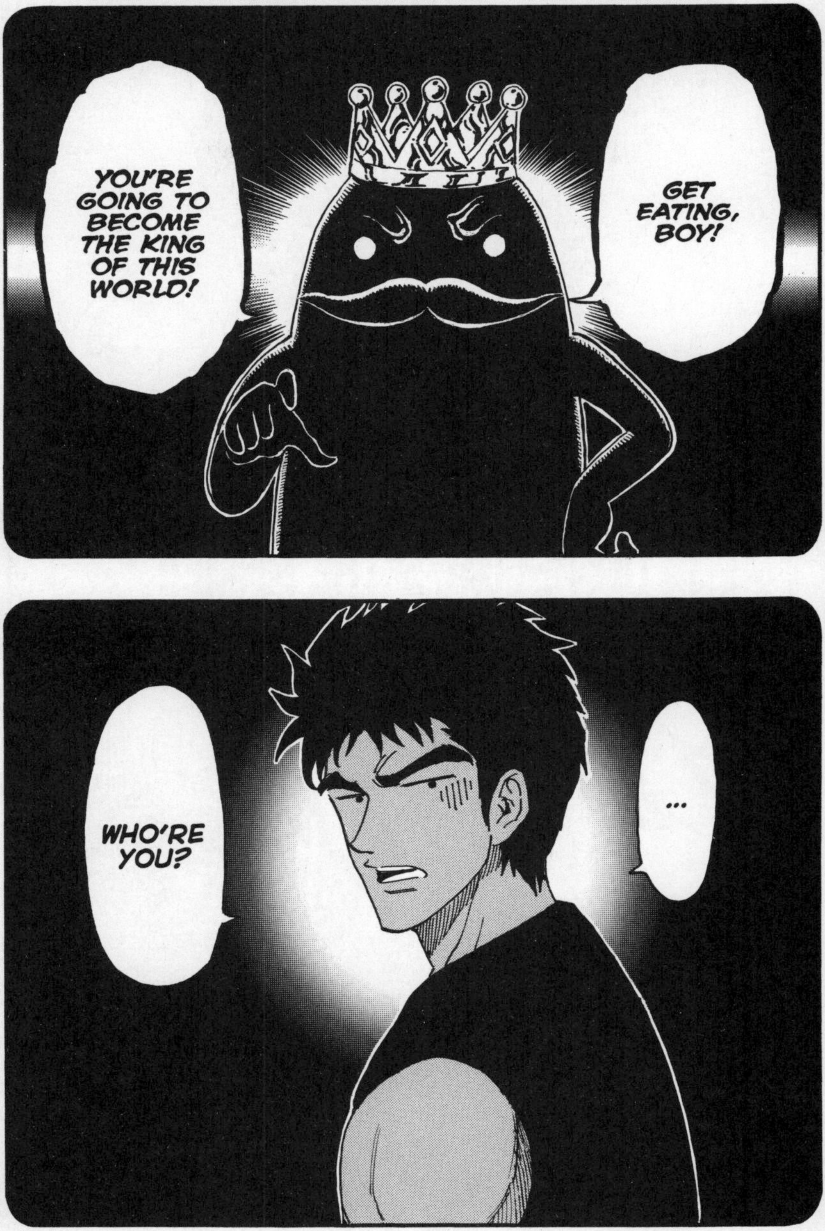
GET EATING, BOY!
YOU'RE GOING TO BECOME THE KING OF THIS WORLD!
...
WHO'RE YOU?

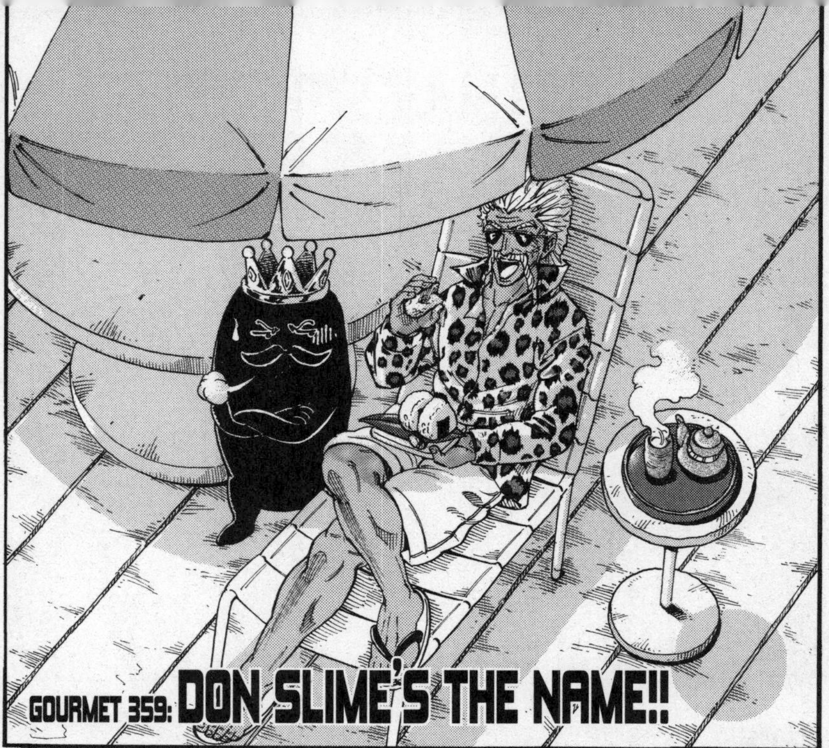
GOURMET 359: DON SLIME'S THE NAME!!

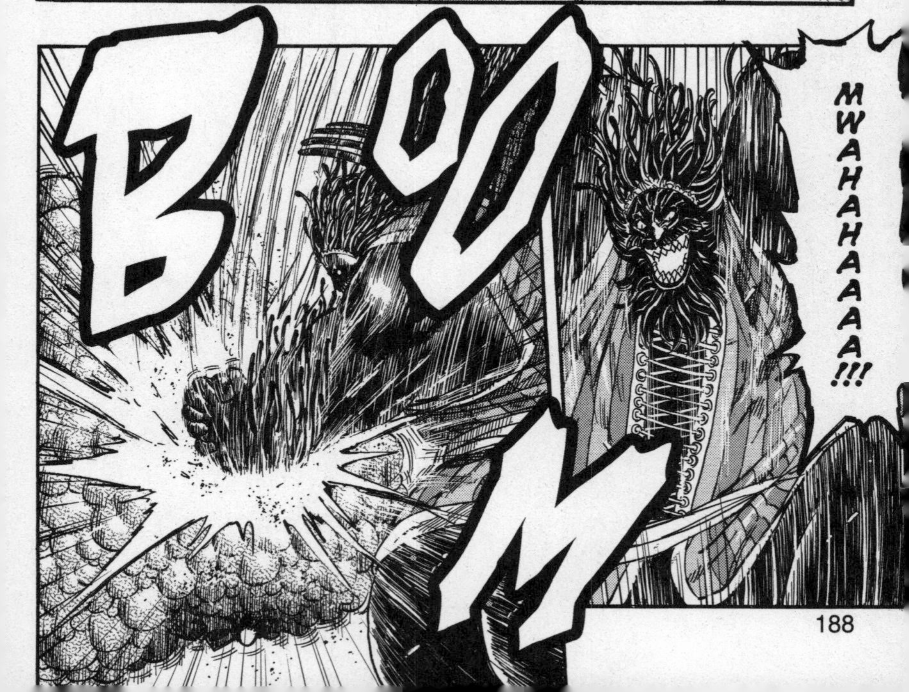
MWAHAHAAAAA!!!
BOOM

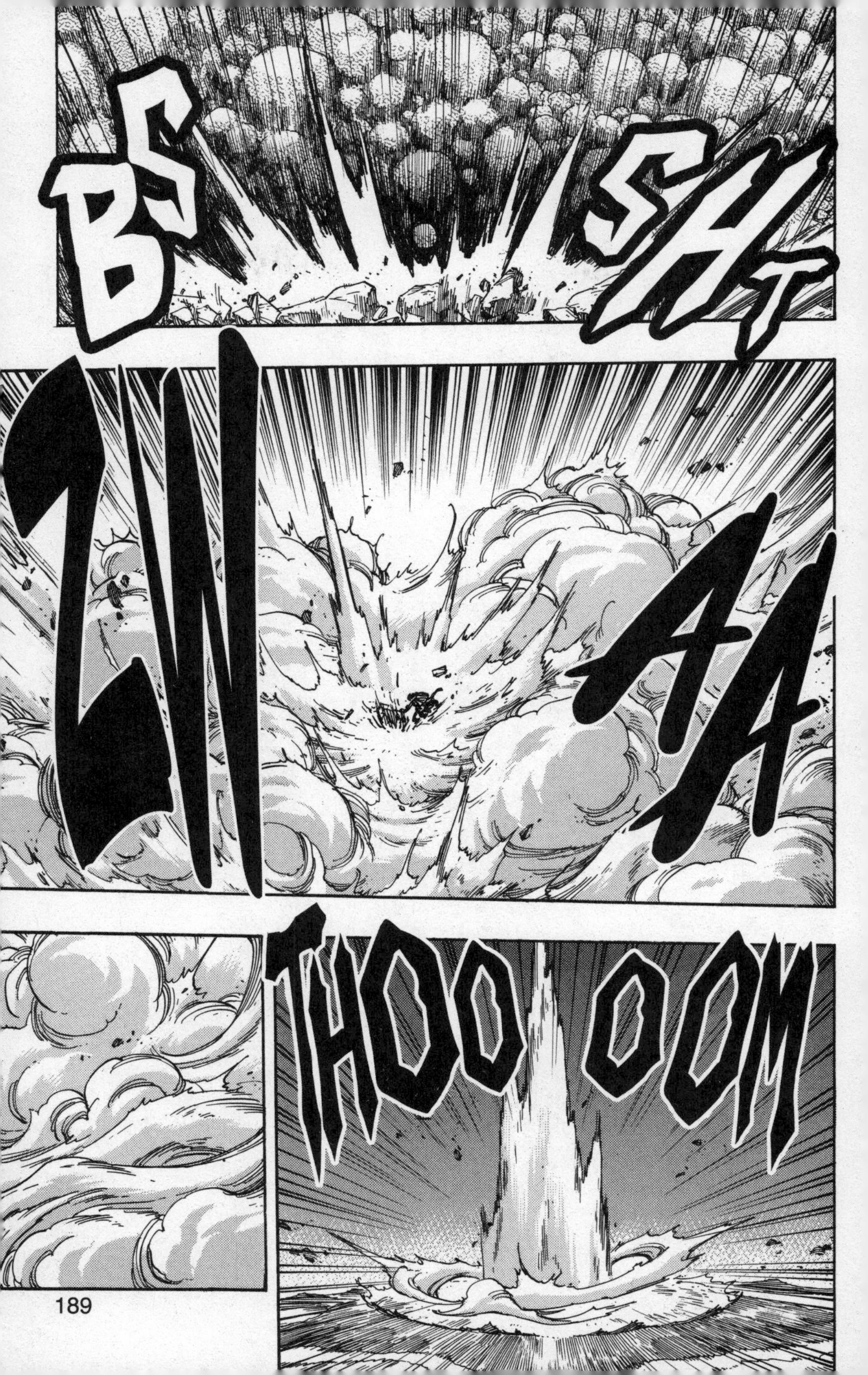
BSSHT
ZWAA
THOOOOM

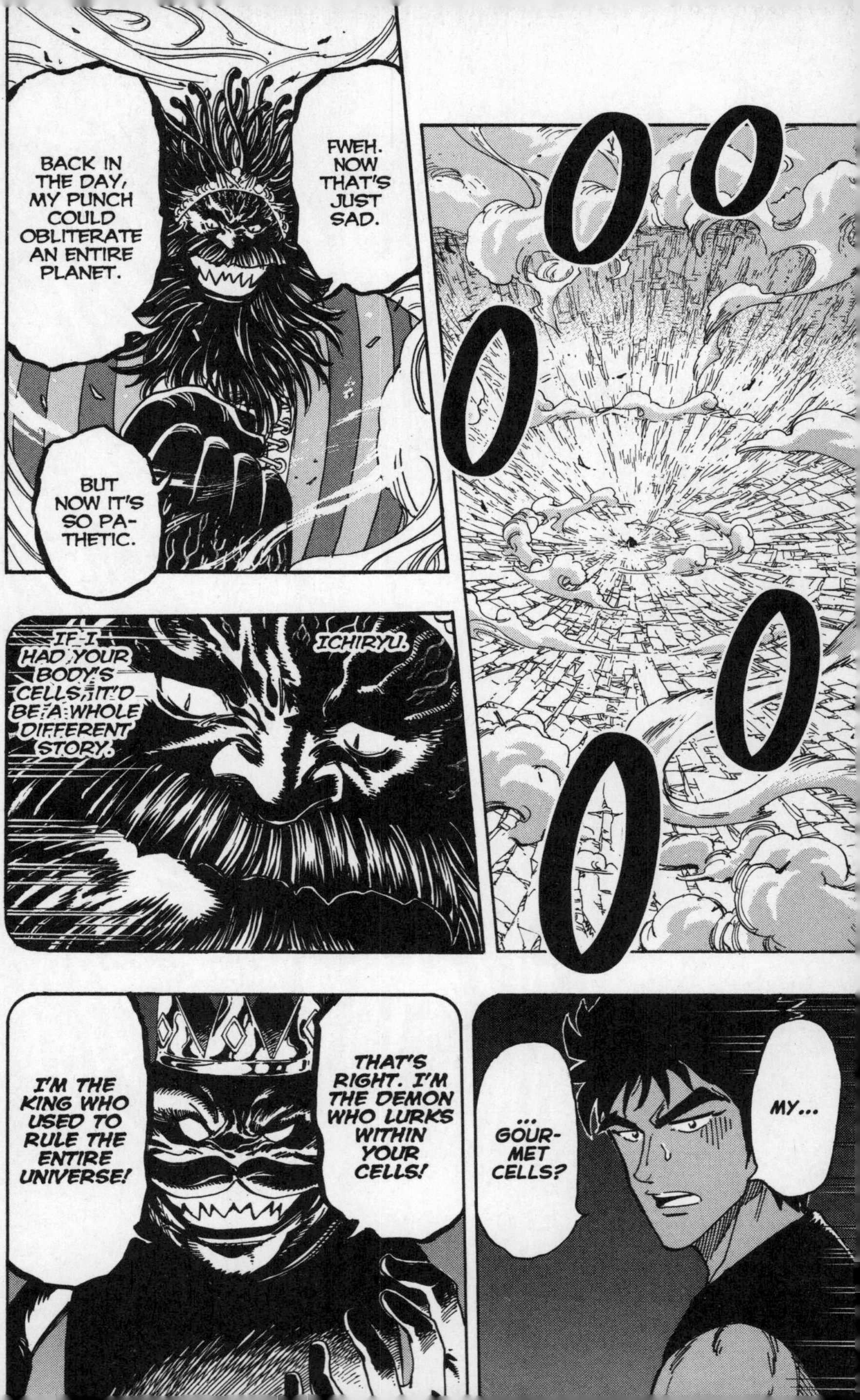
OOOOOO
FWEH. NOW THAT'S JUST SAD.
BACK IN THE DAY, MY PUNCH COULD OBLITERATE AN ENTIRE PLANET.
BUT NOW IT'S SO PATHETIC.
ICHIRYU.
IF I HAD YOUR BODY'S CELLS, IT'D BE A WHOLE DIFFERENT STORY.
MY...
... GOURMET CELLS?
THAT'S RIGHT. I'M THE DEMON WHO LURKS WITHIN YOUR CELLS!
I'M THE KING WHO USED TO RULE THE ENTIRE UNIVERSE!

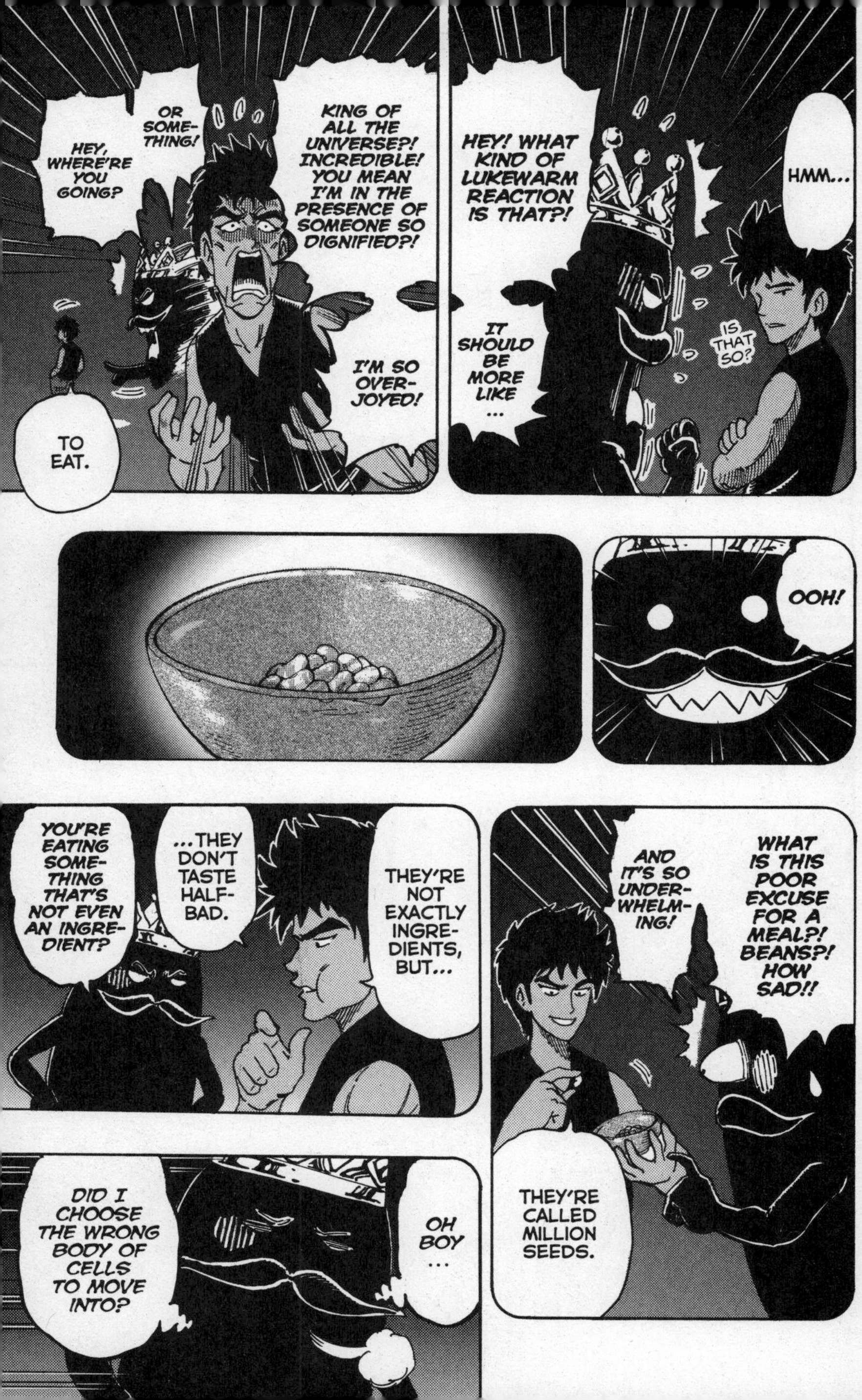
HMM...
HEY! WHAT KIND OF LUKEWARM REACTION IS THAT?!
IS THAT SO?
IT SHOULD BE MORE LIKE ...
KING OF ALL THE UNIVERSE?! INCREDIBLE! YOU MEAN I'M IN THE PRESENCE OF SOMEONE SO DIGNIFIED?!
I'M SO OVER-JOYED!
OR SOME-THING!
HEY, WHERE'RE YOU GOING?
TO EAT.
OOH!
WHAT IS THIS POOR EXCUSE FOR A MEAL?! BEANS?! HOW SAD!!
AND IT'S SO UNDER-WHELM-ING!
THEY'RE CALLED MILLION SEEDS.
THEY'RE NOT EXACTLY INGRE-DIENTS, BUT...
...THEY DON'T TASTE HALF-BAD.
YOU'RE EATING SOME-THING THAT'S NOT EVEN AN INGRE-DIENT?
OH BOY ...
DID I CHOOSE THE WRONG BODY OF CELLS TO MOVE INTO?

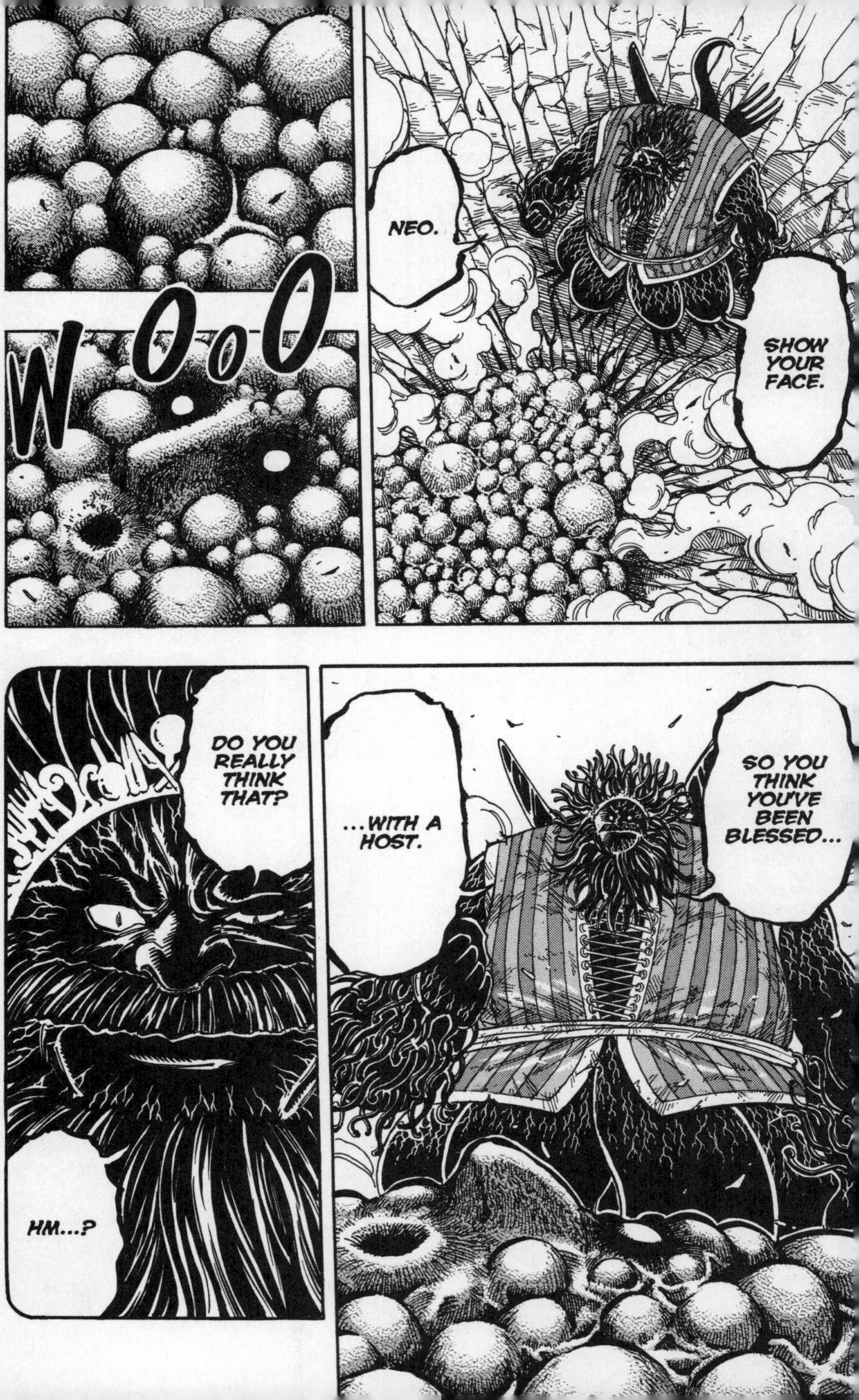
NEO.
SHOW YOUR FACE.
WOOO
SO YOU THINK YOU'VE BEEN BLESSED...
...WITH A HOST.
DO YOU REALLY THINK THAT?
HM...?

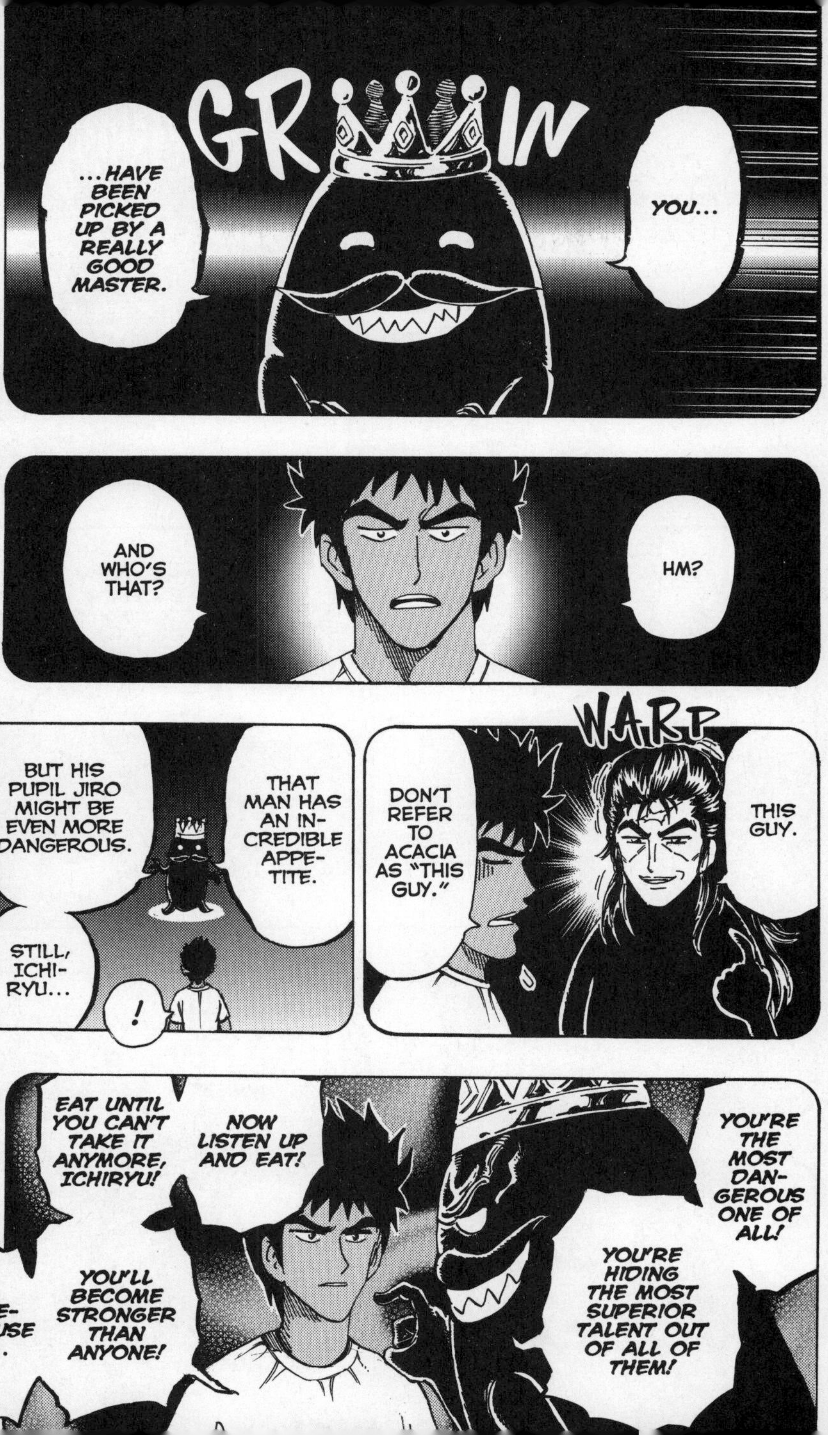
GRIN
YOU...
...HAVE BEEN PICKED UP BY A REALLY GOOD MASTER.
HM?
AND WHO'S THAT?
WARP
THIS GUY.
DON'T REFER TO ACACIA AS "THIS GUY."
THAT MAN HAS AN INCREDIBLE APPETITE.
BUT HIS PUPIL JIRO MIGHT BE EVEN MORE DANGEROUS.
STILL, ICHIRYU...
!
YOU'RE THE MOST DANGEROUS ONE OF ALL!
YOU'RE HIDING THE MOST SUPERIOR TALENT OUT OF ALL OF THEM!
NOW LISTEN UP AND EAT!
EAT UNTIL YOU CAN'T TAKE IT ANYMORE, ICHIRYU!
YOU'LL BECOME STRONGER THAN ANYONE!
BECAUSE...

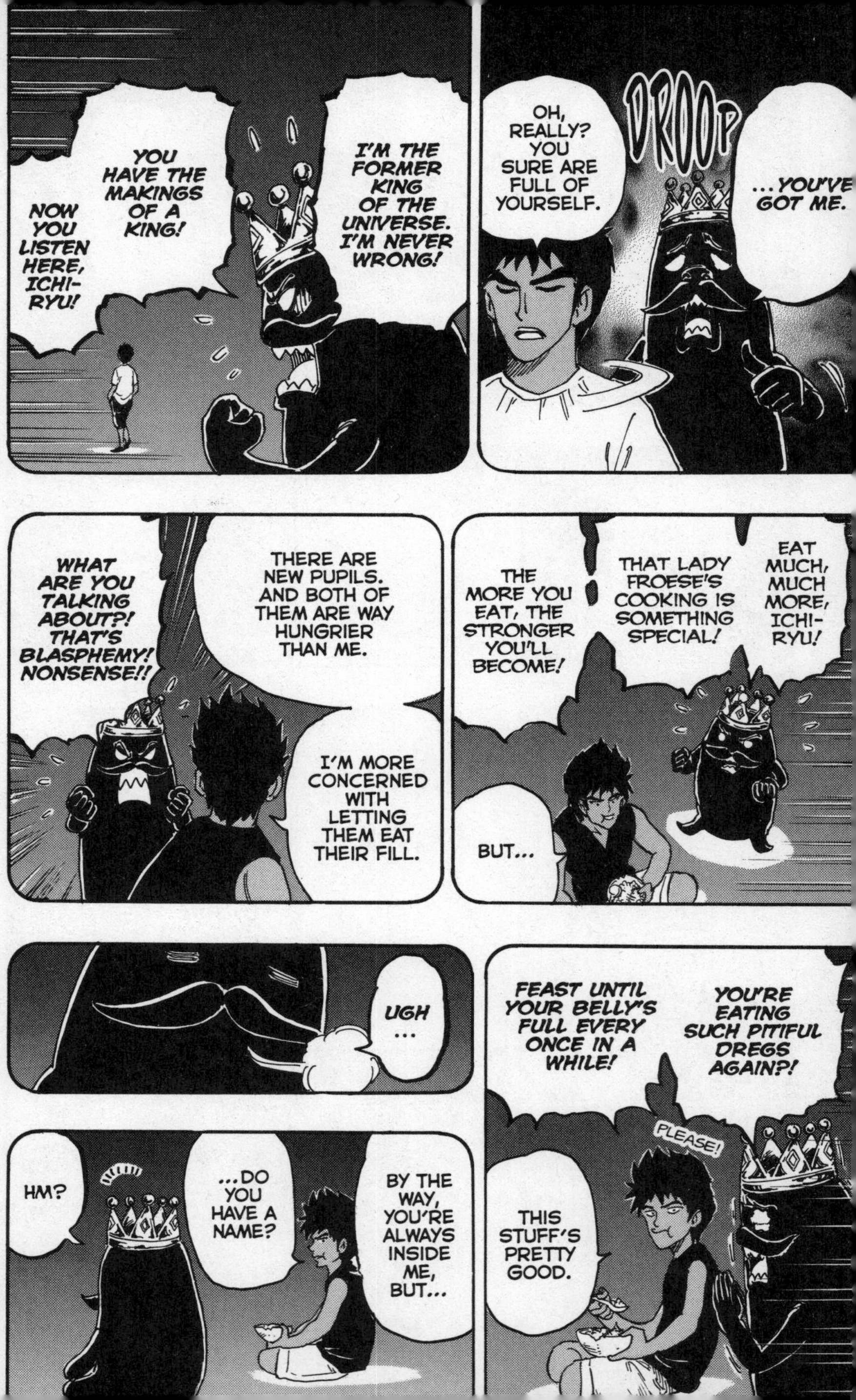
...YOU'VE GOT ME.
DROOP
OH, REALLY? YOU SURE ARE FULL OF YOURSELF.
I'M THE FORMER KING OF THE UNIVERSE. I'M NEVER WRONG!
YOU HAVE THE MAKINGS OF A KING!
NOW YOU LISTEN HERE, ICHI-RYU!
EAT MUCH, MUCH MORE, ICHI-RYU!
THAT LADY FROESE'S COOKING IS SOMETHING SPECIAL!
THE MORE YOU EAT, THE STRONGER YOU'LL BECOME!
BUT...
THERE ARE NEW PUPILS. AND BOTH OF THEM ARE WAY HUNGRIER THAN ME.
WHAT ARE YOU TALKING ABOUT?! THAT'S BLASPHEMY! NONSENSE!!
I'M MORE CONCERNED WITH LETTING THEM EAT THEIR FILL.
YOU'RE EATING SUCH PITIFUL DREGS AGAIN?!
FEAST UNTIL YOUR BELLY'S FULL EVERY ONCE IN A WHILE!
PLEASE!
THIS STUFF'S PRETTY GOOD.
UGH ...
BY THE WAY, YOU'RE ALWAYS INSIDE ME, BUT...
...DO YOU HAVE A NAME?
HM?

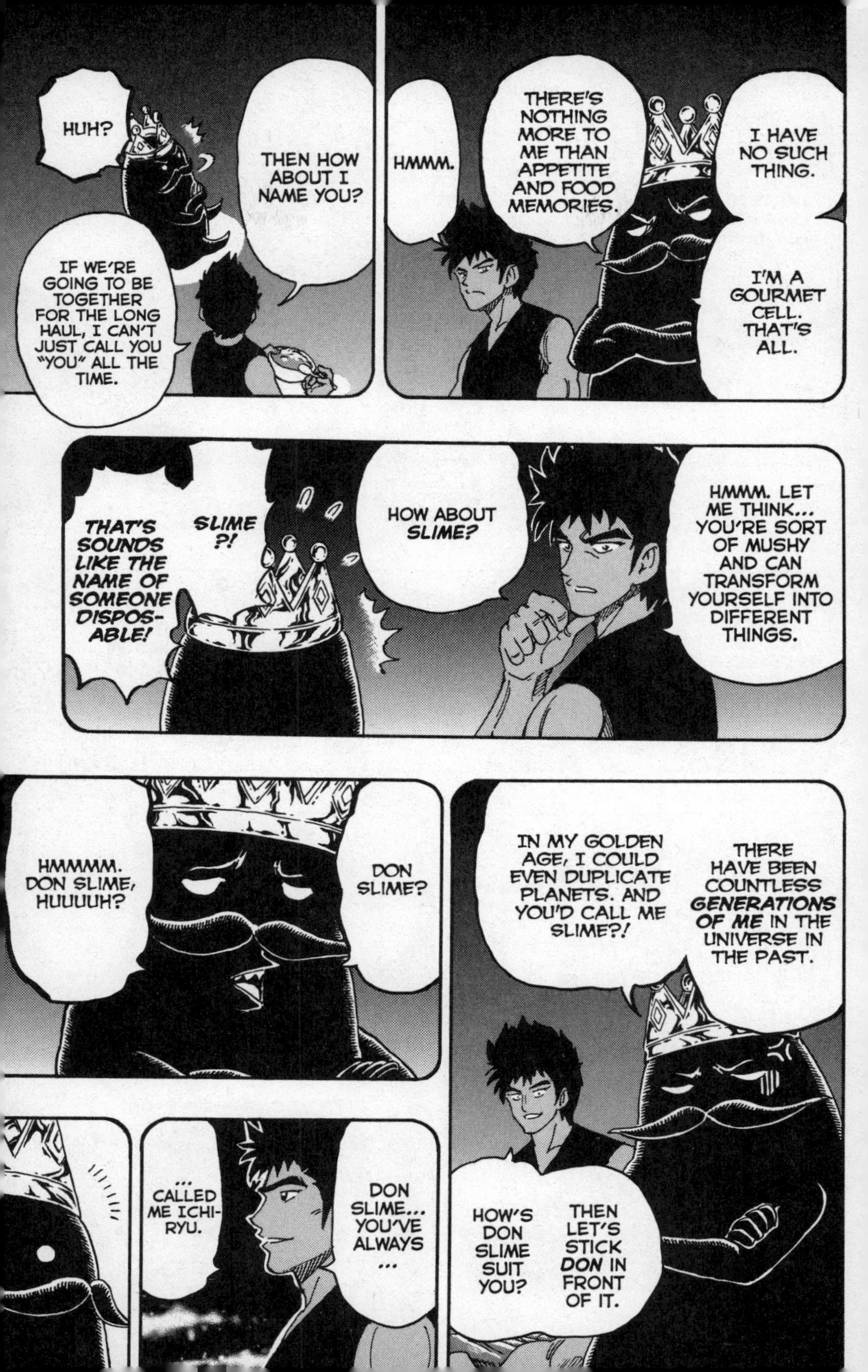
I HAVE NO SUCH THING.
I'M A GOURMET CELL. THAT'S ALL.
THERE'S NOTHING MORE TO ME THAN APPETITE AND FOOD MEMORIES.
HMMM.
THEN HOW ABOUT I NAME YOU?
HUH?
IF WE'RE GOING TO BE TOGETHER FOR THE LONG HAUL, I CAN'T JUST CALL YOU "YOU" ALL THE TIME.
HMMM. LET ME THINK... YOU'RE SORT OF MUSHY AND CAN TRANSFORM YOURSELF INTO DIFFERENT THINGS.
HOW ABOUT *SLIME?*
SLIME ?!
THAT'S SOUNDS LIKE THE NAME OF SOMEONE DISPOS- ABLE!
THERE HAVE BEEN COUNTLESS ***GENERATIONS OF ME*** IN THE UNIVERSE IN THE PAST.
IN MY GOLDEN AGE, I COULD EVEN DUPLICATE PLANETS. AND YOU'D CALL ME SLIME?!
THEN LET'S STICK ***DON*** IN FRONT OF IT.
HOW'S DON SLIME SUIT YOU?
DON SLIME?
HMMMM. DON SLIME, HUUUUH?
DON SLIME... YOU'VE ALWAYS ...
... CALLED ME ICHI- RYU.

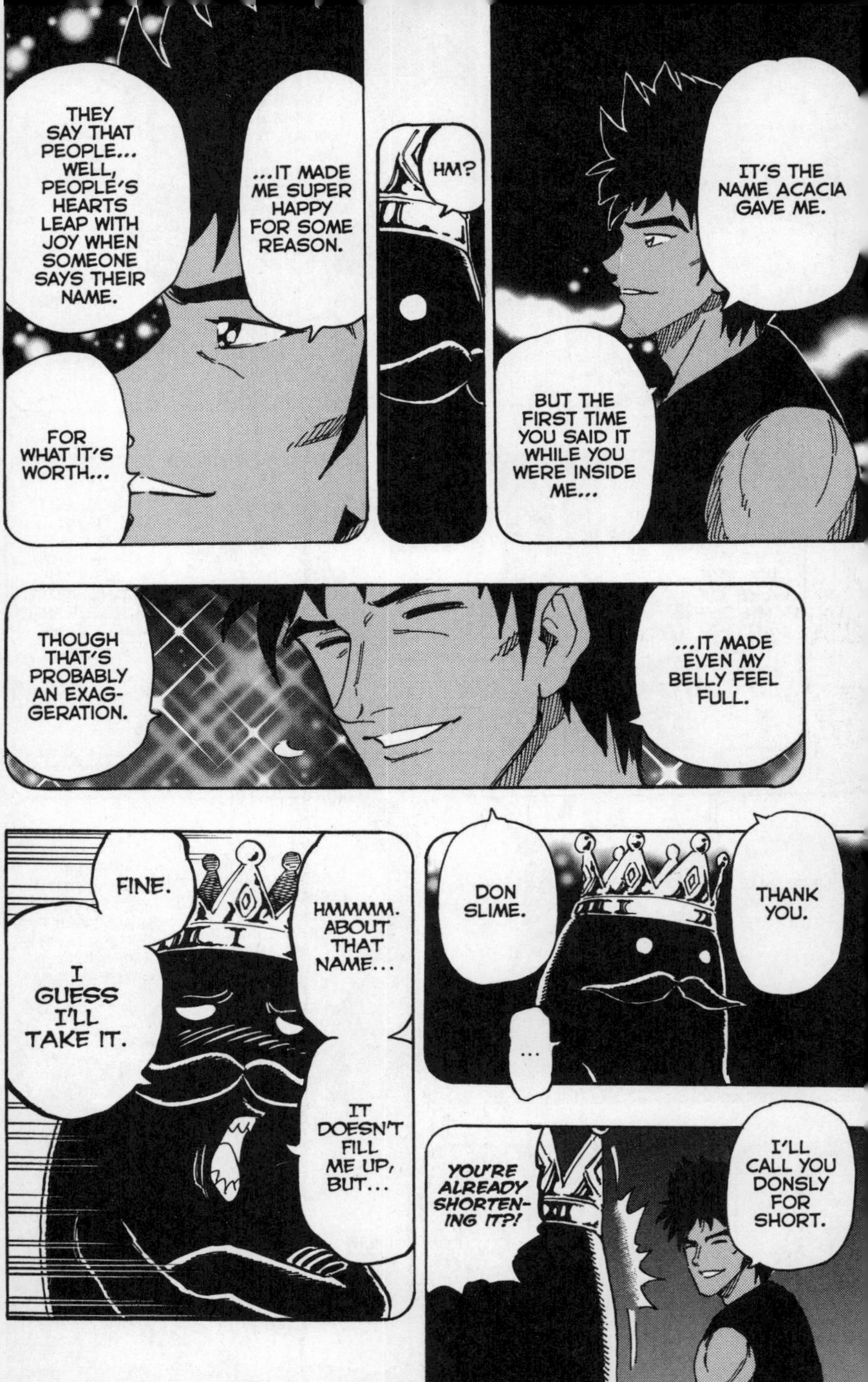
IT'S THE NAME ACACIA GAVE ME.
BUT THE FIRST TIME YOU SAID IT WHILE YOU WERE INSIDE ME...
HM?
...IT MADE ME SUPER HAPPY FOR SOME REASON.
THEY SAY THAT PEOPLE... WELL, PEOPLE'S HEARTS LEAP WITH JOY WHEN SOMEONE SAYS THEIR NAME.
FOR WHAT IT'S WORTH...
...IT MADE EVEN MY BELLY FEEL FULL.
THOUGH THAT'S PROBABLY AN EXAG-GERATION.
THANK YOU.
DON SLIME.
...
I'LL CALL YOU DONSLY FOR SHORT.
YOU'RE ALREADY SHORTEN-ING IT?!
HMMMM. ABOUT THAT NAME...
FINE.
IT DOESN'T FILL ME UP, BUT...
I GUESS I'LL TAKE IT.

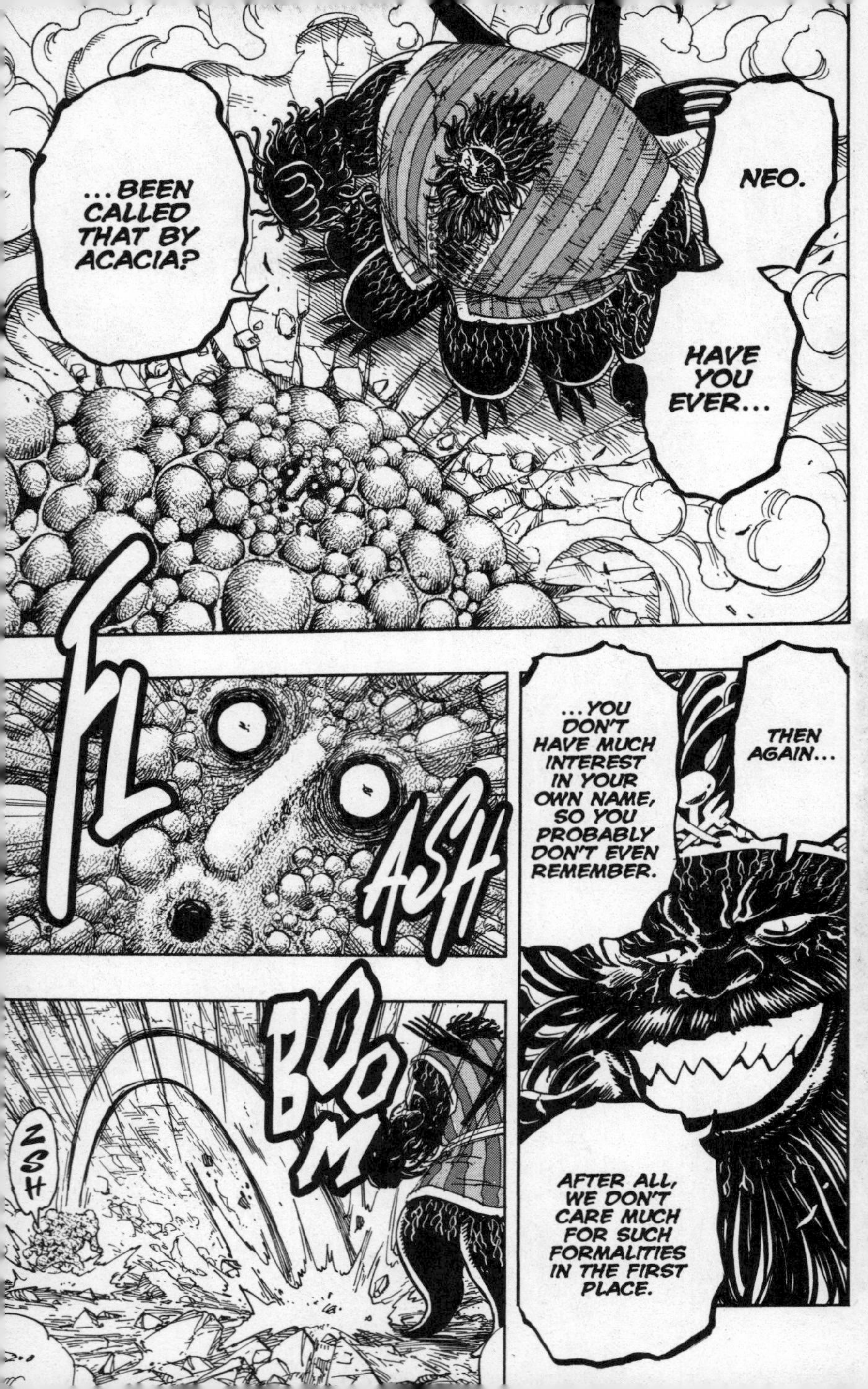
NEO.
HAVE YOU EVER...
...BEEN CALLED THAT BY ACACIA?
THEN AGAIN...
...YOU DON'T HAVE MUCH INTEREST IN YOUR OWN NAME, SO YOU PROBABLY DON'T EVEN REMEMBER.
AFTER ALL, WE DON'T CARE MUCH FOR SUCH FORMALITIES IN THE FIRST PLACE.
FLASH
BOOM
ZSH

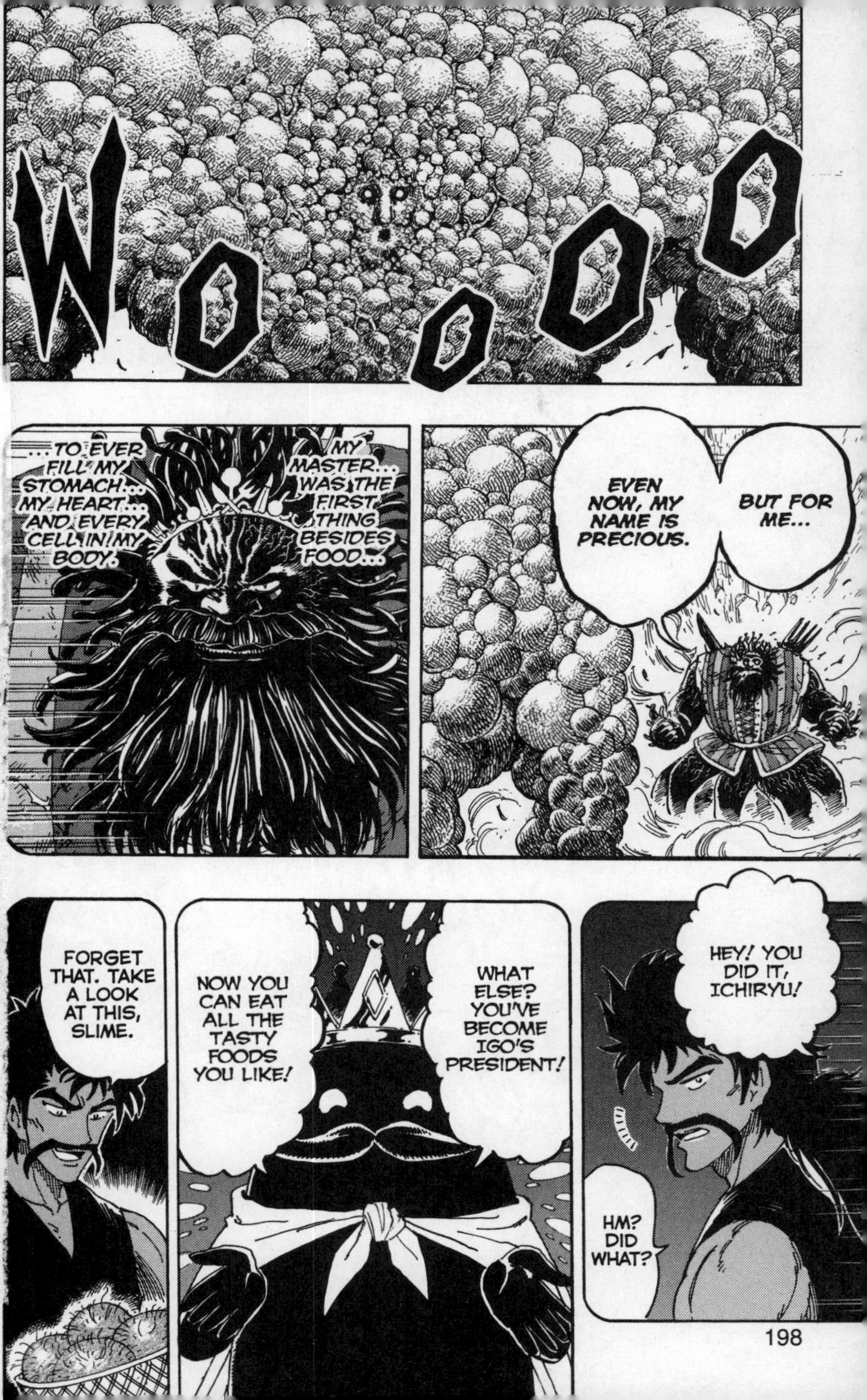
WOOOOOO
BUT FOR ME...
EVEN NOW, MY NAME IS PRECIOUS.
MY MASTER... WAS THE FIRST THING BESIDES FOOD...
...TO EVER FILL MY STOMACH... MY HEART... AND EVERY CELL IN MY BODY.
HEY! YOU DID IT, ICHIRYU!
HM? DID WHAT?
WHAT ELSE? YOU'VE BECOME IGO'S PRESIDENT!
NOW YOU CAN EAT ALL THE TASTY FOODS YOU LIKE!
FORGET THAT. TAKE A LOOK AT THIS, SLIME.

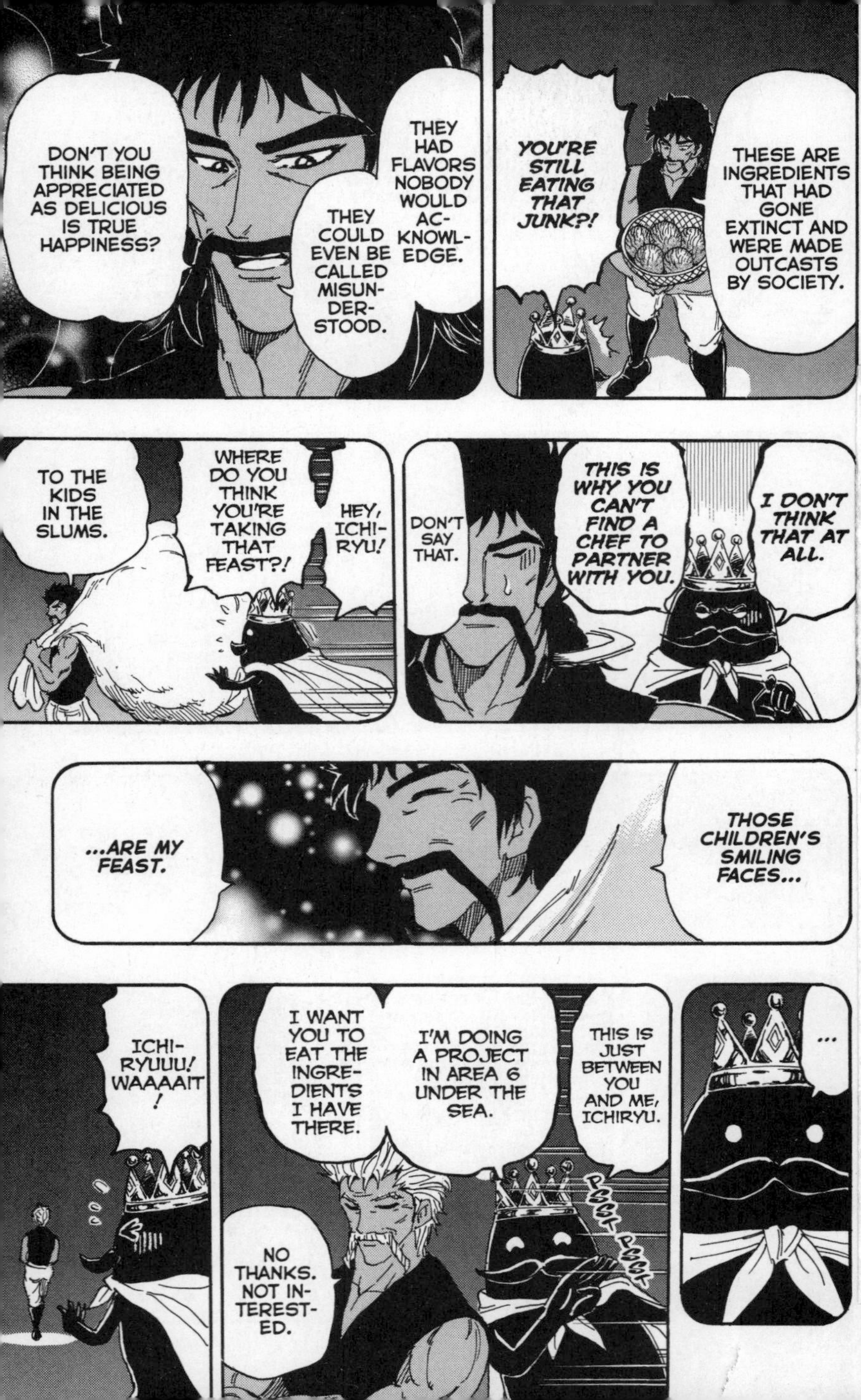
THESE ARE INGREDIENTS THAT HAD GONE EXTINCT AND WERE MADE OUTCASTS BY SOCIETY.
YOU'RE STILL EATING THAT JUNK?!
THEY HAD FLAVORS NOBODY WOULD ACKNOWLEDGE.
THEY COULD EVEN BE CALLED MISUNDERSTOOD.
DON'T YOU THINK BEING APPRECIATED AS DELICIOUS IS TRUE HAPPINESS?
I DON'T THINK THAT AT ALL.
THIS IS WHY YOU CAN'T FIND A CHEF TO PARTNER WITH YOU.
DON'T SAY THAT.
HEY, ICHIRYU!
WHERE DO YOU THINK YOU'RE TAKING THAT FEAST?!
TO THE KIDS IN THE SLUMS.
THOSE CHILDREN'S SMILING FACES...
...ARE MY FEAST.
...
THIS IS JUST BETWEEN YOU AND ME, ICHIRYU.
PSST PSST
I'M DOING A PROJECT IN AREA 6 UNDER THE SEA.
I WANT YOU TO EAT THE INGREDIENTS I HAVE THERE.
NO THANKS. NOT INTERESTED.
ICHIRYUUU! WAAAAIT!

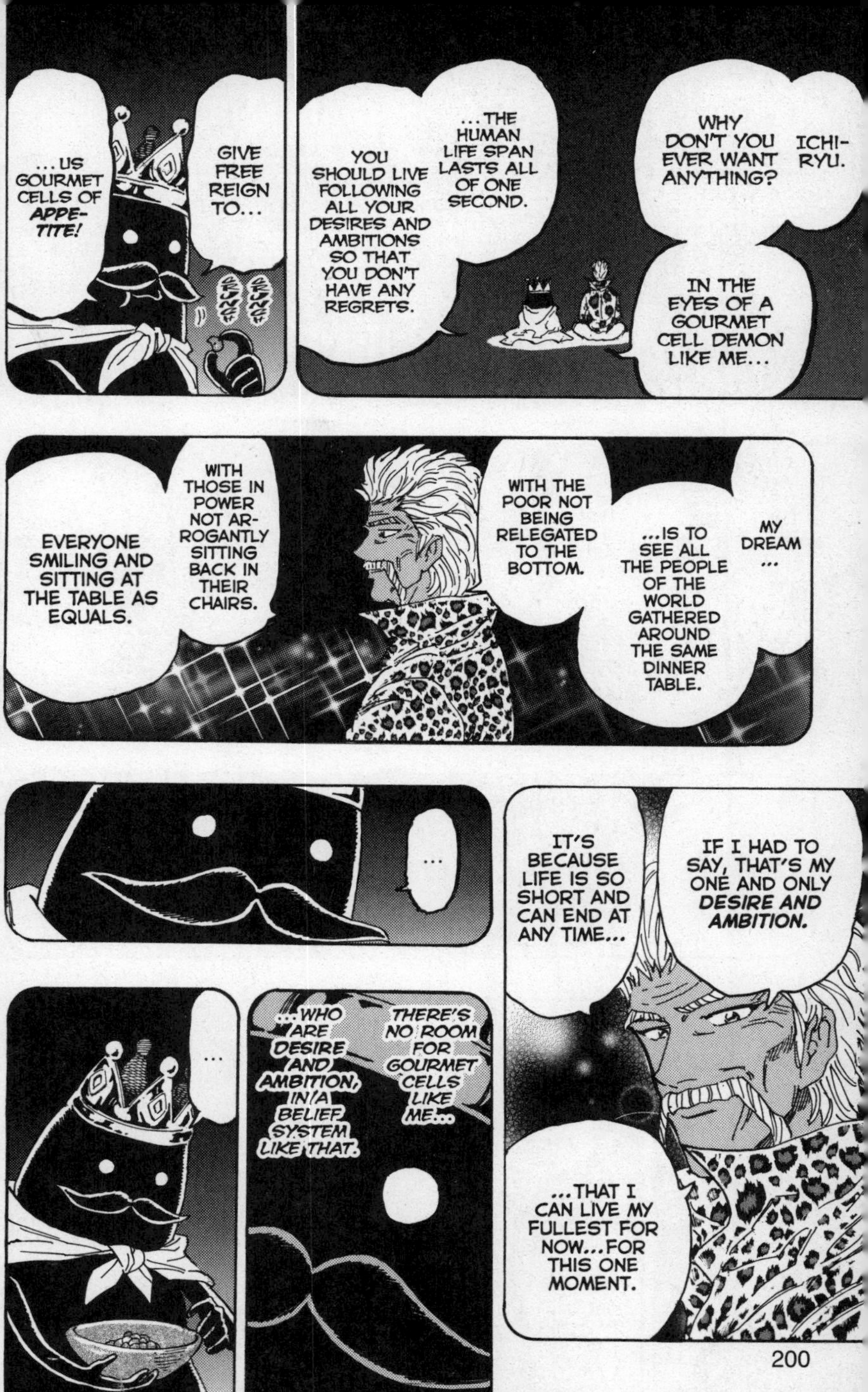
ICHI-RYU.
WHY DON'T YOU EVER WANT ANYTHING?
IN THE EYES OF A GOURMET CELL DEMON LIKE ME...
...THE HUMAN LIFE SPAN LASTS ALL OF ONE SECOND.
YOU SHOULD LIVE FOLLOWING ALL YOUR DESIRES AND AMBITIONS SO THAT YOU DON'T HAVE ANY REGRETS.
GIVE FREE REIGN TO...
...US GOURMET CELLS OF *APPETITE!*
CRUNCH CRUNCH
MY DREAM...
...IS TO SEE ALL THE PEOPLE OF THE WORLD GATHERED AROUND THE SAME DINNER TABLE.
WITH THE POOR NOT BEING RELEGATED TO THE BOTTOM.
WITH THOSE IN POWER NOT ARROGANTLY SITTING BACK IN THEIR CHAIRS.
EVERYONE SMILING AND SITTING AT THE TABLE AS EQUALS.
IF I HAD TO SAY, THAT'S MY ONE AND ONLY *DESIRE AND AMBITION.*
IT'S BECAUSE LIFE IS SO SHORT AND CAN END AT ANY TIME...
...THAT I CAN LIVE MY FULLEST FOR NOW...FOR THIS ONE MOMENT.
...
THERE'S NO ROOM FOR GOURMET CELLS LIKE ME...
...WHO ARE DESIRE AND AMBITION, IN A BELIEF SYSTEM LIKE THAT.
...

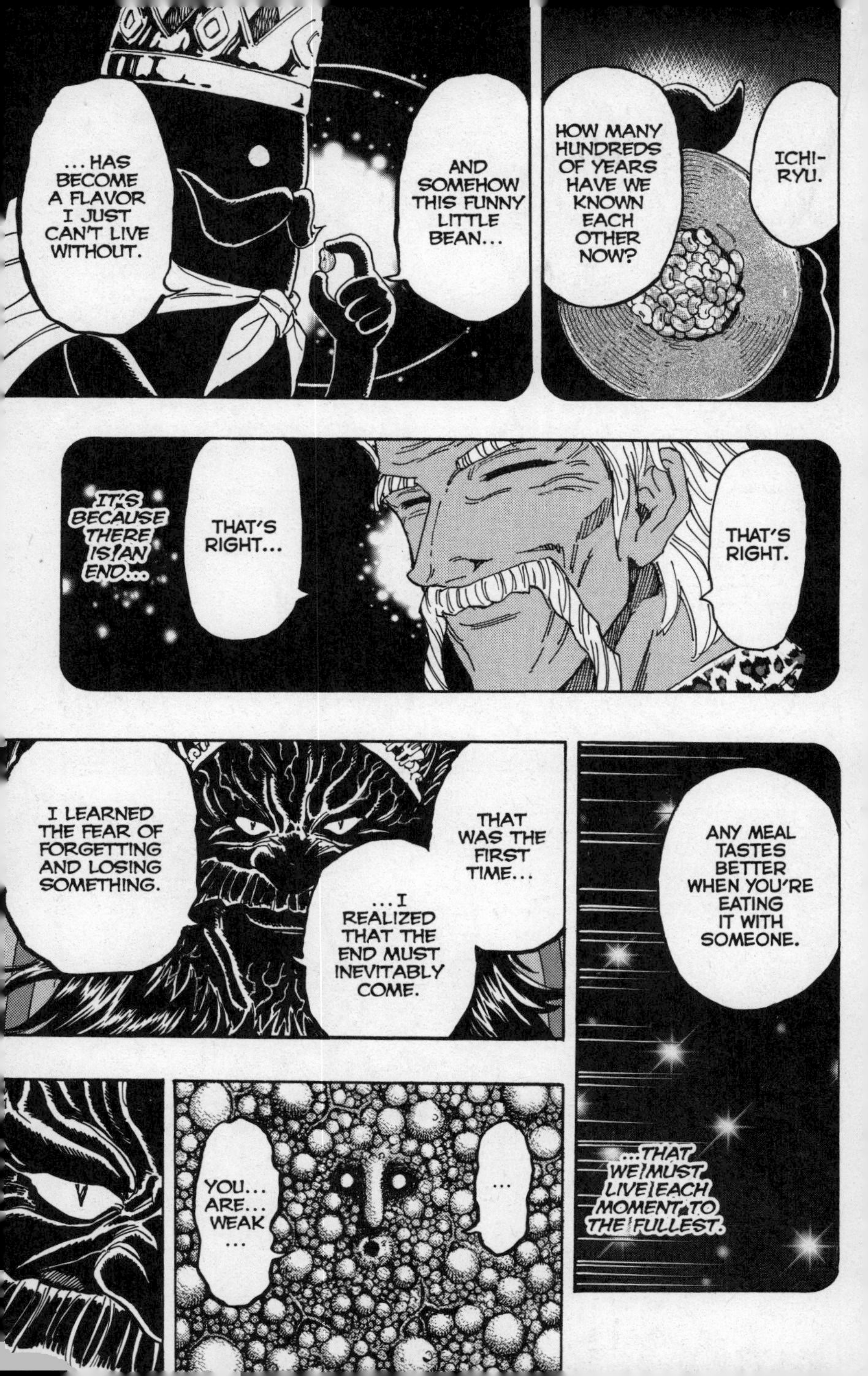
ICHI-RYU.
HOW MANY HUNDREDS OF YEARS HAVE WE KNOWN EACH OTHER NOW?
AND SOMEHOW THIS FUNNY LITTLE BEAN...
...HAS BECOME A FLAVOR I JUST CAN'T LIVE WITHOUT.
THAT'S RIGHT.
THAT'S RIGHT...
IT'S BECAUSE THERE IS AN END...
ANY MEAL TASTES BETTER WHEN YOU'RE EATING IT WITH SOMEONE.
...THAT WE MUST LIVE EACH MOMENT TO THE FULLEST.
THAT WAS THE FIRST TIME...
...I REALIZED THAT THE END MUST INEVITABLY COME.
I LEARNED THE FEAR OF FORGETTING AND LOSING SOMETHING.
...
YOU... ARE... WEAK ...

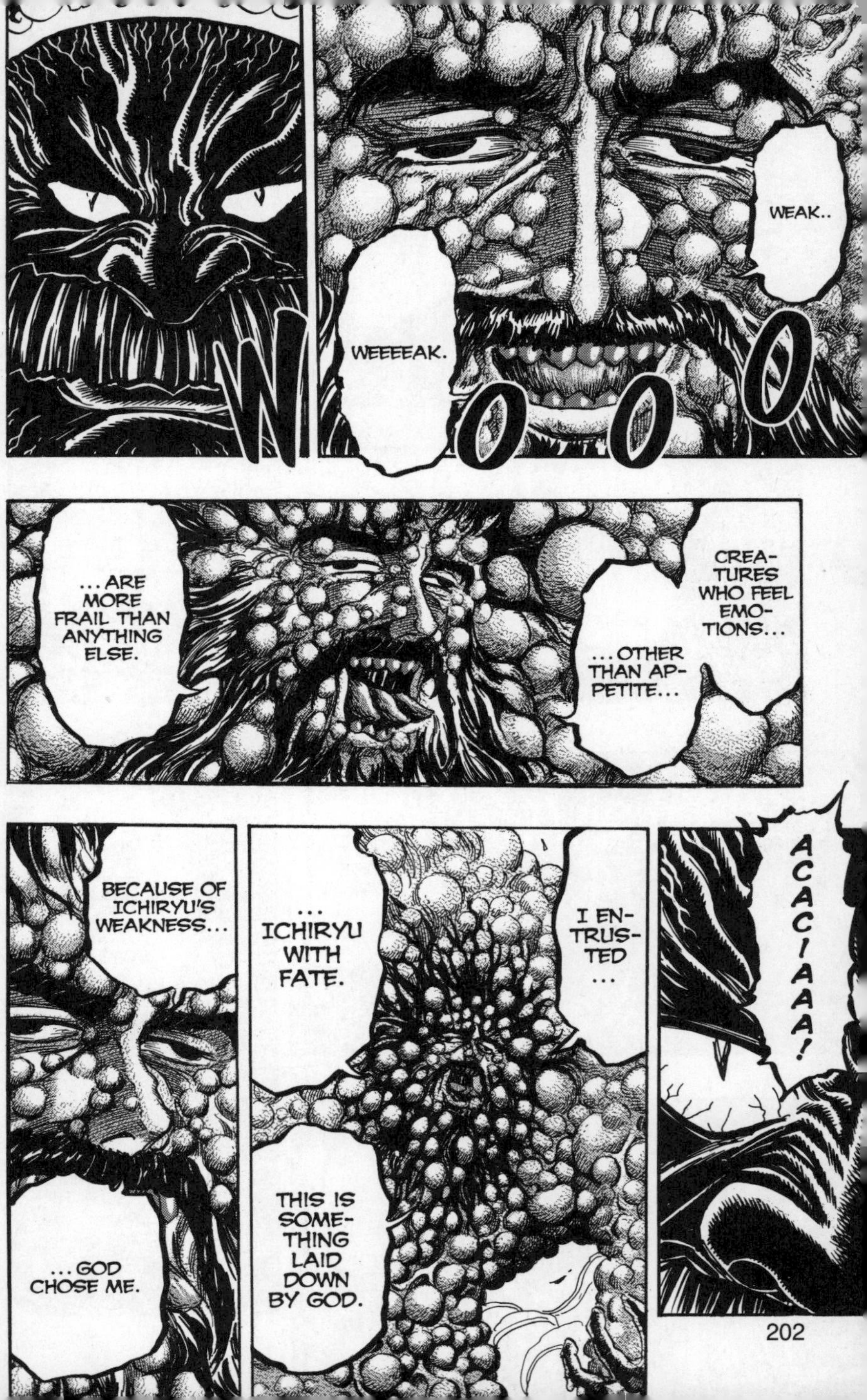
WEAK..
WEEEEAK.
WOOOO
CREATURES WHO FEEL EMOTIONS...
...OTHER THAN APPETITE...
...ARE MORE FRAIL THAN ANYTHING ELSE.
ACACIAAA!
I ENTRUSTED...
...ICHIRYU WITH FATE.
THIS IS SOMETHING LAID DOWN BY GOD.
BECAUSE OF ICHIRYU'S WEAKNESS...
...GOD CHOSE ME.

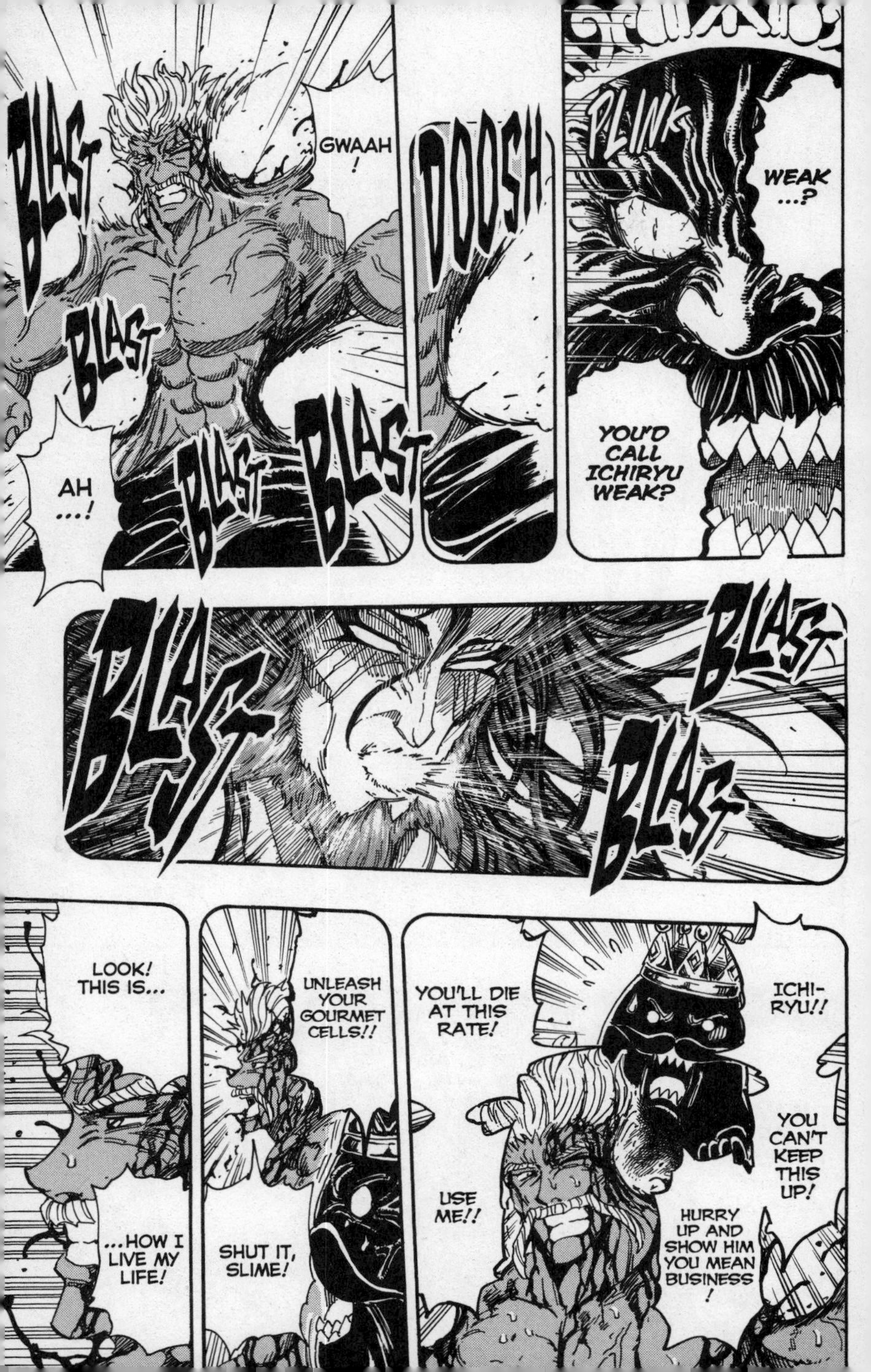
PLINK
WEAK ...?
YOU'D CALL ICHIRYU WEAK?
DOOSH
GWAAH!
BLAST
BLAST
BLAST
BLAST
AH ...!
BLAST
BLAST
BLAST
ICHI-RYU!!
YOU'LL DIE AT THIS RATE!
YOU CAN'T KEEP THIS UP!
HURRY UP AND SHOW HIM YOU MEAN BUSINESS!
USE ME!!
UNLEASH YOUR GOURMET CELLS!!
SHUT IT, SLIME!
LOOK! THIS IS...
...HOW I LIVE MY LIFE!

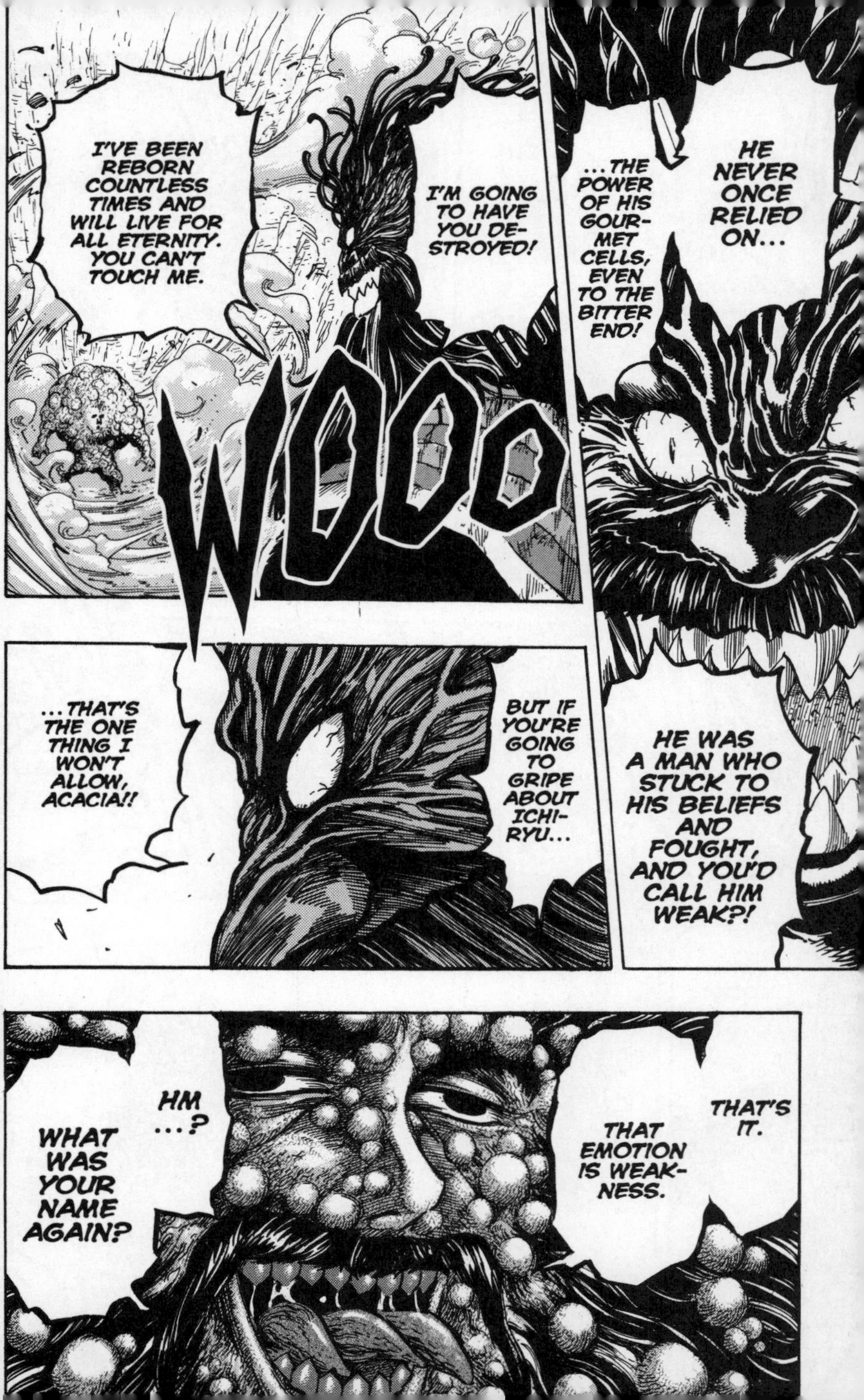
HE NEVER ONCE RELIED ON...
...THE POWER OF HIS GOURMET CELLS, EVEN TO THE BITTER END!
I'M GOING TO HAVE YOU DESTROYED!
I'VE BEEN REBORN COUNTLESS TIMES AND WILL LIVE FOR ALL ETERNITY. YOU CAN'T TOUCH ME.
WOOO
HE WAS A MAN WHO STUCK TO HIS BELIEFS AND FOUGHT, AND YOU'D CALL HIM WEAK?!
BUT IF YOU'RE GOING TO GRIPE ABOUT ICHIRYU...
...THAT'S THE ONE THING I WON'T ALLOW, ACACIA!!
THAT'S IT.
THAT EMOTION IS WEAKNESS.
HM ...?
WHAT WAS YOUR NAME AGAIN?

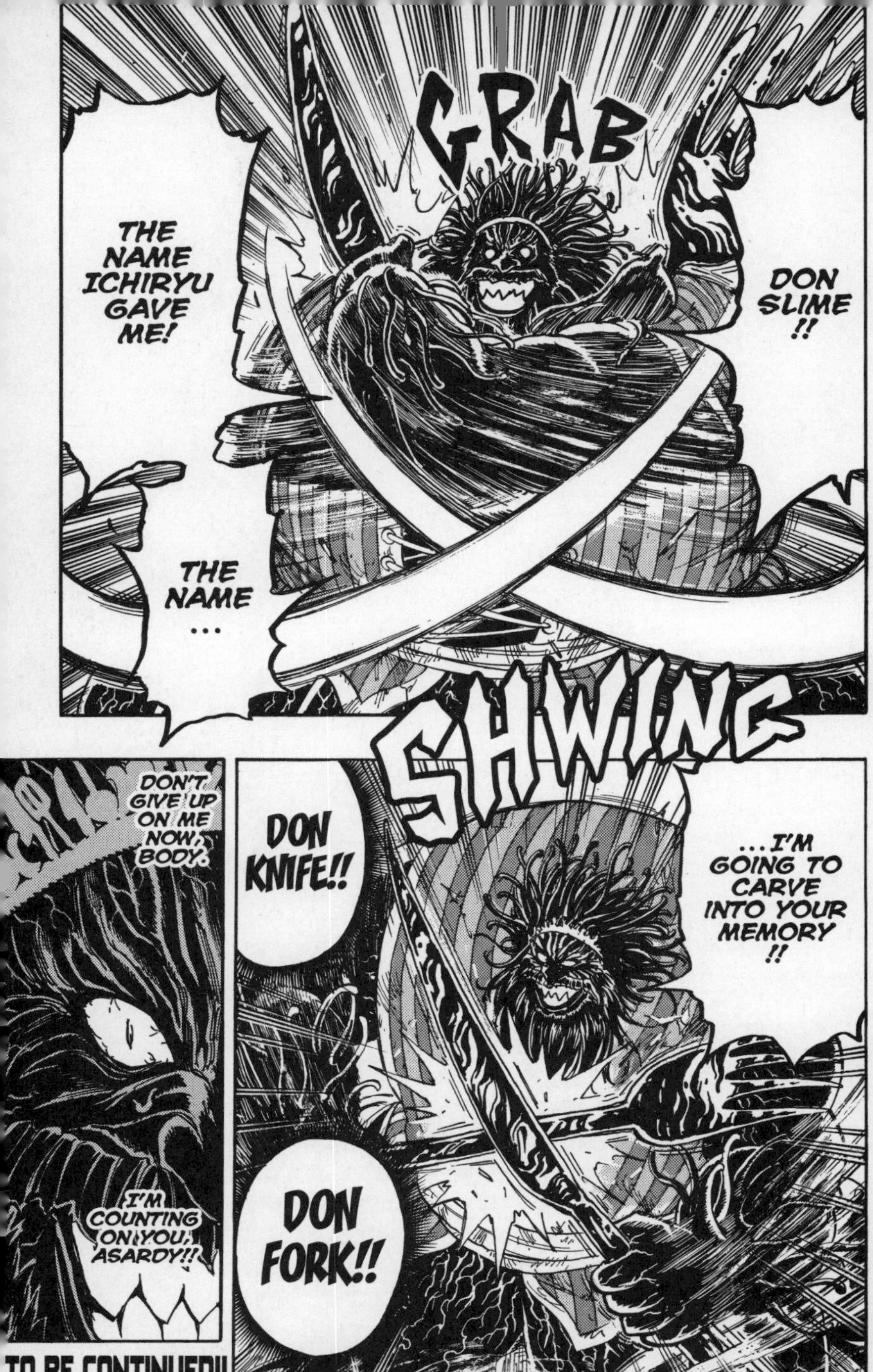
GRAB
DON SLIME!!
THE NAME ICHIRYU GAVE ME!
THE NAME...
SHWING
...I'M GOING TO CARVE INTO YOUR MEMORY!!
DON KNIFE!!
DON FORK!!
DON'T GIVE UP ON ME NOW, BODY.
I'M COUNTING ON YOU, ASARDY!!

TO BE CONTINUED!!

COMING NEXT VOLUME

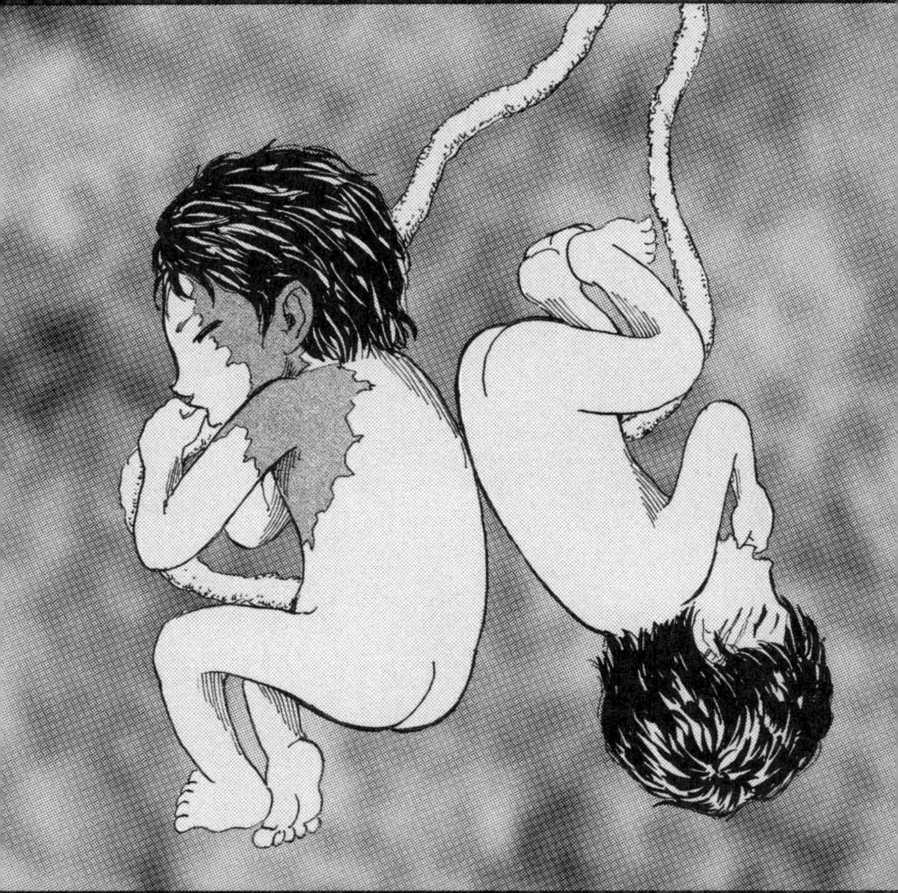

THOSE TEARS!!!

In the final moments before the Gourmet Eclipse, Toriko and the gang are finally reunited and partake in the parts of Acacia's Full-Course Meal that have been captured so far. What sort of power will the Full-Course Meal impart to Toriko and his friends? Meanwhile, things are getting a little too slimy for Don Slime as he goes head-to-head against Neo, who gets more and more powerful with every bite! With the end of the world looming overhead and the coming of God imminent, will everyone be ready for the disasters to come?

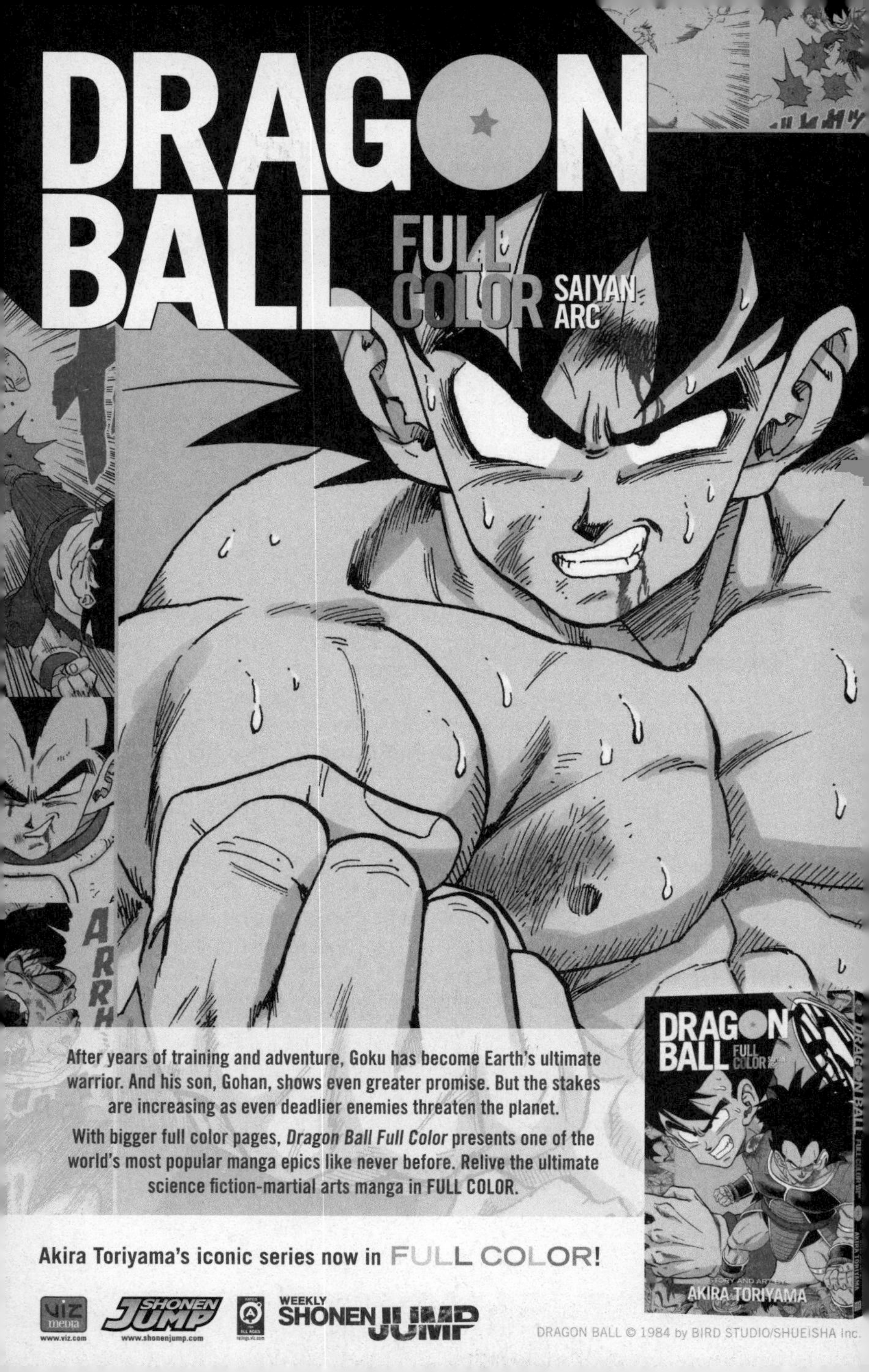
DRAGON BALL
FULL COLOR SAIYAN ARC
ARRH
After years of training and adventure, Goku has become Earth's ultimate warrior. And his son, Gohan, shows even greater promise. But the stakes are increasing as even deadlier enemies threaten the planet.
With bigger full color pages, *Dragon Ball Full Color* presents one of the world's most popular manga epics like never before. Relive the ultimate science fiction-martial arts manga in FULL COLOR.
DRAGON BALL FULL COLOR SAIYAN ARC
STORY AND ART BY
AKIRA TORIYAMA
Akira Toriyama's iconic series now in FULL COLOR!
viz media
www.viz.com
SHONEN JUMP
www.shonenjump.com
ALL AGES
WEEKLY SHONEN JUMP
DRAGON BALL © 1984 by BIRD STUDIO/SHUEISHA Inc.

You're Reading in the Wrong Direction!!

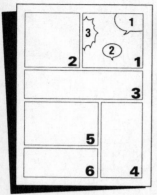

Whoops! Guess what? You're starting at the wrong end of the comic!

...It's true! In keeping with the original Japanese format, **Toriko** is meant to be read from right to left, starting in the upper-right corner.

Unlike English, which is read from left to right, Japanese is read from right to left, meaning that action, sound effects and word-balloon order are completely reversed... something which can make readers unfamiliar with Japanese feel pretty backwards themselves. For this reason, manga or Japanese comics published in the U.S. in English have sometimes been published "flopped"— that is, printed in exact reverse order, as though seen from the other side of a mirror.

By flopping pages, U.S. publishers can avoid confusing readers, but the compromise is not without its downside. For one thing, a character in a flopped manga series who once wore in the original Japanese version a T-shirt emblazoned with "M A Y" (as in "the merry month of") now wears one which reads "Y A M"! Additionally, many manga creators in Japan are themselves unhappy with the process, as some feel the mirror-imaging of their art skews their original intentions.

We are proud to bring you Mitsutoshi Shimabukuro's **Toriko** in the original unflopped format. For now, though, turn to the other side of the book and let the adventure begin...!

—Editor

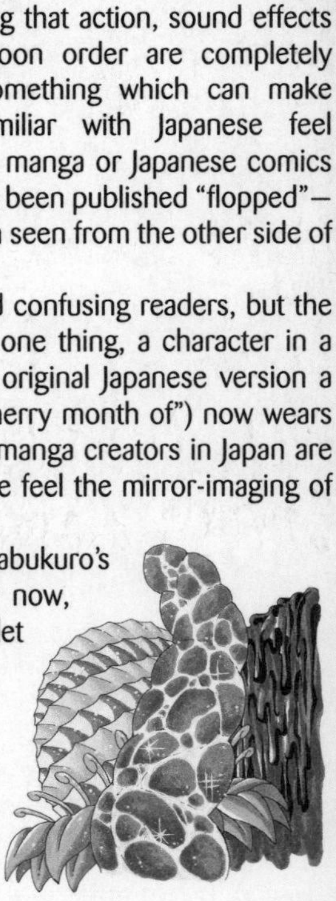